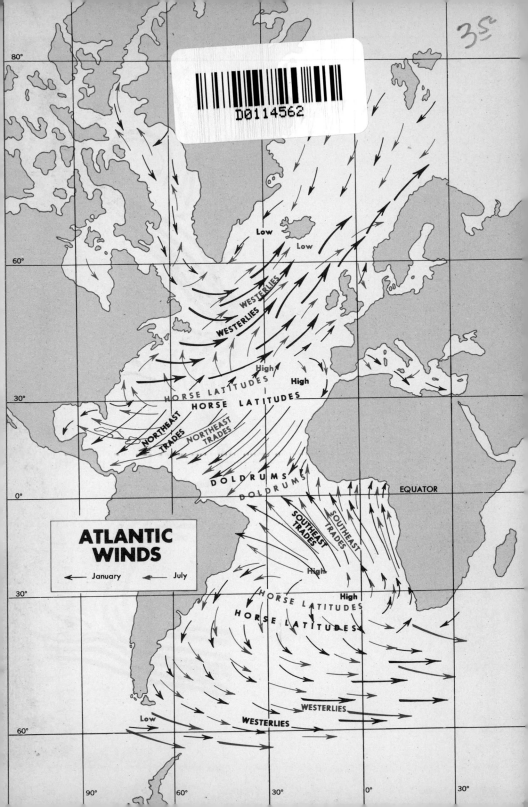

ATLANTIC WINDS

January ← ← July

The Atlantic

A HISTORY OF AN OCEAN

The

Also by Leonard Outhwaite

ATLANTIC CIRCLE

UNROLLING THE MAP: The Story of Exploration

LEONARD OUTHWAITE

Atlantic

A HISTORY OF AN OCEAN

Coward-McCann, Inc.   New York

To Lucille Conrad Outhwaite

Love's own self was the deep sea's daughter,
Fair and flawless from face to feet. . . .

Swinburne

Contents

Part I: Portrait of an Ocean

1	About this Book	11
2	The Structure of the Atlantic	18
3	Behavior of the Atlantic	37
4	The Meaning of the Atlantic	55

Part II: Discovery and Early History

5	River of Ocean—Primitive	73
6	Atlantis—Birth and Death of Science	93
7	First Across the Atlantic	103
8	The New World in the North	117
9	Iberian Conquest	132
10	Guns and Gold; Faith and Food	152
11	To Their New Homes	170
12	Ships and Cargoes	185

Part III: Modern History

13	The Whalers	199
14	The Slavers	217
15	The Packets	232
16	Seaman's Ocean—Lt. M. F. Maury, USN	249
17	The Clippers	262

18 Fore-and-Aft   279
19 The Coming of Steam and Steel   293
20 Words Under Water   312
21 "Just for the Hell of It"   324
22 Speed, Elegance and Luxury   339
23 Atlantic Warfare Yesterday   357

Part IV: The Atlantic—Today and Tomorrow

24 Flying the Atlantic   392
25 Atlantic Warfare Today   414
26 Atlantic Health, Wealth and Sanity   442
    Acknowledgments and Suggestions for
      Further Reading   461
    Index   467

Part One

PORTRAIT OF AN OCEAN

Chapter 1

ABOUT THIS BOOK

A NOVELIST may employ many devices of art and skill in capturing the interest of a reader. The historian has no such choice. At the very beginning the reader of a book of fact has the right to demand, and the author a duty to supply, a plain statement about the book.

This, then, is a book about the Atlantic Ocean. It is a book that attempts to gather within its covers the main facts about this ocean: its place in the world of nature and of man; how this ocean was discovered and used by early adventurers and explorers; who sailed upon it in times past; what were their purposes; what ships did they use; where did they mean to go and where did they actually land; how did the ocean itself affect their travels; how did trade develop and conflicts of interest arise all about this broad water; what societies have grown up around the Atlantic shores; what nations have arisen; what are their present prospects and their future hopes?

It appears that an attempt to organize the available information on these points and a number of others and to set it forth in an orderly account must, so far as it succeeds, be reckoned a history of an ocean.

It was with some surprise and more than a little timidity that I realized some time ago that I was writing a history of the Atlantic. Confirmed and settled landsmen express surprise that an ocean could have a history. Having little experience with it they think of the ocean as uniform and inactive and as playing little part in human experience. As one who knows and loves the ocean my surprise was of an entirely different kind. I was surprised because while hundreds of millions of people have crossed the Atlantic and taken up residence about its shores and while it remains a central important factor in the life of scores of nations, no one seems to have collected the information and assembled it into a unified history of the Atlantic or to have shown how the ocean has operated and continues to operate in human affairs.

One might well hesitate to undertake a subject that dealt with so great an area; that involved a knowledge of so many kinds of information; that developed through such millennia of time. Cautiously I went on collecting information, thinking about the problems and writing enormous masses of material. This book has been through many changes. There have indeed been several books that finally came together. At one time there was a book about the physical geography or oceanography of the Atlantic. There were also volumes on voyages and discoveries, on ships and seamen and their adventures. There came into being also materials and observations on the Atlantic wars and the place of the Atlantic in world strategy.

All of the materials were in themselves interesting and some exciting; all were useful but the whole structure was unsatisfactory because there was no relation between the parts and no serious attempt to tell a connected story. There are a number of good books on oceanography but the oceanographers have seldom taken time to tell us how winds and currents have affected the voyages of ships, the progress of discovery, the outcome of naval engagements, the flow of commerce. Similarly there are excellent books on particular technical subjects such as the building and rigging of ships; there are books on voyages of discovery and adventure; on naval battles; on shipwrecks and disasters; and so on—in each of these classes we need the basic interpretation that links the detailed events to the character of the ocean on one hand and the development of social history on the other. Most books of history are written by landsmen who neglect the ocean because they know so little about it. Nor have the seamen themselves done very much to supply us with a general ocean history. Most of the seamen when they commence writing find it difficult to break away from technicalities. They tend to overburden us with the details of some special subject. Admirals Mahan and Morrison would serve as notable exceptions to prove the rule.

So it seems there was a place for an ocean history and the book has finally been written as such. I have great sympathy with the modern Samuel Butler who said that he never decided what subject to write about. He waited until a book came up to him and tapped him on the chest and insisted on being written. Even so I would never have completed the book had it not been for two encouraging factors.

The first factor was that those who read the early efforts or who listened to the story as I put it together believed in the final outcome.

The second factor is my experience with the Atlantic and my belief in it. For some years I was fortunate enough to have sailed about the Atlantic in my own ship. Either then or at other times I have visited many of its ports; crossed it on many different courses and in many different vessels from antique square-riggers to the fastest of modern ships, from great leviathans to snug little "tabloids." I have been on my feet for days while my ship fought through hurricane winds on the high seas and I have made up for this by drowsing away a season in a cozy little cove. I have seen the northern seas gray with ice shaken in the grip of a winter gale and seen the ocean a sheet of molten gold under a tropic moon. These are all aspects of the same ocean and they are things never to be forgotten.

The early efforts were by no means wasted but they have been cut down and condensed. The important change however is that an attempt has been made to relate each part to every other part so that it can be seen that the ocean and its shores, the winds and currents, the ships and the men that sailed them all played concerted roles in the great drama that is human history and human civilization.

To assist the reader in becoming familiar with the ocean and with this book I have gone through it and have set out below some score of special statements. There is no room in this chapter and no attempt is made here to tell the full stories, list the evidence or set forth the arguments in support of these ideas. They are listed because they should be looked at together and because they tell in part what the book is all about. Indeed, I would be disappointed if the reader accepted these points without question but greatly pleased if curiosity or doubt lead him to the main chapters where there is an opportunity to trace out the structure, character and life story of our ocean.

1. We have grown up with an arbitrary and false notion about the world. In writing and in making maps we have split the Atlantic, creating an eastern and a western hemisphere, an old world and a new one. This has obscured the historic and present importance of the Atlantic to the welfare and safety of the world.

2. It is just as accurate and much more useful and illuminating to divide the world into a water hemisphere and a land hemisphere. The

surface of the water hemisphere, as the name implies, is practically entirely composed of ocean. It contains only 6 per cent of the land area of the world including the uninhabited Antarctic continent and it includes only a small fraction of the people and of the natural resources of the world.

3. The land hemisphere contains 94 per cent of the land of the globe and most of the population and the physical resources of the world.

4. The Atlantic Ocean is central to the land hemisphere. The Atlantic touches all five of the great continents and its shore line is made up of parts of their coasts. The only major land mass that it does not touch is Australia.

5. The Atlantic Ocean is the major drainage basin of all the major continents and by an overwhelming percentage it receives the waters of the major river systems of the world. Since the watershed of the western continents lies far to the west and the watershed of the eastern continents lies far to the east, practically all of the productive agricultural lands of the temperate zones of the earth lie along rivers that drain into the Atlantic basin.

Sir John Murray estimates that the continental areas drained by rivers emptying into the Atlantic are about twice as great as those emptying into the Pacific and Indian *combined*.

6. The Atlantic Ocean has a greater continental shore line than the Pacific and the Indian Oceans combined.

7. In the Old World in classic times the writers and the military leaders gave the name "Mediterranean" to a sea. They recognized its importance because it was surrounded by practically all of the important nations of the then-known world. So today we might give the name "Mediterranean Ocean" to the Atlantic because it is surrounded by the world's major land masses.

8. The Atlantic story tells how man first learned to travel on the seas and on the ocean. It shows that the ocean has had an important effect on the way in which men think and feel and behave. The use of the sea has compelled man to develop some of his most important arts and sciences. The Atlantic story shows how structure and the behavior of the ocean have entered into human history; how the great winds and currents of the Atlantic have assisted man in some directions and held him back in others; how they have helped to determine the routes followed by the explorers, the colonists and the traders.

9. Often the routes which the early settlers followed across the Atlantic set the pattern for later travel and exploration on the continent.

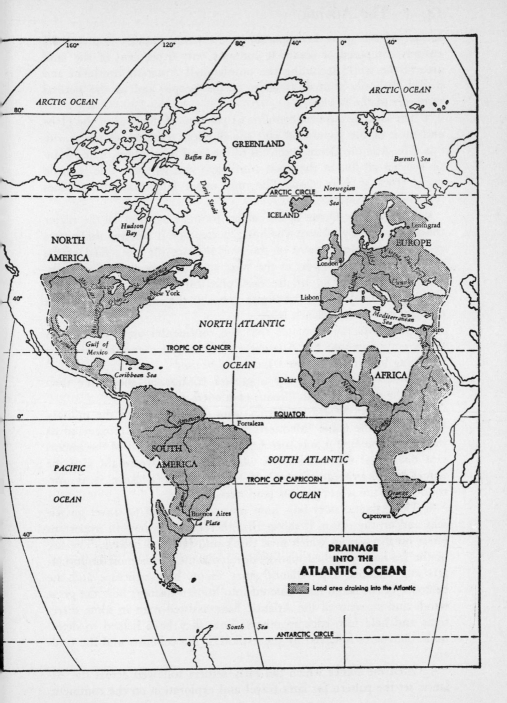

DRAINAGE
INTO THE
ATLANTIC OCEAN

Land area draining into the Atlantic

There was more than a Mason-Dixon Line that separated the North from the South; there was also the Gulf Stream and the Gulf Stream came first.

10. That the Atlantic is actually a highway of culture has been demonstrated over and over again when it has proved easier to carry people, religions, political ideas and scientific inventions across the ocean than to transport them over the few miles of man-made barrier that separate one European country from another.

11. The regular and highly organized system of winds and currents in the North Atlantic were largely responsible for the routes followed by the early European sailors in their quests for the Orient and the western continents. The winds and currents accounted also for the sequence in which discoveries were made.

12. The natural organization of the Atlantic assisted the Europeans and Americans in maintaining contact with each other and in establishing natural avenues of communication and trade. The Atlantic Ocean is a natural highway to all the continents and peoples grouped about its shores.

13. In the course of history hundreds of different types of ships have been developed to serve man's needs of travel and transportation. The vast majority of these ship types have been designed for Atlantic trade and built in Atlantic ports even when they were finally used for trade in other oceans. Likewise, most of the developments in seamanship and navigation have taken place on Atlantic voyages.

14. From their origin in the Atlantic basin men and ships and other methods of communication, arts and sciences, doctors and teachers and even political theories have gone out to all parts of the world. Our modern world of science and also of political and personal liberty is in origin an Atlantic world—the anthropologist would call it an Atlantic culture area.

15. Air travel across the Atlantic has become one of the most stirring enterprises of our time; it has not substantially altered the patterns of communication long established on the sea but it has accelerated and confirmed them.

16. The Atlantic is not a natural defense to any one nation or people; it is only of service to those who understand its essential character and have the energy and intelligence to utilize its natural advantages.

In two World Wars, control of the Atlantic has been threatened and the re-establishment and holding of that control proved a necessary and essential step to victory. Disruption of free and easy Atlantic travel would seal the doom of modern western society.

17. The nation or nations that control the Atlantic will control the heart of the world.

The importance of this area is increased rather than diminished by modern methods of warfare. Even if for military purposes we should hang satellites in space or control rockets from the moon, it is the Atlantic basin they would be sent there to defend.

Chapter 2

THE STRUCTURE OF THE ATLANTIC

THROUGHOUT their history people of the western world
have been familiar with the Atlantic—when they spoke or wrote of
"going to sea" or "crossing the ocean" it was upon the Atlantic
Ocean or some of its seas that they were about to embark. This was
first true of all Europeans and later became true also of settlers in Iceland, Greenland, Canada, the United States, the east coast of Central
and South America, the west coast of Africa. To millions of people,
to hundreds of thousands of families, to states and nations, the crossing of the Atlantic became an important historic event and the Atlantic their particular and almost personal ocean.

This familiarity has its drawbacks. Today the word "Atlantic"
will bring to mind a different image for each different reader. To
some it will mean the heaving gray waters of a dirty but busy harbor;
others will think of a clean rocky cove in Maine with little islands in
the offing; or a flat sunlit beach in Florida; or the standing waves of
Pentland Firth; or a harbor in Brittany that is over twenty feet deep
when the tide is in but is dry sand when the tide is out and the
ocean is just a blue line out there. Millions will think of it only as a
rather narrow strip of water connecting New York harbor with the
ports of the English Channel.

Each of these is a true but very specialized view of some part of
the ocean. Clearly before we can describe the structure of the Atlantic

we need a more general and comprehensive definition of our subject.

Two entirely different ways of looking at an ocean and of defining it are possible. Each way has some advantages for particular purpose, but, naturally, the definition of the Atlantic that we wish to adopt is the one that is current today and that is generally accepted by geographers, oceanographers and navigators.

One way restricts the ocean to the main mass of its waters, a vast open sea. This view emphasizes the distinction between the broad reach of ocean waters that stretch between continents and ocean waters that touch or penetrate the shores of the continents, peninsulas, islands, etc. This view tends to separate·the main ocean from its related seas, sounds, bays, straits and other tributary waters. This view implies that all shoreward, lesser or tributary bodies of water are different from the ocean and require a different treatment or that they are not sufficiently important to be taken into account. This view was more popular in the past than it is today and at that time there were geographers who carried the process of division even further speaking of a "North Atlantic" and a "South Atlantic" as though they were separate bodies of water existing independently of each other. It would be an exaggeration to say that the geographer or historian who separated an ocean from its adjacent and tributary seas was like an anatomist who said that a man consisted of head and trunk and that arms and legs, hands and feet could be ignored. Still it is quite probable that the tendency to give separate names and separate consideration to many different bodies of water delayed the recognition of the organic and integral character of the Atlantic and the systematic study that scientists have brought to bear on it in recent decades.

The other view acceptable to modern scientists is that an ocean consists not only of the deep and wide expanse of its main mass of waters but also of adjacent seas and tributary waters such as Mediterranean Seas (of which several are recognized including the original Mediterranean) and bays, gulfs, channels, etc. When this view is adopted and applied, a clear and more simplified view of the oceanic waters of the world emerges and it appears that these are naturally divided into three great ocean systems: the Pacific, the Indian and the Atlantic.

This way of dividing and defining the ocean systems aside from the major virtues of completeness, clarity and conformity with the general geological structures of the earth has other advantages. It recognizes that some of our older attempts to name and separate bodies of water while arbitrary and unimportant still had a certain convenience. In fact the scientists themselves still use expressions like "North Atlantic" and "South Atlantic" because these are convenient to describe geographical areas and the conditions found therein. They would insist, however, that the North and South Atlantic are not independent oceans but interdependent parts of the same ocean, with the South Atlantic at one level sending great masses of water into the Caribbean and so into the North Atlantic balanced by receiving waters coming directly from the North Atlantic at another level.

Science and common sense agree that an ocean means the main body of water together with all of its adjacent seas, gulfs, sounds, etc. There are a number of reasons for this usage including the following: First, it is sometimes difficult to tell where a sea leaves off and an ocean begins. Second, because there is in nearly all cases a free and continual exchange of large volumes of water between adjacent seas and the ocean itself. This introduces a third reason because while the ocean affects the adjacent sea, the adjacent sea also in some degree affects the character of the ocean. Finally, because the value of an ocean in great measure depends upon these lesser waters which are so important not only to the plant and animal life of the ocean but also to the life of man.

The Atlantic Ocean, then, consists of a large diversified and intricate system of salt water almost entirely surrounded by the land of six continents including Antarctica. The land margins of the Atlantic begin in the southeast quarter of the ocean at the Cape of Good Hope and include all the west coast of Africa. Then, in the Mediterranean, the north coast of Africa, Asia Minor and Turkey, the margins of the Black Sea, the southern coast of Europe, and in the Atlantic once more, the western shore of Europe from the Straits of Gibraltar to the North Cape, then the north coast of Europe and Asia as far as Bering Strait.

Bering Strait as a matter of fact constitutes but a narrow rift in the continental bulwarks of the Atlantic. As we shall see later in greater detail, Bering Strait is not only narrow but also shallow and the volume of water flowing over the sill inconsequential from the point of view of the oceanic system.

The boundary then becomes the northern shore of Alaska and Canada including the extensive indentation at Hudson Bay, Labrador and the eastern shore of Canada, the eastern shore of the United States into the Gulf of Mexico and the irregular contours of Central

America, the long sloping shoulder of South America which terminates in Cape San Roque and the eastern shore of South America to the Horn where the continental bulwarks of the Atlantic terminate.

South of Cape Horn and south of the Cape of Good Hope the geographers supply a somewhat arbitrary limit to the Atlantic. South of the Horn the Atlantic is separated from the Pacific by an imaginary line which is the shortest one that can be drawn from the Cape in longitude 70° west to the South Shetland Islands. This line is less than 800 miles in length and is not entirely arbitrary for there is an underwater ridge which joins South America with the Antarctic continent. South of Cape Horn the line runs at 20° east until it reaches the Antarctic continent, and the shores of Antarctica form the extreme southern margin of the Atlantic Ocean. Thus six continents lend a part of their shores to form the bulwarks of land that almost completely surround our ocean.

This physical structure quite justifies the designation of the Atlantic as the *Mediterranean Ocean.*

Barents Sea, the Greenland Sea, the Norwegian Sea make up very broad channels between the Arctic Sea and the Atlantic proper. The channels between northern Greenland and Ellesmere Island are extremely narrow and the channels through the Canadian Arctic Islands are many and narrow. In the Atlantic proper the S-shaped effect is created by a western indentation of the east. Within this basin of land lie the many and diverse bodies of water that together make the complex Atlantic Ocean. To name and describe all the waters of the Atlantic is fortunately not required here for it would be a long task. It is interesting, however, to recall the main features of this Atlantic, noting how varied is their character and how wide is their extent about the earth.

It will simplify matters if we first look at the Atlantic as it might be seen from the air or as it does appear on a globe. Then what we later see below the surface will be more easily understood.

Evidently people expect every ocean to be round or oval or oblong for they so often express surprise when they come face to face with the real but highly irregular shape of the Atlantic. It is always helpful to remember that the main body of the Atlantic has the general shape of the letter S and even recent technical writers on the ocean have found it useful to refer to this shape. It helps the accuracy of our picture if we add that the S is rather broad and straight, but the double curve is clearly there. Also while the letter is fairly shaped in the upper or northern portion of the Atlantic, for here the continents draw together, it is rather lost in the southern portion, for South Africa and the tip of South America trend away from each other, and the base of the S is lost in the broad Antarctic waters.

The upper or northeastern point of the S lies between Greenland, Iceland and the British Isles. Then the whole Atlantic swings boldly westward to match the westward bulge of the Iberian peninsula and Africa and the westward retreat of the North American shore forming a broad gulf between Nova Scotia and the West Indies. Then the curve to the east to round the eastward projecting coast of South America. The narrow constriction of the S at its middle point comes between Cape Verde, the most western point of Africa, and Cape São Roque, the most eastern point of South America. Beyond this on the eastern shore, the eastern curve of the African coast into the Gulf of Guinea seems to preserve the shape of the S and on the west the falling away to the west of the east coast of South America below São Roque also suggests this form. As we have already noted the southern portion of the Atlantic S degenerates and the base is missing.

However imperfect the S, it helps us to understand and remember facts about the Atlantic that otherwise would seem puzzling. For example, that the east coast of North America is nearly in north-and-south line with the *West* coast of South America and lies between 1,000 and 3,000 miles to the west of the easternmost point of South America. The 80th meridian west longitude just grazes the east coast of Florida and passes over the extreme western tip of South America. Practically all of South America lies *East* of this meridian. Cape São Roque lies at 35° west longitude and in the North Atlantic is just halfway across the Atlantic between London which is 0° and Cape Cod which is 70° west. The longest east-to-west line that can be drawn in the main body of the North Atlantic is approximately that from Mogador or Agadir in Morocco to Jacksonville or St. Augustine in Florida, a distance of about 5,000 miles. In contrast the shortest crossing, say between Freetown in Africa and Natal (near Cape São Roque), is only 1,800 miles.

We cannot leave this topic of the general form of the main Atlantic without at least a brief mention of a very fascinating theory. This is the theory of continental drift advanced earlier in this century by a geologist named Alfred Wegener.* Schoolboys have often observed that if the east coast of North and South America were moved east and

---

* Wegener, Alfred, *The Origin of Continents and Oceans,* Tr. J. G. A. Sperl from 3rd German edition, E. P. Dutton (1924), N. Y.

the west coast of Europe and Africa were moved west they would meet and more or less mesh together like the parts of a jigsaw puzzle. Labrador, Greenland and Iceland would fold against the Scandinavian Peninsula and the British Isles. The Scandinavian Peninsula in turn would fold into the Baltic area and the British Isles would fill up the North Sea; Newfoundland–Nova Scotia would perhaps fit into the Bay of Biscay; the westward bulge of Africa would nestle into the Caribbean area and the eastward bulge of South America tuck into the Gulf of Guinea. So there would be one big continent instead of many continents separated by wide oceans.

While this schoolboy fantasy is admittedly crude and superficial, Wegener, looking at the same area and the same general conformities, thought the idea merited serious study. He emerged with the theory that at some time in the distant geological past all the continents were together forming one solid land mass. Then rifts developed and the eastern continents started moving eastward while the western continents moved westward into their present positions.

This, of course, sounds absurd for we tend to think of a continent as a solid, rigid and uniform section of the earth's basic crust. And we tend to be confined to a short time scale. Wegener pointed out that rocks and soils composing the continents were lighter, more porous and less rigid than the deep, dense, heavy, rigid layers of rock which formed the basic shell of the earth underlying both continents and oceans. In common with other geologists he showed that great blocks of the earth's crust as seen in the continents are continually subject to movement and do adjust themselves to pressures as though they were afloat on some heavier medium. He pointed out that many changes in substances that are impossible in a short space of time become possible over a long time span. Thus glass and many metals seem rigid in the instant that we look at them; if we hit them a smart blow they break; but if we support them only at one end, under their own weight over a very long period of time they will tend to bend and even to flow. Wegener argued that in time even continents could float and drift. The geological time scale is so vast that it seems to provide time enough for even such movements.

At one time precise measurements taken in Greenland and in Europe seemed to show that Greenland was moving away from Europe at almost the exact pace predicted by the continental drift theory and Wegener's stock went up, but there have not been any general confirmations. At present Wegener seems neither to be accepted nor quite rejected. I am informed that a number of quite respectable geologists and geographers continue to take an interest in his theory or in some modified form of his many lively ideas.

In any event human life moves on a more limited scale and none of the facts or observations of this book depend upon either the acceptance or rejection of the Wegener theories, but it is almost impossible to forget Wegener when we look at the form of the Atlantic either above or below sea level.

The main Atlantic is extended by three large Mediterranean seas. Northward there lies the Arctic Mediterranean (which used to be called the Arctic Ocean) made up of the main polar sea, which has a shape somewhat resembling a half-moon, and smaller bodies of adjacent waters such as the White Sea, the Norwegian Sea, etc. There are very good and simple reasons for regarding the Arctic waters as part of the Atlantic and for separating them from the Pacific. Between Scotland and the Faeroes, Norway and the Faeroes, the Faeroes and Iceland are broad sea channels hundreds of miles in width and with a depth of 1,500 feet over the sills. Through these channels the Norwegian current and other arms and extensions of the Gulf Stream system pour warm waters into the Arctic basin so that the coast of Norway even to the North Cape and the south coast of Iceland are free of sea ice throughout the year and even the shores of islands in the eastern part of the Arctic basin are ice-free part of the year. Between Iceland and Greenland, Greenland and Laborador are also broad channels and through these, cold currents run out of the Arctic into the main Atlantic so that there is a very free and continual exchange of waters between the ocean and the sea. On the other hand the Arctic basin is almost completely cut off from the Pacific. Bering Strait, which separates the two, is only thirty-five miles wide and is generally shallow with a maximum depth of 160 feet.

The eastward extension of the Atlantic is, of course, the classic Mediterranean, and its own extension the Black Sea. The Black Sea is a specialized body of water, perhaps the most remote and inactive of all the adjuncts of the ocean. There is some exchange of water between the Mediterranean and the Black Sea. Through the Bosphorus, only two miles wide and 120 to 270 feet in depth, run two rivers of water one above the other. A stream of light water with little salt runs out at the rate of 12,000 cubic meters per second and a stream of heavy, salty Mediterranean water runs in below it at a rate of 6,000 cubic meters per second. Altogether this is very little for a sea. The Mississippi River for example runs 120,000 cubic meters per second. Even this exchange is for the most part confined to surface waters. The bottom inflow is so small compared to the deep waters of the Black Sea that renewal of water below ninety feet would take 2,500 years. Below 600 feet the Black Sea contains no oxygen at all but much ill-smelling hydrogen sulphide.

The Mediterranean proper, as we shall see, participates actively in the life of the Atlantic.

The westward extension of the Atlantic is the Caribbean–Gulf of Mexico system. These two basins are now regarded as making up an American Mediterranean.

Small Mediterranean seas in the Atlantic system are the Baltic and Hudson Bay, and the marginal seas are the well-known North Sea, English Channel, Irish Sea and Gulf of St. Lawrence.

The Atlantic system also contains one unique curiosity. The Sargasso Sea is more—and less—than a legend. Even the oceanographer still refers to the Sargasso Sea though it is only an area in the Atlantic. It is a sea without earthly shores, a body of one kind of water surrounded by walls of other kinds of water.

How does this vast and complicated ocean system compare with the other oceans? In absolute figures it is larger than the Indian Ocean and much smaller than the Pacific. The area of the main Atlantic rated in square kilometers is 82,441,000; the Indian is 73,443,000. The main Pacific at 165,246,000 is almost twice the size of the Atlantic in area.

This is a statement in absolute size of the main oceans. However, the interest of an ocean depends not so much on its absolute size as on the supplementary waters and its relationship to the land and the service it performs between continents. Here the Atlantic is in a special position. The Indian has practically no adjacent seas, a mere 1,476,000 square kilometers; the vast Pacific 14,000,000 square kilometers of adjacent seas; the Atlantic 24,022,000.

The reach or extent of the Atlantic and its adjacent seas is also interesting. In an east-to-west direction along a slightly bent line, say such as would be followed by a ship sailing on Atlantic waters from the Suez Canal to the Panama Canal, the Atlantic extends over 8,000 miles or the equivalent of one-third of the distance around the world measured at the equator.

In a north and south direction the axis of the Atlantic may be said to lie along the 150th meridian east longitude and its extension the

30th meridian west longitude. Along this line from the mouth of the Indigirka River in Siberia to the Weddell Sea area in the Antarctic, the Atlantic extends *more than halfway around the globe.*

These measures have for the most part concerned the surface of the sea, the area that has been of the greatest practical importance to man. To become familiar with the nature and behavior of the upper layers of the ocean and to have taken accurate sounding to the 100 fathom mark (600 feet) was an accomplishment that took centuries of human effort. The importance of the 100 fathom mark is that the sharp break between the shelf on which a continent sits and the steep slope in the deeper ocean usually is found within this limit and frequent soundings within this mark are of greatest service to the navigator.

Until 1920 deep-sea soundings were very difficult to make and only some thousands of soundings existed for each ocean where hundreds of thousands were needed. It was thought, therefore, that the continents sat on their respective shelves; that somewhere between the 80 and 100 fathom line the shelf itself terminated sharply and that the continental slope began which descended in a steep but regular fashion to the ocean floor; the ocean floor was flat, monotonous, slightly undulating. Differences in depth in various oceans were recognized and some deep areas had been reported and to these were assigned the name "abyss," but changes in depth were gradual.

The practical development and application of sonic depth finding around 1920 changed all this. The continental slopes were discovered to be cut by "gorges" and "canyons," the ocean floor to be broken into "ridges," "basins," "trenches," etc. In limited areas mountains have been revealed that are quite as steep and rugged as mountains ashore. Millions of soundings are now available, in fact they accumulate more rapidly than they can be checked and plotted. Day by day oceanographers in private agencies and government departments are busy exploring and mapping this new, remote and unseen world beneath the ocean surface.

Though our chief concern is with the upper layers of the ocean we should be aware that the world beneath the waves is not as inactive or remote as we sometimes suppose. It is an integral part of the entire ocean and even the shapes found in the bottom of sea or ocean may influence behavior at the surface. We have neither time nor space to explore this matter in detail but even a few examples will make us more familiar with the whole Atlantic.

To begin with a simple matter our surface view of the area of a sea or other body of water may be very misleading as an index of its inner character, depth and volume. Thus on a globe if we examine the North Polar Seas (Arctic Mediterranean) we can see that they are almost exactly three times the area of the Caribbean–Gulf System (American Mediterranean); yet under the surface at least half of the Polar waters are shallow and the American Mediterranean is nearly all deep, so it holds more than half as much water as the Polar Mediterranean. Again the area of the Baltic is more than one-third the area of Hudson Bay but it holds less than one-sixth as much water.

Underwater the Polar Sea is an area of great contrast so we might start our underwater glimpse of the Atlantic here. The deep part of the Polar basin lies off the Alaskan coast and the adjacent coast of the Canadian Arctic Islands and Greenland. It is egg-shaped with the point of the egg aimed at Alaska. In this basin Sir Hubert Wilkins obtained a sounding of 5,440 meters, or about 17,650 feet. Other soundings give lower values but the basin is known to be deep particularly as contrasted to the areas off Siberia and Russia and that north of Scandinavia.

On the average a continental shelf is thirty miles wide but the seas off Siberia are so wide and shallow that the continental shelf is as much as 800 miles away from the coastline.

There is an interesting point connected with these shallow northern seas. It is generally recognized that the tides which we see along our seacoast are the local evidences of two tidal waves on opposite sides of the earth which sweep around the open oceans of the earth every twenty-four hours and that these tidal waves are created by the combined gravitational pull of the sun and the moon.

As between the sun and the moon, the moon, though much smaller, is so near to us that it plays the major part in creating the tides as it circles around the earth.

Astronomers and geophysicists have pointed out that this gravitational pull is not a one-way street. While the moon is exerting a force to move and drag the tides around the world, the tides in their turn are exerting an equal hold and drag on the moon. It has recently been calculated and pointed out that a large part of this drag, this tidal friction, must be attributed to the shallow northern seas and that they contribute somewhere between 70 per cent and 80 per cent of this drag.

One of the gateways into the Polar seas is the broad passage between the Shetland and the Faeroe Islands. Here we have an opportunity to illustrate how a feature on the bottom of the sea can influ-

ence the life of the ocean and also how far-reaching and yet how delicate are the adjustments of the sea.

Between these islands there is a ridge on the bottom of the sea
named the Wyville Thompson Ridge in honor of one of the early
English oceanographers. The ridge lies 1,500 feet below the surface
and over it the warm waters of the Gulf Stream pour into the cold
Norwegian Sea. Of course at the surface temperatures are about the
same on either side of the ridge, but below the ridge there is a warm
side and a cold side. Studies show that though they are separated
by a very short distance and though the same water flows freely over
them, the creatures living on one side of the ridge are almost completely different from those living on the other side. Only 11 per cent
of all the species counted are found on both sides of the ridge.

It was also over this ridge in 1929 that Helland-Hansen found the
Atlantic water entering the Norwegian Sea to be warmer, saltier and
somewhat greater in volume. He thought about this and then announced that this should have far-reaching effects. He predicted
that two years after his observation the effects should be felt as far
away as the Barents Sea. Sure enough two years later, 1931, the seas
around Spitsbergen were free of ice for an area twice as large as
usual. Also fishing boats off Spitsbergen caught codfish in successful
commercial quantities, which had not happened before in over half
a century.

The Wyville Thompson Ridge is part of a line that extends from
Iceland to the Faeroes, from the Faeroes to Shetland and then to Scotland. South and west of this the main Atlantic begins. Here in the
great Atlantic basin a remarkable structure has in recent years
emerged with new clarity—this is the Mid-Atlantic Ridge. This runs
in an irregular line midway between the continents, dividing the Atlantic into two vast long valleys—an eastern valley and a western valley. The ridge rises to varying depths below the surface of the sea but
it extends in an almost unbroken fashion from Iceland in the north
to the island of Tristan da Cunha in the south. Indeed, many but
not all of the Atlantic islands are simply the loftiest summits of this
vast submerged mountain chain. Such peaks are Iceland, the Azores,
St. Paul's Rocks, Ascension, St. Helena, Tristan da Cunha.

Between the island peaks the ridge is submerged to an average
depth of 9,000 feet below the surface of the sea but it would still be
an impressive mountain range if viewed from the valley of the sea
itself. Between St. Paul's Rocks and Ascension there is a considerable
break in the chain like a mountain pass.

Romantically inclined people hearing of the Atlantic Ridge have suggested that this may be the remains of the lost and mythical continent or island of Atlantis now sunk beneath the waves. The scientific evidence seems to be the other way about: that the ridge is not old land that has sunk but new land that is rising.

Incidentally this was the view of Wegener. Not much was known about an Atlantic Ridge when Wegener propounded his ideas but he argued that it was natural that the eastern and western continents would part along a line of basic weakness in the earth's crust. Along that line of weakness vulcanism would take place and new materials would be thrust up. He argued that the volcanic character of the Atlantic islands such as Iceland, Azores, Canaries, St. Paul's Rocks, etc. was evidence in favor of his theories. At least in some quarters the emergence of the Mid-Atlantic Ridge has aroused a new interest in Wegener's ideas.

The conventional view, of course, is that the heavy blocks of rock that compose the base of the seas and the light blocks of the continents sorted themselves out in the basic formulation of the earth's crust and have remained more or less fixed. Even the conventional view admits vertical movement—balancing movements away from or toward the center of the earth, which have changed the relations of the sea to the land—but Wegener was arguing for floating and sliding movement.

The Atlantic Ridge though it is the most extensive is not the only ridge by any means. Minor ridges of lesser height or greater depth, whichever way you wish to put it, branch off from the Atlantic Ridge and serve to separate the Atlantic into a series of basins and depressions. Also there are independent ridges such as Bermuda to which we have already referred and sharp spurs at Madeira, the Canaries, the Cape Verdes.

The deep waters of the Atlantic are then divided by the great Mid-Atlantic Ridge and on either side of the ridge there are spurs or lesser ridges running east and west which serve to mark off a number of ocean basins, each of which has a special name. The names used are those of some nearby land or of some important island group. Thus there is an Iberia basin, a Canaries basin, etc. The basins all vary in size and shape and many of them have special features which create very dramatic underwater scenery; thus the Sierra Leone basin is relatively small, a sort of Rhode Island among the basins and on the other extreme, the North American basin which is vast enough to embarrass a Texan. In the eastern Atlantic there are ten basins that run from the West European basin in the north to the Antarctic basin in the south.

Here we might round the Mid-Atlantic Ridge and coming up the west side of the Atlantic we would travel over another ten basins from the South Antilles basin up to the Labrador basin with a detour into the Caribbean basin and Gulf.

Thinking about this general structure of the Atlantic raises an interesting point. It would seem natural to look for the deepest portions of the ocean far away from the continental shelves and somewhere toward the bottom center of the great open ocean spaces. It is always a bit of a surprise to find that they are in all cases close to land and usually close to some curving chain of volcanic islands. They are deep and they may have a considerable length particularly in the Pacific but they are never wide and thus deserve the description "trench."

The trenches should probably not be thought of as the deep parts of an ordinary ocean basin but rather as a special feature of the underwater landscape. Studying bathymetric charts and submarine profiles it is natural to think of them as mountains in reverse or upside-down mountain chains. Undoubtedly they are an evidence of some fundamental and long-established weakness in the basic shell of the earth. Here the basic tectonic forces that crinkled the mountains and islands upward at the same time crumpled the trenches downward.

There is such a trench close to the north shore of the island of Puerto Rico, a sort of sword cut in the bottom of the sea. Here the Atlantic reaches its greatest depth of 8,750 meters or about 28,000 feet. Not far away and even more closely associated with the land is another slot between Jamaica and the southeast coast of Cuba. This is known as the Cayman Trench and reaches a depth of 7,200 meters or 23,748 feet.

How deep is the ocean? From the point of view of imaginative writing of poetry or of philosophy it has been very useful to be able to refer to the ocean as a realm of unknown mystery and great depth. It has been an area of useful comparisons against which man could express or extend his knowledge and his feelings. Long before and long after Moby Dick the ocean has been set up as one of the perpetual challenges of the human spirit.

What has been a gain to poetry has, however, been a distinct loss to science. From a scientific point of view, one of the most important things to say about the Atlantic or any other ocean is that it is excessively shallow. The scientist in his own work no doubt recognizes the comparative shallowness of the oceans but neither he nor his interpreters seem to have made an effort to convey to the general reader how shallow the oceans really are.

It is easy enough to understand how this situation has arisen. A man swimming from a sandy beach may properly say the ocean is deep when he can no longer touch bottom. A primitive man sailing in a canoe will say the ocean is deep when the irregular stone suspended from a thong that he lets down from the bow of his vessel will no longer take hold on the bottom. A fisherman on the Grand Banks may properly think that the waters in which he is fishing are pretty deep if he has tried for a sounding with his lead line and missed bottom.

Up to a few years ago all ocean depths were measured, even from research vessels, by letting down a heavy weight at the end of a long line payed out from a stationary or drifting ship until the weight actually reached the bottom of the ocean. This required infinite patience, skill, knowledge, good fortune with the weather and a generous amount of time. The student of the sea who made such soundings could understandably say that from his point of view the ocean was deep.

In recent years all this has changed. Methods have been invented for measuring the oceans and the seas by bouncing sonic and supersonic waves to the bottom of the ocean. The waves are created at the ship or the station and the length of time that it takes them to reach the ocean bottom and return gives a measure of the depth which may be read almost instantly and continuously. The result is that the mapping of the ocean floor has recently gone on at a terrific pace and has rapidly built up a fairly accurate knowledge of the shape and depths and limits of the ocean basins.

Of course, even before this had happened, the oceanographers had a good general idea of the depth of the oceans and they already knew that compared with the size of the earth and to the vast extent of the oceans, they were in fact very thin and shallow bodies of water. I am a great admirer of the oceanographers and an enthusiastic follower of the work that they are doing and nothing that I say here is intended in any way to diminish the credit and the support which they deserve from the public. Still I cannot help wishing that they and the more popular writers had done a little more to let the general public in on a trade secret. In an astronomical or geographical sense the oceans are very shallow.

In part the oceanographers are victims of two of their own professional habits. Each of these habits has a good historical and logical reason and each has produced good results. However, the accumulated effect of using both of these devices in oceanography leaves the general observer with an exaggerated sense of the shape and character of the oceans.

The first of these devices is the use of rather dramatic technical names. In the old days when deep sea soundings were developing slowly and the work of oceanographers was just beginning it was easy and natural to pick up some popular phrase and use it in a technical sense. Thus we had "the continental shelf," "the continental slope," "the deep," "the abyss," "the trench" and a number of other words that stir the popular imagination and suggest great depth. Such terms now have become purely technical phrases and have a technical meaning to the oceanographer. Their effect on the general reader is forceful though not exact.

The second of these devices is the use of highly exaggerated profiles, charts, diagrams and three-dimensional models to illustrate the structure of the ocean and its retaining floor. In these representations the vertical scale or depth is greatly exaggerated in relation to the horizontal scale or breadth. Sometimes the ratio is as much as 1 to 200. The ordinary observer always inevitably forgets the figures and remembers only the deep impressive pictures of the chasms. He carries away the impression that the oceans are very deep, whereas he ought to conclude that the use of such a scale is necessary because the oceans in a physical sense are very shallow.

At all events, at the present time, the prevailing popular impression seems to be that there is an enormous difference in elevation between the mountains of the continents and the depths of the seas with great chasms separating the continents one from another. The picture of the earth which many people carry around with them suggests that the earth is shaped something like a ball of wet clay that has been grasped by a strong hand which has pushed up some areas which we call continents and has left deep finger marks that have somehow gotten filled up with water, and these we call the oceans.

In order to correct our images I propose for a few moments to project a cold, impersonal, or if you prefer, an inhuman view of the ocean. Possibly this should be called an astronomer's view of the ocean.

Let us consider the ocean in relationship to the earth. We will use round figures which we can easily remember. They will be a little inaccurate, but for our purpose this does not matter, because the thing we are after is a matter of comparative and not absolute size. Let us assume the earth has a radius of 4,000 miles, diameter of 8,000 miles and a circumference of 25,000 miles. Of course, scientists will point out that the earth is not a sphere but to a certain degree an "oblate spheroid of rotation." We come to this point in a moment.

Now let us reduce this earth to a size we can easily look at. The eye height of the average human being is not too far from five feet five inches, so let us take a block of steel of sufficient diameter and turn it down as smoothly as we can into a sphere that has a five-foot diameter and is perfectly smooth everywhere. Now this sphere will represent the earth and on it, keeping to scale, we will show the continents and the oceans. How much metal do you think we should cut away to represent the deepest sea? How much metal do you think we should have to build up to represent the highest mountain? The answer is rather surprising. The highest mountains in the United States would be represented by a little roughness 1/50 of an inch in height. The highest mountain in the world, Mount Everest, a little over 29,000 feet, would be represented by an elevation of 1/25 of an inch. The deepest depth ever measured in any ocean is a little deeper than Mount Everest is high. It occurs, not in the Atlantic, but in the Pacific. The Philippine Deep runs to about 33,000 feet. So this would be represented by a little scratch in our globe about 1/25 of an inch in depth.

To get a clear image of these relationships, let us imagine that we are representing on our globe the sum total of the height of Mount Everest and the depth of the deepest part of the Philippine Deep as lying right beside each other. We could represent this by a flat piece of cardboard stuck on our globe. Standing some ten feet away from our five-foot globe, we could see that the cardboard was there. Of course, actually the highest mountains and deepest seas are separated by thousands of miles. If our globe represented these in proper scale, we would possibly notice a slight irregularity in outline here and there. If the light were coming from the right direction and we saw the roughness, we might infer that the mechanic who turned our metal globe had had a slightly unsteady hand or that his tool was dull and had slipped a little.

Incidentally, while we have the globe before us it is interesting to note that on this scale the difference between a sphere and the oval shape we referred to could hardly be detected. It works out something like one part in 300. It would take a very sharp eye indeed to detect the difference between a five-foot sphere and a five-foot ellipse that truly represented the earth's proportions.

Now to get back to our ocean, we have already referred to the fact that if the mountains and the continents themselves were all shaved away and dumped into the depths of the sea so as to make a perfectly round sphere, the ocean would cover all the land to a depth of one and one-half miles. This is an important statement because it does give us an impression of the amount of water in our oceans. But on our five-foot globe, water a mile and a half deep would be represented by a very thin film indeed.

A Dutch astronomer, Van den Bergh, put the matter something like this. Take a new soccer ball and blow it tight, roll it quickly through a puddle of water and pick it up. Our earth is about as wet as the soccer ball you now hold in your hand.

Of course, not all the moisture of the earth is at any one time all in the oceans. There is always some of it in the air in the shape of clouds. From the human point of view, we have become accustomed to think of the clouds and atmosphere as being very high indeed just as we think of the mountains and the sea as very high and deep. Sometimes it looks to us as though the moon were racing through the clouds, but here again poetic imagery has gotten the better of reality. The envelope of air or atmosphere that surrounds the earth is more dense at sea level, and as we progress upward, the atoms of the gases that compose our atmosphere get farther and farther apart. On account of our interest in rocket flight, the upper air is intensively studied today and extraordinary new facts are turning up about it. But for general purposes we may say, sixty miles above the earth our atmosphere begins to approach a vacuum; about as good a vacuum as we can create in a laboratory with an ordinary vacuum pump. On our five-foot globe the air would be represented by a sort of smoky film that would disappear entirely half an inch away from the surface of the globe. On this same scale the moon would be 160 feet away. All of the useful air, the air in which man can breathe, the winds can blow, the clouds can scud, the lightning flash and the thunder roll, the rain and snow and hail fall back upon the earth, all the airy drama that directly affects man . . . would take place in a thin film 1/25 of an inch high.

There it is, a sort of abstract extraterrestrial view of the earth and the oceans. Looked at in this way, perhaps neither the ocean nor man seem, for the moment, to be very important. We have built up our picture of the five-foot globe in order to acquire a certain perspective regarding the proportions of our earth. To emphasize these proportions, we have talked in terms of a steel ball. That was all right for our purpose, but now we shall have to make certain corrections. Though the interior of our earth is actually very dense and under great compression, the surface of the continents are made of rock and dirt and sand which contrast, of course, with the ocean water. Photographs have now been taken of the earth from a V2 rocket in flight and they begin to show how the earth actually looks as we move out into space. It does look like a very solid smooth ball. The curvature of the earth begins to be apparent but the outlines of the oceans and seas and lands are apparent too. Clouds appear as a very low-lying fuzzy scum, drifting here and there over the sea. An observer on the moon with a good pair of field glasses could, after a period of time, create a very good picture of the structure of our earth. He could do so, not because of the difference in height of the structure of the earth, but because land and water receive and reflect light in quite different ways. Now one of the most significant things that an astronomer on the moon or some planet would notice and record about our planet is that it *did* have an atmosphere and that it was *wet*. If he had about the same scientific equipment that our astronomers have, the astronomer on Mars would conclude that the earth is very unusual and interesting because it could sustain life—including human life. Even from the astronomer's point of view, these thin oceans are therefore of the greatest importance.

This five-foot globe representing the earth can leave with us not only a vivid picture of the mountains, the seas and the atmosphere, but also a just and useful sense of their true proportions. It relates us to reality, it shows us how vast in area and how thin in depth is the stage setting in which man has been performing the human drama. This vision of the earth is not exaggerated; though it seems hard to believe, it is in fact an understatement.

Though the shell of the earth from mountain height to abyss is but a thin eggshell in space, man's hold on life hangs on a still thinner film. It is not all levels of the earth or depths of the sea that are useful to living creatures. Photosynthesis, the process by which sunlight builds up in plants the ingredients that are required for the process of living by all creatures, and other chemical and bacteriological actions that are essential to life are confined to a film that, on our globe, would be so incredibly thin as to be ultra-microscopic. In the case of the oceans there is some depth to the zones on which life is dependent; in the case of topsoil on the land, it is so thin as to be almost immaterial. It is not surprising that a flush of rain or a puff of air can endanger life over a large area by washing soil away into the rivers and the seas.

It is important, from time to time, to be able to adopt a cold view with respect to man's place in nature. It is equally important not to let a cold view become a fixation. After all, it is in this filmy scum of rock and sea and air wrapped around the dense core of the world that we live out our destiny of privation or richness, of war or peace. This is our ultimate base and we must preserve it as well as master it. The knowledge that we are held to so thin a paring of the world's space and that we stand so insecurely upon the margin of a vast universe does not destroy the human view or the human responsibility. Man need not be too humble because, so far as he can know, he is the only actor on the stage. He has traveled about the globe and today is peering into the sky and the sea. He has discovered and so, in a way, helped to create the universe. From the human point of view, the lands are still fruitful, the heavens beautiful and the oceans deep.

We have come to a more realistic picture of the Atlantic Ocean. It is not a great reservoir of water filling up a pool or trough gouged deeply out of the earth as we have so often imagined. It is in fact a vast but thin sheet of water curving around the world between the continents. With related seas it stretches over 12,500 miles in a north-south direction or more than halfway around the world and on an irregular line from the eastern end of the Mediterranean to the western end of the Gulf of Mexico over 8,000 miles or over one-third of the way around the world at the equator. The average depth or thickness of this very irregular sheet is only 3,332 meters or a little over two miles. Even the North Atlantic without its shallow seas has an average depth of less than four kilometers or two and one-half miles. So when the depth of the ocean is compared with its extent it is seen to be on the average no thicker than the paper this book is printed on.

Yet within this thin sheet the Atlantic carries on an intense and complicated life of its own. At the surface move winds and weathers, currents and tides; below the surface the ocean is made up of distinct and recognizable masses of water with known limits and depths and each marked from the other by special characteristics.

We may think of these waters as the parts or organs that make up the body of the ocean. However, since each part enters actively into the life of the ocean we may properly deal with them in the next chapter which considers the behavior of the Atlantic.

Chapter 3

BEHAVIOR OF THE ATLANTIC

ATLANTIC behavior is full of strange tricks and curious surprises. This, at least, is the way matters appear to the observer who is making his first acquaintance with this ocean. Meeting some odd performance for the first time he will first feel he has come upon a unique freak or singular accident; when the event is repeated he feels that man must have a hand in it; finally, as he becomes familiar with habits and patterns of the ocean, what at first seemed accidents turn out to be orderly parts of the ocean's behavior when viewed over long distances and considerable periods of time.

Here, to begin with, are some cases in which the Atlantic has acted in its own natural fashion on natural objects, without human intervention. Later we can consider cases where the ocean has acted on man-made objects and more complicated events where man and ocean act together.

In Central America, from Panama on up into Mexico, the year is divided into a wet season and a dry season. Every year during the wet season some of the great trees of the tropical forests along the rivers come to a violent end. Some are blown down and fall into the river; others standing on the banks have the earth washed out from beneath their roots by the rising waters of the river until the banks collapse and they topple into the stream. In either case some of these trees will be carried downstream and delivered into the Caribbean or the Gulf of Mexico where the Atlantic Ocean takes charge.

After an appropriate interval of months or years some of these trees of various Central American species have turned up as driftwood along the beaches of the European coast. The first student who found and identified one of these trees no doubt thought that he had come upon a rare curiosity, but further study has shown that such trees and timbers have turned up in Europe over centuries and have been found in many places all the way from the Atlantic coast of Spain to Norway and the North Cape. In fact examples have been found far in the Arctic seas collected from the shores of Spitsbergen, Novaya Zemlya and other coasts.

The Atlantic makes this complicated delivery of lumber in the following way: The logs discharged by the Central American rivers into the western Caribbean are driven by prevailing winds and currents northwest between Yucatan and Cuba; they are then in the Gulf of Mexico and could here be joined by trees from northern Yucatan and the eastern coast of Mexico; after a loop through the Gulf they

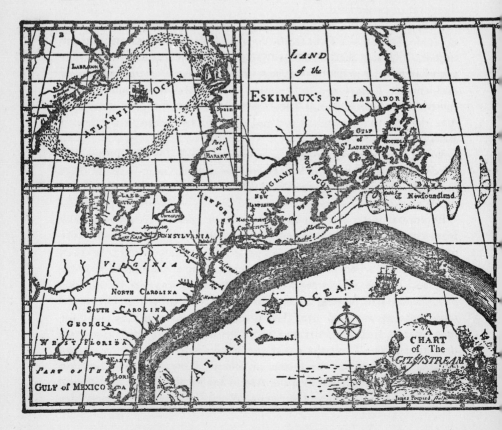

are caught up in the Florida Current which is the beginning of the Gulf Stream and carried rapidly between the north coast of Cuba and Key West in Florida; then north between the east coast of Florida and the Bahama Bank; the Gulf Stream then carries them north and east in a wide arc; out in midocean the Gulf Stream gradually loses some of its speed and spreads out in area (technicians now refer to this portion as the North Atlantic Drift); but it is recognizable as simply a continuation of the Gulf Stream and our Central American logs continue leisurely northward and eastward toward the European coast; then the drift begins to divide and separate in smaller currents; one of these continues to curve in a clockwise arc and would deliver logs to the Bay of Biscay, the Portuguese or the Spanish coast; another flows past Ireland and Scotland and on up the west coast of Norway past the North Cape and on into the Arctic; one current, still warm, flows north and then west in a counterclockwise fashion and is known as the Arminger Current, running south of Iceland in the direction of Greenland.

Thus the Atlantic without human assistance accomplishes a natural intercontinental export-from-America import-into-Europe trade in timber. The fact that men have used these timbers when they were sound *after* their arrival in Europe and that at least one ancient medieval church (*stavekirk*) in Norway is reported to contain Central American timber does not alter the nature of the original case. Nor does the fact that nowadays cut and sawn timber occasionally appears along with the natural product.

While this may sound like a unilateral trade in which the New World gives and the Old World receives, the Atlantic is really more impartial and offers another deal under which the East gives and the West receives.

Explorers and other travelers who have visited Greenland have, from time to time, commented on the fact that the Greenland Eskimos on both coasts made carvings out of wood, used it in their weapons and, when they could get it, in their structures such as canoes and houses. This was often a puzzle to the travelers for no trees of sufficient size to yield a piece of timber had grown in Greenland within the memory of man. The answer, of course, is that the Eskimos have been using driftwood and that this wood to them is a treasured possession. The woods that the Eskimos have used have almost invariably come from the forests of Siberia. Trees from the Siberian forests have been carried into the Arctic Sea by rivers like the Ob and the Lena in the spring and summer. When the freeze-up comes, they become embedded in the ice pack and after drifting across the whole Arctic are carried by the currents to both the east and west coasts of Greenland.

This current drift across the Polar Sea has carried more than ice and driftwood. One of the travelers who noted the Eskimos' use of driftwood from Siberia was a tall young Norwegian named Fridtjof Nansen then making the first crossing of the Greenland Ice Cap. He thought about the driftwood and also about the case of the *Jeanette*. This was an American ship that had entered the Arctic Sea by the way of Bering Strait, had been caught in the ice and wrecked and abandoned off the Siberian coast. Wreckage from this ship and even a box containing some of the ship's papers turned up in Greenland. Out of such evidence Nansen developed his plan for freezing the *Fram* in the ice and crossing the Pole, and Nansen's example stimulated the Russians in recent years to fly a party to an ice island located at the Pole where an observation station was set up. The drift of the ice island followed prediction and the observers stuck with it until it finally disintegrated in a sea of slush off the southeast coast of Greenland.

In all the above cases we have fairly simple situations in which prevailing winds and currents combine to carry floating objects in set courses. The surprise comes because the objects travel so regularly and so far.

Let us look now at the surprising result the Atlantic can produce when it sets to work on more complicated materials. This in fact is the extraordinary case of the ship that simultaneously followed two different courses.

The American sailing ship *Fred B. Taylor* up to a certain June night in the year 1892 had a quiet and undistinguished career going about the sea on useful but routine errands. Then the vessel's strange and lingering death won for her a special mention in the annals of the ocean. On June 18 she was at sea bound from Le Havre to New York in ballast about one hundred miles southeast of Nantucket Island, in 40° 19′ north latitude, 68° 33′ west longitude. Suddenly the North German Lloyd Line *Trave* bore down on her, hit her amidships and cut her in two. In fact, *Trave* literally steamed right through *Taylor* leaving one half of the sailing ship on her starboard and one half on her port side. The mate was killed in his bunk and the carpenter drowned. The rest of the crew were ultimately rescued. As for *Taylor,* nothing could be done to sail or direct her and no form of salvage was undertaken.

For a while the two abandoned halves of the *Fred Taylor* drifted along together. Then they began to separate. We shall name the parts *FT1* and *FT2* because each part seemed to assume a new life of its own worthy of record. *FT1* and *FT2* now were moving on almost directly opposite courses and each started a lengthy journey.

FT1, after slight hesitation, moved toward the northwest. Then she took a long run north which, after a month or so, brought *FT1* south of Matinicus Island and east of Mount Desert Island off the northern coast of Maine. Then, turning a little south of west, *FT1*

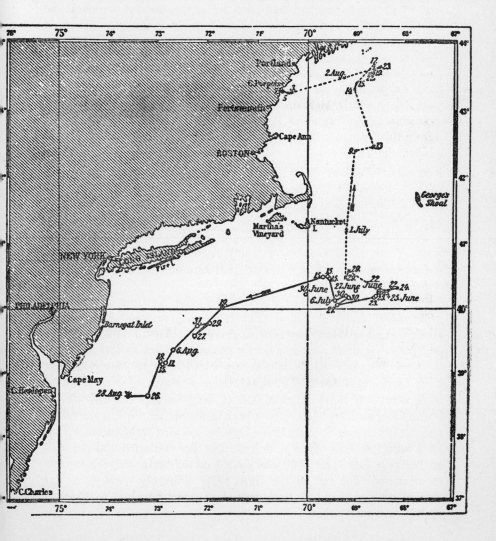

swung into the Gulf of Maine and on August 7 grounded on Cape Porpoise.

Selecting an entirely different course, *FT2* jogged off southwest. On two occasions, at the end of June and at the end of July, *FT2* reversed the direction of travel for a day or so. Even with these delays, *FT2* arrived off Cape Henlopen below the mouth of Delaware Bay on August 28.

So the record comes to this: starting from the same time and place, in fact starting as the same ship, two half ships without any kind of human interference, under what appear to be the same natural conditions, travel for months in almost opposite directions. When they stranded they were 350 miles apart!

Here again the mystery is cleared up by detailed knowledge and observation of the ocean's behavior.

FT1 was the stern of the vessel. It was high built, compartmented, floated relatively high out of waters. The prevailing winds off the coast in spring are from the southwest and even high winds come from this quarter. *FT1*, therefore, rides the winds and the harder they blow, the farther she travels northeast. Only she goes to the north and not very much to the east because, though chiefly driven by the wind, she is also afloat on a current that pushes her toward the west. The result is her northward course until, well "down-east" in Maine, she becomes the tired victim of northeast winds and a current setting into the Gulf of Maine, which combine to drive her ashore.

FT2 was the bow and forward portion of the vessel. It lay low in the water offering little surface to the wind. It was chiefly in possession of the current. The current here is a large eddy that lies between the Gulf Stream and the American coast and that moves in a counterclockwise fashion. As the old sailorman used to say, it moves against the sun. *FT2*, therefore, traveled in an arc in a southwesterly direction.

FT2 while steadily in the grip of the current was not entirely free from the effects of wind and weather. On two occasions, that is on the last few days of June and of July, strong southwest winds set *FT2* back on her heels; in fact reversed her course. In each case, however, as soon as the winds abated the hulk took up her westward drift to her destiny.

Almost on the equator and some 600 miles east of the coast of Brazil there is a mountain peak that rises from the floor of the sea and sticks its head above the ocean to form a steep and desolate little island known at St. Paul's Rocks. The Rocks lie in the narrow part of the Atlantic, midway between West Africa and Brazil. On a certain day a ship being near this island was in latitude 1° 44' north and longitude 27° 16' west. At this place and at a certain time ten bottles were dropped overboard from this ship. Each bottle was carefully sealed and each contained a card with an address and appropriate instructions for returning a report from wherever they might be discovered. Eight of these bottles were never reported. After 377 days one of the bottles was reported having landed on the east coast of Nicaragua in Central America. After 196 days one of the bottles was reported from the coast of Sierra Leone in Central Africa!

This is a real teaser for, in this case, the bottles were identical and we cannot assume that one bottle would be acted upon by the wind while the other bottle would be acted upon by the current. Note that drifting objects here were not the results of an accident as in the *Fred Taylor* case. The bottles were carefully prepared and this obviously suggests an experiment. However surprising the drift of the bottles may seem to us they were not surprising to the men who threw them overboard. They were in fact conducting an experiment to establish a boundary between the Atlantic North Equatorial Current which runs westward and then northwestward along the northern coast of South America into the Caribbean and the so-called Guinea Current which is a great eddy setting eastward into the Bight of Benin. Some of the bottles were supposed to go east and some west but it must have been something of a surprise to show that the currents going in opposite directions flowed closely beside each other. Experiments either ashore or afloat do not always work out as neatly as this one.

Bottles in currents have often contributed to romance as well as to science. There was, however, a recent case that didn't quite come off. A lonely Texas soldier was returning home from a south European port on a ship which seemed to him interminably slow. On impulse, he wrote a note, stuffed it in a bottle, corked the bottle and threw it overboard. He went home and after a time, I suppose, forgot about the message; but the Atlantic took charge and some combination of the North Equatorial Current and of the Gulf Stream in due course delivered his message to a supposedly beautiful colleen who was herding sheep near the sea in Ireland. The boy and girl corresponded and he made a trip to Ireland to see her. It was a wonderful story and of course it attracted front page notice. It should have ended, "The sea brought the lovers together and they lived happily ever afterward," but unfortunately romance seems to have vanished in a puff of publicity.

The floating bottle carried by ocean currents has over the years been a great aid in the study of the oceans. Of course many of the bottles launched are never found or they fall into the hands of ignorant or careless people and are never reported. The bottles that are recovered have provided a great deal of information about the direction and extent of ocean currents and the date of report or arrival may also indicate an average speed or rate of travel.

Besides bottles and other sealed containers the drift of many other objects have been traced over the Atlantic. Since most of these objects were large enough to be real and active dangers to ships traveling along shore or across the ocean, captains were usually eager to trace and report them. The list of such objects includes logs and timbers, wreckage, derelicts, icebergs.

Almost from the beginning of ocean navigation captains have kept logs or other systematic records of their voyages, recording therein at regular intervals the state of the weather, direction and strength of the wind, the condition of the sea, the course or direction of the ship, her speed; later as instruments became available there were also records of soundings, barometer readings, air temperatures, water temperatures, etc. etc. There were also brought forward an estimate of the ship's position (dead reckoning) or when conditions were favorable a statement of her exact position (fix) determined by observing fixed objects ashore—lightships, lighthouses, capes, objects ashore (coastwise pilotage) or by observing sun and stars (celestial navigation). Now when the observed position differed from the dead reckoning position, the navigator could assume that a surface current at sea or a tidal current near shore were responsible. A head current could set the ship back, a favorable current advance it or lateral currents set it to either side—but in any case the direction and speed of the current could be calculated.

Often, of course, in the old days these ships' logs were crude and inaccurate, but as more and better instruments became available (chronometers, patent logs, sounding machines, etc.) and as navigation methods were more systematically taught and used, knowledge of the sea improved. The large-scale scientifically directed study of ships' logs began about one hundred years ago and out of it grew books and charts that first gave a general, comprehensive and practically accurate picture of the winds and weathers, the seasons, the storm systems, the surface currents, etc., of the sea.

The early work may have been crude and rather limited to surface conditions, but it was also broad and constructive; as it owed its materials and direction to practical men it also was of value for practical purposes as in the management of vessels, navigation and the development of superior trade routes. Later research at sea has not only refined the methods and extended the results of earlier study, it has also plunged into new regions, developing knowledge of the ocean slopes and bottom, of the several separate kinds of water masses that make up the undersurface body of the ocean and the way in which these waters behave in relationship to each other.

We may acknowledge at once the theoretical importance and the intellectual fascination of the new works in oceanography. A single example will suffice to indicate what is involved and we select quite arbitrarily the newly developing field of oceanic (really sea bottom) geology. In those days neither governments nor private institutions were supporting systematic research at sea and even vessels assigned to some special inquiry were a rarity. Nowadays both governments and private institutions provide special vessels, instruments of great complexity and cost, and special opportunities for all manner of ocean research from the surface of the sea to geological strata below the sea's bottom, and professionally trained specialists carry out studies of great refinement and fascinating mathematical accuracy. It is interesting to remember, however, that in the beginning ocean meteorology and oceanography were made possible by the co-operative contributions of many thousands of practical navigators.* Since only about 30 per cent of the surface of the earth is dry land and 70 per cent is below water and since many geological strata now exposed on land were formed under sea and many strata formed as dry land are now underwater, it seems reasonable to believe that there will be serious gaps and flaws in geological history until submarine geology is further developed.

We may also admit that present studies though they may seem remote can and have produced practical results as in submarine sound and supersonic devices including sonar, submarine navigation, and devices for defensive and offensive submarine warfare. Who knows what lies in store in the development of the ocean as a source of raw materials, of food and of power?

* The chapter on M. F. Maury contains some further information on this period.

Our proper first interest, however, is in that broad bold picture of conditions found at the surface of the sea and at moderate height above and depth below that surface—the realm where the ocean of air and the ocean of water react upon each other. It is in this realm that man has lived and explored and traveled and traded and fought. It is the conditions found in this realm in all parts of the Atlantic that have influenced human history. They have acted on human conduct whether man was conscious of them or not and often in the beginning of Atlantic history the voyagers were unaware of the systems of winds that could hold them back or hasten their voyages, the currents that could swing them off their intended course. Later as men organized their experiences and their knowledge they made expert use of Atlantic conditions—avoiding calms and side-stepping hurricanes, going west in the northeast trades and back in the belt of prevailing westerlies and edging into the current systems that could speed them on their courses.

The winds are largely if not totally responsible for the most important Atlantic currents such as the Gulf Stream system. Recent computations, at least, have shown that the force available in the wind system was of an order sufficient to account for the current system. It seems therefore that the winds of the Atlantic north of the equator deserve first attention.

At the equator itself is the belt of the dreaded doldrums. This is an area of inactive or fitful air lying between the strong and steady northeast trades of the Northern Hemisphere and the strong and steady southeast trades of the Southern Hemisphere. It is the belt of many and prolonged calms but also of sudden squalls; of drought and heat punctuated by sudden torrential rain. It was an area dreaded by the captains and men of the old sailing ships for here they could be caught without wind and therefore without power to progress or fill sails to steady the ship, which therefore rolled noisily and incessantly in the long sea swells while the sails and rigging wore out with the constant motion; the deck planks shriveled and warped; the food ran out; the water evaporated in the casks; the captain drove his men, shifting sail to catch every hatful of wind that came along; the men grumbled or fell sick. Anything could happen in the doldrums and often did. At times even steady breezes sprang up and a ship slipped through without perils or hardships and also without stories to tell on reaching port.

In general the doldrums lie along the equator but this is not always exactly correct. They do lie between two trade-wind belts and since the trade winds move some degrees of latitude north or south with the seasons it follows that even the doldrums also shift a little.

The Northern limit of the doldrums is the southern limit of the northeast trade winds. This limit shifts and is never precisely defined, but in September, at the time of the equinox, it will be found at about 10° north latitude in mid-Atlantic. The trades there form a broad band which extends northward to about 30° north. However, in the eastern Atlantic the northern limit swings up to include all of the African coast and also part of the Spanish coast, terminating near Cape Trafalgar. On the west it is described as ending at Cape Canaveral, a midpoint in the east coast of Florida.

Within this broad band the prevailing wind comes from the northeast and may blow from this quarter steadily with good force (average force four on the Beaufort scale) day after day. This is of course a general statement based on averages of figures reported by many ships over many years. In practice the wind might blow anywhere between north and east, but it could be expected to blow from this quadrant about 80 per cent of the time. Three or four per cent of the time even in the center of the belt there will be calms, light airs or variable winds. The rest of the time brisk winds of short duration might be expected from any quarter of the compass. This is so high an average of favorable winds as to insure a relatively quick passage to any ship bound from European ports to southern ports of the American Atlantic coast or to Gulf ports or to the Caribbean. Many captains of sailing ships bound from European ports to Norfolk, Baltimore or even New York have found it just as fast and far more comfortable to take their vessels "south about" through the trades than to buck the winter westerlies on a more direct course.

Life in the trades is usually drawn and described as fair and comfortable. It can be so but it can also be boisterous and rough. Storms are not excluded from the trades area and I know from personal experience that when meteorological conditions give them an extra push they can create hard work and discomfort for a small ship.

It is important to observe that the trades though called northeast vary their direction according to a regular plan. All along the west coast of Africa as far as Cape Verde winds come from the north even more frequently than from the northeast. Between Cape Verde and the West Indies they come from the east more frequently than from the northeast. As they approach the American coast north of the Windward Islands and about the Bahamas they blow from the east and southeast as much as from the northeast.

This shows that the northeast trade wind system is not in fact confined to a belt of latitude but that it tends to form itself into an arc and in that arc the bend is to the right if your back is to the wind or in a clockwise direction. The arc indeed is part of a complete though sometimes weakly expressed circuit of winds for the trades do not suddenly come to an end in mid-Florida. Even north of Florida out at sea there are prevailing easterly and southerly winds to speed a northbound vessel on her course. There is a weak spot around Hatteras but above 40° north, say around the latitude of New York, the band of the prevailing westerlies has begun.

Just as the northeast trades begin off the African coast with winds from the north rather than the northeast so the westerlies begin off the American coast with winds from the southwest rather than west. Moving east and then northeast a ship finds herself in the area where the westerlies do prevail and this extends into the upper fifties, say about the latitude of Scotland.

The westerlies are real enough but they are not as regular and well defined as the trade winds and the tendency to swing to the right is not noticeable. There is a weak area of variable winds off the Bay of Biscay but a little southward at Cape Finisterre the winds again are from the north and northeast and are blowing down the line of the Spanish and Portuguese coast. They have been called the Portuguese trades and they feed directly into the northeast trades. In fact they can hardly be distinguished from the northeast trades with which we began our circuit of this part of the Atlantic.

The area between the northeast trades and the westerlies contains a permanent barometric "high" near the Azores and in general the winds of this region are light, variable and disorganized.

North of the westerlies there is again an area or belt of variable winds and in summer even a strip with a fair proportion of easterly winds. In the north the great land masses of the continents crowd together and leave only the basin of the Polar Sea between them.

The weather in the sub-Arctic and even in the Polar Sea (now called the Arctic Mediterranean Sea) is greatly influenced by the land areas and does not have an oceanic character.

Until recently systematic information on Arctic weather has been scanty but is now accumulating rapidly. The huge Thule air base and other air bases and stations are adding to this body of information. In this connection it is interesting to remember that the establishment of the Thule base involved the voyage, up and back, of a fleet of some seventy ships. Flights over the Pole that a short while ago were acclaimed as feats of exploration are now routine assignments. All this will result in a new formulation of information on Arctic weather, winds and currents.

With the winds systems of the North Atlantic in mind it is easy to understand the main features of the current system, for the latter is a result of the former. Owing to the fact that water is a denser, steadier and literally more conservative element than the air, the great ocean currents move with a regularity, a far-reaching influence, a persistent majesty that make the wind systems seem flighty and temperamental. The wind systems can blow over the land as well as the water and they are re-formed by influence of the land; the ocean currents are confined to the ocean basins and are therefore more highly organized. Also contributing to this organization is the fact that the ocean currents are more directly responsive to earth's gravitational and rotational forces. For all these reasons we should not expect the ocean currents, even the wind-driven currents, to correspond exactly with the pattern of the winds. It is the surface currents created directly or indirectly by winds that we shall chiefly notice but there are also currents that chiefly appear because of the earth's rotational force and thermal currents due to the slow heating and cooling of great masses of water. These types of currents affect not only the surface of the sea but its depths also. It takes a thick volume even to begin to describe the form and behavior of ocean currents so great is their variety and so complex their behavior. Fortunately, it is enough for our purpose to note their general form and a few special circumstances.

Along the equator there are in mid-Atlantic no special currents to note. Under the northeast trades lies the North Equatorial Current flowing straight to the west. A part of this current turns northwest as it approaches the West Indies and flows north of the Windward Islands and east of the Bahamas, where it becomes the Bahama Current. North of the islands this current flows along beside the Florida Current which has come northward between the Bahamas and Florida. They mingle and bend toward the northeast and east and are here together called the Gulf Stream. In mid-Atlantic again this great flow of water loses some of its speed and spreads out and is now known as the North Atlantic Drift. Progressively as it moves along parts of this drift turn southeast and south and rejoin the North Equatorial Current. One branch continues east until it strikes the African coast and bends south through the Canary Islands where it joins the colder waters of the Canary Current; but an important part of these joined streams bend westward and become again a part of the North Equatorial Current. So with the North Atlantic currents we have made a complete right-hand or clockwise circuit of this portion of the Atlantic, a circuit caused by the winds but complete, well defined, fully organized.

But the Florida Current that comes up between the Bahamas and Florida and that Floridians and unregenerate mariners will no doubt continue to call the Gulf Stream—where does that come from and what gives the whole system its drive and power and direction?

Let us return for a moment to mid-Atlantic in the center of the North Equatorial Current. We are moving straight westward with the current pushing us along and the northeast trades at our back. Now the part of the current that is on our right swings away farther to the right but soon additional water from the South Atlantic sweeps in from the left and the whole stream, with the east winds still pushing, passes between the Lesser Antilles and on into the Caribbean. Here, with the Central American coast blocking the way, the waters of the current pile up. With increased speed they flow through the only available exit, the narrow Yucatan Channel. Part of this stream may make a circuit in the Gulf of Mexico, but the gulf also is continually receiving this large volume of wind-driven water so the greater volume of all the flow that has come through the Yucatan Channel swings quickly around the west end of Cuba and, still picking up speed, rounds the end of Florida as the Florida Current: in other words the start of that Gulf Stream system whose course we have already traced.

Though it may seem strange that there could be any appreciable difference in "sea levels" or that so large a body of water as the Gulf of Mexico could be affected in this way, it is in fact true that sea level in the Gulf of Mexico is higher than sea level on the Atlantic coast. By measurement sea level in the gulf at Cedar Keys, Florida, is nineteen cm. or about seven and one-half inches higher on the average than sea level at St. Augustine, Florida.

The current itself also accounts for a strange unevenness in sea level. Owing to the rotation of the earth a current running like this one will sort out light water from heavier water in its composition and in the Northern Hemisphere the light water will slope up on our right hand if we face in the direction toward which the current is running. It has been calculated as a result that sea level on the north coast of Cuba is forty-five cm. or almost eighteen inches higher than sea level at Key West, Florida.

The volume of water moving in these currents is so great that it is usual to figure the volume of water carried by the current past an imagined line *each second*. Anyone with zest for nice large figures can translate this into volumes per minute, hour, day or any larger unit curiosity might dictate. Between Miami and the Bahama Bank the current carries 26,000,000 cubic meters of water per second. Should you stand on the levee of the Mississippi River at New Orleans and look across it to the far shore it would seem to you a vast and rapid flow of water. It would take 217 Mississippi Rivers to equal the flow of the Florida current even here at its narrowest point. The current flowing outside the Bahamas, the Bahama or Antilles Current, adds another 12,000,000 cubic meters per second. This great stream seems to drag along with it other masses of water for off Chesapeake Bay the volume transport has been computed as 74,000,000 cubic meters per second and even higher.

In the center of this great circuit of North Atlantic currents is a quiet current-free area which includes the area known as the Sargasso Sea. We have already spoken of the northward extensions of the North Atlantic Current (European part of the Gulf Stream system) when we were tracing the voyages of the Central American driftwood.

With so much warm water moving northward one might expect that there should be some exchange or balance—some cold water moving south—and there is. On both sides of Greenland there are southward flowing currents of cold water coming out of the Arctic Mediterranean. The East Greenland Current runs rapidly and carries along with it masses of pack ice and icebergs. One branch of this current continues south beyond Cape Farewell with its dangerous load. The other branch hugs the cape and having bent around it starts flowing northeast as the West Greenland Current. Before reaching Davis Straits it turns west and joins another southbound current to continue as the Labrador Current. The Labrador Current continues south across the Banks; around Newfoundland and ever on along all the Atlantic coast, running between the coast and the Gulf Stream. Of course as it progresses it warms up gradually and loses some of its speed and power but lingering traces have been detected along the shore as far south as Georgia.

We have been speaking of the surface currents of the North Atlantic and here warm, northward flowing currents seem to predominate over one important southbound cold Labrador Current; but we should remember that lighter, warmer waters will ride on the surface and that denser and colder waters tend to sink and to form the intermediate and deep waters of any ocean. Atlantic intermediate water is formed off Newfoundland and sinks and moves south slowly under the surface currents. Atlantic deep bottom water is formed on either side of south Greenland. It sinks to the very bottom of the ocean and begins a movement southward over the bottom surface that is so slow it has been described as a "creep"; but eventually it will arrive near the equator.

To these must be added a very special type of water known as the Mediterranean which, as we might expect, originates in that sea; but we should hardly expect it to form a distinct level or carpet in the Atlantic spreading out in all directions and being recognizable almost as far as Bermuda. To understand how this is so, we must recollect the peculiar conditions in the Mediterranean.

If you were looking from the Rock down on the Straits of Gibraltar, the only connection between the Atlantic and the Mediterranean, you would observe that the waters seem to be flowing continually from the Atlantic into the Mediterranean and that so far as you could see, there would be practically no water escaping from the Mediterranean into the Atlantic.

The mystery is solved—as mysteries so often are—by looking beneath the surface. Here we should find that at greater depth there was a flood of water pouring out of the Mediterranean into the Atlantic. What happens here is that the Atlantic water coming in is light and not very salty. The column of fresh water flowing into the Mediterranean is not very great. On the other hand, the region is warm and sunny, therefore the evaporation is great.

The incoming Atlantic water, therefore, spreading out on the surface evaporates and becomes saltier and heavier and so sinks down to form a carpet of saltier and heavier water and finally to form the stream that rushes out of the Straits of Gibraltar under the lighter Atlantic surface water. It finds its own level of temperature and of saltiness and spreads out across the Atlantic in a fanshape pattern. This Mediterranean water keeps its identity amid the other Atlantic waters and has been identified off Bermuda.

The right-handed or clockwise circulation of currents in the North Atlantic is of course due to the rotation of the earth about its axis. The same force that produces the right-handed swerve in the Northern Hemisphere will produce a left-handed swerve across the equator in the Southern Hemisphere. The South Atlantic winds and currents are therefore very similar in general pattern to those of the

North Atlantic except that their revolution is left-handed or counter-clockwise. The trades are southeast trades and they drive a South Equatorial Current. Part of this turns southward as it approaches the South American coast and becomes the Brazil Current. The Brazil Current continues south until it meets a cold current coming up from the direction of Cape Horn. Then it swings east and becomes the Antarctic Current. Off the west coast of South Africa the cold northbound Benguela Current appears flowing north even into the Bight of Benin.

The South Atlantic currents have one unique feature which is not repeated elsewhere. The east coast of South America culminates in a point at Cape São Roque, the coast retreating away to the northwest and southwest. This wedge divides the South Equatorial Current and an important part of it is deflected northwest. At least 6,000,000 cubic meters per second of it cross the equator and continue northwest to join the North Equatorial Current and pour into the Caribbean and eventually become part of the Gulf Stream system.

This chapter began with some examples of what the winds and currents of the Atlantic could do to inert and inanimate objects like trees, bottles, wrecked ships, etc. It is easy to understand that such powerful and far-reaching forces will also exert their influence to help or to hinder the voyage of a ship even when driven by sail or engine and even when it is directed by man. The Atlantic will be at work even though man is not always aware of the forces that are assisting or arresting his progress.

Parts II and III of this book examine many of these relations between man and the Atlantic at different periods of history. It would be impossible to summarize these at this point; but because we now have some of the main Atlantic features in mind it might be interesting to pick some examples more or less at random:

The winds and currents of the Mediterranean affected the location of colonies from the time of the Phoenician on down; also the order in which different parts of the Mediterranean basin were developed; many special features of Mediterranean oceanography are reflected in classic myths, in Homeric literature, etc.

The early discovery of the American continent by the Norsemen and their voyages along the Atlantic coast become more intelligible and creditable when we examine how their outward and southward passages would be assisted by winds and currents. The relationship of currents to the shores of Greenland and the upwelling of water at the west Greenland shore determined the locations sought out by at least four successive groups of voyagers: Eskimos, Norse, Danes, Yankee and other whalers.

The Portuguese mariners under Henry the Navigator were encouraged and able to undertake their explorations of the west coast of Africa with crude vessels because their outward passages were always aided by favorable currents and the Portuguese and northeast trades; the Benguela Current almost blocked them farther south until Diaz dared to take his ship offshore.

Cabral made an independent discovery of South America while on the way to India because the southeast trades and the South Equatorial Current carried him off course.

So it goes right down to our days: the *Savannah,* the first powered vessel to cross the Atlantic, was more assisted in her crossing by a judicious use of the Gulf Stream than by her steam power plant.

During World War II submarines came into the Mediterranean without using motors or propellers, and thus without being detected by sound, by submerging a little but letting the everpresent surface current carry them in. They left the Mediterranean by submerging to somewhat lower depth and letting the flood of everpresent heavier, saltier water carry them out over the sill into the broad Atlantic. . . .

These are scattered and not always important examples of the way in which the ocean has influenced human undertakings and also of the way in which men with knowledge of the ocean have used it to their advantage. The remainder of this book shows in a more leisurely and systematic fashion the part the Atlantic has played in human history.

Chapter 4

THE MEANING OF THE ATLANTIC

IT WOULD be almost impossible to write of the main physical features of the Atlantic—its structure and its behavior—without at least suggesting that these features are important to us as individuals and as nations. Some of the physical scientists, however, have achieved such a high point of abstraction that the human value of their work has all but been ignored. Here we claim no such abstract skill or purpose. Even though in the recent chapters we wished mainly to present a picture of the physical ocean, we have not tried to disguise the fact of its human importance. It would, indeed, be surprising if many readers had not anticipated our general point of view regarding the meaning of this ocean: the Atlantic is the world's most important ocean; it is the central fact in our historic past and in our hopes for the future.

In the present chapter we shall try to summarize in some detail what physical features of the Atlantic are important to human beings and why they have this significance. Even the readers who already accept a general belief in the importance of the Atlantic may find it interesting to check the details of this belief and perhaps to add points to our necessarily abbreviated analysis. Other readers may be surprised or in doubt. They may well say: "All right! If the Atlantic has this importance why haven't we heard more about it? Why isn't it plain in maps and in writing?"

These questions deserve an answer. We shall proceed then in this

way: first, we shall name certain ways of making maps and of looking at things, tricks of thought and unfounded beliefs that obscure
the value and importance of the Atlantic; second, we shall present a
new way of looking at the world and a new division of hemispheres
that make plain to the observer why the Atlantic is so important;
third, we shall list the functions of the oceans and show how well
the Atlantic performs these functions. A function, of course, is something an ocean does or performs, and here we mean not only what
the ocean does in nature but also what it does for man. What the
Atlantic does, and has done, for us is its meaning to us.

The reason why so many of us fail to recognize the importance of
the Atlantic at once is that most of us have grown up in—and even
been trained into—certain artificial ways of looking at the world.
The ways of looking at the world are embodied in maps—the kind
of maps that glare down at us from schoolroom walls and even from
the halls of colleges and that appear too frequently in all but the
most modern atlases.

The first misfortune in the use of maps is the too common dependence upon the Mercator projection. The Mercator projection is one
of the oldest and most widely used and misused methods of trying
to reduce a round globular world to conform with a flat sheet of
paper or the page of a book. The Mercator projection is the one that
makes the round world fully occupy a long flat quadrangular area. It
draws the meridians of longitude as though they were parallel to
each other though they should actually converge and cross each other
at two points—the North and South Poles. Thus as we move away
from the equator either north or south distances and areas become
progressively distorted in an east and west direction and the Poles,
which are points and really have no east-and-west extension at all,
are stretched out until they are made equivalent to the equator. Join
the east and west ends of a world Mercator map and you will see
that our globe has been reduced to a cylinder. This Mercator map
has certain technical uses for navigators: it is useful for areas near
the equator; even in higher latitudes it is useful for limited areas.
However, when it is used, as it so often is, as an introductory or general picture of our world, the result is misunderstanding and confusion. It is almost an ideal device for misrepresenting the relationships between the oceans and continents of the world.

One of the commonest alternatives to the Mercator map is also to
be regarded as a major misfortune. This is the map that shows the
globe as two round flat circles touching each other only at the equa-

tor, representing an *Eastern* and a *Western Hemisphere* with the *Old World* on the right and the *New World* on the left. This corrects some of the defects of the Mercator map; it does draw the meridians so that in each half of the representation they are seen to intersect at the pole; it avoils the distorted largeness of high latitude areas and the relative dwarfing of equatorial areas; it does come nearer to representing the continents in their true shapes and proportions. But it also, unfortunately, does violence to the oceans. It splits the Atlantic wide open, leaving only a margin of water around the continents of either hemisphere. It thus not only destroys the unity and integrity of the Atlantic but also makes it appear that the Atlantic serves to split and separate the hemispheres. This psychological impression is in the main unreal and even contrary to the fact for as we shall see demonstrated in many ways the Atlantic has served mainly to unite the continents and to serve as a highway between them.

The disregard or disrespect for the ocean expressed, perhaps unconsciously, in these maps is also found in much of our modern writing and teaching. Earlier in our history most American citizens lived on or near the Atlantic seaboard and many of them had but recently crossed the ocean to establish homes here. Most of them were in some way directly or indirectly dependent upon the ocean and quite conscious of its importance to them as a source of food and fuel, as a channel for their trade, a highway for their contact with the rest of the world and a wide frontier to be defended. As we have expanded to fill up a large part of a continent the proportion of landsmen who seldom or never see the sea has increased and the proportion of those that dwell on or along the sea has diminished. This change in knowledge and interest is no doubt reflected in our writing and thinking. More and more our history, our literature, our political theorizing, our news has been written by landsmen for the benefit of other landsmen. The good seamen, the fine naval leaders, the merchants and those who know the science of the sea are still with us, but they are outnumbered and it is difficult for them to be clear and articulate and eloquent about their problems where a common background of information and interest has ever to be created anew and almost rebuilt from the ground up. It is not true that the Atlantic is less important to ourselves and to other nations than it was in the past. It is probably more so, but the relative number of people who understand this importance has decreased.

The materials for understanding exist. There is indeed a vast new literature of the Atlantic and the other oceans, new ships, new trades, new methods of navigation, new methods of naval warfare, new relations of land and sea and air. They have all been expressed—somewhere or other. The trouble is that most of the writing is scattered and technical and not available to the ordinary citizen reader. Just here the author wishes to remind the reader again that the facts and points of view expressed in this book are not his discoveries or inventions and that he does not believe they are novel. They have mostly been expressed before, but by technicians writing for other technicians in half a dozen different realms of knowledge. The author's chief task and pleasure has been to dig up these scattered facts and theories and points of view, to try to express them simply and to relate them to each other.

So much for the negative side to account for ignorance and misunderstanding.

On the positive side let us take a fresh and different view of our whole world. There is really only one realistic and satisfactory way of seeking out and studying the relationship of land and water areas of the world and many other related facts. That way is to turn between our hands a carefully made geographical globe which represents in true proportion the main features of our world but shows them in reduced and manageable size.

Now as we turn the globe in our hands and study it one thing becomes clear: though the main facts of the earth are all there before our eyes and between our hands, we can see at any one time only half a world or a little less. We are compelled to look at the globe in hemispheres—one at a time. But we are not compelled to use the old and arbitrary division of the world into Eastern and Western Hemispheres. This intensifies a separation which is rather arbitrary in nature and which is gradually losing such historic importance as it may once have had.

Instead let us seek out two new hemispheres which will correspond with very important geographical facts and will give us new ideas regarding the character of the world and its peoples. The most interesting way to see these hemispheres is to find them for yourself on your own globe.

To find the first hemisphere turn the globe so that the southeast corner of New Zealand is the center of the world and directly under your eye. The exact center should be Antipodes Island.

You are now looking at the Water Hemisphere. The reason for the name is clear. It is almost entirely composed of the Pacific and

Indian Oceans with the extreme southern end of the Atlantic added to overwhelm an already overbalanced score. Land for human habitation is scarce indeed. Antarctica, barren, mountainous, ice-crammed, is the most prominent land mass. Australia, New Zealand, New Guinea and the tip of South America with a far scattering of tiny islands make up the rest. All of the land in this Water Hemisphere, including uninhabited Antarctica, totals less than six per cent of the land area of the world. In this whole half of the globe resources are scarce, people are scarce, contacts are difficult, travel drawn out and history a fragment.

Now give the globe a half-revolution. Adjust it so that London is directly under your eye. Here again the exact spot the geographer would select is off the mouth of the Loire River in France but London is easier to remember. You are now looking at the Land Hemisphere. It contains 94 per cent of the land areas of the world. It contains by some staggering percentage practically all of the world's natural resources and almost the total of all land areas lying in temperate climate. No wonder that this one half of the world contains all but a small fraction of the entire population of the world—96 per cent!

Now as your eye runs south see how the Atlantic opens out and lies as a broad channel between the four continents—Europe, Africa, North and South America.

The position of the Atlantic at the center of the earth's land mass is in itself important enough to warrant our concentration on this subject as individuals and as a nation. However, the outline map does not tell the whole story; there are further facts that add to the importance of this ocean. Perhaps the easiest way to convey these facts is to ask: what do we expect of an ocean? What does it do for us? What services does it perform? Does the Atlantic do these things well?

There does not appear to be any standard or generally accepted list of the functions of an ocean. The oceanographers present many of the facts in great detail but their approach is abstract and they do not appear to be much concerned with the comprehensive utility of an ocean. The following list of functions of an ocean is offered here with no idea that it is authoritative or complete but only as a convenient method of presenting certain important facts:

Collection or Drainage: The first and obvious function of an ocean is to serve as an area for the collection of surplus waters that the land does not use or retain. In this sense, the ocean is the destination of the brook, the river, the bay and the sound. As Swinburne has it, "Even the weariest river winds somewhere safe to sea."

Now before proceeding to the consideration of other functions let us see where the Atlantic stands with respect to its service as a drainage recipient. The easiest way of doing this is to make a tour along the shores of the Atlantic, considering the major river systems that flow into it. We may start with the Cape of Good Hope and, neglecting some smaller streams, the first river we come to is the Congo. Farther on in the bight we have the mighty Niger. The Gambia and the Senegal are smaller streams but drain a large, relatively dry area. The northwest quarter of Africa is relatively dry with no big river systems but in the Mediterranean there is the Nile. Also reaching the Mediterranean by way of the Black Sea, consideration should be given to the Dnieper and the Danube. The only other river in the Mediterranean worthy of inclusion is the Rhône. We may refer to the drainage of Spain and Portugal though the rivers in themselves are not considerable nor are those of the French Atlantic coast such as the Garonne, Loire and the Seine. In Germany there are the Elbe, Oder and the Rhine—the latter the largest as well as historically the most important of the northern European rivers. The drainage of the Scandinavian countries, while large in aggregate volume, produces only few and short river systems. In the Arctic coasts we encounter some of the world's largest and longest river systems such as the Dvina, Pechora, Ob, Yenisey, Lena, Yana, Indigirka and the Kolyma.

In passing to the Arctic coast of America we come to the Mackenzie and the drainage of the Hudson Bay system. Below Labrador the St. Lawrence accounts not only for the major drainage in eastern Canada but also, through receiving the overflow from the Great Lakes, of a large interior region of the continent. However, although important to their area, the Penobscot, Kennebec and Connecticut can hardly be reckoned as major river systems on the world scale. The Hudson-Mohawk system should be included because of the relatively large area it serves, and on the same account the Delaware, the Chesapeake and collectively the Potomac and the other rivers that flow into Norfolk Sound.

In the gulf, the Mississippi-Missouri system constitutes one of the world's greatest rivers—judging not only by the volume of its waters but also by the area served. The Rio Grande is important only on account of the area served, since the volume of its waters is not significant. On the South American coast we come again to the rivers of the major class: the Magdalena, the Orinoco, the Amazon and the La Plata system.

The mere listing of river names is impressive. The impression can be strengthened and left as a permanent part of the reader's mental equipment if he will take the slight trouble of taking a pencil and following on a globe or map of the world the headwaters and the continental divides of all these rivers that by one route or another pour their waters into the Atlantic Ocean. In Africa, for example, the line runs well to the east so that there is a very short coastal plane along the Indian Ocean and only one moderate-sized river, the Zambesi. Continuing in this fashion through the other continents, it will be seen that the mountain systems of the world for the most part lie relatively close to the non-Atlantic side of all the continents.

The rivers of China and of India, and on the American continent the Columbia, the Sacramento and the Colorado represent the total of the world's major non-Atlantic rivers. *Half of the land mass of the world is represented in the collective Atlantic drainage basin.*

Renewal: As soon as the sea receives the waters of the river it commences their restoration and renewal. The muds and silts are deposited as deltas, bars and shoals. On rising coasts these will perhaps emerge again as shore and finally land. The waters themselves are acted on by the tides and the waves. They are churned up, aerated, nutritive substances consumed by the many marine creatures of the shore, small particles attacked by the bacteria of the sea. The Atlantic performs these services for the world's widest, most productive, richest, busiest river valleys and coastal plains.

Storage: In this function as in that of renewal, the Atlantic performs the service of storage for the same major continental areas.

Temperature: We have noted already how the oceans are the determining factor in the earth system of winds and weather. In the matter of temperature they make the earth habitable to man. Here their function is that of conservation and balance. Most of the sunlight that the world receives falls upon water, and fortunately water and moist air absorb heat more slowly and give it up more slowly than land surfaces or dry air.

The ocean and its related waters therefore serve as a temperature balance wheel modifying the shift of temperature between day and night and also from season to season.

Were it not for the oceans and the moisture-laden atmosphere which they create, we should be as badly off as our satellite the moon. Here, without moisture and without atmosphere, the temperature where the sun is shining will reach 200 degrees Fahrenheit above zero whereas in the shadows or in the dark area of the moon it will drop as far below zero. On earth we never carry our climate to quite such extremes, but in the hilly part of the western Sahara Desert the daily temperature variations are extraordinary and unwary travelers can suffer both from sunstroke and frostbite within twenty-four hours. To a certain degree fluctuation of daily temperature is a feature of all arid deserts remote from the sea. The centers of the continents that are relatively dry are marked by extremely hot summers and extremely cold winters and other features of what is known as a "Continental Climate"—that is to say, a climate so far inland that it is relatively free from the temperating influence of the ocean.

It may seem surprising or even doubtful that a stream of water running slowly somewhere offshore, or a surface of water out at sea, could warm the moving winds or even temper the climate of half a dozen nations. It is surprising until we remember the great thermal capacity of water—the capacity to absorb, hold, transport, heat. The texts on oceanography are full of complicated computations on exactly what happens when the Gulf Stream cools as it moves along. For general purposes it is enough to remember, as we noted in a previous chapter, that the thermal capacity of air is to that of water about in the ratio of 1 to 3,000. So it takes 3,000 times as much energy to warm a cubic foot of water one degree as to warm a cubic foot of air one degree. It works the same way in reverse. Thus one cubic foot of Gulf Stream water cooling one degree will raise by one degree 3,000 cubic feet of air.

Now, referring again to our globe or outline map, notice how the Atlantic and all its supplementary waters invade or surround the European continent with the Black Sea and the Mediterranean, the North Sea and the Baltic. The European continent indeed has the form of a large peninsula, so that almost all parts of it are subject to the modifying effects of the Atlantic waters. These effects are more marked in the northern part of Europe for two reasons. First, because of prevailing westerly winds, and second, because of the sweep of the North Atlantic Drift, which is the natural continuation of the Gulf Stream. Europe is an air-conditioned continent—the Atlantic serving to warm its air, to moisten it and help it to circulate much as machinery conditions the air of a building.

Because of these same prevailing westerly and southwesterly winds, the effects of the Atlantic are less marked on the American shore though the ocean does exert a temperating influence even along the Atlantic seaboard, and the deep indentation in the continent created by the combined effects of the Caribbean Sea and the Gulf of Mexico influences the southern part of the United States. That the presence of the Atlantic can influence the temperature and climate even in cases where the prevailing winds blow from the land to the ocean does not seem to be very well understood.

Rainfall and Moisture: The water that the ocean is continually receiving through the flow of rivers from the continents must be restored to the continents again in order to preserve the cycle and the plans of nature. This is taken care of by evaporation of the water along the shores of the continents and also in the open sea. In general, what we have said about temperature control applies also to moisture control.

The Atlantic with all its seas, gulfs and other ramifications is continually renewing and refreshing the moisture content of the air so that the lakes and rivers may be supplied through the fall of rain and snow, fogs and mists and other forms of water transport and precipitation. It is worth special mention that the function of the Gulf Stream is not only to keep the waters of northern Europe warm and the harbors open but also to keep the climate wet. At first we might suppose that the most rapid rate of evaporation took place where the sun was usually shining and the air was generally warm and that evaporation was generally low or negligible in temperate and northern climates.

The story is not quite as simple as this. A study has been made and a curve drawn to show the rate of evaporation from the open Atlantic all the way from 50° north to 50° south. The highest rate of evaporation comes in one band a little north of the equator and in another band a little south of it with a slight depression at the equator itself. It is a minor but interesting point to note that the section in the tropics seems to reflect the fact that wind, as well as warmth, adds to the rate of evaporation; therefore, the areas of maximum evaporation are in the zone of the trade winds and not at the equator which is marked by the doldrums—a region of calm and fitful winds.

The important point however is that the total evaporation in the tropics is much less than we might expect and evaporation in the middle and higher latitudes is much greater. The reason for this is that a high rate of evaporation takes place whenever the water is warm and the air above it relatively cold. In the tropics, of course, the warm water that is flowing north and south and being driven by the belts of trade winds has to be replaced by colder water coming up from lower levels of the sea. On the other hand, in northern latitudes, wherever and whenever surface water is relatively warm and the air cold, there will be a high rate of evaporation usually visible as mists or fog. This effect is not confined to the ocean and we can remember it any time that we care to look at the smoking surface of a mountain lake in the early autumn. Before we leave this section it will be worth noting that in the Western Hemisphere the Atlantic contributes water content to the air over the land chiefly in the tropics and the great trade wind belts. On the other hand, on the European side, the Atlantic contributes its moisture chiefly in the region of the prevailing westerlies. This should make it clear that the areas of land that largely receive their *precipitation from* the Atlantic have a quite different pattern from that of the areas of land that contribute their *drainage to* the Atlantic.

The preceding functions of an ocean may be considered as natural functions—those that are world-wide in character and that create the general conditions of human life. To these we may add a set of functions from which man benefits directly and in which he directly participates. It will be enough to refer to each of them briefly in this place in order that we may have a summary of the major characteristics of the Atlantic. How these functions have operated in detail and how they have served man in the past form part of the stories and histories in the next section of this book.

Food: Wherever man has lived on the seashore or adjacent to the sea, it has supplied an important part of his living resources. Even the most ancient and primitive people have derived the most important part of their food supplies from the sea. The inventive and ingenious Eskimos serve as a particular example since they have derived from fish and animals of the sea practically their entire diet. At the same time, the sea animals have supplied them with oil for warmth and illumination, furs and skins and membranes for their clothing, bedding and the lining for their houses and even bones and ivory for their weapons, their ornaments and their arts. They are perhaps an extreme example.

Almost any part of the sea will sustain a reasonably large population along its shores and supply them adequately with foodstuffs that are not only nutritious but also contain all the required vitamins and minerals. In such a diet shellfish, crustaceans and small shore fishes play an important part. Through most of history the sea has made a very significant contribution to the total human menu. However, in recent centuries mankind has been increasing numerically at an explosive rate in many parts of the world such as India and China. Particularly in sections removed from the sea the bulk of the population starve or reach early death through the prolonged and cumulative effects of undernourishment. It has been repeatedly suggested that a further exploitation and use of sea products could help to relieve this misery. Recent studies of the world's food resources seem to show that such a program is not as easy to carry out as it at first sounds for the following reasons: (1) The population grows at such a high rate that it is doubtful that new methods of fishing and taking other natural food products from the sea can keep up with such an increase. (2) The sea is not equally fruitful in all its parts—the tropics are less productive of sea life than the northern waters and the open seas are but scantily populated, particularly in the forms of life that are readily accepted as human food. The rich fisheries are along our coasts and on banks and shoals.

A more recent suggestion is of an entirely different character, namely, that detailed studies of ecology—that is to say the natural relations of plants and animals with each other and with their environment—in shallow waters and along the shore will show how sea products essential for human nutrition can be increased. In short, this is a proposal to develop methods for farming the sea just as we have long since developed methods for cultivating the soil. Possibly it is true that the sea cannot naturally and speedily be expected to alleviate the hunger created by runaway population growth. It is equally true that throughout history and right up to the present time the oceans have liberally supplied and enriched the diet of nations and races that had an easy access to the sea; particularly the Atlantic has been bountiful to man. Later sections of the book will deal specifically with special topics such as the Channel fisheries, the North Sea and northern fisheries, the Icelandic fisheries, the Grand Banks and shores of America.

Ocean Products Other Than Food: Quite apart from food, the ocean has supplied man with many utilities and luxuries. Among the utilities have been oil of the whale and the seal used both for illumination and lubrication, and also among the utilities have been salts and chemicals. Among the specialties and luxuries that have had historic importance are such interesting curiosities as "whalebone" which brought a fantastic price when it went into the making of corsets. It was the only material then available that made it possible for ladies to assume the interesting and complicated contours that were then regarded as the height of fashion. The ocean has also yielded countless acres of furs to keep the ladies warm and stylishly attired and the whale has yielded ambergris to serve as a base for their perfumes.

A chapter in the next section of the book deals with the chief types of whales and the types of vessels that have hunted them.

Travel and Transport: The ocean is the great highway of mankind. Man's farthest journeys and most successful journeys have been made by way of the sea, and all of the continents, subcontinents and major island groups of the world were *discovered, developed and colonized by people traveling in sailing vessels.* The oceans have always been and still are the prevailing means of international trade and the cheapest method of transport ever devised.

What has made the Atlantic so important in human exploration, colonization, communication, trade, travel and general progress depends partly on this ocean's central position among the continents, but two other factors are almost equally important. One is the length and complexity of the *Atlantic continental coast lines, greater than the other two oceans combined.* This provides easy junction of land activities of man and ocean transport—the ports, harbors and safe anchorages. The second factor is the river systems and drainage basins that we have already examined. The rivers supplement the ports and open up the continents, providing the natural channels by which articles of trade reach the interior valleys and the products of the land flow to the sea and so to world markets.

There are a number of quite satisfactory maps of all the methods of transport and travel of the world which show quite clearly that the North Atlantic is the greatest highway ever developed in human history both for the transportation of goods and for the travel of people. A major part of the remainder of this book is devoted to the history, development and meaning of this great natural channel of contact.

The central position of the Atlantic has inevitably exercised a powerful influence on human history. In order to avoid the possibility of creating the impression that this is an argument in favor of a form of geographic determinism, the idea may be rephrased. History in the western world, that is to say in the major continents which surround the Atlantic Ocean, has been a drama of nature in which man and the ocean have each played a leading part.

The Atlantic has been the scene of some of man's most intense efforts and ingenious inventions. To begin with an elemental matter directly connected with the ocean itself, it is interesting to observe that practically every type of ship known to man and all the major uses of ships and most of the improvements for the mechanical propulsion of ships had their origin in Atlantic ports and their first use in Atlantic waters. The most noticeable exception to this general rule is the Chinese junk which already in the days of Marco Polo (thirteenth century) was a very large and elaborate vessel used both in the transport of goods and of persons. Apparently it had an independent development in the Orient, as did also the outrigger canoe and its special development the flying-outrigger.

Successive developments in the types of Atlantic ships have brought successive changes in the character and continuity of human history. Improvement in ship design or construction or management has brought a larger sphere of the world within range of European influence. At first these were slight changes that resulted merely in knitting the shores of Europe closer together across such bodies of water as the Mediterranean, the Baltic, the North Sea and the Irish Sea. Iceland, Greenland and the shores of America came within range. Then a succession of improvements heralded the century of major world exploration and laid the foundation for the collection and construction of a coherent knowledge of the whole world.

It is perhaps self-evident that the Atlantic ports have been the scene of departure of the greatest adventures and explorations. We are not equally aware that from such ports have departed the great migrations of human history from the days of Hanno and Himilco down to the days of the "transatlantic ferry." There are many fascinating matters to consider, some of which seem so far to have received relatively little attention. Such are the relationship between the growth of population in Europe and transatlantic travel; the relationship between the development of practical, portable firearms and the development of world-wide navigation; the relationship between transatlantic travel and transport and the development of political and economic freedom on both the European and the American shores of the Atlantic.

The Atlantic has also been the highway for expansion of the arts and sciences. The originators and proponents of many discoveries, inventions and beliefs have found it easier to cross the Atlantic than to step across an international boundary line in Europe from one country into another.

The pictures of the land and water hemispheres and the resultant picture of the central importance of the Atlantic Ocean may appear novel to many people.

Possibly the discovery of the air has had something to do with our forgetting the importance of the sea. In less than half a century aviation has had a spectacular development: the attempted flight of the Atlantic by Harry Hawker; the flight of Alcock and Brown; the round-the-world flight of the NC4's; Lindbergh and many successive adventurers by air have each in turn been the cause of public interest and enthusiasm. Today, transoceanic flights, though still a novelty for some travelers, have become a commonplace experience for others. In this time the airplane has also proved its usefulness in war both in independent operation and as an adjunct to the older services. In time of peace, in transport and in commerce, the airplane can perform valuable services, though at relatively high cost. It is largely, therefore, confined to operations in which speed of delivery justifies the high economic premium. Any examination of air routes and shipping routes at sea or air routes and railroad routes ashore will show that air travel and transport for the most part parallels rail and steamship services and that it must be regarded as a supplement to their activities rather than as an entirely independent medium. All types of air services are, however, a very small percentage of other travel and transport.

We can all be enthusiastic proponents of the intensive development of the airplane as an instrument of travel and the development of an air arm as an instrument of warfare. We can do this without in any way forgetting or jeopardizing our recognition of the fact that preservation of the United States as a nation or as a member of an associated group of Atlantic nations depends upon the maintenance of naval and marine and maritime services.

Probably also a curious line of thinking that developed before and during the last war has, in some measure, influenced our attitude toward the ocean. This is thinking connected with the word "Geopolitics." In the early years of this century a British geographer, Sir Halford J. MacKinder, propounded the theory that while in the past political and economic control had largely rested in the hands of the maritime nations, the development of mechanical means of transport on land would, in the future, make it possible for a nation controlling a large core of land and being land-based to dominate a continent. He went further and made this more specific. He drew a map in which he showed that the core of the greatest land mass in the world was the great plains in the center of Eurasia. He predicted that the country that controlled this area, to which he gave the highly colored designation "Heartland," could expect to control the great central land mass of the Eurasian continent and finally to dominate the world.

MacKinder's ideas were seized upon by a German general named Haushofer just before World War II. Haushofer appropriated them and embellished them with Nazi philosophy and expounded them under the title "Geopolitik" which he claimed constituted a new science. The theory was so simple that Hitler could understand it and so biased that he could accept it as part of his deluded system.

Despite its obvious errors and the fact that it was discredited along with many other elements of Nazi philosophy, the MacKinder-Haushofer view has probably had some influence on our thinking. There is a point at which the MacKinder view looks quite impressive, but on examination the concept of the so-called "Heartland" turns out to have many difficulties. In the first place the territory is so far removed from the shores of the ocean and the general centers of population that transportation to and from the area is a distinct problem. In the second place land transportation is many times more expensive than water transportation and probably always will be. In the third place only a fraction of the so-called "Heartland" is endowed with natural resources; some of it, in addition to being inaccessible, is arid; a great part of it is subject to the extreme climate characteristic of the interior of a continent.

Reduced to its simplest terms, the Mackinder idea can be recognized as the extreme of landlubber thinking. It advances the opinion that any area of land must be more valuable than an equal area of water. Actually, as far as our present position is concerned, as long as we and our allies and natural associates preserve the integrity of the Atlantic and the access by all forms of travel from the seacoasts into the interior of the various countries, we will be secure. We will retain our access to the oceans and through the oceans with the world. Even though some portion of central Asia may become developed as a mining and industrial area, the territory as a whole will probably remain what it has always been—backward, remote, difficult of access, rural, primitive, uneducated, superstitious and emotionally erratic, the serf of the cities nearer the seaboard, the victim of tyranny. The nation or nations that control the Atlantic and the lands adjacent control the future.

It is plain today that the Atlantic is the world's most important ocean; a newer and larger Mediterranean for all the continents; the heart and highway of human intercourse. The Atlantic Ocean has been not only the background but also the actual stage on which the most important events in history have been worked out including the migration of peoples and cultures, the development of new systems of communication, the evolution of sciences and the achievement of political and religious liberty.

The Atlantic has a meaning that is important to all the peoples about its shores. In trying to make this plain we have made some rather large and sweeping statements. It is not enough to say that certain things happened. We shall want also to see why and how they happened. The next two parts of this book deal with the history of the Atlantic, the growth of the Atlantic peoples, the events that have taken place on and across the Atlantic and about its shores. They are events in which the ocean has not been a passive element in the story but has contributed to the development and outcome of the plot.

Today there is much honest confusion and still more cynical devaluation of history and historical accomplishments. Now that monarchy and inherited responsibility for the direction of people at all levels have all but disappeared from the earth, the unbridled scramble for control of the masses is on. Avid demagogues find it convenient, even necessary, to destroy or belittle the accomplishments of all former rulers and leaders. In this they are aided and abetted by discontented and envious peoples who through lack of experience or ability find it difficult to measure up to the standards of beauty, accomplishment, coherence, control and liberty that men have set for themselves over the centuries. Yet historic events have a way of repeating themselves—if not in identical shapes at least in similar patterns, and the problems of the future are often only the unsolved problems of the past in a new disguise.

Many believe, or profess to believe, that the purpose of history is only to celebrate the past—whereas in reality it is to guard the future. This is why we invite the reader's careful attention to the two following parts on the history of the Atlantic and why we have added a final part restating the crucial value of the Atlantic to us for today and tomorrow.

Part Two

DISCOVERY AND EARLY HISTORY

Chapter 5

THE RIVER OF OCEAN—PRIMITIVE

I T IS natural to feel that the literature of the sea begins with Homer. He was the first to sing at length of the hopes and fears and triumphs of one of the great seafaring people; his stories are full of the wonder and beauty of "the wine-dark sea" and of the feelings of seamen which are properly a mixture of fear and courage, of avoidance and desire. He has the feeling of the sea and his characters are often recognizable seamen. It seems reasonable to believe that where his seamanship seems confused or wrong this is due to the scribes and translators and not to the author.

Homer reflects also the natural association between beautiful women and the sea. It is inevitable that the goddesses of beauty, love and fertility—Aphrodite of the Greeks and Venus of the Romans—should be sea-born creatures. Beautiful mortals also have always been associated with fine ships, and when Homer records the flight of Helen with Paris he is contributing a link in a long chain of such associations in fable and history which may have begun with the fleet of exploration of Hatshepsut, the beautiful Egyptian queen, and which continued with Cleopatra and her barge; Isolde and her fateful voyage; Gudrun the fair, and the Norse dragon ships that carried her on the first serious attempt to colonize America. Somehow the history-making beauties have always succeeded in boarding the record-breaking liners and the story continues to our own day when yachts fast and beautiful have turned up in our anchorages with appropriately qualified ladies.

73

There is more to the Trojan wars, however, than even the magic of Helen's beauty. It was an English poet who asked of Helen, "Is this the face that launched a thousand ships and burnt the topless towers of Ilium?" In Homer, however, the facts often outrun the fantasy; thus in the Iliad, the very catalogue of the ships belies the fable. It shows us that ships and the sea were permanent and essential to the Greek way of life and that against this background the fatal beauty of Helen is an episode. The catalogue of ships is the work of a devoted enthusiast. To the modern student it may seem a dull record but to the ancient Greeks it was lively news.

This fleet was not a temporary accident. The people who could construct it and bring it together at one time and place were old hands at ship construction and navigation. The attack on Troy represents a large-scale concerted effort at naval transport in the interests of war. History and archaeology agree that the Trojan War of Homer is best interpreted as an episode in a long-drawn-out effort of the Greeks to maintain control over trade and transport in the Aegean. In this interest they would need also to control the Hellespont, which was at once both entrance to the Black Sea and an all but complete land bridge into Asia. The strong settlement at Ilium was a threat to such control.

Homer was a literary man rather than either a historian or a geographer or indeed a captain of ships and armies, yet his is the chief record and the chief insight into the geography of his time. His object was entertainment and he was speaking to the people and for the people and therefore probably he was reflecting only what was common knowledge mingled with myth and tradition. A glance at the map taken in conjunction with the views of the historians and scholars will show the limitations of his geographic knowledge even when he thought he was carrying his listeners far afield.

The Greek islands and the plains of Troy Homer knows. Here is relative reality. Beyond that, three definite localities can be reasonably assigned as forming the scenes of certain more imaginative passages in Ulysses' travels. Scylla and Charybdis are a dramatized and exaggerated description of the Strait of Messina with its characteristic currents; the Aeolian Islands, with the Lipari Islands are still there; the land of the Lotus Eaters, a portion of the Tripoli coast, for here a form of the lotus was eaten and regarded as a delicacy. It would be nice to know if the lotus has narcotic properties but there seems to be no evidence of this point.

Beyond, Homer's geography gets vaguer and vaguer. Phoenicia

and Cyprus and Egypt are shadowy. He has in mind a general but distorted picture of the Mediterranean shores. The places are there but their relations are askew. He knows of the Black Sea but not what lies beyond it. He sees the whole world as a flat disk with the Mediterranean at its center, the countries forming its shore. Travel only a short distance from the shore and you become lost in the lands of storm and mist and fabulous monsters. A step too far and you may find yourself at the door of Hades. Sail beyond the known landmarks and you are the sport of Neptune, who rules the "river of ocean" that flows all about the outer world.

For Homer, and for generations of Greeks that succeeded him, the sea was always the Mediterranean. The shores of the Mediterranean were all that was known of the world and in the west the sea terminated at the Pillars of Hercules which we know today as the Straits of Gibraltar. The river of ocean lay without and flowed all about the disk-shaped world. The river of ocean represented the outermost limits of knowledge—a realm of fable and fantasy; an area inhabited by threatening Gods and unknown dangers. The river of ocean thus represented a primitive idea that, in the same form or in a slightly different form, was shared by many people not only in the Mediterranean basin but elsewhere. It not only continued as a popular idea after the Greeks extended their geographic knowledge and began to build up some scientific knowledge of the world, but it persisted and moved outward as knowledge moved. It spread over Europe in the Middle Ages and for centuries directly and indirectly influenced what people thought about the Atlantic and what they were able to do about it. It was the shape of the enemy that had to be met and overcome, not once but repeatedly, by knowledge and science.

One of the charms of Homer and indeed of the later Greeks is the extent to which their thinking could encompass and combine primitive superstition and worldly sophistication. Reading history we are sometimes puzzled to find that superstition and knowledge live side by side; we assume that where truth has been discovered, superstition will automatically be eliminated. We should be less naïve, remembering that today, despite our efforts at universal education, there is a wide gap between what we can know and what we prefer to believe.

The Greeks later controlled the Mediterranean and were succeeded by the Romans. The Greek language became the medium through which the histories of many people in and about the Mediterranean were collected and recorded. Thus we are always apt to begin our accounts with the Greek literary tradition. It is clear however that the Homerian Greeks were not the first sailors though we have accepted them as our point of departure. At the time of the siege of Troy, large fleets of ships were already in existence. It is clear therefore that there must have been a very long previous history of ship building and at least coastwise sailing in the Mediterranean.

In considering how far back the earlier histories of shipping may run, there is an important point that can guide our thinking and what will help to make the span of history intelligible to us. This point of view, accepted by most major historians, anthropologists and archaeologists, may be stated in this way: the farther back we go in time the slower will be the rate of technical progress. The corollary to this is that the farther down we come in time toward our own day and the more numerous are the peoples and nations that have access to a common body of knowledge, the faster are the steps by which our arts develop.

We may illustrate these points by referring to the development of types of vessels. The ordinary Mediterranean merchant vessel changed very slowly. Though it was a little larger and heavier, the commercial vessel of Julius Caesar's day was not radically different from the early Greek sailing ships though a period of almost a thousand years lay between them; but on the other end of the scale, between the time that the packet ship was first developed and the time when the clipper ship emerged there was a mere span of forty years; and the period between which the clipper ship emerged and the time when it was superseded by the steamer is still shorter. So when we ask how long was the period of history of ships that preceded the Homeric Age, we have to make allowance not in terms of hundreds of years, but of thousands of years.

Homer never acknowledged his debt to other storytellers and likewise the Greek shipbuilders never acknowledged where they got their art. Rudyard Kipling put it in a ballad that is pure Cockney:

> "When 'Omer smote 'is bloomin' lyre
> E'd 'eard men sing by land and sea,
> And wot 'e thought 'e might require
> 'E went and took—the same as me." 7

Both the stories and the ships seem to have owed a part of their origin to Greek contacts with the Minoan civilization. The Minoans, of course, occupied the island of Crete and made it the heart of a considerable Mediterranean empire long before the emergence of

Greece as an important power. The fact that they were able to establish upon an island a large society exercising control over a considerable area in itself indicates that they were a maritime people. But we do not need to work on inference, they were a people skilled in the arts as well as in seafaring and they left us a succession of drawings of their vessels. Even the carved stones they used for seals more often than anything else carried the picture of a ship.

As archaeology unrolls their story, it is apparent that they knew much more about ships than the early Greeks and that they utilized their knowledge more effectively. By the year 2000 B.C. the Minoans had a steady contact with Egypt and examples of their pottery are fairly common in that country. By 1500 B.C., that is 500 years before Homer, they had contact with the island of Cyprus. The inference is that the first venturesome Minoans sailed straight south to the African coast and then followed this eastward to the Nile. After they began trading with Cyprus it was customary to pass by way of Cyprus and so to the eastern shore of the Mediterranean and then south to Egypt. By the year 1200 B.C. they were voyaging to Sicily and southern Italy, for Minoan coins of this period have been found in both locations. They seem to have passed through the Strait of Messina, for one of the kinds of stone out of which they built their great palace at Knossos came from the Aeolian Islands. They may have passed through the Straits of Gibraltar and been the first to reach the Atlantic seacoast in the south of Spain. This was the region that was later known as Tartessus. By the year 1000 B.C. their knowledge was passing and their power broken; they were victims of the Achaean and Dorian raiders, so the Greeks probably benefited to a certain extent from what the Minoans already knew.

Considering the extent of the Minoan voyages of the year 2000 B.C. as well as the archaeological record, it is conservative to assume that the Minoans were sailing the east end of the Mediterranean in the year 3000 B.C.—that already brings us back 5000 years from today. We do not know where and when the Minoans derived the patterns of their ships but we do know that they were in touch with the Egyptians. In fact, by the year 2000 B.C., judging from the archaeological record as revealed by their pottery, there was already a considerable trade between the two centers of civilization, so that brings us to the Egyptians.

Seven hundred and fifty years before the time of this trade, an adventurer named Hannu was sent on a voyage by King Sahuri, who was then ruling Egypt. A record of his exploits is engraved in the rocks above the town of Hamamat, which is 420 miles up the Nile above Cairo. From here he departed and here he returned. He crossed the desert to the city of Coptos (Cosseir), a port on the Red Sea. From here he sailed to the eastern end of that sea—a region then known as the land of Punt. The port of this land was Seba or Sheba. Here Hannu traded and also apparently collected booty for the Pharaoh "out of fear and dread such as he inspired in all nations." The total amount of goods was so great that he had to build additional vessels in the port of Seba in order to take back to Egypt the cargo which included spices and precious stones for the statues of the temples, 80,000 measures of myrrh, 6,000 weight of gold-silver alloy, 2,600 staves of precious wood, probably ebony. This was in 2700 B.C.

Twelve hundred years later, that is in 1500 B.C., Queen Hatshepsut sent out a similar expedition to Punt which likewise was recorded in pictures and stories on the temple walls at Ded-el-bahari. These expeditions to Punt were both ventures on a very great scale but we may infer that lesser trade expeditions were probably quite common in the intervening years. In any event, the building of sailing ships for voyages running the length of the Red Sea and probably also for covering portions of the eastern Mediterranean was possible in the year 2750 B.C. The ships were large and could carry a large number of people and a relatively large cargo as the records show. We must infer therefore that the ships were of a recognized pattern and that back of them rested a maritime history.

We do not know what manner of vessels plied the Mediterranean and the Red Sea before Hannu's expedition for there are no drawings that we can definitely identify with earlier vessels plying the sea, but from what we know about the character of the nations that occupied Persia, Mesopotamia, the eastern end of the Red Sea and Egypt, we can infer that they traded with each other both by land and by coasting voyages for thousands of years before the date of Hannu's expedition. In Egypt we have drawings of relatively large ships that are at least as old as 6000 B.C. We are certain that such ships were cruising the Nile and it is probable that others like them were sailing the Mediterranean.

This we know, that ships were operating in Egypt 8,000 years ago. They already have lines that suggest the Egyptian ships of thousands of years later—ships with raised bows and sterns. They require a number of oarsmen and could apparently also provide space for passengers or cargo or both. There seems to be provision for a steersman and a permanent steering oar.

We cannot be certain that all ships of this type were built in Egypt. Trees, such as could provide planks for shipbuilding, were always scarce and sometimes nonexistent in Egypt. Later we know the Egyptian ships were often built up of short pieces of timber and this is why they used the heavy truss of twisted ropes which is so prominently shown in the temple drawings. We already know that Hannu had a fleet of ships built in Punt for his voyage home. These earliest pictured ships therefore may well have been built in Tyre or Sidon (as these cities were later called by the Phoenicians) or timber from Lebanon may have been shipped to Egypt and the vessels built there. No doubt the ships shown were used chiefly on the Nile but there is no inherent reason why they would not also serve for voyages between Egypt and other sections of the eastern Mediterranean coast. From the size and character of the ship of 6000 B.C. we must conclude that shipbuilding and operation already had a long history. It seems reasonable to draw the inference that simple ships were being sailed and rowed about the shores of the Mediterranean and making passages to some of its islands centuries before this.

Vilhjalmur Stefansson, who in recent years has given much attention to the question of early voyages, would put the date of the first navigators much earlier than this. In any event, this is a history

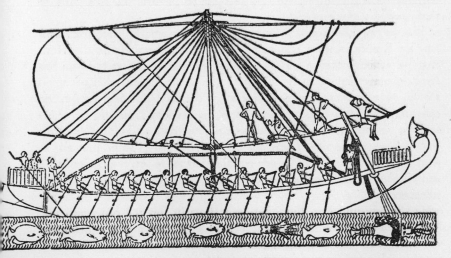

EGYPTIAN SHIP

about which we have no details. We can only draw inference from what we know about primitive navigation in other times and places.

Though the history of Egypt and the eastern Mediterranean, of Mesopotamia and Persian territory is very ancient indeed, there is no reason for assuming that it was in this region that the ship was invented and navigation first arose. In fact, we shall have to extend our Mediterranean horizon to see what developments may have been taking place elsewhere in early times. Rather than taking an arbitrary jump in time and space, we will do this by following some of the early Mediterranean voyagers.

It is a curious circumstance of history that one of the longest sailing voyages in the Atlantic carried out by early Mediterranean navigators was also one of the first ones, and that the vessel entered the Atlantic by sailing around the Cape of Good Hope from the Indian Ocean. The record of this trip is preserved by the author Herodotus. Herodotus visited Egypt about 150 years after the trip was supposed to have taken place and obtained the following account of the voyage:

> Libya shows that it has sea all around except the part that borders on Asia—Necho, a king of Egypt, being the first within our knowledge to show this fact; for when he stopped digging the canal which stretches from the Nile to the Arabian Gulf he sent forth Phoenician men in ships, ordering them to sail back between the Pillars of Heracles until they came to the Northern [Mediterranean] Sea and thus to Egypt. The Phoenicians therefore setting forth from the Red Sea sailed in the Southern Sea [Arabian Sea and the Indian Ocean] and whenever autumn came, they each time put ashore and sowed the land wherever they might be in Libya as they voyaged, and awaited the reaping time; having then reaped the corn they set sail, so that after the passing of two years they doubled the Pillars of Heracles in the third year and came to Egypt. And they told things believable perhaps for others, but unbelievable for me, namely that in sailing round Libya they had the sun on the right hand. Thus was Libya known for the first time.

Necho ruled in Egypt about 600 B.C. and was responsible for initiating the building of a canal between Bubastis, on the Nile, and the Red Sea. Necho did not invent the idea of creating a continuous waterway between the Mediterranean and the Red Sea. The first canal had been completed by Seti I and Rameses II between 1300 and 1350 B.C. This is over 3,000 years before the Suez Canal was opened in 1869 A.D. With the passage of years this canal filled with sand. In Necho's time the attempt at a new canal is said to have cost the lives of over 120,000 slaves involving Egyptians as well as foreign captives. Necho's canal was not actually finished until the time of Darius Hystaspis (521 to 486 B.C.). No doubt Necho was trying to strengthen his hand and divert attention from the slow progress of his project when he ordered the Phoenicians to sail around Africa.

It will be noted that Herodotus rejects the story because the voyagers said that when they were sailing around Libya (that is, Africa) from east to west they had their sun on their right hand—that is, to the north of them. From our point of view this, however, is one of the details that makes the story credible, for this is exactly what would be notable to Mediterranean voyagers who for the first time found themselves in the latitude of the Cape of Good Hope. It is not likely to have been invented in view of the state of geographic knowledge in Egypt and Greece at that time.

Also enhancing the credibility of the story is the fact that the passage was made from east to west and not in the reverse direction. An examination of the pilot charts will show that a coasting voyage of this kind enjoys favorable winds and currents most of the way. An attempt to sail around Africa from west to east was made by Sataspes in 485 B.C. and two attempts were made by Eudoxus in 146 B.C. and all these attempts were met by failure. On the other hand there is the historic record of a young Portuguese named Botelho who made the passage from India around Africa to Portugal in a seventeen-foot boat. The German scholar Müller and the English geographer Rennels have both made detailed examinations of the probable route of Necho's sailors. They both believe that Necho's ship, traveling from east to west, was the first vessel to round Africa and sail through the South Atlantic.

The more direct approaches to the Atlantic were also developed by the Phoenicians. Before the year 1100 B.C. they had probably a fair knowledge of the western Mediterranean for in that year they established the colony of Utica on the African shore. Near this site 300 years later they established the larger and more important colony of Carthage.

From Carthage about the year 500 B.C. the Phoenicians engaged in mammoth undertakings to establish colonies on the shores of the Atlantic both to the north and to the south of the Straits of Gibraltar. Hannu was the leader entrusted with the expedition to explore and establish colonies southward along the African shore. A Greek translation of his own account of the trip says that it involved the use of sixty vessels, each of them driven by fifty oars. Thirty thousand men and women are said to have made up the expedition as a whole. This seems an incredible number. However, even if we make a liberal discount in the numbers as being due either to error or intentional exaggeration, we still have left the framework of a large undertaking that moved over a very extensive territory. In this connection it is worth noting that Hamilcar, who was the father of Himilco, invaded Sicily with an expedition involving 3,000 ships and 300,000 men.

Hanno is credited with having established a colony near the site of the present city of Mehedia and having established a temple and colony near Cape Cantin. Beyond the cape he reported a river and swamp frequented by elephants and it is assumed that this was the Tensift River and it is thought that the island which he called Cerne was Herne Island. His trip is assumed to have carried him to Sherbro Sound with a terminal landing on Macauley Island. Here he reports capturing strange beings called "gorillas." From this point they began their homeward voyage.

Somewhere between 800 and 700 B.C. the Phoenicians had established a colony on the Atlantic coast in what is now Spanish territory. The city was Gades, where the city of Cadiz is now located, and the general region in which it was located was referred to as Tarshish or Tartessus. Departing from Carthage, also about the year 500, Himilco, the brother of Hannu, was to carry a large expedition northward beyond Tartessus. We have no clear record of Himilco's undertaking; what we know about it is derived from the writings of Avienus and on examination proves to be a strange mixture of fact and of romantic embroidery. Avienus was writing in 300 A.D. Fortunately, about 400 years before that Pliny provided a briefer but much more reasonable reference to Himilco's undertaking. Himilco certainly explored the coasts of Spain and Portugal and possibly went farther than this. He reports that the natives of those parts were accustomed to come and go to a region to which the name Oestrimnis was assigned. Islands in the bay of this region were called the Oestrimnides. In these islands men mined and smelted tin and lead. They were said to be visited from all directions by people sailing the ocean in small boats constructed of hides sewn together and stretched over a wooden frame. This filled Avienus with unbelief. It is probable however that this is our first literary description of the large ancient vessel called the curragh which was in common use in ancient Ireland and probably also on other shores.

The account refers to a people called Hierne who inhabited the island, apparently the Irish people, and refers to another island called Albion. According to Avienus, Himilco said that the seas in all these parts were inhabited by terrible and threatening serpents or monsters of the deep but also that the winds over these seas were sluggish and fitful; that the seas themselves were so clogged with seaweed that they impeded the progress of a ship and also that they were so shallow as to be continually muddy. Voyages were said to take an incredibly long time. Stefansson believes that the terrifying descriptions of navigation in the Atlantic were not the result of superstition or cowardice on the part of the Phoenicians but were a part of a studied policy. They were invented to mislead and terrify Greek sailors who were potential competitors in colonization and in the development of trade, particularly trade in the metals in which Phoenicians seem to have specialized.

A more developed and realistic account is supplied by the Greek navigator, scientist and explorer Pythias who made a very extensive voyage in 330 B.C. The part of his trip that interests us for the moment is that he visited and described the tin mines and the island on which tin was stored. The island might well have been St. Michael's in Mount's Bay. Pythias is impressed with the way in which the miners dig galleries in the earth, following the vein of metal-bearing ore. He observes that the miners are friendly, gentle and intelligent. He attributes this to the fact that they have a very extensive trade and that this brings them in contact with people from many foreign nations.

Pythias' own book is lost so that what we know of him always reaches us from quotation, but this passage seems to be plain enough. He is saying that the people of Cornwall are notable as good businessmen with an urbane and cosmopolitan attitude which comes from dealing with people of many different nations. In other words, Cornwall is the site of an extensive trade by sea from many different directions. This is simple confirmation from a classic literary source of what we have in our own day learned from extensive archaeological explorations. At least as early as 500 B.C. sailing vessels produced in northern Europe were connecting the continent with Cornwall—Cornwall with Ireland—Ireland with Scotland and so on in a widening circle which apparently also included the Scandinavian countries.

H. O'Neil Hencken of Harvard University is one of the archaeologists that have specialized in the early Bronze Age and in earlier European archaeology. He believes that not only was the trade of 500 B.C. very extensive but that contact between the islands and the continent was being made by long and direct voyages. In other words, travelers from France would lay a course from the Isle of Ushant direct to Ireland and likewise voyagers to and from Spain and Portugal were accustomed to lay a course at sea which carried them directly to the Scillys and Cornwall. Thus they would avoid making the laborious passage around the shores of the Bay of Biscay such as is supposed to have been followed by Himilco.

On the basis of archaeological and cultural evidence over a wide area that covers the continental coast and also localities in Great Britain as well as Ireland, Scotland and all the outer islands, Hencken believes that there was extensive travel by boat as early as 3000 B.C., but the spread of the culture which was characterized by such monolithic structures as cromlechs and the "Druid Circles" and so forth implied the existence of ready and efficient marine travel before the year 2000 B.C. At that time and at the beginning of the Bronze Age there was a flourishing period of navigation and trade. There appears then to have been a recession in activity and communication until about 1200 B.C. but thereafter a revival of interest which was apparent to Pythias. It is possible that the establishment of overland trade routes through France and other parts of Europe accounted for the falling off in water transport.

The existence of early and extensive travel by sea in northern Europe is also attested to in the works of Prof. A. W. Brøgger in the University of Oslo. Professor Brøgger, during his lifetime, was responsible for the reconstruction and preservation of the Viking ships that have been discovered in Norway. He also devoted years of study to the origins and development of navigation in northern Europe. He believes that there was extensive communication on the high seas at the end of the so-called Stone Age and before the beginning of the Metal Age in northern Europe. He bases his belief not only on representation of early vessels carved in rock but also on widely distributed archaeological evidence. This includes the evidence of extensive trade not only across the Baltic but also in all directions across the North Sea, involving communication between Norway and the island groups such as the Faeroes, the Orkneys, the Shetlands and the shores of Scotland.

Statements such as these may seem unfamiliar or even incredible to people who have been brought up entirely in our large centers of population. Their eyes will be accustomed to tall skyscrapers and to ships of enormous tonnage and horsepower. They will probably view with suspicion the belief that very early and simple vessels could undertake any voyages at sea. On the other hand, those who have some experience with societies that are removed in space and in technology from our own will have a much better understanding of the accomplishments of our ancient ancestors of the late Stone Age and early Metal Age. The following facts have a direct bearing on what probably took place four or five millennia ago.

The Eskimo people, both in their western limits in Alaska and in their eastern limits in Greenland, at the time of their first contact with western civilization could be described as being in a Stone Age of culture. Modern anthropologists are properly reluctant to use general classifications such as Stone Age as applied to a particular people. This is understandable since the Ages as represented in the history of any particular people may have occurred at quite different times and really represented quite different stages of development. Still, here we use the expression to mean that until their contact with European society, the Eskimo people were apparently quite devoid of any knowledge of the use of metals.

Still they built extremely strong and seaworthy boats and took them on long voyages in some of the coldest and most stormy waters to be found anywhere. Two distinct forms of Eskimo ship were employed and each served a different purpose—the kayak was the small, lightweight, decked-in canoe used by the men in hunting for seals, fishing and so forth. The other form of boat is the umiak. This is a relatively large boat consisting of a framework made of wooden poles and bent and shaped ribs and other shorter pieces of timber. Over this framework is stretched a skin or shell; this shell is built up of the dressed skins of many animals sewn together with waterproof seams. Considered as a whole, the umiak has pointed ends, relatively straight sides and a relatively flat bottom. It is light in relationship to its capacity and extremely buoyant. While both forms of Eskimo boat are capable of lengthy passages in open sea and also in waters covered with drifting ice, the umiak particularly is noted for its capacity to carry heavy loads through high winds and large seas. It is primarily intended for the carrying of freight and a large number of passengers too. While the form and size of the ancient Irish curragh is not exactly known, it apparently had certain affinities with the Eskimo umiak. It is known that the Irish monks of the Middle Ages and other early Irish travelers made extensive and successful voyages in such skin boats. It is generally believed that it was in vessels of this type that the Irish reached Iceland and were reported there by early voyagers from Scandinavia. A small vessel made up of such hides stretched over a wooden frame is still in use by the fishermen of the Isle of Arran (Scotch southwest coast) and is believed to be a small and late survivor of the curragh type of construction.

From another part of the world comes the history of extremely long voyages in the open ocean made by people who had no knowledge of the use of metals and who employed what is commonly regarded as a primitive method of transportation. These people are the Polynesians and their vessel is the outrigger sailing canoe. Dr. Peter Buck, from New Zealand and partly of Polynesian ancestry, after many years of study first at the University of Hawaii and later at Yale University succeeded in working out an extensive and connected chronological account of the voyages and migrations of the Polynesian people over vast areas in the Pacific Ocean. They successfully completed such passages as those from Tahiti to Samoa, Tahiti to Hawaii and also from the central Polynesian groups to New Zealand.

Of course the Polynesian voyages are not an integral part of Atlantic history but indirectly they have an important bearing on our story. The Polynesians, though highly developed in literature and philosophy, are technicologically a Stone Age people surviving into modern times. They made their great voyages before they had any knowledge of metals or contact with Europeans and their inventions. Close study of all branches of the Polynesian people has recently made it possible to establish a chronology for their migrations and to document the story of their migrations. Thus it has been established that people with relatively simple culture such as the Polynesians and the Eskimos were able to make very long voyages in the open Pacific and in stormy Arctic portions of the Atlantic. The fact that two people of simple mechanical culture are known to have made long sea voyages does not, of course, prove that other pre-scientific people made similar voyages on other seas and at other times. It shows that there is no inherent reason why such voyages could not have been made; it makes it more difficult to deny them and easier to accept them. In fact the acceptance of Stone Age voyages across the Bay of Biscay, the North Sea and other Atlantic waters is essential to any rational reconstruction of European pre-history.

Formerly some scholars and many laymen denied the possibility of regular sea voyages by primitive people on the ground that they had no system of navigation. The argument ran that even though it were proved that the curragh, the umiak and the outrigger canoe were occasionally capable of long sea passages, the people using them, lacking navigation, would still be incapable of building up migration and trade.

This argument never had the general value and authority that is attributed to it. For a long time it has been accepted that celestial navigation is not an absolute requirement for ocean travel. Today, as well as in the past, sailors have made very successful passages steering by the wind, utilizing permanent wind systems like the trades or periodic systems like the monsoons. In recent years the argument has lost what little force remained to it because we have discovered that at least one people of simple culture did develop and use an effective and natural system of celestial navigation. It seems probable that the same or a somewhat similar system was employed by other early navigators.

Again it is the Polynesians who have supplied us with information as to the system they developed and utilized. The system which they employed has been explained by the aviator and navigator Harold Gatty in a volume that is now generally available. This is the so-called *Raft Book*. Gatty, with the aid of scientists and other advisors, prepared this book to serve as a guide and method of navigation for aviators operating over the Pacific during the period of World War II and also for the use of others who might for various reasons find themselves at sea on a life raft or in a lifeboat. Editions of the book prepared during the war were as nearly as possible waterproof both with respect to the text and with respect to simple equipment supplied with the volume that could be used in elementary navigation.

Gatty states that the essence of the Polynesian system was the recognition of the importance of the zenith star, the star directly over the observer's head. This is in sharp contrast with what we may call scientific methods of navigation, all of which have depended on devising and using instruments for determining the observed height of a celestial body such as a star above the observed horizon. Gatty has ascertained and proved that it is possible, with the unaided eye, to determine either ashore or afloat with a relatively high degree of accuracy which is the zenith star. It may be that our ability, with a little experience and practice to determine this position, is in some way dependent upon our human practice of walking upright and thus having perpetually to accommodate ourselves to the preservation of our balance against the force of gravity. In any event, it is possible for most people to tell which star, if any, is immediately overhead. In case of doubt, the accuracy of observation may be increased by looking upward and walking around in a circle if on land, or rowing about in a circle if afloat.

A knowledge of the patterns of the stars together with a recognition of which star is overhead, permits the observer to ascertain his own location on the earth. Gatty points out that if then the observer knows that some other star is immediately over some island or point of land he will, by directing his course toward that star, also be directing his course toward the desired point of land. The navigators among the Polynesian people are said to have studied the stars in their relationship to various islands so that they had a precise knowledge and tradition which enabled them to know which stars habitually passed over which islands.

There is a curious corollary to this method of navigation, namely that the navigator who pursues it and who sets his course by a star automatically follows a great circle course. When European navigators began to travel across the Pacific they would occasionally observe and refer to the fact that Polynesian canoes apparently had taken great circle courses. How this could have been done was a great mystery to these European navigators who had always depended on optical instruments, chronometers and compasses in setting their courses at sea.

The fact that the Polynesians used the principle of the zenith star as a method of navigation suggests the possibility that other prescientific people who are known to have made extensive voyages on the seas, out of sight of land, employed the same method.

Western sailors of today steering a ship at night usually guide themselves by a star. This has nothing to do with the zenith star method of navigation. This modern usage sets the course and gives direction to the steersman by our conventional methods of navigation. When the steersman is on his compass course he observes a star just in line with his masts or the stem of the vessel. He steers by that for a while and this relieves him of the strain of continually following a compass. This is what Masefield referred to when he said:

> *"All I want is a tall ship*
> *And a star to steer her by."*

This is beautiful but it is not zenith star navigation. Still, so many

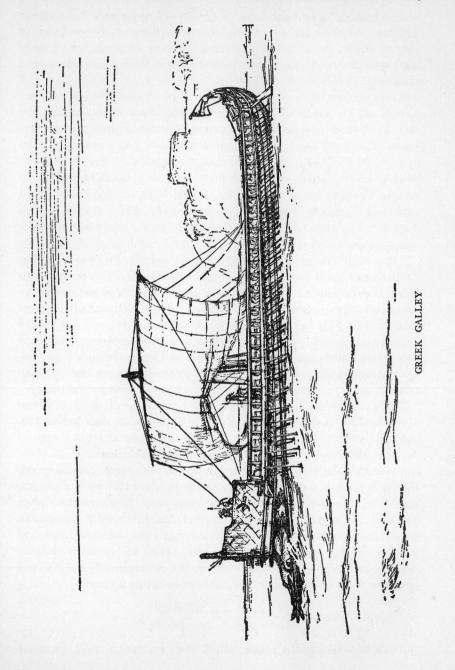

GREEK GALLEY

languages contain references to "guide stars," "lode stars," "steering by a star" and corruptions like "hitching your wagon to a star" that in time past they may have applied to an old, simple, effective and widely known method of navigation—roving the seas with the aid of the zenith star.

Thus, step by step we have extended our knowledge of early ocean travel, giving it wider scope in space and placing its origins farther back in time. Homer provides us with pictures of the early Greek navigators and their ships and the literary historians have been content to begin their accounts of ocean travel at this period. Even then, Greek ships were well developed and capable of traveling all about the eastern Mediterranean. The forerunner of the Greek ship was undoubtedly the Cretan ship which is known to have made passages to Egypt and probably benefited by Egyptian experience with ships and we have pictures of Egyptian ships that are at least 8,000 years old. We must not suppose that the Egyptians were the first or only navigators of these early periods. The Egyptians had no forests from which they could cut large ship's timbers. Such timbers were imported into Egypt by the Phoenicians who, of course, had to have ships of their own to carry on this trade. Egyptian records frequently acknowledge their dependence on the Phoenicians. Thus it was Phoenician men in Phoenician vessels who in 600 B.C. under the Egyptian King Necho made a passage around Africa sailing from east to west. They, therefore, were the first to discover and sail the South Atlantic. By 700 B.C. these people had established colonies on the shores of the Atlantic both north and south of the Straits of Gibraltar in Europe and Africa.

Again, they were not the only mariners in this region for here they found an extensive trade carried on across the seas by middle and northern European people traveling in vessels of their own construction. This is confirmed by the Greek navigator Pythias who in about 330 B.C. made a voyage to Scotland and Iceland. The trade that Pythias observed was no doubt a direct survival of an extensive system of ocean travel that was well established before the age of metals began. Around the year 2000 B.C. there seems to have been a golden age of seafaring when European sailors from Scandinavia to Spain made voyages across such open ocean waters as the North Sea and the Bay of Biscay. This extensive system of travel is said to have had its origins in the period around 3000 B.C. This is as far back in time as the archaeologists now take us but it is clear that a long period of coastal travel must be allowed before sea voyages were attempted and that the origins of such coastal voyages are lost in the mists of time.

*　*　*　*

In all these voyages the Mediterranean Sea itself played a part. In the first place this sea is made up of two very distinct parts, for the southern part of Italy and the island of Sicily separate the western from the eastern Mediterranean. In the second place though the ocean tides are of little effect in the Mediterranean, and surface and deeper currents are felt acutely only in the straits of Gibraltar and Messina, the wind systems are organized and persistent.

Thus the earliest Egyptian and Phoenician and Minoan voyages were confined to the eastern Mediterranean. It represented a distinct breakthrough for each people when first the Minoans and then the Greeks came into the western Mediterranean. Homer's account of Scylla and Charybdis are fanciful exaggerations but they reflect the fact that early navigators had real troubles with adverse winds and unpredictable currents at the Strait of Messina and dreaded this passage.

All these early navigators learned to know and use the favorable wind systems of the eastern sea, waiting for favorable seasons for their voyages. They made little reference to absolute or compass directions (they did not in fact have compasses) but classified their ports and their courses according to the name of the wind that was used for the voyage. This should not be surprising to New England readers. Nowadays most people, thinking of a map, talk about going "up north" or "down south" or even "up to Maine" but real New Englanders still talk about "down east" or go "down to Boston" or "down to Maine." This usage grew up at a time when most New England travel was carried out in sailing ships. Prevailing winds in these latitudes are west and southwest so if you leave Philadelphia or New York or Connecticut for Boston or Maine you go "down the wind"; on the return journey you would "beat up to New York."

From Greece the downwind passage led southward toward the African coast. Then there was a choice of an easy run under still favorable winds eastward to Egypt or a somewhat less favorable run westward under Sicily to Tripoli or Tunisia. Between southwest Sicily and Africa there is a broad passage. Here at most seasons of the year there was some likelihood of an unfavorable wind but also enough variable winds so that with a little patient waiting the broad waters gave an easy passage to the west. Beyond this point variable and even favorable winds at most seasons carried voyaging ships all the way to the Pillars of Hercules (Straits of Gibraltar).

On the map a direct or northern route between Greece and Rome looks invitingly short but was beset by headwinds and navigational dangers such as those at Messina. The longest way "southabout" was in practice the shortest way home.

The Minoans went this way; so did the Phoenicians and the Greeks after Homer. Virgil knew the facts of navigation as well as the facts of life when he brought Aeneas to Carthage and the court of Queen Dido before the stormy passage to Rome.

Later in the seventh and eighth centuries the Islamic conquerors came this way, sweeping across the North Africa coast from Egypt to Spain both by land and by sea. At sea they followed the same winds and came to the same ports that had successively served the Minoans, the Phoenicians, the Greeks, the Romans.

Even ashore the winds and conditions of the Mediterranean Sea have left their imprint in the living cities and the dead ruins of successive civilizations. Thus it is the eastern and the southwestern shores of Sicily that are crowned with the temples and palaces of successive cultures. So also is the north shore of Africa from Tunis to Gibraltar.

The waters of the Mediterranean are circumscribed; its currents persistent but moderate; its weather settled and mild for long periods. Even so we can see that the conditions influenced the voyages of the early and simple ships, holding them back on some courses and nudging them along on easier but longer ones. In this arm of the Atlantic we can see on a limited scale how the characteristics of the sea helped to determine the course and sequence of historic movement.

Here men learned to work with the sea, to accept the easy way when the hard way had almost defeated them. Here they met and learned to use some of the forces that they were to encounter on a larger and rougher scale when they set out on the broad Atlantic.

Chapter 6

ATLANTIS—BIRTH AND DEATH OF SCIENCE

THE peoples of western and northern Europe were the first to sail freely in the open Atlantic but it was in the Mediterranean that a scientific knowledge grew and flourished and died. The classic authors present us with the first recorded picture of a real world that is in recognizable agreement with modern knowledge. Their knowledge reached reality but it began in myth and ended in dogma. Even the name of our Atlantic has its origin in a land of fable.

The women of this land were beautiful and the men were brave; the soil was fertile and the climate was kindly to man. Strong kings ruled over the country and it was wonderful to see how satisfactory life could be in a well-ordered society. This, said Plato, was the island of Atlantis which rose out of the ocean beyond the Pillars of Hercules and this was the way life had been lived about 9,000 years ago.

Then this island paradise had been engulfed in a great catastrophe. Suddenly the island had sunk in an earthquake and the waters had risen in a great storm that swept over the land and destroyed all the people. No one would ever find Atlantis again or even be able to sail there because there were sandbanks near where Atlantis had once been. All this is supposed to have been told to Solon, the lawgiver, by an old Egyptian priest 150 years before Plato's telling of the story.

Plato's Atlantis is an early and attractive Utopia. It is one of the stories that makes a great appeal to many people. It has been widely circulated from Plato's time to our own day. It has stimulated conjecture and discussion which is no doubt exactly what Plato intended it to do. Some writers have supposed that Plato's Atlantis must have been based on a memory of some real event and, with this in mind, they have suggested a number of changes in the story.

One of the more reasonable conjectures is that there did circulate in Egypt a fable of an island that disappeared. This referred to the island of Crete where, as we know, the Minoans built an advanced and powerful society and from which they sailed in their own ships to trade with Egypt. When the Achæan and Dorian Greeks overran Crete the trade with Egypt ceased so completely that the legend grew that the island had sunk beneath the waves.

Other less comprehensible conjectures flourish. Perhaps Plato, when he spoke of the Pillars of Hercules, didn't really mean the Straits of Gibraltar. If this is so, then he didn't mean the Atlantic Ocean as the location of the island. Possibly instead he meant a coast near a place where there had been a temple to Hercules. This could have been a place along the North African Mediterranean coast and maybe there had been colonies of early Greeks or Phoenicians and maybe the coast had suffered from volcanic shock or other changes so that sand and the desert had encroached and finally maybe they hadn't meant to refer to 9,000 years, but to some other time scale, and so on and so forth. As you can see, this is the kind of game that can become very complicated.

The sciences of geology and oceanography show clearly that there never could have been in the Atlantic, within the lifetime even of the earliest human forms, a continent or a large island which disappeared beneath the sea. The studies of history and anthropology, on the other hand, would show us how easy and how universal is the human habit of developing fables and legends and that the legends and fables that have no basis or relationship to natural fact are just as frequent as those that do. It seems much more sensible to conclude that Plato is simply trying to interest his students of philosophy and, with this in mind, invents an attractive allegory or illustration. In this respect it is like his use of the banquet or his figure of the people who had to guess at reality by studying the shadowy images which were cast on the walls of a cave.

It is interesting to note that Plato's legend of Atlantis seems to reflect a more intelligent and sophisticated knowledge of the world than the primitive river of Homer's world. Plato's own words seem to make it clear that he really means that there is a large and naviga-

ble ocean lying beyond the Straits of Gibraltar. He and his audience
can apparently take it for granted that men can sail there and that
men could find islands in the ocean. Notice also that Plato can apparently talk to his audience about a time span for human history that
runs to 9,000 years, which is considerably better than Bishop Ussher
could do 2,000 years later. Bishop Ussher, you remember, was the
English divine who decided that the world had been created on a certain day in the year of 4004 B.C.

Whatever we may assume about Plato's intentions, his fable about
Atlantis popularized the idea of there being islands in the ocean and
established a tradition that continued for thousands of years.

The best of the classic geographers included in their writing a great
deal of scientific information about the world, as we shall demonstrate
in a few pages. However, when they ran out of real information they
were reluctant to stop writing. Instead, they found it interesting to
repeat stories and legends and hearsay evidence. To Plato's Atlantis
other classical writers added stories about the Fortunate Islands
which were located out in the Atlantic; others talked about the Hesperides. Some of these islands were supposed to be inhabited either by
the gods or by the demigods or extremely fortunate human beings.
Some ideas of this kind survived into the Middle Ages and continued
or were reborn during the Revival of Learning. The Irish added stories about St. Brandan's Isle and about an island called Antillia and
Hy-Brasil. The very early maps used to assign a location for some or
all of these islands, but the map makers seldom agreed with each
other as to the probable location of the various named islands. As
knowledge about the Atlantic Ocean increased and became more accurate, maps gradually developed and the islands got moved farther and
farther away. Occasionally, as we know, a mythical name got assigned
to an island or a group of islands; thus, there was a time when the
Canary Islands were also called the Fortunate Islands.

It is extremely difficult for the human mind to contemplate empty
space or a completely empty ocean. The writers and map makers
were yielding to a natural impulse if they assigned names to islands
in the Atlantic. It is probable also that they were counting on reasonable inference even if not reported fact. We have seen already that
Pythias' account was known to many ancient writers even though
these did not always agree with him. They did accept the fact that
Pythias and others knew about Ireland and Great Britain and island
groups lying between them, and also north of Scotland as far as the
island that Pythias referred to as Thule. It is said that a group of

Phoenician coins were discovered about one hundred years ago on the island of Madeira. These coins were said to have been examined by archaeologists and to have been identified as the coins of the fourth century B.C. Unfortunately, the circumstances surrounding the discovery were not beyond question and the coins themselves were carried away before they could be given judicious study. It is possible, however, that Phoenician sailors got at least as far as the island of Madeira. Sertorius, 80 B.C., was a Roman who was an exile in "Gades" (Cadiz) in Spain. He reports that a group of sailors brought home a ship and told of having been to the "Fortunate Isles" which lie in the Western Ocean. They described two islands which were said to lie 10,000 stades, or about 1,000 miles, from the African coast. They said that the islands were protected from winds from the north and the east, but received winds from the west and the south. From these directions, the winds were gentle and brought plenty of rain so that the grounds of the islands were fertile. This description could apply to Madeira, there being two chief islands in the Madeira group. But the distance which Sertorius reports would be quite wrong for the Madeira group though it would be right for the Azores.

The first authentic record of European occupation of the Canaries was made by Juba, 25 B.C. to 25 A.D., who lived and ruled in North Africa, and is therefore referred to as a Numidian. He was the second person of this name; his father, after he was defeated by the Romans in 46 B.C., committed suicide. The son was taken to Rome by Julius Caesar where he acquired an education. Octavius, that is Augustus Caesar, allowed Juba to resume the rule of his father's kingdom, and later Juba was made king of Morocco. Juba married Cleopatra Selene, the daughter of Cleopatra and Antony.

Juba promoted an expedition to the Canary Islands and, based on the findings of this expedition, supplied a good description of the islands of the group. This included a description of the characteristic trees of the island, of the active volcano on Teneriffe, called by the Portuguese Pico de Tyede, and of the "banner cloud" which condenses on the leeward side of that peak. The islands were described as being inhabited by dogs, and this is thought to have accounted for the name which is still attached to this group. Goats and lizards were also found. Signs of human habitation were reported, but no human beings were seen. Is it possible that they were there, and retreated before the invaders? We do not know, but it is certain that when the Portuguese rediscovered the Canary Islands they were inhabited by a savage, primitive and very interesting tribe known as the Guanches.

The Guanches are usually considered to have been a division of the Berber people of North Africa. Henry Fairfield Osborne, the paleontologist and anthropologist, quoted with apparent approval a lengthy extract from a French authority who had spent some time on the problem of the Guanches and suggested that they showed strong affinity with the race of Cro-Magnon. Of course, this view would imply that the Guanches had been on the Canary Islands for a very long period of time. However this may be, it is clear that at least two and possibly three expeditions had visited the Canary Islands before the Portuguese rediscovered them. Plato's myth of the lost island or continent of Atlantis is firmly associated with the name of our ocean, but he was not the first of the Greek scholars to write of the ocean.

Hesiod in 750 B.C. had talked of the "Isles of the Blessed" and of the "Hesperides" and of "Erythia"; all islands that were supposed to exist in the outer ocean. This was the first appearance of the idea of islands which persisted for so long, and reappeared so frequently in the history of the Atlantic Ocean. Following Hesiod there grew up in Greek geography the idea that the surface of the earth could be divided into zones—the zones representing, in a general way, the crude division of the earth into belts of latitude. The belt at the extreme north was so cold that life there was impossible; and the belt directly under the sun, that is corresponding with our idea of the equator, so hot that that also would not support life. Teachings like this, which had little relationship to the real world, were accepted in Classic times even by persons who were otherwise knowledgeable and scholarly. The love which the Greeks had for a logical order and system produced splendid results in mathematics, such as the geometry of Euclid, and in their architecture and in some of their decorative arts, but when they came to geography it misled them, for they often preferred their rigid theories to the reports of travelers who had made themselves acquainted with the real world. The idea of the uninhabited polar region and the uninhabited tropics survived the Classical period and was revived with the Revival of Learning. Stefansson believes that in one modification after another this idea has persisted right down to our own day because of the veneration that European scholarship has usually given to Greek learning.

Herodotus, around 450 B.C., supplied us with the account of the Phoenicians who went around Africa in the time of the Egyptian King Necho. We are grateful to him for this service, but it is interesting to observe that the reason he was skeptical about this passage around Africa was that he preferred to believe that no human life could survive a passage through the tropics. Nonetheless, Herodotus added considerably to our knowledge of the Atlantic Ocean. Tidal movement in the Mediterranean is so slight as to have escaped the attention of most of the classic writers, and Herodotus is the first to give us an account of tidal action in the Indian Ocean and in the Atlantic.

Pythias, who lived in Massilia, the present French city of Marseille, in the closing years of the fourth century B.C. was not only one of the greatest of classic scholars, but also one of the greatest explorers of the ancient world. Somewhere between 325 B.C. and 310 B.C. he projected a voyage in Atlantic waters. Since his voyage was to be a long one, he felt that he needed to know all that he could about the earth and the heavens. Like many of the learned Greeks of his time he appreciated that the earth was not flat, but a sphere. He established two reference points to guide him on his travels—that is, he ascertained the position of the polar star and he made an observation of the exact latitude of his own city, the port from which he was departing on his travels. At the time of the solstice he erected a perpendicular pointer which, for purposes of measurements, was divided into 120 parts. Then he measured the shadow of the sun at high noon which turned out to be 41 and ⅘ths parts. Converted into degrees of arc this would give a reading of 70° 47′ 50″. In common with Eratosthenes and Hipparchus he knew about the inclination of the ecliptic 23° 51′ 15″. Subtracting this from the altitude of the sun he obtained 46° 56′ 35″. To obtain his latitude he would therefore subtract this from 90° which gave him a reading of 43° 3′ 25″. He then had to make a correction for half of the diameter of the sun; this could be considered roughly as 16′ which would be added to his reading to give a latitude of 43° 19′ 25″—roughly the present latitude of the observatory at the port of Marseille. Among his other scientific accomplishments Pythias reported observation of the tides of the Atlantic made during his long voyage and attributed them to the moon.

In the previous chapter we have already referred to Pythias' voyage to England because it throws light on the extent of ocean navigation in the North Atlantic before his time. Pythias provides an account of his trip around the British Isles and shows that he knew also about Ireland. It is now believed that he sailed also to Iceland and traveled far enough beyond Iceland to come in contact with the drifting ice pack. The name he used for Iceland was Thule.

Pythias' own books, one of them entitled *The Ocean,* have been lost, but he is quoted in the works of many other classical scholars. What he had to say seems at first to have been accepted and believed, but later, though he was often quoted, he was usually discredited because what he reported did not agree with accepted theory. Pythias' work was reinforced by the work of another Greek geographer, Eratosthenes, who lived from 239 to 196 B.C. Eratosthenes left a description of the known world from the shores of the Atlantic to India in a gazetteer in which he attempted to assign the latitude and longitude of places throughout this expanse. Naturally his latitudes were fairly good, whereas his longitudes were erratic because he lacked an accurate mechanical method of keeping time. Eratosthenes not only believed in a round world but also gave us the first accurate measurement of its circumference.

He did this in the following way. He knew that at the summer solstice the sun stood directly overhead at a place on the Nile called Syene. Syene was the ancient name for the city in Egypt now known as Aswan. At this time and place the sun shining down on a vertical well cast no shadow at all. Erecting a vertical pointer at Alexandria, where he was working, he took an observation of the earth's shadow at the time of the summer solstice and calculated that the distance from Alexandria to Syene represented the 150th part of a great circle. The average of repeated measurements between Alexandria and Syene gave a value of 5,000 stadia. He therefore calculated that the circumference of the earth was 250,000 stadia, which converts into 25,000 miles.

Admittedly there exists some doubt about the definition and use of the term stadia and consequently about its conversion into our miles. It is possible that both the measures of Pythias and of Eratosthenes may have been less accurate than would appear from these rough calculations. The point is that both of these ancient scholars had a clear idea of the character of the world in which they lived and used correct theoretical methods in their calculations. They represent a high-water mark in classical geographic knowledge.

Unfortunately for the progress of science Posidonius, who lived about one hundred years before Christ, also believed in a round world and made a calculation of it as being only 18,000 miles in circumference. Posidonius somewhat atoned for his error in the calculation of the earth's circumference by recording the first deep-water sounding. He reported that the Sardinian Sea was 1,000 fathoms in depth.

Ptolemy was the author of the last of the classical geographies and it was his work that was later used and accepted by the Renaissance scholars. Unfortunately, Ptolemy followed Posidonius, giving the earth's circumference as 18,000 miles. This had far-reaching effects on the knowledge and history of the Atlantic Ocean before the great Age of Discovery in the fifteenth century. Before the discovery of America people knew fairly accurately about the size of Europe and the Near East, and roughly about the distances to India and other parts of the Far East. When they subtracted these distances from 18,000 miles it gave them a very erroneous figure for the distance they would have to travel sailing westward to arrive at China, Japan or India. No doubt Columbus was following this line of reasoning in establishing his belief that he could quite easily reach the Indies by sailing westward across the Atlantic.

The Romans consolidated the Mediterranean world and in the process of doing so built serviceable ships both for conducting their wars and also for transporting goods on the Mediterranean. Toward the end of the Roman Empire Rome itself did not raise enough agricultural products to supply its large population. Each year great quantities of grain were transported from Egypt and from other colonies. It is said that the annual imports of grain from Egypt ran to as much as 20,000,000 bushels and a great number of vessels must have been employed in this trade.

The Romans, however, did not venture on the far-flung ocean voyages such as are reported by Pythias' voyage or the voyages in the Indian Ocean connected with Alexander's campaign in India.

The Romans seem to have made a very limited use of ships along the Atlantic shores of Europe. When Caesar was sweeping northward in Europe and was carrying out the campaigns in Gaul, he was marching by land and depending mostly on land transport. When he commenced the invasion of England he assembled a considerable fleet of ships for the short crossing of the English Channel. Some of these he collected from his local enemies and some were built under his directions, just as he did when he required a bridge or a road. He speaks particularly of the ships of the Veneti which seem to have been able craft as far as their sailing ability is concerned. No doubt they were a product of that long history of sailing in northern waters to which we have already alluded. Caesar's vessels were able to conquer the ships of the Veneti with the methods developed in galley warfare in the Mediterranean, that is by ramming them, by grappling, by cutting their rigging and boarding them in hand-to-hand struggle, but Caesar notes that these ships were apparently superior sailing vessels. He says that when they turned in the direction of the wind they were able to outdistance the Roman ships and escape. As Corson has recently suggested, this seems to indicate that the north European sailors had already, at the beginning of the Christian Era, learned how to build a ship that could be sailed to windward.

The Roman civilization that Caesar established in England was later cut off from its home in the Mediterranean when the Goths and the other northern European tribes moved southward, and this suggests the extent to which the Romans were dependent on overland transport. With the coming of the northern hordes, the geographic knowledge and the use of the sea that had been a part of the classic tradition lapsed and died. The Goths swept southward into Europe in 378 succeeded by the Visigoths in 395. At the same time the Huns came into the Mediterranean area by way of Asia Minor. In 406 the Vandals crossed the Rhine into Gaul, made their way through Spain and into North Africa, coming around to attack Rome through Sicily and the Mediterranean islands. Wave after wave of northern barbarians disposed of what was left of Mediterranean civilizations. The Gothic woe had descended on Europe.

After the fall of Rome the growth of the Christian Church made possible the preservation of some of the traditions and records of classic learning. Scholarship found a certain refuge in the monasteries and cloisters but even this was of dubious value. In its struggle for survival and expansion the Christian Church often insisted on theology rather than science being made the test of geographic knowledge. Ptolemy and Aristotle represented all that was left of classic geography and in time even their teachings were distrusted and altered. Medieval maps give us a vivid impression of this flat and shrunken world. Jerusalem becomes the center of the known world. Strange characters and demons appear on the fringes of the land and the oceans in one quarter of the map, while elsewhere there will be a representation of Adam and Eve evicted from the Garden of Eden.

What happened to geographic knowledge is perhaps well illustrated in the work of Cosmas who, in the middle of the sixth century produced a work under the title *Christian Typography*. In his youth Cosmas is supposed to have traveled extensively and thus earned the title "Indicopleustes" meaning the traveler who had been to India. When he became a monk Cosmas produced his work and denounced and condemned the idea of a circular world. He insisted that the world was flat and oblong. The sun did not travel around the world;

day and night were accounted for by the fact that the sun circled around a conical mountain. The difference between the length of the day in summer and winter was due to the fact that sometimes the sun circled around the base of the mountain and sometimes around the top of it.

Modern scholars have pointed out that if we examine the records of scholarship and science carefully it is possible in almost every age to point to the writing of one or more gifted men who believed that the world was round and who did not share the traditional ignorance of their time. This is probably true but it is of doubtful value. The important point is that these scholars had no influence on the men of their time. The bulk of the people, including the leaders of enterprise, believed that the world was flat and behaved accordingly, and the seas and oceans were filled with nameless and unspeakable terrors, the dangers of which increased in proportion to their distance from the familiar land.

Chapter 7

FIRST ACROSS THE ATLANTIC

THEY called them the Summer Sailors. They made the warm days in spring—that had ever before been a joy to Irish hearts—a period of apprehension or terror. No one could say where or when they would appear but all knew that, year by year, some section of the coast would be visited by barbarian heathens.

In some quiet dawn the warm sea breaking along the shore would be sending up thin veils of mist to hide the harbor cove and the little town along its shore that lived by fishing in the sea and grazing cattle in fields that sloped seaward. It might be that Ilah, who had gone into the fields to milk the kine, would be looking up to see the early sun shining on the mist and instead, there over the mist her eyes would fasten in horror on the grotesque head of a sea serpent. For a space all would be silent while she helplessly watched the horns, bright eyes and the red mouth move steadily and silently into the cove. Then, faintly over the sound of the waves along the shore, she could hear from the ship beneath the dragon head the muffled movement of the oars in the tholes, the creak of the steering oar as it turned a little on its boss, and low gruff voices. She couldn't decide whether she should scream to warn the village or keep quiet and try to save herself. Then she realized she was already screaming and it was too late. The ship had grated to a stop on the shingle beach, the big men dropping and jumping from her high prow and spreading out into the fields. The girls who had come into the field would be taken like herself; the cattle taken or killed; there would be fighting. What would happen to the village? For her part she would kick and scream, though she had heard of girls who had forgotten to scream and been carried off laughing instead.

Sometimes it was not a single boat creeping to shore silently in the dawn. Sometimes it was a whole company of ships coming in the evening, with the last of the sunset picking out the strong colors of the sails and glinting on the helmets and arms of the men, with the bellowing sound of horns and wild shouting from ship to ship. That was the worst, with fighting all along the shore and in the fields; the burning villages lighting up the night clouds and smoke still rising when the ships sailed away at dawn.

Thus, for an age in history, the sailors from the north harried the coasts of Europe. That was the less pleasant phase of their energetic activity, their knowledge of the world, their undoubted ability. To the people they oppressed they seemed like a new visitation of fate but their voyages and their ships had ancient foundations.

Once the Vikings (also called Norsemen, Normans, etc.) started their voyages they spread far and fast. They came from various parts of Norway, Sweden, Denmark. In theory at least, those from Norway took the outer passage which brought them to the islands, Faeroes, Hebrides, etc., Scotland and Ireland and from Ireland to France; the Danes took the middle passage to the low countries, the east coast of England and France; the Swedes took the eastern passage across the Baltic into Slavic territory where they founded colonies at Novgorod (862) and Kiev (900) and pressed on to Byzantium (Constantinople).

By the middle passage the Danes made the first recorded attack on England in 787 and within a century Guthrun, the Dane, by the Peace of Wedmore, divided England with Alfred the Great, holding for himself all of England north of Watling Street (London to Chester) and Scotland.

By the outer passage they swept over the Faeroes, Orkneys, Shetlands, Hebrides to Scotland and Ireland. They first appeared on the Irish coast about 795 and established colonies and trading posts at Dublin (840), Waterford and Limerick from whence they carried on operations against the French coast—Normandy.

In practice the orderly scheme suggested above was not strictly adhered to; it only represented tendencies. The Viking movements were somewhat confused in origin, route and objective. Yet by 841 they had appeared in the French ports and converged in strength in Normandy. By 845 Hrolf, the Ganger, was engaged in a massive attack on Paris. By a spirited defense Count Odo saved Paris but had to concede to Hrolf, also called Rollo, possession of Normandy. Rollo was christened as Robert and under him colonization and occupation began. Within a century Normandy, though independent, had adopted the French language and the French legal system.

Not only Paris but also Hamburg, Utrecht, Nantes, Bordeaux, Seville and other cities were the subjects of Norman attacks. By 843 they were appearing in the Mediterranean whose islands were then in the hands of the Saracens and other Islamic people. It was the Norman Harald Hardrada and his Scandinavian crews in Byzantine ships who beat the Saracen pirates off the coast of Anatolia and then attacked the Islamic ports all along the North African shore. In 1038-1040 with further Byzantine help he beat the Saracens of Sicily in two decisive battles. Twenty-six years later this same Hardrada turned up in Northumbria to aid Tostiq in an attack on Harold, the newly selected king of England. Rushing north Harold defeated Hardrada at Stamford Bridge; rushing south again he found that William and his Norman French had already landed on the Channel and his exhausted troops lost the battle of Hastings (1066).

In the Mediterranean the Normans insinuated themselves between two powerful factions of the Christian Church—the Roman and the Byzantine—and in fact played a part in developing open hostility between them. Having accepted Byzantine support in the attack on the Saracens of Sicily, they shifted ground and then accepted papal support in attacks on Saracens in Italy. With support from the papacy they also took parts of southern Italy from Byzantium. In 1060 they took Reggio, completing the conquest of Calabria. After they took Otranto in 1068 and Bari in 1071 the Byzantine rule in Italy had come to an end.

Then the Normans themselves proved hard to dislodge. Between 1081 and 1085 Robert Guiscard and his son Bohemund tried to establish a Norman empire in the Balkans. They won the battle of Pharsalus and took Durazzo, they conquered a large part of Macedonia but were turned back at Larissa. It took the combined Venetian and Byzantine fleets to defeat them near Corfu. Even so the Balkan project was not abandoned until Guiscard died and his sons fell to quarreling. Bohemund and his successors played an important and not unprofitable part in the Crusades.

The Viking ship was not a sudden new development and there is no uncertainty about its characteristics and its structure. A number of examples of the Viking ship have been discovered and carefully unearthed and preserved in Norway. They include the Gokstad ship, the Osberg ship and other variant forms, and a number of them are now assembled and displayed in the museum at Bygdoe near Oslo.

Even the earliest of the Viking ships is already a highly developed vessel. The sizes of the ships, their graceful lines and seaworthy qualities; the skill and strength shown in their construction; the attention devoted to mechanical detail such as the method of securing the permanent steering oar and of closing the thole holes when the vessel was under sail; all these imply a long history of seafaring and shipbuilding experience.

Not only the character of the Viking ships but also the ways in which these ships were used by the Norwegians, the Swedes, the Danes and the colonists during the great age of Viking expansion suggest that they were already bold and experienced seamen. We shall see in a moment how rapidly and how far they traveled.

We know already that there was a background for this age of development and that this background included not only the Norse but also other people who dwelt about the North Sea and the Baltic. From classic sources there are Caesar's references to the seafaring people in Gaul and beyond Gaul to the north. There are classic references to the trade that centered about the Cornish tin mines and the traders that came from all points of the compass to carry away the tin to their own countries. These include references to the large skin boat known in ancient Ireland as the curragh, a shrunken form of which has survived in Ireland but which seems in pre-Christian times to have had a much wider distribution.

Pythias, traveling in the last quarter of the fourth century before Christ, gives a detailed description of the Cornish tin mines and of the effect of widespread trade and travel on the character of the miners and merchants. Pythias sailed around England and Scotland. He also sailed to the island of Thule, which was apparently Iceland, and left an observation on the character of the ice field. So far as the classic records are concerned, Pythias discovered all these things for himself and for the Mediterranean civilization of which he was a part, but it is important to notice that these are not discoveries from the point of view of the North Sea people. Pythias himself reported that when he was along the Scottish coast, or in the islands beyond it, he was told quite accurately the direction in which Thule lay and the average length of time it took to get there in a sailing vessel.

Back of Pythias, we are dependent largely on archaeological records, and here we find that the interpretations of the archeologists help to explain the background for the Viking voyages. It is generally accepted that the Bronze Age in southern Europe and the Mediterranean ran a different course from the Bronze Age in northern Europe. The use of bronze in northern Europe seems to have been at least as old as 2000 B.C. The speed with which the Bronze culture spread in northern Europe and the way in which bronze tools, ornaments and other objects were distributed can only be explained by a very extensive system of trade around and across the North Sea, involving the Hebrides, the Orkneys and other island groups and, of course, including Ireland.

What is true of the Bronze Age is also true, in a measure, of the distribution of products of the Iron Age that preceded it. Even if we move back into the Stone Age in northern Europe, including extensive areas in the Scandinavian peninsula, the archaeologists who deal with this period believe that there was then a very extensive use of seagoing vessels in the North Sea, and along its shores. During his lifetime, Professor A. W. Brøgger was in charge of the Viking ships and conducted extensive studies in the arts and industries of this period. He also devoted much time to the late Stone Ages and their artifacts. These included drawings, carved in rocks, of ships of considerable size. Brøgger believed that vessels, such as represented in the rock drawings, were used not only for coastwise voyages but also for connections across the North Sea, so that the record of a developing seamanship in this part of the world is very old indeed.

We return now to the records of written history. It is the skin boat, or curragh, of the Irish that was probably used by the earliest northern sailor known to us by name—the Irish priest Brendan. No doubt he was a great traveler, but he could not possibly have completed all the voyages that are attributed to him or lived through as many adventures as cluster about his name. Stripped of its more exuberant and extravagant details, there is enough factual description left to make it seem probable that on one of his trips St. Brendan encountered either the glaciers or the icebergs along the eastern Greenland shore and visited the south shore of Iceland.

Discuil, in 825, produced a work on geography which refers specifically to the theory that the earth is round and deals with its measurement under the title *Mensura Orbis Terrae*. In this volume he speaks of a voyage to Iceland as though it were an accepted matter and not a singular or rare occurrence. This voyage, described by Discuil, took place some thirty years before the time he was writing— that is, at the end of the eighth century. It is, apparently, a recollection of a conversation with one of the monks who had made the trip. They remained in Iceland from February to August. He describes the mountainous character of the country and says that at the time of the summer solstice there was continuous daylight; where they were the sun hardly set at all. He said that it was so light, even at midnight, you could see well enough to pick lice off your shirt.

About the same time, the Scandinavians were extending their operations, which included colonizing the Faeroe Islands. By 860 they also had reached Iceland. There were apparently a number of expeditions that were referred to in tradition, and when we come to the written record credit seems to be divided. One of the earliest of the Icelandic sagas is the Landnamabok which describes the colonization of Iceland and the way in which its land came to be occupied by the different chiefs and their families. According to this saga, a Swede named Gardar, accompanied by a few dependents and servants, made the trip to Iceland in 860. He built a house or shelter there and therefore referred to the place where he spent his time as Husavik. At the same time a Norwegian named Naddodd is also reported to have made the trip to Iceland, and called it Snowland.

In 865, Raven-Floki, accompanied by Herjolf and Thorolf, made the first attempt on the part of the Norwegians to colonize Iceland. It appears that they were entranced by the great numbers of fish in the streams and the sea and all hands spent their time fishing. Like many other fishermen before and since, they neglected their duties ashore. They forgot to raise and harvest crops for themselves and their cattle. Their attempted colonization was not a great success and when they returned to Norway, as not infrequently happens among travelers, they disagreed. Their opinions on Iceland ranged from that of believing it was a wonderful country for colonization, little short of an earthly paradise, to that of holding that it was a very poor country, hardly able to sustain life.

The opinion that it was a good country seems to have won out, for presently a large expedition set out from Norway to establish a colony on Iceland. The official date for this settlement is given as 874 but Professor Hermannsson of Cornell, a leading Icelandic scholar of today, believes the date to have been several years earlier.

There are two rather interesting quirks to this important bit of history. One has to do with the name, which has been so misleading to people throughout history. Actually, Iceland has a rather mild climate. The major part of the island enjoys an open and warm winter, and the ports and shores are free of ice throughout the year. Mountains stretch across the northern part of the island and here there is considerable snowfall and sometimes ice in the harbor. This, however, has no bearing on the selection of the name. The ice the Norwegians referred to had nothing to do with the land but only with the sea. The Norwegians had never seen ice in the sea, either low floating ice floes or lofty bergs. The Norwegian branch of the North Atlantic Drift keeps the entire coast of Norway free of ice at all seasons of the year. On the other hand, though the coasts of Iceland are free of ice, both bergs and floes can be seen from its mountains, and also observed from any ships that sail around Iceland. It was the surprise of finding ice in the sea that led the early colonists to accept for their country a name that has always been a handicap.

The other curious circumstance is this: that though the Norwegians and Icelanders credit themselves with the discovery and colonization of Iceland, in the very same records they refer to the fact that the Irish had been there before them. Memory of this fact is even preserved in their place names. The Norwegians always referred to the Irish as Westmen. A small island lying off the south shore of Iceland is still called the Vestmannaeyjar or, as we would say, the Irish Island. By this time the Norsemen had occupied a considerable territory in Ireland; the colonists in Iceland, of course, felt themselves superior to the Irish. They occasionally took Irish girls as wives; more frequently they carried them off as slaves or servants. Therefore, any travels or discoveries that the Irish may have carried out in Iceland merit only a casual reference in the sagas, whereas they, themselves, must be reckoned as the real discoverers and colonizers. Whatever the social theory, the fact seems to be that the Irish and the Norse had been in contact with each other for a considerable period of time, and that the Irish constituted an important strain in the population of Iceland. The attitude of the Norse toward the Irish elements in the population were considerably altered by the adoption of Christianity and by the development in Iceland of representative government.

In terms of distance involved in travel, and of its geographical location, Iceland is closer to America than it is to Europe. The move to Iceland was an important and decisive step in the first migration from Europe to America. It is, therefore, natural and appropriate that their geographic progress should have been accompanied by a forward step in social organization and the development of political institutions. The Icelanders felt themselves to be free of the mother country. They determined to develop their own system of government and of laws. With this in mind they sent one of their scholars to Norway to carry out a three-year study of its laws and legal system. The purpose back of this step, and the spirit of the study, are important. The object was not to make a slavish imitation of the Norwegian system but to find out which of the Norwegian laws should be rejected and which could be adapted to the purposes of the new country. They also adopted a parliamentary form of government which was the beginning of an independent democratic system. The Parliament was called the Althing, or meeting of the leaders and representatives from all sections of the country. Its first meeting was in 930 at a spot called Thingvelir, in a natural volcanic amphitheater in the hills looking out over a coastal plain. This was a democratic assembly in the sense that all parts of the country and all interests were represented there but the leaders who met there were the titular heads of families rather than elected representatives. Naturally, there was not, at this time, universal suffrage, and in many ways the social organization of Iceland continued to bear the marks of its feudal origins. It was, however, the start of a democratic system, and in 1930 a great international meeting took place on the plains of Thingvelir to celebrate the thousandth anniversary of the oldest uninterrupted parliamentary system in the world.

Long before the Althing met, the Icelanders were aware that other lands might lie to the west of them. As early as the year 900, Gunnbjorn Ulfsson, on a trip around Iceland, reported several small islands and said also that he had sighted a large island with mountains, which is supposed to constitute the first reference to Greenland. Whether Gunnbjorn actually sighted Greenland or not is of no great importance for, in any event, the sailors of Iceland were bound to have an interest in the lands and seas that might lie to the west of them. They might even have seen Greenland, for it is reported that, from the highest mountain in northwest Iceland, it is possible, under favorable weather conditions, to see some of the mountains in Greenland. It only needed some special circumstance or incentive to start the Icelanders off to the west.

The circumstance was that in 982 an aggressive and vigorous man named Eric got into trouble. He was nicknamed "Eric the Red" and seems to have had a hasty temper and to have had the misfortune of killing his opponent in some personal feud. This was quite in the family tradition, for Eric's father before him had killed a man in Norway and this accounted for his being in Iceland. Eric's penalty was that he was to be exiled from Iceland for a three-year period.

Accordingly, he decided to look for the land that Gunnbjorn had first reported. Sailing directly to the west he saw Greenland spread out before him and approached its west coast. It was almost inevitable that he should try this for it was the land that lay nearest to him, but it was equally inevitable that he should meet with difficulty and no success. He encountered the ice fields and the steady resistance of the Labrador Current. The current made it natural for him to try to follow the coast in a direction south and west and so he came around Cape Farewell and, traveling north along the west coast, he found icefree waters, an easy approach to the shore and a number of good harbors. Here was vegetation and enough good soil to support animals and men. There were fish to be caught in the sea and seal to be hunted. To the Eskimo he assigned the name "Skrellings."

This was no mere summer sailing; Eric was an important person and must have been so or he would not have had a ship at his disposal. The conventional ship of his period would be somewhat less than one hundred feet long. Even with mast and sail, it would require oarsmen—that is, a crew of thirty or forty retainers. For a three-year stay he would take with him farm animals and equipment. During his three-year stay he thoroughly explored the west Greenland coast as far as Disko Island.

Eric returned to Iceland in 985 and told them of the land he had discovered, which he called Greenland. He knew the advantage of a good name and hoped to promote interest in his new country. In 986 he started back for Greenland with twenty-five ships, a large company of men with their wives and servants and the animals and equipment that they might need to establish their farms in the new country. They encountered head winds and heavy storms. Some of the ships were lost at sea and some returned to Iceland. Eric, with fourteen ships, reached Greenland and commenced the establishment of the settlers. Two general areas of colonization were established— an eastern settlement and a western settlement. This is a little misleading because both the settled areas were on what we would have called the west coast of Greenland and we would have called one the southern settlement and the other the northern settlement.

From this beginning Greenland had a steady growth. It is estimated that, in time, the population grew to about 10,000 and that as many as 280 farms were developed and occupied. The Christian religion, which had won popular acceptance in Iceland by the year 1000, spread also to Greenland and, for centuries, it was the western outpost of the Catholic Church. Ecclesiastical administration of Iceland was first conducted from Hamburg, and, at the end, was transferred to Nidaros in Norway. Nidaros was the old name for the city later called Trondhjem. Not only the interests of the Church but also the interests of trade were represented in frequent communications between Europe and Greenland during the next several centuries. Adam of Bremen, in 1070, wrote the history of the Church of Hamburg. He writes as though a general knowledge of Iceland and Greenland could be taken for granted and refers to voyages made to Vineland. He refers also to the fact that a Norwegian king, Harald Hardrade had made an expedition to Spitsbergen and thus, in another way, reflects the wide range of navigation of the time. But this is getting a little ahead of the story.

Eric had two sons. One of them, Lief by name, in the year 999 sailed to Norway by way of the Scotch Islands. He spent the winter in the court of the king, Olaf Tryggvason, and the king, who was an ardent churchman, persuaded him to take with him two priests in the following spring when he set sail for Greenland. The usual procedure would have been for Lief to sail for Iceland and then to proceed to Greenland but he decided to make the passage direct. In addition, owing either to poor weather or to some slip in his navigation of the open ocean, Lief missed Greenland, and the first land he saw was either Newfoundland or a part of the Labrador coast. He then turned around and sailed in a northeast direction and arrived at the colony which his father had founded. This is the first authentic record of an uninterrupted crossing of the Atlantic.

On his way back to Greenland Lief rendered assistance to a vessel in distress. Because of this, and other accomplishments, he earned for himself the title of "Lief the Lucky." He used the name Vineland for the land that he had discovered.

On Lief's return he started preaching Christianity and, during the winter, plans were made for an expedition to the land that Lief had discovered. This expedition met with consistently bad weather. The contrary winds carried them so far back that they saw Iceland, and at another time saw birds coming from Ireland, but they could not succeed in getting to the west. The ship returned with Eric and his son but with nothing accomplished.

Thorstein Eriksson married a beautiful young woman named Gudrid—the wedding taking place at his father's home, Brattahlid. After the wedding, the newly married pair went to Thorstein's farm in the northern settlement. Here there was a great deal of sickness, and during the winter Thorstein died. Gudrid went to live with Eric and was treated by him as a daughter. In the meantime, a merchant and navigator by the name of Thorfinn Karlsefni had set sail for Greenland. He had a good vessel and a crew of forty men and was accompanied by another ship. They all celebrated the winter together at Eric's place and after Christmastime Thorfinn and Gudrid were married. The rest of the winter was spent in discussing and preparing an expedition to the country Lief had discovered and which he had called Vineland the Good. The expedition was to consist of two ships—one, that of Karlsefni, the other with Bjarne and Thorhall. There was also another vessel with some of Eric's people aboard. Gudrid and a number of other women sailed with the ships. Altogether there were 160 people in the ships.

First they proceeded north to Disko Island and then, sailing to the southwest, came to a rocky shore which they called Helluland—the land of flat stones—usually supposed to be Labrador. Sailing a day and a night, they came to a forested country which they called Markland. This was probably the southern portion of Labrador near the Straits of Belle Isle, or a part of Nova Scotia. After this they sailed for a long way and came, after a time, to a region where there were many bays and fjords, and sandy rather than rocky shores. They found an island surrounded by strong currents and thought the country good. They had not made sufficient preparation for the winter however and, during the winter season, ran short of food. One ship with Thorall, the hunter, separated from the rest of the party and, after battling heavy west winds, was driven to Ireland. It was later reported that he died there. Karlsefni, Bjarne and the rest of the party sailed a long way to the mouth of a river having a lake, or pond, in its lower reaches. This place they called Hop. This was a very prosperous region. After a meeting with some natives, which passed without incident, the explorers settled down for the winter in houses they had built above the lake. There was no snow and the domestic animals were able to go through the winter outdoors. In the spring there was a peaceful meeting with the natives and there was an exchange of skins for woven cloth. The natives went away, but later returned and there was a pitched battle during which the explorers lost several men. One of the women, Freydis by name, though she was pregnant and considerably hampered, took a sword from one of the fallen companions and prepared to attack the natives. The natives retired.

Karlsefni decided that, with so many natives all about them, it would be dangerous to create a settlement here, even though the land was extremely productive. They sailed back and spent a third winter at the island where there were powerful currents. During this winter there were quarrels, and cliques formed, owing to the presence of the women. After this winter, they returned to Markland and then to Greenland where they spent the winter with Eric the Red. Karlsefni's son, named Snorri, was born during the first winter of the expedition and was three years old when they returned from America. The date was about 1006.

* * * *

Where was Hop? Exactly how far south along the American coast did the Norsemen travel? Thousands have asked such questions and literally scores of scholars after careful and prolonged study have attempted to provide answers. All agree that the Norsemen spent some season on the northeastern coast of North America but no one quite agrees as to which parts of the coast they sailed past or which harbors they visited. Locations are proposed and defended all the way from Nova Scotia in the north to North Carolina in the south.

One thing seems reasonably established, the climates of Iceland, Greenland and the American coast have changed between the year 1000 and the year, say, 1900. The winters in all three sectors were milder and there was less fast ice in the winters and drifting ice in the summers to interfere with navigation. Miss Rachel Carson after reporting Pettersson's studies dealing with the influences of ocean tides and currents on climate accepts the idea that in Viking times the water was warmer and the weather milder in the northern North Atlantic than it was before or has been since.

If this were so the Viking voyagers were affected in two ways. First they would have had a longer cruising season during the summers, and second they would not have had to travel farther south than the southern coast of New England in order to find open winters during which the cattle could shift for themselves outdoors; where grapes would ripen in the summers, etc. Here we may note that Means has examined the so-called Old Stone Mill in Newport in great detail and presented a reasonable argument for accepting it as a Norse tower.

However far south the Vikings may or may not have sailed along the American coast it is now generally admitted that at least one Norse party penetrated the continent as far as Kensington in Minnesota.

Even if we do not assume a radical change in climate the Norse voyagers to America were not meeting the terrible conditions that some readers conjure up for them. It is often supposed that in sailing westward they would be meeting persistent head winds out of the west such as English sailors later encountered when they wished to sail from the Channel to New York. Actually in the latitudes of Norway, Iceland, Greenland and Labrador summer winds are light and variable and often favorable to a westward passage. Daylight for some months is almost continuous, there being only a few hours of twilight darkness. They had the benefits of the westward flowing Irminger Current which is a recurring element of the Gulf Stream system. It would benefit them by its flow on certain courses but chiefly it aided them by tempering and warming the Atlantic climate.

Beyond Iceland the Viking voyagers would have benefited directly from various ocean current systems. It is now supposed that in those days the east coast of Greenland was relatively free of ice and that the earliest crossings were made directly westward with first landings on the Greenland east coast. Later as ice increased these landings in east Greenland were abandoned. In any case ships approaching the Greenland coast would be easily carried south by the East Greenland Current. Keeping sufficiently near shore they would have no difficulty rounding Cape Farewell, the southern tip of Greenland, for the current itself rounds the Cape and continues flowing to the north as the West Greenland Current.

Along the west coast from Farewell almost as far north as Disko the voyagers in summer would find icefree harbors and open land ashore and an almost incredible wealth of life in the sea. Along this shore in addition to the West Greenland Current there is an upwelling of cold deeper waters bringing with them foodstuffs and chemicals for the plankton; the plankton and smaller creatures in turn providing luxuriant fare for the greater fishes and the seals, the walrus, the whales. This combination of currents of harbors and of life in the sea made the Norse seek this shore and its waters as a place for settlement as before them it had attracted the Eskimo. Later, Hans Egede sought it out as did the missionaries and settlers who followed him, and over the centuries there were drawn here also the whalers and sealers of many countries.

Again as the Norse ships left west Greenland and approached Labrador they would pick up the Labrador Current and this would help to carry them south to Newfoundland and Nova Scotia, and even beyond as far as time and inclination led them to travel along our coasts.

So the mild seasons and the currents of the sea could have assisted the voyages of the Vikings and undoubtedly were used by them to the utmost; but beyond all geographic and climatic advantages they had within themselves the tradition and spirit of adventure.

Chapter 8

THE NEW WORLD IN THE NORTH

THERE is a chapter still missing in the school and general history books. This is the chapter that deals fully and justly with the great accomplishments of all the peoples of northern and western Europe in discovering, colonizing and otherwise utilizing the seas and lands of the northern part of the Atlantic including, in its proper setting, the Norse discovery of the North American Continent.

This is an accumulative story of early beginnings, of long development, of ample sweep and perspective, full of heroic effort and great accomplishment. It is difficult therefore to understand its long neglect. Most of the elements of this story have been known for a long while though the story continues to grow and factors have been added in our time both by students abroad and by Stefansson and others in this country.

Please note that the statement in the above paragraph is that the story of the northern sea routes to America is "neglected" not "omitted." One cannot say that the story of Lief Eriksson and the voyages to America are omitted. It is now customary to include or refer to the Norse voyages to parts of the North American coast. The neglect lies in giving the facts no background or development. The treatment or attitude suggests that the historians have come to accept somewhat reluctantly the facts that Lief's discovery of America and Karlsefni's attempted colonization are real. The suggestion remains that though these early facts in American history are accepted, they are of no importance, whereas Columbus' voyage and the Spanish claims are to be taken at their full face value.

Owing to a lack of background material and explanation the reader is usually left with a set of particular conclusions—all false:

1. The Norse discovery of America was an isolated affair—an accident.
2. That interest in and contact with North American seas and shores ceased thereafter.
3. That the northern routes from Europe to America were impractical or at least not utilized.
4. That there was no wealth or economic benefit to Europe in the north to compare to the Indian gold of Central America and Peru.

The story of the northern sea routes to America has a very respectable antiquity—it is in fact medieval. Though its effects continue into modern times, its essential spirit is medieval. It has its heroes, its romances, its humor but in the main it is the story of many anonymous heroes of practical purposes, of great tasks undertaken and carried out in the interest of daily living. Perhaps that is the trouble. It contrasts with the story of the later southern routes to America which is Renaissance in time and spirit—individualistic, romantic, flamboyant!

Whatever the reason, the early general development of the north Atlantic is neither generally known or understood yet the facts are reasonably clear.

Europe was in contact with North America about five hundred years before Columbus sailed and the contact was neither accidental nor temporary. It is a natural part of a long development which began in the Stone Age when the Norse were already building ships for ocean travel and engaging in trade across the North Sea. At this time, of course, there were pictures but no written records so the evidence on this part of the story is archaeological. There is written evidence that Norse enterprise at sea was in vigorous development at a later date for the annals of Alfred the Great contain an account supplied by Othere (Ottar), a Norse sea captain, giving a spirited account of a developed whaling enterprise engaged in by many men and ships. He also supplies information regarding a voyage around the North Cape to Muscovy.

Norse ships indeed, over a period of several centuries, kept expanding the range of their voyages. Their westward progress was marked by stages at which they successively reached the Orkneys, the Shetlands, Scotland and Ireland. When they arrived in due course in Iceland, they found the Irish had been there before them but it was they who colonized it and built there an independent nation. The Icelanders in turn colonized Greenland and proceeded to the continental shores of America. It is true that Eric the Red, when he closed with the American continent, said he did so because he overran his course to Greenland. It is, however, very misleading to say that America was discovered by accident. His statement may have been an excuse and his passing Greenland deliberate. At most, the "accident" would apply only to Eric as an individual and not to the Norse captains as a whole for they continually sailed beyond the known ranges and if it had not been Eric's ship it would have been some other Norse captain's. Certainly Lief's voyage and the colonizing voyages of Karlsefni and the others were deliberate.

The attempts at colonization were neither brief nor haphazard. They lasted some years and involved careful preparation of many men and ships. Why did they fail? Because they lacked guns and powder; the Spaniards succeeded because they had both—a point to be discussed later.

There was at the time neither mystery nor secrecy about the existence of a large New World in the north and west. Who knew about this New World? The Roman Catholic Church knew about it for centuries, punctuated by periods of neglect or lapses of memory such as afflict many administrations. So many educated men having access to church records would know.

At the time of the discoveries the Archbishop of Hamburg was responsible for ecclesiastical administration in Iceland. A history of the Church of Hamburg was written in 1070 by Adam of Bremen. Adam is, therefore, interested in Iceland and Greenland; he is, in fact, well informed about these territories. He also specifically refers to the voyages to Vineland. So far as the Church is concerned, there appears to have been a continuing interest in Greenland and Vineland. The annals of Iceland show that Bishop Eric Knupsson of Greenland made a visit to Vineland in 1121. In 1126, the bishopric of Iceland was transferred to Nidaros, the city which was later called Trondhjem in Norway.

As late as 1381 there was a resident bishop in Greenland but none is known after this date and contact with the western world seems to have diminished. However, at least two Popes became distressed about the alleged lapses of the colony in Greenland.

The Church in Greenland was becoming a problem to Rome. Pope

Nicolas, in 1448, wrote a letter deploring conditions in Iceland and referring specifically to the destruction of parish churches by the natives. In 1476 two captains of vessels, also acting as governors, by the names of Pining and Pothorst, went to Iceland and later, on instructions, went to Greenland—the purpose being to protect trade from the depredations of the Eskimo population. They were dispatched by King Christian I of Denmark but he was acting at the request of and in concert with the king of Portugal.

The year of the Pining and Pothorst voyage to Greenland was also the year in which Christopher Columbus, according to his son Ferdinand, went to Iceland and also traveled in the sea beyond without finding ice.

In 1492, before Columbus announced his discovery of islands in the Atlantic, Pope Alexander the Sixth, who was a member of the Spanish Borgia family, wrote a letter regarding his concern over the young Christians growing up in Greenland. After Columbus' return, no further letters regarding Greenland appear to have been written.

Governments also showed a lively interest in the new west. In 1261-1262, both Greenland and Iceland were persuaded to accept the sovereignty of the king of Norway. Subsequent to this, Norway tried to divert trade between Iceland and Greenland and to serve always as an intermediary. About 1348 a small ship from Greenland, with seventeen men aboard, arrived in Iceland having been carried there by strong winds from the west. They had been in that part of Labrador called Markland. This is only one of several historical citations which show that the Greenlanders continued to visit the North American continent where they found a source of timber for their houses and ships. These men were taken to Bergen, presumably because it was thought that they had violated the trade agreement.

In 1354 King Magnusson, having heard reports which tended to show that the Greenland colony was drifting away from Christianity and accepting the ways of native life in Greenland and in Labrador, felt it necessary to correct this situation. He appointed Powell (Paul) Knutson to command an expedition—to take the ship *Knor* and proceed to Greenland. This expedition apparently sailed in 1355 and the expedition, or a part of it, is believed to have returned in 1363 or 1364. However, its exact fate remains unknown unless we accept the work of a present-day scholar, Mr. Hjalmar Holand, who believes that this expedition, in pursuit of its assignment, traveled to Labrador and then, in pursuit of its object, penetrated the North Ameri-

can continent and left a record of its wanderings and its fate in a
runic stone that was discovered in 1898 grown into the roots of an
aspen tree in Kensington, Minnesota. The stone records how eight
Goths and twenty-two Norwegians, on an exploring journey, had
traveled to this point and how ten men had already been killed by
the Indians. They had left ten men behind at a sea or lake coast to
look after their ship—fourteen days' journey away. The date of the
stone was 1362.

I included a brief summary of Mr. Holand's work in my volume
entitled *Unrolling the Map* and, more recently, Dr. Stefansson has
reviewed the case in his volume, *The Great Explorations and Discoveries*. Linguistic scholars find difficulty in accepting the language
of the stone but this difficulty may be accounted for by the mixed
origin of the travelers and the circumstances under which it is supposed to have been created. On the other hand, geologists, forestry
experts and archaeologists who have worked with Mr. Holand, find
an even greater difficulty in believing that the stone itself and the circumstances under which it was found could have been faked. Despite
the linguists, the Kensington stone remains, at least, one of the lively
mysteries; possibly it represents a basic record in the exploration of
the American continent.

In 1432 Henry VI of England and Eric of Pomerania, who was
then king of parts of Norway, Sweden and Denmark, entered into
a treaty which provided specifically that England was not to trade
direct with Greenland. The mere fact that such a treaty was thought
necessary shows two things. First, that the Greenland colony and its
products were sufficiently important to engage the attention of two
European countries. It also shows that there was contact not only
between Greenland and the Scandinavian countries but also between
England and Greenland.

As a matter of fact, we know from other sources that the Greenland products that passed in trade to Europe were furs and hides
and rawhide thongs made from the various sea animals and fish. The
light-colored American Arctic falcon, often referred to as the gyr-
falcon, was also captured and tamed. It was highly prized in the sport
of falconry and exchanged as an honorable gift between princes.

In addition, at about this time Europe had another contact with
America that was of considerable importance. The historians of the
whaling industry report that the seamen of the Bay of Biscay, chiefly
the Basques, commenced whaling locally in the thirteenth century.

At the end of the fourteenth century they had extended their operations as far as the coast of Newfoundland and a little later than this they were whaling in the waters between Greenland and Labrador.

The Iceland fisheries had already been well developed and each year attracted vessels from European coasts. English ships and English merchants, particularly those from the port of Bristol, served as middlemen in trade that grew up between Portugal and Iceland. Icelandic records refer to these English vessels and also note that they were seen passing beyond Iceland in the direction of Greenland. Thus, by the middle of the fifteenth century the whaling vessels were simply one element in a growing number of North Atlantic voyages and the Norse voyages had already resulted in a number of products from American waters annually entering European trade.

It is sometimes stated and often assumed that there were long periods after the Norse discoveries during which there was no interest in the New World and no voyages were made. Now it is true that there were periods, both before and after Columbus, when there were *no recorded* crossings but this may well be because there were no quarrels or disasters or because the Church and the princes were otherwise occupied. It seems reasonable at least to assume that once the trading, the fishing, the whaling were established, those sturdy and unassuming fellows, the trader, the fisherman and the whaler, went steadily about their business and kept out of the news.

Nor were larger plans by more important people lacking. Several such names and plans began before Columbus and carried through afterward. Thus a Portuguese named João (John) Vaz Corte-Real was working with the Danish government and it is believed that he traveled to the Grand Banks on the American coast in 1472-1473. It was the sons of this man who later carried out extensive expeditions to the American coast.

England also was pursuing an interest in the northern route. The instigator in this case was Giovanni Caboto, a naturalized citizen of Venice who moved to England in 1485 for the express purpose of conducting voyages across the Atlantic to the northwest. He petitioned the British government for patents and privileges in any lands that he might discover during his voyages. This was some six years before Columbus sailed on even his first voyage. It was natural that Cabot should associate himself with the port of Bristol and also natural that it took some years for Cabot to establish himself in England and to gain the support and privileges he required. In 1496, letters patent were issued to him authorizing him to sail and to claim for

England any lands he might find. These letters also gave him the authority to colonize and a trade monopoly on the territories he might discover. He sailed from Bristol in 1497 in a small ship named the *Matthew*. There were only eighteen men in his crew. His landfall was probably on Cape Breton Island and he cruised about the mouth of the St. Lawrence, discovering an extensive coast and persuading himself that this was not simply an island. One result of Cabot's voyage was to discover and report the richness of the fisheries on the Grand Banks.

In 1498 Cabot sailed again with a large ship supplied from London and with four vessels from Bristol. We are imperfectly informed regarding the fate of this expedition but we do know that Cabot and the vessel in which he traveled were lost. It is believed that John Cabot, on his second trip, followed the Labrador coast into Davis Strait. His son, Sebastion Cabot, made an attempt in 1509 to find a northwest passage. The significance of John Cabot's voyages is that he made an independent discovery of the North American continent and laid the foundation for later British claims to discovery and colonization in this part of the world. He also confirmed the richness of the American fisheries. It is quite possible that these fisheries would have grown in any event but his report no doubt hastened their development. It is certain that in the early years of the sixteenth century the French, Dutch, Portuguese and English were sending fleets to fisheries off the American coast.

Cabot's work was reinforced by the voyages of the Corte-Reals, the sons of John. The first expedition in 1500 was under the leadership of Gaspar. It touched at the Azores and at Iceland and then proceeded into the Denmark Straits to the northwest of Iceland. Here they encountered the natural difficulties of this part of the ocean which, as we have already seen, influenced so many other voyagers. He also proceeded to round Cape Farewell and pursue the west Greenland coast almost to the Arctic Circle before he returned. In 1501 he returned with three ships and picked up the Labrador coast in the vicinity that the Greenlanders called Markland. They turned south and came to the region of very large trees. Here they encountered natives—either Eskimos or Indians—and captured fifty of them to take back as slaves. After passing the Straits of Belle Isle, two ships returned to England while Gaspar Corte-Real himself headed south with the intention of seeing how the lands along which he had been sailing related to the islands Columbus had discovered and reported. He was never heard from again. His brother, Miguel, went in search of him and discovered and named St. John's Harbor in Newfoundland. From here the three ships of the expedition disbursed to search different parts of the coast. Two of the ships kept an appointment in St. John's in August but Miguel and his vessel were lost.

It is interesting to relate these voyages to the work of Christopher Columbus. Columbus' voyage of 1492 was a significant and memorable event but it was not, as usually claimed, a discovery of the American continent and it is no detraction to point this out. All that he did, and all that he claimed to have done, was to discover some islands in the sea which he believed to be near the coast of Asia. It was not until the third voyage of 1498 that Columbus picked up a portion of the South American coast and it was not until 1502 that he reached the Central American coast around Panama. Columbus did not believe—and did not want to believe—that a great continent and a great ocean lay between his ships and the Orient. On the other hand, Cabot and Corte-Real were sailing along the mainland of North America at exactly the same time that Columbus and Vespucci were picking up the coast of South America. They met with less recognition and acclaim but they were more realistic. They knew that they had discovered a very large land mass, possibly a continent.

It took a number of further voyages to demonstrate that the old Vineland, Labrador and other lands of the northern explorers were actually connected with the new Florida of the Spaniards but an important contribution was made by a man named Verrazano. Verrazano was a Florentine who, after extensive travel, drifted into the employment of the French. In 1524 he fitted out four vessels and set out from the Brittany coast to sail to China. A succession of storms forced him to return. After this he was able to repair one vessel and man it with about fifty men. He arrived on the American coast in latitude 34° north—that is, near Cape Hatteras. Following the coast northward, he apparently saw Barnegat Bay and shortly afterward arrived at New York harbor. Thus, he was in New York and at the mouth of the Hudson River before Henry Hudson. He gives a lively description of the bay and of the coming and going of the Indians between the various shores of the harbor. Leaving New York, he sailed between Block Island and Martha's Vineyard and came into Narragansett Bay where Newport now stands. He sailed along the New England coast and touched Newfoundland, which had already been visited by Breton sailors, for Aubert had been to the St. Lawrence in 1508. Verrazano's long and successful voyage aroused a good deal of attention and accounted, in part, for the voyages of Jacques Cartier.

In 1534 Cartier made his first voyage going west with two ships and a complement of sixty men. Cartier went through the Straits of Belle Isle and found a harbor in the river beyond. While at anchor here, a big fishing barque from La Rochelle came into the neighboring anchorage. Here is a fine example of the unheralded presence of fishermen. Cartier is credited with discovering the St. Lawrence but fishermen are already using it as an anchorage. Cartier explored Gaspé and Chaleur Bay. He went up the river as far as Anticosti Island. He sailed again the next year, traveling up the St. Lawrence as far as Montreal. He wintered there and returned successfully.

In 1541 there was another expedition in which Cartier set out from St. Malo with five vessels. Nominally, Roberval was supposed to have joined this expedition and to be in charge of it but it was Cartier who carried the matter through. Again he spent the winter on the St. Lawrence but did not succeed in two attempts to get beyond the La Chine rapids.

Verrazano's voyages, together with those of Cartier, laid the background for the French claims to American territory.

Cartier's voyages started from the same ports that were used by the fishing fleet and followed the same courses that were used by fishing vessels, including, as we have seen, the approaches to the St. Lawrence River.

In much the same way Martin Frobisher, beginning in 1576, made three attempts to discover a northwest passage which carried him to Greenland, to Labrador and finally even into Hudson Strait. The story of Martin Frobisher's becoming diverted by so-called "fool's gold" of Labrador and of his returning with a shipload of iron pyrites to England is so well known as not to require repetition here. We should not lose sight of the fact, however, that his original intention was to find a way to the Orient by a northwest passage. From the time of Frobisher on, for centuries, there was continuous discussion and planning in England and elsewhere in Europe as to the methods of reaching the Orient by way of a northwest passage. From this time also there were frequent attempts by many exploring expeditions to discover the passage.

It was only ten years after Frobisher's efforts that John Davis commenced his voyaging. In 1585 he was on the west coast of Greenland; one of his ships, the *Moonshine,* having as master John Ellis. Together, they made friends with the Indians and Davis left an extensive account of his voyage. The vessels crossed to Baffin Land and then proceeded southward on the Labrador coast. The next year, with an expedition of a somewhat different composition, Davis was back and renewed his acquaintanceship with the natives of Greenland. Davis' account strengthens the general idea that the Norse colonists of Greenland, or at least a considerably large portion of them, adopted the ways of the Eskimo and intermarried with them.

After Davis there was a period of sixteen years before Henry Hudson took up the search. In 1607, sailing on behalf of the Muscovy Company, Hudson determined to reach China by sailing over the North Pole or near it. He found his progress blocked by Greenland and the ice barriers. Instead of turning south with the current as all voyagers had done before this time, Hudson turned north and when compelled to do so by the ice, turned east. He sailed as far as 80° north and in the process of doing so came on Spitsbergen. Hudson, in his report, recommended the development of hunting and fishing in the north and probably encouraged the development of Spitsbergen as a whaling center. A second attempt in 1608 to sail to the northwest brought Hudson no better success.

It was in 1609 that Hudson received his backing from the Dutch East India Company instead of the British, who had heretofore backed his voyages. His vessel, the *Halfmoon*, was extremely small and his crew numbered no more than eighteen or twenty men. In May he attempted a northwest passage. Amid fog and ice the crew grew quarrelsome and resistant. Hudson proposed that they try a passage either through Davis Strait or else accept the suggestion of Captain John Smith of Virginia that a passage existed on the American coast in about 40° north latitude.

They decided on the latter alternative. They stopped at the Faeroe Islands in May and were off Newfoundland in June. Here, in a gale, one of the *Halfmoon*'s masts snapped off and went overboard. A new mast was fitted on the coast of Maine—probably in the Kennebec River. The record noted good fishing for cod and a possible trade in furs. He continued along the coast of Maine around Cape Cod and by August was in Delaware Bay. When this proved disappointing he turned northward and so came to New York harbor in September. Verrazano had already been here but Hudson improved on the former voyager's performance by sailing up the river as far as Troy and Albany where he found his way blocked. In this year 1609 Champlain, sailing for the French, had explored another American river—the St. Lawrence. He had turned up the Richelieu River and entered Lake

Champlain. This year the routes of Hudson and of Champlain thus came within less than 100 miles of each other.

On his way home, stopping at Dartmouth in England, the *Half-moon* was seized by the British and Hudson and any English followers he had were commanded to sail in the interests of England—not of Holland.

Hudson had not found the way to China though he had discovered the river which bears his name. His chief contribution, indeed, was that he had fully disclosed that there was no passage anywhere in the latitudes along which he had sailed and thus he confirmed the character of a large portion of the American continent.

In April, 1610, Hudson started his fatal voyage in the *Discovery*. This time he was determined to explore the passage west of Greenland that Davis already had reported. He forced a dangerous and difficult passage into the straits that bore his name. Surmounting the difficulties such as fog and ice that blocked their progress seemed to have resulted in a sense of doom rather than a feeling of triumph. He was again faced with resistance, if not mutiny. By August 3, however, he was able to report that a great sea extended to the westward. This was Hudson Bay. He explored the eastern side of the bay and carried the ship through the winter but in the spring, under the leadership of Henry Greene, mutiny blossomed. On June 22, 1611, Hudson and eight members of the crew were set adrift in an open boat. This was the last heard of Henry Hudson. Greene, the mutineer, was killed in a fight with Eskimos before the ship left the American coast. A handful of survivors reached England and were imprisoned.

Before commencing his ascent of the St. Lawrence River and his discovery of the lake that bears his name, Champlain, in 1604, and in the succeeding season, conducted an extensive survey of the Atlantic coast. He began at Cape Breton, worked around the southern coast of Nova Scotia and explored the Bay of Fundy and Passamaquoddy Bay. He explored the St. Croix River. In successive seasons he carried his surveys and his maps as far as Cape Cod and later as far as Vineyard Sound. The rest of Champlain's work was continental exploration and colonization.

In 1611, two British ships of exploration, both seeking a northwest passage, met in the center of Hudson Bay. By agreement, Foxe explored the western side and James the eastern, wintering in the extension of Hudson Bay that bears his name.

Thus, these not very well-known voyagers, meeting in Hudson Bay, bring to a close a cycle of history that began with the Viking voyages. They added a last little touch to the greater work that Champlain and Hudson and Verrazano and other early voyagers, including the Norse, had undertaken, completing such survey of the north and east coast of America as could be made by ships at sea. The Norse discovered the New World that they called Vineland and that we call North America; the other voyagers mentioned in this chapter in one way or another helped to give it form. In defining the land they also defined vast tracts of our Atlantic Ocean. They discovered the northern islands and also the sweep of the ocean where there were no islands. Over hundreds of years and by many voyages they proved the northern sea routes navigable and useful. By discovering the whaling grounds and the fisheries of the North Atlantic they added incalculably to the wealth and welfare of the world. There has been much talk of the wealth and treasure of the Indies, of Mexico and of Peru. It was great but it was soon exhausted. The value of the *annual* catch sent from the banks to England greatly exceeded the value of all the Indian gold ever shipped in galleons to Spain.* The gold has disappeared but the fishing banks are still helping to feed a hungry world.

Our voyagers too laid the foundations for a great nation; even this brief record shows the background that made it natural for the French and English to meet in Canada for the exploration and development of that country.

* * * *

In order to secure a sense of connection and chronology, comments on the characteristics of particular ships have been omitted in the foregoing portion. Yet a knowledge of the ships the men sailed in adds interest to their story.

Many centuries intervened between the time when the Vikings started westward across the Atlantic until the English sailors were cruising in Hudson Bay. Naturally, over so long a period there were a number of changes in the design and construction of ships. The ships in which the English, French and Dutch sailors explored the American coast were quite different in character from the Viking type of ship in which Eric and Lief had sailed. In the years between 1000 and 1500 A.D. there had been a considerable development of ship design in all the ports of Europe. The Norse vessel, though it reached a considerable size and was capable of carrying horses and other animals as well as men and their goods, was essentially an open type ves-

* See page 122, *Unrolling the Map.*

sel with a very small amount of decked-in space. Originally it was a ship to be rowed but it became also a sailing vessel. It was a double-ender, having relatively sharp lines both at the bow and the stern and with both the stem and stern prolonged upward. Amidships, the vessel was broad with relatively flat floors. The lines of the Viking ship were sweeping and graceful, producing a vessel that could be easily driven—that could carry a considerable burden and still remain buoyant and seaworthy. The "clinker" or "clincher" type of construction added considerably to the strength of this vessel.

The medieval ship that was very extensively used farther south in Europe had a quite different form. Whereas the Norse vessel was relatively long and narrow, the medieval vessel of the French, English, Dutch and German coasts was relatively round and bowl-shaped with a blunt bluff bow and stern. These ships depended largely on the use of sail and soon were using several masts whereas the Norse vessels held to the single mast, set amidships, carrying one large sail hung from an elevated yard. The medieval ship was largely a cargo carrier and a general utility boat. On the occasions when it was used as a war vessel, special structures were erected at the bow and stern that could carry fighting men on platforms raised above the general deck. These structures had walls like an old-fashioned fort and were known as the "forecastle" and the "aftercastle." In time they became permanent structures so that there were additional decks fore and aft and this, in turn, set the pattern for the later vessels with many decks such as we see in the Spanish galleons and the English war vessels of the eighteenth century. The term "aftercastle" has disappeared but the forecastle survives as the contraction "fo'c's'le" which is the name for that portion of the ship used by the crew as living quarters. It was formerly the forward section of the upper deck but now may be located anywhere.

The medieval type of sailing ship from the French seaports and the Channel ports of England was extensively used during the period of the crusades to carry pilgrims to Malta and other ports in the Mediterranean on their way to the Holy Land.

Beginning with the ship of a very generalized pattern, local differences began to develop in the different countries. The Hanseatic League grew up in northern Germany. An increasing volume of trade between the Hanseatic ports called for larger and heavier vessels and this, in turn, demanded an increase in sail area. Holland and the Low Countries generally specialized in ships adapted to shallow waters as well as ships that could sail the open sea, and they experimented also with ships that could be maneuvered in canals and inland waterways. The Dutch, therefore, developed many different types of hulls and also of sail plans, including the extensive use of fore-and-aft sails.

The ports of England began to develop trade with the continent including not only the French ports that lay across the Channel on the peninsulas of Normandy and Brittany, but also Bordeaux and the other Biscay ports. In times of peace, English vessels also went to Spain and Portugal. England has never been a wine-producing country and so an important part of the trade with the continent was the carrying of wines to the English ports. In fact, this trade accounted for the first practical measurement of the capacity of a ship. The large barrels in which wine was stored and shipped were called tuns. The vessels were rated according to the number of "tuns" they could carry. At first this was just the number of casks that could be stowed away in the hull of the vessel. Later, there were both "tuns" and "tunnage"—the latter term being used to describe cargo capacity. After many changes in the use of terms, the word "ton" emerged as a measure of the amount of enclosed space in a vessel that could be used for stowage and a ton was described as sixty cubic feet of space.

Wooden vessels have a short life and encounter many griefs and accidents. Even in the nineteenth century a vessel that was in operation twenty years after it was built could be regarded as having reached a ripe old age and the life of medieval and Renaissance vessels was shorter still. Occasionally an old ship has been found embedded in the mud of some harbor and thus preserved, but we should know very little about the history of these ships were it not for the fact that drawings of ships have appeared in the old illuminated manuscripts, in tapestries, paintings, coins and the seals of governments.

The local government of a port city was strong and important in the days when national governments were relatively weak and changeable. Each city had its own seal and these seals usually consisted of a picture of the ship that was characteristic of that harbor. Thus a twelfth-century seal of the port of La Rochelle on the French coast illustrates the first use of permanent reef points for shortening the area of a sail. There is a seal of 1244 of the city of Elbing in northern Germany which shows an early—possibly the first—use of a permanent rudder hung from the stern of the vessel. The early trading vessels had two masts but in the year 1400 a vessel of the Hanseatic League named the *Brindle Cow* was built with three masts.

At all periods of history exploration and colonization have been regarded as marginal and risky enterprises. There have been a few exceptions, but for the most part explorers have not been very wealthy or powerful people. The companies they have been able to organize have not as a rule been financially strong and the support that they have received from kings, princes and governments has been grudgingly given. The ships in which the early explorers reached the American coast were not especially built for transatlantic crossings. They were ordinary cargo vessels of their time—often not even the best examples of such vessels. This accounts for the small numbers of the crews and the small size of the ships in which Verrazano, Cartier and Hudson carried out their long voyages.

Chapter 9

IBERIAN CONQUEST

FIVE hundred years elapsed between the time the Norse first completed the crossing of the Atlantic by the northern routes and the first crossing of the Middle Atlantic by Columbus. In the fourteenth and fifteenth centuries first the Portuguese and then the Spaniards began to do for the Middle and South Atlantic what northern nations did for the North and Arctic Atlantic. They may have been late in starting, but once under way their ships traveled with all sail set and a "bone in their teeth."

Sometimes a man will drift through life leading a worthy but unregarded existence until one day he finds himself or an idea takes possession of him; then he begins to live with all his powers and to flourish. This is exciting and heartening when it happens to a man; when it happens to nations, the whole world watches and waits.

In the fifteenth and sixteenth centuries two small nations of Europe came alive, strode forth to establish worldwide empires and gave rise to independent states. In the beginning the small kingdoms of Portugal and Spain shared the Iberian Peninsula. They also shared the Atlantic seaboard. It was from the ocean that they drew their strength and the Atlantic was their highway to adventure and conquest.

In the early years of the fifteenth century neither Portugal nor the several states that were later united under Spanish rule were of great importance in European politics or European trade. Since the time of the Crusades, Europe had been extending its geographic knowledge. Part of this knowledge was due to the Crusades themselves that had brought both the royal leaders of the Crusades and many common people in touch with powerful and far-reaching organizations of Islam.

Part of the knowledge had come because Europe had for centuries been surrounded by powerful Asiatic empires. The great growth of the Mongol Empire had brought to northern and eastern Europe a terrifying realization of the strength and danger that lay in the Orient. Travelers like Carpini, Rubruck and Marco Polo, as well as other priests, missionaries and traders had from time to time lifted the curtain on the vast drama of Far Eastern civilization. Despite the wars and the conquests and the difference of philosophies and ethnic hostilities, articles of trade such as spices, drugs, silks and other textiles continued to flow into Europe from the Orient. The channels by which they flowed were both northern and southern land routes across Asia and also by sea through the Near East and into the Mediterranean. When the Mongol Empire broke up into a number of independent states, the Ottoman Empire arose as another hostile threat to Europe. Trade was interrupted but it did not cease. The trouble was that it was carried out with irregularity, with great risk and with interposition of countless intermediary agencies, all of which resulted in multiple charges and high cost. The parts of Europe that chiefly received and benefited by this trade were the eastern European countries nearest to the trade routes and city-states in the Mediterranean, such as Venice and Genoa. The last European nations to be reached by such a flow of trade were Spain and Portugal and Spain was relatively cut off from the rest of Europe and Portugal was cut off from Spain. In addition both countries, while they may have gained in knowledge, had suffered in national pride under the Moorish rule from which they had only gradually liberated themselves.

Perhaps in such a position it was natural and inevitable that they should begin to look to the ocean. The trouble was that the knowledge of their time told them that the Atlantic Ocean, which they fronted, was at its best void and profitless and at its worst full of mythical shapes and unknown dangers.

Ignoring for the moment prehistoric travel, for at least 600 years of the historic period the northern sailors had been fearlessly crossing seas and oceans. The Irish monks had sailed to Iceland. The Norse had traveled quite regularly between the Scandinavian countries and the shores of England, Ireland and Scotland. Finally they had made the passage to Iceland, Greenland and the American coast. All this they did in ships that were well designed and sturdily built and seaworthy but that had no comforts or conveniences. They did it by primitive methods of navigation. They did it without benefit of scientific instruments or much help from previously organized knowledge. Their earliest voyages were made in open waters and under the tempering influences of the Gulf Stream, but their remote voyages were made in cold waters, in cold weather and often against adverse winds. Considering all their relative disadvantages it is wonderful evidence of their courage and independence that they traveled so far.

By contrast, the Portuguese and the Spaniards of the early fifteenth century had many advantages. They had ships that ran to as much as 200 tons burden that already were decked over and had permanent protection for the crew against wind and weather, and also protected space for storage. These vessels had three masts carrying lateen sails which were handier going to windward than a square sail hung from an awkward yard.

On the geographic side they had many advantages. They enjoyed relatively mild climate, their ocean and their inland waters as well were free of ice throughout the year. They had many rivers and good harbors. Spain had ports on the Bay of Biscay, like San Sebastian, Bilbao and Gijon. Portugal on the Atlantic itself had harbors from Coruña and Vigo in the north to Lagos and the mouth of the Guadiaña in the south. In between lay Oporto on the Duero River and the Tagus rolled down past Lisbon. Spain again had Huelva, the Guadalquiver which made a seaport even of Seville and the wonderful harbor of Cadiz which had been a shipping center since the days of the Phoenicians. Once at sea, they had the advantage of northeasterly winds, sometimes called the Portuguese trades, and provided they were going south and west, as indeed they did, they had advantage also of an ocean current moving in that direction. A glance at charts showing surface currents and prevailing winds will show how the ocean favored the Iberian navigators on the courses their ships so naturally selected.

They also had the advantage of some early knowledge of the science of navigation, including the use of the compass. The compass seems to have come into use in Europe during the twelfth century. It was found first among the Genoese and Venetian sailors who were trading with the Saracens and other Eastern peoples.

Early European compasses were little more than small magnetized bars placed on corks, floating in a small basin of water. They were often referred to as "Genoese Needles" or "Mariners' Needles." Alexander Necham of St. Albans provides the first description in English of a compass. He lived between 1157 and 1217 and by his time the magnetized bars were embedded in a floating card that carried the design of a directional rose or wind rose. A recognizable form of our modern compass was beginning to take shape and navigation by instrument was being developed. These were very considerable advantages and one might expect that the Iberian sailors would have made a fuller use of them and commenced their ocean voyages at an earlier time. There were, however, a number of factors to account for the delays, such as a lingering fear of the Moors and the Islamic peoples in general. Another factor was that of local political struggles and the time required to achieve a sense of national unity. On top of all was the matter of geographic knowledge and belief. The learned men were still bound by too great a deference to the classical geographers and the common sailors were full of natural superstition and folklore surviving from the Middle Ages.

Despite these common attitudes, some groups of courageous sailors from southern Europe did venture into the Atlantic. As we have already seen in the chapters dealing with north European navigation, the Basque whalers were on the Grand Banks by the end of the fourteenth century and later were in Greenland waters. The Portuguese, in the fifteenth century, were involved in trade with Iceland and also utilized Bristol voyagers and traders as middlemen. This contact of Portugal with the northern fisheries appears to have been old and well-established. While the historians do not comment on the matter, it seems quite possible that such contacts may have exerted a considerable influence on Portuguese navigation and helped to build a tradition of seamanship.

History, however, credits one man with being the principal agent in preparing Portugal for her voyage into greatness. Later he was called Henry the Navigator but in the early years of the fifteenth century he was only the third son of King John. He was not likely to reach the throne and was, in fact, only the unimportant son of an unimportant ruler of a not very important state. As a young man Henry seems to have had one strong emotion—hate; and one strong ambition—to beat the Arabs and the Moors.

There was no chance that Henry could command a national army so he decided to create one. He revived an old crusading order. Under its white cross banner he assembled an army. In 1514 he took his followers to Africa and captured the city of Ceuta in Algiers. This was a modest victory but in those days it was, after all, something to have a victory and not a defeat.

When Henry returned to Europe he found that he had become a popular figure on an international scale. Kings were seeking his advice and he could have had the command of an army in England or in Germany.

Henry surprised everybody by rejecting these offers. He had come back from Africa with something more than victory or popularity. He had come back with a great amount of information respecting the Islamic peoples of Africa and also with information about Africa itself. He had learned of their vast political and religious organization, their considerable command of science, their ships and their trade routes. Henry came back with a plan for the development of Portugal. He was certain that prosperity and power for Portugal lay in developing its ships and in a program of trading and conquest.

Henry began developing a systematic study of navigation in the broadest sense; he collected information on ship construction and ship management; on geography; on navigation in the narrower sense. He was always ready to collect new information and he talked with everyone who came into the harbors—even the Moors. He not only collected information—he also collected men. Every time he found a good man, he hired him. After a time, that is, in 1420, he built an observatory, workshop and school for navigators at Sagres near Cape St. Vincent.

In the port of Palos, nearby, he began building ships and sending them on voyages. In 1418 one of his ships discovered the island of Madeira and soon after it was colonized. This was a great satisfaction to Henry and it looked like a proof of his policies. In this single stroke he accomplished at least two things. He showed that there was justification and reward for vessels that would proceed boldly to sea. The other peak of his triumph was that it served to offset what, from the Portuguese point of view, had been a rebuff or an injustice. As early as 1340 Portuguese vessels had rediscovered the Canary Islands, but subsequently (1344) the Pope had awarded the islands to the crown of Castile. So that at the very dawn of the age of Iberian navigation and discovery there had been a basis of competition between the Spanish and the Portuguese and the pattern was set for a long series of rivalries and recriminations.

Then, with Madeira behind him as an indication of accomplishment, Henry began sending his vessels creeping down the coast of

Africa. Here, over the years, his navigators were destined to learn something about the character of the ocean. As far as the Canaries, and even as far as Cape Verde, in most seasons of the year both the tide and the currents would be favorable to his vessels on the out-ward passage. The difficulty would be encountered on their return. Between the Canaries and Cape Verde there would be the handicap and the hazard of the "harmattan." This whole strip of coast forms the western boundary of the Sahara desert and is one long succession of sand banks interrupted only where the Senegal River enters the sea and where the present French port of St. Louis is located. The har-mattan is a wind that blows to sea having crossed the Sahara from the northeast or east. When it is well established it carries with it the dust and the sand of the Sahara. In its extreme form it is a seagoing sandstorm.

There are excellent technical descriptions of the harmattan but they sound overdrawn until one has had the actual experience of taking a sailing vessel through such a wind as I did when I took *Kinkajou* from the Canaries to Dakar in 1929. This coast is notoriously difficult at any time. There are no satisfactory harbors, even for a small ves-sel. There are occasionally periods when enormous swells, technically known as "breakers," sweep in from the ocean upon the coast. Should a vessel happen to come to grief along the coast, there are no facilities and not even water. The coast is largely deserted and the tribesmen, even in our day, have proved inordinately hostile. We were told at Dakar of a number of cases of European travelers—both by sea and by air—having been killed or tortured. When the harmattan is blow-ing operating a vessel along the coast is something like being caught in an English Channel fog except that, in this case, the wind is dry and not wet and the obscuring particles are dust and not vapor. Natu-rally, we kept far offshore to give ourselves as much sea room as possible but even there the harmattan pursued us. There was a murky half-light and even at high noon the sun was nothing but a blurred redness in the sky and it was impossible to take an accurate observa-tion. Everything dried out and filled with grit and sand. Even though the sand was of a very fine texture, it kept accumulating on deck and every few hours we would have to sweep it up and shovel it overboard.

Charles Darwin when he was sailing in the *Beagle* encountered one form of harmattan. He found in it material for scientific observa-tion and left in his journal an interesting account of this strange phenomenon.

In 1427 Diogo de Seville, in command of Henry's vessels, began the discovery and exploration of the Azores, which continued until 1431. An Italian chart of 1351, the Medici Portolano, showed some islands in the ocean that might have been intended as a representation of the Azores, but it is even more probable that they were simply imaginary islands since, as we have seen, classical geographers often referred to such mythical islands as Atlantis and the Hesperides. The islands may have been discovered on the first extended cruise of the Portuguese ships in the Atlantic beyond the longitude of Madeira, but it seems more likely that their discovery was due to the fact that Henry's vessels had for some time been adventuring into the Atlantic.

In 1425 Henry sent out an expedition that was bent on conquest rather than mere discovery. It was the intention of the expedition to take the Canary Islands away from Castile. He also tried to secure the islands by negotiation so that he could have a base for further expeditions in Africa and be free of rivalry in the development of African trade.

Another attempt at conquest was made in 1450 to 1453 but when a treaty was finally drawn, after Henry's death, it provided that Castile (Spain) retain the Canaries while Portugal was assigned the West African coast, Guinea, Madeira and the Azores.

That, however, is getting ahead of the story. In the meantime, Henry's progress down the African coast was slow. It took a decade of effort before one of Henry's vessels passed Cape Bojador in 1433, but a year later they had gone as far as the Senegal and in 1445 Diniz Diaz discovered and rounded Cape Verde. Relative to the desert coasts that lie north of it the name is well chosen for on the cape and about the shores of Dakar harbor there are some palm trees and other signs of vegetation that look bright to eyes that have been gazing only on water and sand, though no one could say that the vegetation of the cape was luxuriant. From this point on, Henry's captains were rewarded in their long search of the African coast. They came into a strip of coast where the African natives were eager for trade. Soon as many as twenty-five ships a year were making the passage between Portugal and the African coast.

Henry's work was now in full stride and in 1455 an Italian captain in his employ, named Cadamosto, explored Africa extensively by sailing up both the Senegal and the Gambia Rivers. He was also responsible for the discovery of the Cape Verde Islands. The busy trade with the African coast continued until Henry's death in 1469. By this time the African movement that Henry had sponsored had produced at least three results of historical importance. It had been demonstrated that man could sail in tropic waters and visit tropic shores without falling ill or being burned to death. Up to this time many European scholars, following the classic geographies, had actually believed both that the tropics were uninhabitable and also that they could not even be crossed by any living person.

The second result was that the Portuguese had begun the development of African slavery. Slavery, of course, was not unknown before this time and in many countries of Europe serfs and certain classes of servants and prisoners of war lived in a virtual state of slavery. The beginning may have been relatively innocent. Portuguese captains returning home with their ships loaded with gold and ivory and other exotic goods of the West African country probably desired simply to include with their cargoes some Negroes to satisfy curiosity and to serve as examples of the inhabitants of this part of the world that was then new to Europe. After they had served their initial purpose the Negroes were no doubt put to work on Portuguese soil and gradually the idea of a prosperous trade in Negro slaves took shape. Henry the Navigator tried to forbid the slave traffic but it seems to have grown despite his efforts and to have developed into a set pattern after his death.

The third outcome was that, even leaving slavery out of account, Portugal found the development of West African trade and the establishment of trading posts profitable. Portugal began to be a thriving maritime country. We have seen already that she was establishing contact with England and with Iceland and simultaneously was sending her ships to the Atlantic islands and to West Africa. Year by year she was building larger and stronger vessels and sending them on very extensive voyages. It was a matter of policy that so far as Africa was concerned some voyage each year should advance into new territory. Henry had seen a part of his dream come true and had established policies that were for a time to convert little Portugal into the position of a world-wide empire.

Alfonso V, on Henry's death, made a contract with a trader named Gomez under which the latter was permitted exclusive development of the Guinea trade for a five-year period. Gomez undertook to carry forward the work of exploration for at least 100 leagues each year. Under this arrangement in 1470-71 a Portuguese station was put down on the Gold Coast. In 1472 Fernando Po discovered the island named for him and other ships crossed the equator and even reached two degrees south. In 1481, João II came to the throne and resumed the exploration as a royal enterprise. In the eighties his ships reached the Congo River and pushed southward along the coast. Whatever may have been Prince Henry's intentions it was clear now to João that Portugal was to develop a route to India. With this in mind, Pedro de Covilhã was sent to India by way of Cairo and Aden. Returning from India, he explored the east coast of Africa as far as the Zambezi River.

Progress down the West African coast had been steady rather than rapid. Below Cape Verde and the bulge of Africa many navigational difficulties were encountered. In the Gulf of Guinea and the Bight of Benin there was always the possibility of encountering the doldrums and the calms extending over a wide area and with the tropic sun adding its weight to the burden already borne by a becalmed vessel. Below the Gulf all up and down the West African coast a vessel attempting to benefit by land and sea breezes would be encountering the continual adverse set of the current. To the princes and the masters of trade in Portugal the progress of the ships against these adverse conditions no doubt seemed slow. To the captains and crews of the vessels time would not seem so important. The discomfort and irksomeness of the voyage would be continuously offset by the novelty of discovery along the shore. The men that made these voyages would be seeing for the first time the strange products of the West African coast which in those days were so unfailing and abundant—the gold so plentiful, the great ivory tusks of the elephants that then were ranging near the west coast, the exotic fruits and vegetables, the oil kernels and other products of the coast, the kola and other strange stimulants of the tropics, the rich diversity in form and color of the many Negro tribes inhabiting the coast and the interior, the strange languages and the barbaric music, the mouths of the great rivers like the Niger and the Congo leading into a continent that was still a vast mystery.

Possibly the traders were so busy with new sights and scenes that they were not unhappily conscious of the inevitable delays, but there were other men who were in a hurry to be finished with Africa and on their way to India. The most important man in a hurry was Bartolomeu Diaz. It was really he that set the crown on the great work that Henry had commenced in the beginning of the century. Diaz was carrying on a great tradition. He was a relative of João Diaz who had rounded Cape Borgedor and Diniz Diaz who had discovered Cape Verde.

Diaz commenced his career trading for ivory on the Guinea coast.

Later he commanded a ship sailing to the Gold Coast and for a while he was superintendent of the royal warehouses at Lisbon. Officially Lisbon is now intent on the passage to India and Diaz leaves the port in command of a fleet of three ships on a mission to carry the exploration of Africa as far as possible. To him the adverse sailing all down the West African coast must have seemed irksome indeed, but he succeeded in pushing his vessels to 26 degrees south where, on Diaz Point, he erected a landmark—a part of which is still standing.

Leaving the point, he decided also to avoid if possible the tedious conditions along the coast so he pushed out into the ocean and headed south and there in the current of the westerlies he encountered a stiff gale and kept his ships driving before it for thirteen days. There were other storms and still he held his course to the east. Then he turned north to re-establish contact with the coast. On February 3, 1488, he came into Mossel Bay. He followed the coast long enough to be certain that it ran eastward and a little north and in following the coast he came to a river to which he gave the name Great Fish River. By this time his men were weary and complaining and his supplies were getting dangerously short so he turned back following the coast line. In this way, sailing to the west and a little to the south, he came to a mountainous shore and a great cape which the king, hearing Diaz's report, christened the Cape of Good Hope.

In this single voyage he had demonstrated the advantage of sailing in the open sea, he had added 1,260 miles to the known coastline and he had solved the riddle of the African route to India. He had done more than that. He had for the first time demonstrated to the Europeans that there was a way out of the Atlantic Ocean. Of course, 2,000 years before this the Phoenician sailors under King Necho had demonstrated that there was a way *into* the Atlantic but the Phoenicians had been forgotten, or where they were not forgotten they were discredited. To all intents and purposes, Diaz defined the eastern and southern limits of the Atlantic Ocean and opened the gateway to Asia.

Diaz had already proved himself a great seaman and a devoted servant of Portuguese interests. When he sailed home with Good Hope in his lockers, he had every reason to expect recognition for his good work and the backing with which to pursue further voyages. Instead of that, he found that he was to suffer from one of the occupational diseases of navigators and explorers—neglect of his interests at home during the time of his service abroad. Despite the fact that it was Diaz's voyage joined with Covilhã's travels that demonstrated the route to India he was not given command of this voyage. This was assigned to Vasco da Gama, a man of wealth and position, who had assiduously sought the favor of the king.

While Diaz was not powerful enough to claim his just reward, he was still so important and so well informed that he would not be neglected. He was assigned to assist in preparing the ships and expedition and da Gama had the full benefit of his advice and his knowledge of navigation. Diaz made the voyage as far as the Canary Islands but there he was ignominiously left behind while da Gama made the broad sweep through the Atlantic and around the Cape to East Africa and India.

Later it was Diaz's fate to assist another voyager to fame. In 1500 he helped Cabral organize his expedition to India and was in command of one of the vessels. They touched at the Cape Verde Islands and then, in keeping with the ideas of navigation that Diaz seems to have developed, they swung boldly out into the Atlantic before heading south. It was on this trip that Cabral and Diaz made an important and independent discovery of the eastern projection of South America. The record says that they were carried to this point by a succession of storms which would be augmented also by the prevailing westerly set of the surface currents. As we have already noted, this explanation is in keeping with the character and structure of the Atlantic Ocean.

Attempts have been made to demonstrate that the Portuguese at this time already knew of the existence of the South American coast and that they shrouded their knowledge in secrecy, but there is no conclusive evidence on this point. In any event, Diaz was the first man to have touched both the shores of the South Atlantic and it was upon this discovery of the South American coast that the Portuguese later successfully based their claim to the occupation and colonization of Brazil. Leaving the Brazilian coast the Cabral fleet crossed the ocean to the Cape of Good Hope where Diaz and his ship were lost in storms while rounding this great landmark of the world which he had discovered.

The fate of the Portuguese Empire in the east is not an inherent part of this story. It is pertinent, however, to point out that the Portuguese ships were the first vessels built on Atlantic shores to circulate freely in the world's other oceans. In 1501 da Gama took a fleet to the mouth of the Red Sea and to India with the intention of blocking the Red Sea route and after that, for a period, the Portuguese had the Indian water and the Indian trade for themselves. Four years later,

Francisco de Almeida went out as the first governor and established Portuguese forts at Calicut, Cananor, and Cochin. In 1509 he won a victory over the Moslem fleet and destroyed it. A year later Alfonso de Albuquerque made Goa the capital of the Portuguese Empire in India and within a year he had taken Malacca and thus opened up communication with Siam, the East Indies and China.

In 1542 two Portuguese vessels reached Japan and before 1560 the Portuguese had established a permanent settlement at Macao near Canton. At the same time they were, of course, holding and developing their African interests. They had been inland in Africa as far as Timbuktu. They had been 200 miles up the Congo River and had entrenched themselves there. On the east coast they had established Mozambique and sent missionaries far up the Zambezi River and had other stations on the East African coast.

With such a start and such a momentum of accomplishment, the Portuguese naturally attracted to themselves additional proposals for voyages and the services of men with new ideas. Just here, while the Portuguese Empire was still in its early growth, some defect in the system began to reveal itself—possibly it was complacency or preoccupation, possibly it was lack of imagination. Certainly it was an inability to judge the talents of men and to deal with them justly.

In those days nationalism was less marked and rigid than it is today. Along with this, although the patriotism or loyalty of individuals was probably as frequent as it is today, it had more channels for expression. It was quite common for military leaders as well as common soldiers to become mercenaries and offer their services to some king or country of which they were not a subject. The same thing was true of navigators and explorers. We have seen already how Verrazano, an Italian, sailed for the French and how John Cabot, another Italian, found his opportunity in England and particularly with the merchants of Bristol.

In at least two cases these changes of allegiance were startling and far-reaching. Columbus in 1483 or 1484 laid his plans for a westward voyage to India before João II of Portugal. Fernão de Magalhães, whom we call Magellan, who was a native of Portugal likewise made his original proposal for his great voyage to the Portuguese court. Both these great adventurers, that later revealed to Europe the true character of the world, were rejected by Portugal and both later found support in Spain. Naturally after this there was hostility between the countries that cast a long historic shadow and naturally also the initiative in new ventures passed to Spain.

So much has been written about the life of Columbus and about his four voyages that it is all but impossible to deal adequately with these subjects in a book of the present scope. Despite all the writing and the research, Columbus was and remains today a figure of mystery and this is part of the strong hold he exercises both over the technical historians and the popular imagination.

One of our sources of information about Columbus' early activities was the life of him written by his son, Fernando, yet the historians believe that this record is full of inaccuracies. We do know that he had traveled widely and that he had access to many sources of information including the information that Portuguese navigators and travelers had amassed. We believe he was in England in 1477. In 1478 he was in the Madeiras and in 1480 he married the daughter of the hereditary captain of Porto Santo of those islands. We know that he had read Marco Polo and that he had marked a copy that was in his possession with many notes. We know that he believed in a globular world and that he announced his intention of reaching China and the Orient by sailing to the westward.

His son has asserted that he had visited Iceland and sailed in the sea beyond that point. What motive his son would have for falsely asserting that Columbus had made a voyage to Iceland is not clear but if he made the voyage to Iceland, it seems more than likely that he would have heard of the Norse voyages to Greenland, Markland and Vineland. Whether he expected to find lands to the westward before reaching Asia in the latitudes in which he sailed is open to doubt and conjecture.

On his first voyage, Columbus, leaving the Portuguese coast, sailed southwest to the Canary Islands. Leaving the Canaries, he sailed west on the 30th parallel and then dropped south again until he encountered the Bahama Islands. All of his other voyages proceeded in a southwesterly direction. If we accept the statement of his son that Columbus had been in Iceland and if we assume, as seems most likely then, that he would have heard of the Norse voyages to Greenland, Labrador and other parts of the American coast, we are furnished with a reasonable explanation of the courses that Columbus selected. That is, if Columbus knew even a small part of what was common knowledge in Iceland and Denmark, and what was possibly known to many people in Portugal, then he was following a logical course in sailing well to the southwest from Spain.

His purpose was not to discover land in the west but to avoid land. The shores that the Norsemen describe in their accounts of Greenland,

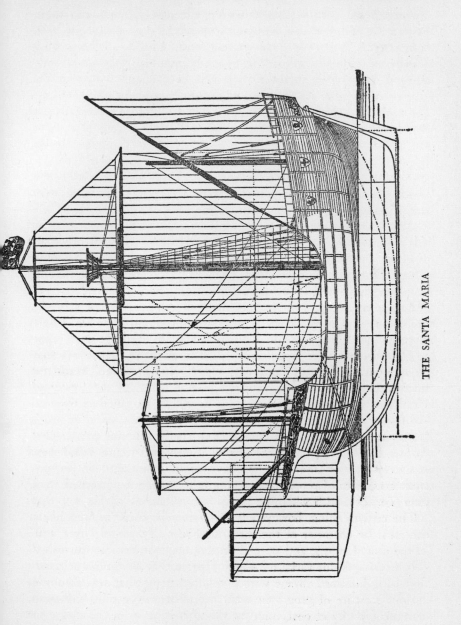

THE SANTA MARIA

Markland, and Vineland did not correspond with the description of the east that Columbus had become familiar with from the pages of Marco Polo. With this interpretation, Columbus' purpose was not to discover lands in the west but to avoid lands until he should arrive at the Chinese or Indian coast.

If we turn to the commission and the contract under which Columbus undertook the voyage, it appears that Columbus probably had a double purpose for two different conditions are provided for. Columbus stated that his purpose was to open up a way to India and he carried letters to the Great Khan, but at the same time he took the precaution of having it firmly stated that he was to be admiral of the ocean sea, whatever that might be intended to mean, and also governor of any new lands he might discover.

Of this we may say either that Columbus had a double purpose or that he was taking no chances. His principal bet was that he would establish a contact with India or China that would rival the route Portugal was already developing, but he was hedging this bet by also protecting himself if he should discover any new lands.

At the very least, there is here revealed some confusion of thinking about the geography of the world and about his purposes. This is not a unique example of double talk or double thinking on the part of Columbus; in fact, some confusion of thought is quite characteristic of most things that Columbus wrote and also most things that have been written about him.

It seems to be now pretty generally agreed that Columbus was very far from being a precise geographer. He did believe that the world was round and that China might be reached by sailing to the west. In fact, he made a great show of this argument, but this was not his discovery and he knew that he could count for support in this view from a number of people from his time including the Italian geographer Torricelli with whom he had communicated.

The curious thing, however, is that while he could be clear about the globular character of the earth, he could at the same time write in the most fantastic and unrealistic way about the lands that he was encountering in his various voyages. His letter to the king and queen respecting his third voyage will serve to anybody interested as a most curious mixture of geography and metaphysics. We must not think that this capacity of developing two conflicting ideas at the same time was necessarily a handicap to Columbus. On the contrary, it was probably by a considerable advantage. It probably made his writings seem quite familiar to the people with whom he had to deal. It permitted him to bridge a gap between scientific teaching and religious teaching and the practical desire for money and rewards which he sought both for himself and for the crown of Spain. Thus, on his first voyage he apparently felt no strain at all in keeping a fictitious log which he showed to his crews and a correct log which he kept to himself, and again he was able to accept from the government an order to treat the natives, whom he called Indians, well and lovingly and at the same time to reconcile this with enslaving them in the islands and also with sending shiploads of Indians back to Seville to be sold as slaves in the European market.

Whatever we may conclude about the mentality and character of Columbus, we must credit him with two important contributions to the definition and history of the Atlantic. Ironically enough, Columbus is usually credited with having discovered the western continents whereas this is exactly the thing that he disclaimed. Throughout his voyages and his writings about them, he held to the belief that whereas he had discovered some islands and a considerable coastline he kept advancing the contention that he would presently sail past these and arrive in Asia proper. Apparently he wanted to sustain this belief even though before Columbus died it was clear to others that large new lands lay in the western ocean.

As we have seen, the Norsemen sailed for hundreds of miles along the North American mainland centuries before Columbus set out and had even attempted colonization there. In any event, Columbus did not sail along the mainland of South America until his third voyage and this almost exactly corresponded with the time when the voyages of Corte-Real and Cabot rediscovered the North American mainland.

Columbus' solid contributions to American history are these: He discovered and colonized the Bahamas and the West Indies. On his third voyage he sailed along hundreds of miles of the north coast of South America and included in this voyage the Central American coast at Panama. Thus, he helped to define a large and important sector of the western boundaries of the Atlantic. Another equally important contribution is not often commented upon. Columbus should also be credited with a scientific and thoroughgoing attempt to explore the ocean itself.

Columbus, during his lifetime, made eight crossings of the Atlantic Ocean. Each one of these going and returning followed a different band of latitude. He never sailed home along the same course that he had employed in the outward voyage and he never repeated a course. Such a diversity of passages can hardly have been achieved by mere accident. It seems natural to infer that this pattern represents a realistic and scientific attempt to investigate the Atlantic Ocean itself.

His most northerly route was the returning voyage in 1493 when he left the north coast of Santo Domingo–Haiti, which he called Hispaniola—and sailed in a northeasterly direction, skirted the Azores, and came to the port of Lisbon. His most southerly route was the outgoing passage in 1498 when he went south past the Cape Verde Islands and closed with the South American coast at Trinidad. Undoubtedly his motive in setting these courses on the way westward was to find a direct passage to India but in each case he could have returned home more directly.

It seems reasonable, therefore, to credit him also with a desire to find the best conditions of wind and weather and current for ocean passages and also with the intention of discovering any intervening islands in the Atlantic that had not been previously reported. Of course, from a scientific point of view, the fact that he did not find intervening islands is almost as important as if he had. His combined voyages served to reveal and define the characteristics of the Atlantic Ocean in its broadest middle section from approximately 10 degrees north to 40 degrees north. His most southerly point would touch the line Caracas-Freetown, and the most northerly the line New York-Lisbon.

The voyages of Columbus were immediately followed up by scores of transatlantic crossings. Despite the fact that Columbus tried to continue in his faith that he had gone near to Asia, the extent and character of the other voyages soon made it clear that new lands of great extent lay in the western ocean.

1497 was the date of the first voyage of John Cabot, already referred to in a previous chapter, and the succeeding year of 1498 was the voyage in which his vessels coasted along the North American shores and the voyage on which he was apparently lost. This was the year in which the Portuguese sent out Duarte Pacheco Pereira. Pereira appears to have sailed extensively along the South American coast. His account of his voyage, written by the year 1505, speaks of a large continent which he says extends from 70 degrees north latitude to 28 degrees south latitude, or roughly from Davis Strait to a point on the coast below Santos, Brazil.

In 1499 Amerigo Vespucci, an Italian, sailing from Spain, explored the coastline of South America from 5 degrees south to 15 degrees north, or roughly from Natal to Honduras. In 1501, on a voyage from Portugal, he picked up the coast again in 5 degrees south and sailed southward to 25 degrees south, that is, to the Bay of Cananea, Brazil, thence southward. The most reliable account, according to recent studies, says that the voyage covered some 800 leagues of the South American coast and reached latitude 50 degrees south (Straits of Magellan).

In the nineteenth century critics in England and America denounced Vespucci as a liar, a boaster and a mean fellow and broadcast the opinion that it was a disgrace and misfortune that the American continents should have been named after him. The reason for this is that two poor and conflicting documents attributed to Vespucci were apparently forgeries. The true and consistent accounts of his voyages which are accepted by modern scholars were embodied in three letters that he sent to Lorenzo de Medici. These letters were written in 1501, 1502, and 1503.

Vespucci was a son of a wealthy and prominent family who received an excellent technical education. He later became a distinguished astronomer and he also made immediate important contributions to scientific navigation.

The geographer, Martin Waldseemüller, naturally and properly placed confidence in Vespucci's integrity and in 1507 he did well in attaching the name "America" to the new continent since it was Vespucci who first reported the true character of a large part of the New World.

In 1500 other voyages to the Brazilian coast were made by Vicente Pinzon who had sailed with Columbus and also by the Spaniard, Diego de Lepe. As we have seen, this was also the year of Cabral's landing on the Brazilian coast.

In 1501 and 1502 Vespucci completed another voyage which carried him at least as far as 32 degrees south latitude. His account of the voyage made it very clear that a New World of great extent had been discovered.

Juan Ponce de Leon, who was the governor of Puerto Rico, reached the American mainland along the Florida coast in 1512. A year later Balboa crossed the Isthmus of Panama and was the first European to sail on the Pacific Ocean.

By this time, of course, passages across the Atlantic had become fairly common and there were frequent sailings between Hispaniola and the ports of Spain. The area of communication had been increased in 1511 when Diego Velazquez conquered and colonized the island of Cuba. In addition to this central stream of traffic, nearly every year saw some voyage that extended the known area of the New World and that gave a more exact picture of its outline.

In 1515 Juan Diaz de Solis, heading a Spanish expedition, followed the South American coast as far as Rio de la Plata. The next year Francisco Hernández de Córdoba discovered Yucatan and gave the first report of the large and wealthy Mayan cities. In 1518 Grijalva commenced the exploration of the Gulf of Mexico which Alvárez Pineda completed by sailing from Florida to Vera Cruz in Mexico and back again.

Throughout the first quarter of the sixteenth century the motive of most of these voyages was still to find a passage that would lead to the Orient but year by year the search became more difficult and though no one liked to admit it, the feeling was growing that a large, dense and impenetrable continent separated the Atlantic Ocean from Asiatic waters.

At the close of the quarter century, Esteban Gomez confirmed the suspicion by making a voyage for Spain which picked up the American coast at Nova Scotia and followed it closely all the way to Florida. Thus, he definitely connected up the country originally discovered by the Norse sailors with the recent discoveries of the Spaniards and Portuguese in Central and South America. In the meantime, of course, all hope of an easy and short western passage to India and China had disappeared.

Magellan originally presented to his own Portuguese rulers his proposal to reach the East Indies by sailing westward. As a youth, Magellan had served for a number of years in the Portuguese fleet in the East Indies. When he was rejected in his own country, he fled to Spain and hastily organized an expedition of which he was the general leader but which employed chiefly Spanish commanders and a fleet of Spanish ships. Hardly had he set out before jealousy and insubordination began to develop which culminated in treachery and warfare during his first winter on the South American coast.

While he was exploring the straits that bear his name, one of his vessels deserted him and returned to Spain. After many difficulties, Magellan emerged from the straits into the Pacific and sailed his vessels across the Pacific to the Philippines. There he met his death in the futile battle between local princes. One of his ships under Sebastian del Cano succeeded in sailing around the Cape of Good Hope and completed the first voyage around the world in 1522.

From the point of view of our Atlantic story, the importance of

Magellan's work was that he defined the limits of the mainland of South America and thus of the southwest boundary of the Atlantic Ocean and he also, of course, for the first time revealed the relationship between the Atlantic and the other oceans of the world.

These years were important not only from the point of view of exploration but also for their development of colonization and of ocean traffic. The discovery of the Grand Banks fisheries and of the whaling and sealing waters between Greenland and America was followed up by annual passages of large numbers of whaling, sealing and fishing vessels coming from Denmark, England, France and Portugal. By 1550, for example, a fleet of 400 vessels was sailing each year from Portugal to the Grand Banks.

On his first voyage, Columbus left some of his companions behind on Hispaniola to hold his claim to the land and this was the first and unsuccessful attempt to found a Spanish settlement in the New World. It was evident at once that the West Indies were a rich find from an agricultural point of view and that they could be quickly exploited by employing the Indians as servants and slaves. Colonization therefore was rapid and this in turn stimulated the shipbuilding industry of Spain and set up commerce between Spain and the West Indies that was to endure for centuries. As rapidly as discoveries and colonization took place, the course of commerce was also expanding to include Florida in the north and the coasts of Panama and South America as well.

Chapter 10

GUNS AND GOLD; FAITH AND FOOD

THE small world that Europe was familiar with in the fifteenth century suddenly expanded to almost double its original size in a brief period of thirty-five years. Between 1492 and 1525 the middle and southern part of the Atlantic Ocean were discovered and took shape; Africa was circumnavigated from west to east; the shores of North and South America were followed from Davis Strait to the Straits of Magellan; the Pacific was discovered and crossed.

In this time too the peoples of Europe began sailing out to occupy all shores of their own ocean—the Atlantic. They did more; they overflowed it and spread abroad over the other seas of the world.

Why did this happen so suddenly? Why did it happen at all? What were the motives and methods? What the results?

To begin with, this was a period not only of action but of high emotion also—hopes of success and fortune, pride of accomplishment but also weariness of effort and fear of defeat. Europe knew for the first time the shape and size of the world. She knew it not only as a matter of thought but also as a matter of feeling. The round world was no longer a vague and inaccurate intellectual idea; it had become quite suddenly a matter of living experience—the routes from north to south, from east to west and back again had been sweated out by weary mariners—they had been won by many futile and a few successful voyages—they had been paid for by hardship, scurvy and other sickness, starvation, torture, death of men and destruction of vessels.

Europe felt she had paid a great and bitter price and demanded a great and bitter reward. Europe began to go everywhere in the world and everywhere she went she took possession of lands and people. Again why?

For centuries Europe had remained static, self-contained, hedged in by powerful enemies. Portions of Europe had even been conquered by non-European invaders as when the Moors held large sections of Spain and Portugal, the Tatars crowded Russia and eastern Europe, or the Ottoman Turks moved into the Danube basin. Then she aroused as though from slumber, her nations seemed to gather strength, they looked out from their shores to new lands, their ships began moving on all the seas of the known world and the known world in the century from 1450 to 1550 more than doubled its area.

The chief reason assigned for the making of far voyages of discovery and conquest was to convert the heathens and barbarians to Catholic Christianity. This was the reason set forth in the proclamations and orders of the sovereigns and it was accepted and repeated by the admirals, the captains, and the general companies of exploration and colonization. It was a genuine, real and vital enthusiasm; however, it was not the only announced reason for such undertakings. In most orders, letters and accounts of the explorers themselves, other purposes appear. Chief among the purposes named are these: to develop trade routes to India or elsewhere in the Far East; to discover and annex lands for Portugal or Spain and later for other countries; to fight savages and heathens where they cannot be converted; to capture and send home gold, silver and other treasure.

These were all acceptable purposes in the intellectual and moral climate of those days. These could be accepted as desirable or at any rate as necessary ends. The spirit of the age was brave and adventurous—it was also ruthless and cruel. For example, occasionally in the records there are statements about the desirability of sending Negro slaves from Africa to Portugal or Indian slaves from the Caribbean to Spain. In those days there were people who disliked slavery. Father Las Casas was one of them who made it his life work to try to protect the Indians from exploitation, cruelty and slavery. Queen Isabella of Spain was another one. Such people, however, were in the minority and various degrees of slavery and servitude were accepted as an almost inevitable part of the consequences of living.

The trouble was that in the execution of the plans the relative value of the different announced purposes became inverted. The advantages of sending slaves back to Europe outran the desire to educate and convert the Africans and the Indians. Once it was discovered that the Indians in Central and South America possessed great stores of gold and silver without appreciating their economic value, the fever for riches speedily outran the desire to establish normal trade or a healthy and successful agriculture and industry.

In part this was due to the way in which expeditions were made up. The exploring and colonizing voyages were all desperate ventures. They were organized in an atmosphere of competition and of desperate haste. They were the ultimate gamble with life and death, fate and fortune hanging in the balance. They attracted leadership that was determined and desperate and the crews were usually made up of adventurers and vagabonds, men who had not succeeded in regular employment and fugitives from justice. Of course, these were not the only types represented on the expeditions, nearly every one of which included priests and missionaries and sometimes other men of education and learning. It was their responsibility not only to look after the religious life of the expedition but also to educate and baptize the natives and in most cases to furnish written reports of the whole transaction. They represented the Church and sometimes also functions of the government. Not infrequently, they were persons of importance and power at home. The difficulty was that on an expedition they were always remote from their source of authority and subordinate to the admirals, the captains, the pilots. What influence they might have exercised came after the fact.

The fact was that most expeditions in the New World were carried out with incredible barbarity, torture and destruction to native societies. They left burned villages and tortured and broken people. It is one of the ironies of history that people who set out to preach a doctrine of love, redemption and salvation should have rivaled or exceeded the barbarity of the savages themselves.

To trace out the details of the contacts between the Iberian conquerors and the people they encountered in the Far East and the New World would produce a chapter of horrors. There is no profit in and no necessity for such an undertaking. Anyone interested in this matter can easily learn the record for themselves by sampling the accounts of the major expeditions. The whole situation in the west is summarized in Bartolome de Las Casas' *Relation*.

The results, which were bad from a moral point of view, were almost equally bad from an economic point of view. What happened in the era of conquest and cruelty was that the native populations disappeared like a fall of snow under March sunshine. Las Casas says, "Whereas there were more than 3,000,000 souls inborn we saw in Hispaniola, there are to-day (1542), not more than 200 of the native population left." Oviedo says that when Pedrarias Davila arrived in the general region of Panama in 1514 there were approximately 2,000,000 living Indians and in 1519, when he began permanent settlement in Panama, the country was almost depopulated.

These populations under a more humane policy could have survived to provide a healthy labor force to establish firm settlements and permanently productive industries. While the gold and silver lasted the policy of ruthless conquest brought to Spain and Portugal and to Europe generally a sudden prosperity, but the supplies of gold and silver were not inexhaustible and then the dearth of stable settlements and healthy populations made itself felt. Misfortunes have a way of reproducing themselves. In the Caribbean and in Brazil and in other parts of the New World the misfortune of exterminating the native population was succeeded by the misfortune of African slavery.

In time, of course, the Spanish and Portuguese settlements in the New World reached a more stable and healthy state in which the missionaries and teachers had an opportunity to establish churches and missions, schools and other intellectual institutions. In the meantime, incalculable damage had been done to religious, cultural and economic progress which could never be repaired.

Before leaving this matter we must observe that the establishment of reasonable and humane relations between European and native society is always most difficult. The difficulties that existed in the sixteenth century were greater than they would be today in many parts of the world. Then the establishment of friendly and humane relations with the Indians, while not impossible, would have been extremely hard. It is worth observing that Las Casas himself in 1521 attempted the establishment of a colony at Cumana in Venezuela which was to carry out his theories of peaceful and humane treatment of the Indians. Likewise, Luis da Cancer, a Dominican, attempted in Florida to establish a peaceful settlement and rule over the Indian nations. This resulted in 1549 in Cancer's being killed and in the subsequent abandonment of his attempt. These and other trials illustrated the difficulties but they are not conclusive because the events that had preceded these attempts at peaceful penetration undoubtedly influenced the outcome.

To balance the account, two additional observations are in order.

We should remember that the European conquerors were hardly more cruel to the Indians than they were to each other when they fell into disagreements. An example of this would be the treacherous seizure of Balboa, the discoverer of the Pacific, and his execution by Pedrarias Davila. Another instance is the fact that Magellan, who was generally regarded as a temperate and humane leader, on one occasion had an insubordinate officer skinned alive; a second man stabbed to death with knives and two others marooned and abandoned in the wastes of Patagonia.

To balance the account, we should also take note of the fact that the Iberian Peninsula had no monopoly over cruel treatment of native populations. We will see shortly that the English at one time went to extraordinary lengths to maintain and establish a monopoly of the African slave trade, or we might examine the rapid and total destruction of the population of Tasmania or the cruelty of our own wars against the Indians in the United States.

Let us return now to a consideration of the reasons, causes or purposes of the voyages of exploration and discovery. In the paragraphs above we have selected some of the reasons and purposes that the sovereigns, the courts and the explorers themselves seemed to have agreed upon and accepted. We also can accept them as being correct so far as the actors themselves understood the situation. We, having now the advantages of some centuries of record and reflection, can see that they are incomplete explanations and they still leave much to be understood and explained.

Religious belief and missionary zeal have a long history and are in fact in almost continuous operation. They were not a monopoly of the people of the Iberian Peninsula in the fourteenth and fifteenth centuries. Likewise, the greed for gold and the desire for quick and prosperous trade is more or less continually present in all manner of people. The more fundamental questions are: why did these motives emerge at this particular time? Why did they operate effectively then when they had not proved equally effective before? Once they began to operate, what sustained them? In asking these questions we should bear in mind that the Iberian conquests were only the beginning of a vast wave of discovery and colonization that in time spread in all the nations of Europe and that continued its movement for some centuries.

To explain events that are of great importance, that involve great numbers of people and that operate over great distances, we should look for very basic causes operating over a considerable period of time. We should look also for a particular set of circumstances developing at a particular time that would leave these causes free to operate.

Naturally one of the basic ingredients of any historic situation is the matter of population. In Europe, from the fall of the Roman Empire up to the fourteenth century, population had been relatively stabilized. Perhaps this should be more precisely stated by saying that there had been a slow but general population increase in Europe over these centuries. Of course, elements of the European population had shifted from place to place; there had been wars, famines and plagues and these had made local differences in the population of various countries. Various areas had high and low spots but over the whole period, population was slowly increasing.

This battle of the people of Europe for survival was a grim one, particularly in the Middle Ages. Birth rates were very high and so were death rates. Many individuals died young and the average length of life was much shorter than it is today. Life was hazardous and unsanitary. This was particularly true in the cities. The numbers of deaths in the large cities of Europe always exceeded the numbers of births; in other words, the populations of the cities never replaced themselves. The only way that a city was able to maintain itself was by a steady stream of people flowing to it from the country districts and the small towns and here, of course, the births exceeded the deaths. This destructive effect of city living was very marked in the ancient cities of Europe. It was decreased by improvements in medicine and sanitation that came in the latter part of the nineteenth century but it continues even today. Even in modern America it is the rural districts that make the expansion of the large cities possible.

In medieval times food for the population was a perpetual problem. Occasionally there were prosperous periods and prosperous areas but over a large part of Europe, people lived on the margin of famine. Methods of producing food were crude and methods of preserving and distributing cruder still. Anything that upset the basic economy of a country produced a large number of deaths; anything like a drought or a set of unusually cold winters could produce a famine and continually millions of people were so undernourished that their lives were shortened.

Despite hazard and disaster the population of Europe was slowly increasing until an extraordinary event upset the balance and produced some unexpected changes in the European living pattern. The changes began with disaster—this was the great plague or Black

Death that swept over Europe in the middle of the fourteenth century. It hit England in the years 1348 and 1349 and the records of the effects and results of the plague are reasonably clear. It is estimated that the city of London alone lost as many as 100,000 people. The loss over the whole of England is estimated by some authorities to have been as little as one-third of the population but others feel that it might have been as high as one-half.

Naturally this produced extraordinary changes in the economy of the country. At first the landholders and lords of the manors seemed to benefit. They collected certain sums on the deaths of their tenants and other sums accrued to them from the new tenants and also land reverted to them where whole families were wiped out; but these were temporary effects. It soon became apparent that the lands were less valuable because there were fewer people to utilize them. Also the revenues from the operation of mills for the grinding of grain, the payments of rents and so forth, rapidly fell off. In many cases stewards reported that tracts of land had little or no value because the tenants were all dead.

One of the most far-reaching results was to change the economic condition of tenants and laborers. The land had not been affected—only the population. There was the same demand for labor and a greatly diminished supply. The laborers and the poorer classes were not slow to recognize this situation and began demanding higher wages and a better return on what they produced. In the next century, on at least fourteen occasions, statutes were passed designed to prevent workmen from making what were regarded as exorbitant demands for wages. Thus, one of the results of the plague was undoubtedly to improve the living and economic condition of the survivors, particularly of the poorer section of the community. In addition to this there was per capita more land to cultivate, better housing and other accommodations and a better supply of food all around.

What happened in England was repeated or even exceeded in other parts of Europe: Venice lost 100,000 people, Florence, 60,000, Paris, 50,000. Authorities seem to agree that in such cities the losses in only three or four months ran as high as one-half of the previous population. It is supposed that Italy lost at least one-half of its population and France about one-third. Some areas did not suffer so severely but the total loss for Europe ran to no less than 25,000,000 people in a few months which represented approximately one-fourth of the people of the entire continent. It took several centuries for Europe to regain the population that it had in the middle of the fourteenth century. The economic and social effects in Europe generally were similar to the effects in England.

There was at least temporarily a relief of pressure, a chance for readjustment, a little more of everything to go around, a little more space and light and air. Of course, from modern standards and from the point of view of present crowded Europe, the land of fourteenth-century Europe did not appear to be overoccupied nor the cities very large compared with the modern metropolis, but this is a wrong set of standards to apply. There is a relativity in society just as there is a relativity in physics.

The technology view of the fourteenth century is very different from our own. Since then, we have had an industrial revolution and our technological progress in agriculture, industry, transportation, medicine and so forth makes possible and tolerable a concentration in population that in the fourteenth century would have been un-bearable. In terms of technology and economy, the fourteenth century was overburdened. In fact, the Black Death itself was probably one of the results of this burden.

The generations that grew up in Europe following the plague had the benefit of relief from the old conditions. They were probably a little healthier, happier, better fed and more hopeful than the pre-ceding generation. They had the benefit of growing up in the more hopeful atmosphere of the age of the revival of learning and the Renaissance which began to spread over Europe. Quite possibly the new conditions of the population facilitated the utilization and spread of the Renaissance ideas and the Renaissance ideas also assisted the population in improving their conditions and their attitude toward life.

Of course, in the beginning, interest in the new philosophy of life was confined to the princes and their courts, to the relatively limited class of specially educated people, to the artists and philosophers. However, there was implicit in this new philosophy and in the arts and the growing sciences an increased opportunity for the independ-ent individual. The Renaissance influence spread not only in a geo-graphical sense from Italy northward into France and England but it also spread in a social sense to different elements in the society. The Renaissance was not confined to the arts or to a set of intellec-tual ideas, it also represented some improvements in technology and in the means and standards of ordinary life.

In a technical sense the term "industrial revolution" has been ap-plied by the historians and the economists to the period that followed the invention of the steam engine and the application of mechanical power to transportation and industry, thus, to the end of the eighteenth century, the nineteenth century and the present. We should not feel, however, that technological improvement had to wait upon this first utilization of steam and it should not blind us to the fact that the industrial revolution was preceded by simpler but very definite improvements in technology and mechanical progress that began in earlier ages and notably in the Renaissance.

Thus, to cite only two examples, Leonardo da Vinci was not only a notable artist but also an inventor and a mechanical genius who anticipated the flying machine and scores of other inventions, and Benvenuto Cellini, who was primarily an artist in jewelry and a gold- and silversmith, took great delight also in general metallurgy and in the casting of the coarse metals including the production of cannon for the siege of Florence.

Among the improvements that came along in this period we may refer to such matters as the increased size and improved design of windmills, notably in Holland, but also quite generally all over Europe; the use of mechanical pumps and hoisting machinery for mines; an interest in transportation and communication between countries with consequent rehabilitation and extension of highways; a new interest in agriculture and horticulture; the development of gardens with better selection of trees and plants and flowers, and of course there were also improvements taking place in the design and use of ships.

All of these changes had their influences on the population of Europe and set the stage for the work of Henry the Navigator and the great century of exploration and discovery.

By our modern standards each of these represented only a slight improvement over what had existed in preceding ages; taken together, however, they had far-reaching effects.

In Europe, increased travel and improved methods of travel and communication tended to improve the volume and variety of food supply and to eliminate local shortages and local famines. Even slight increases in compensations to laborers, artisans and tradesmen were reflected in a more general capacity to buy the foodstuffs which small improvements in agriculture made available and also facilitated the distribution of foodstuffs and of other articles of trade that resulted from Europe's suddenly expanded contacts with all other parts of the world. The prospect of a wider world stimulated European growth;

migration and colonization came along to relieve pressure on European resources.

The fifteenth century saw an increase in the population of Europe. The population that was better fed, better housed, more hopeful and adventurous benefited by what was already taking place on the Atlantic such as the founding of the whale fisheries in the north and the development of the fisheries for cod and other food fishes. The scene was thus set for the next great step in European expansion.

One technological development had the most far-reaching effects; this was the development of explosive arms. The many and frequent wars of Europe stimulated the invention and development both of defensive armament and of offensive arms. The use of incendiary materials and of explosives was very old indeed and developed in the Orient at least as early as in the Mediterranean and in Europe. Once started, the development of effective cannon and of portable personal arms proceeded more rapidly in Europe than anywhere else. It was this development that made possible the spread of European people and of the ideas embodied in their society.

Before the close of the thirteenth century Roger Bacon, the English scholar and philosopher, had developed a formula for gunpowder, but it took many years before gunpowder was effectively used in cannon either ashore or afloat.

The first European guns using gunpowder were crude and dangerous; that is, they were almost as likely to kill and maim the men that built and fired them as to destroy the enemy. The barrels of some early guns were simply long iron bars with angular sides held together by metal bands and hoops. They were breech-loading. Sometimes the breech blew backward; sometimes when the breech held, the barrel blew sideways and sometimes the ball left the barrel in the general direction of the enemy.

Guns were used on ships almost as soon as on land. Mortars were used on galleys in the Mediterranean as early as 1311. They were mounted in vessels of the Spanish fleet in 1359 and in the battle which took place at La Rochelle in 1372, the guns of the Spanish fleet won a decisive victory over England. A few years later, cannon used on naval vessels played a great part in the Venetian-Genoese War.

Various sizes and types of guns for various purposes began to appear during the fifteenth century. By 1500 the advantages of brass cannon in the matter of safety and accuracy had been demonstrated. These were solid castings with bored barrels and were, of course, muzzleloaders. They soon replaced the breechloaders and bound barrels.

From the point of view of Atlantic history, the importance of the preceding paragraphs is that even the early Portuguese ships that crept around the coast of Africa carried explosive weapons. Crude as these were, they were impressive enough to terrify the natives. Joined with the use of helmets, body armor, the crossbow, they were usually enough to tip the balance in favor of the European voyagers.

When da Gama came to the West African coast and to the Malabar coast of India, he discovered that the Mohammedans and the Hindus already knew something about explosives. This they had probably learned from the Chinese, who used explosives at least as early as 1161 when Yu Yun-wen defeated the Chin in a battle fought near the present city of Nanking. The Chinese and Hindus in time developed jet propulsion. The East Indians used rockets. During the wars in India, a British army officer picked up and improved upon the technique and rockets were employed against the United States forces in the War of 1812 so that when we sing "The Star-Spangled Banner" we refer to the "rockets' red glare" without quite knowing what it represented.

Our interest is in the fact that the guns of da Gama's ships were more effective and had a longer range than anything he had encountered in the Far East.

The guns which the great explorers mounted on their vessels were not very accurate and did not need to be. The sound of their explosion was enough to terrify a native population that was encountering Europeans and their ships and weapons for the first time. Many a native leader was terrified by a salute ostensibly fired in his honor. Then guns aroused much the same terror and many of the same arguments that the atom bombs produce today.

Still the early guns and cannon mounted on the ships were not enough in themselves to account for the rapid and successful European occupations all around the world. From the point of view of the explorer and colonizer, what was needed was not so much large pieces as smaller weapons that could move with landing parties and other bodies of invaders, but the smaller weapons were slower to develop.

How much small arms were needed is illustrated by the fact that at least two great and courageous explorers lost their lives under rather similar conditions because while the ships were equipped with guns, they either did not have or did not employ adequate small arms.

When Magellan, sailing around the world, reached the Philippines his ships were provided with cannon but the account shows very clearly that during the battle which he fought at Mactan, the water near shore was shallow and the vessels had to stay so far offshore that the beach where Magellan was trying to effect a landing was beyond range of his guns. Magellan, fighting in armor along the beach, was showered with native arrows that were no more than reeds with wooden points hardened in fire. One of these entered an opening in his helmet and wounded his eye. Native arrows and lances were fired at his legs and he went down in shallow water overwhelmed by a native onslaught.

As late as the end of the eighteenth century Captain Cook lost his life to native warriors on a beach in the Hawaiian Islands under much the same circumstances, apparently again because he was out of the protective range of his ships and had gone ashore in a small boat that was inadequately armed.

The first European firearms were relatively large guns and cannons that could be used in the siege or defense of forts and walled towns and against bodies of massed troops.

The development of small arms came after that of the large pieces. Apparently the first of the portable personal arms was patterned after the earlier and larger models of explosive weapons—it was called a hand cannon. The men who used it must have had great strength and great courage. It was heavy and unwieldy, had a large bore and fired a large bullet feebly. It required two hands for its management; one hand was devoted to holding and aiming the weapon and the other to lighting the charge of powder.

However, with this as a start, lighter weapons were soon developed. Even the lighter weapons still required two hands and the full attention of the marksman because one hand was required to manage the "match" which was used to ignite the charge of powder. The match was simply a length of braided cord, dipped in sulphur, which burned slowly and once lit was serviceable for a considerable period of time. These early single shot weapons were called pistols possibly because they were first developed in the city of Pistoia in Italy.

By 1425, that is in the time of Henry the Navigator, the matchlock pistol began to appear. In this weapon, the match was incorporated in the weapon itself. The match was in a clamp attached to a trigger so that when the trigger was pulled the match came in contact with the powder. Though difficult to load and to keep in operation, this was a weapon that could be fired with one hand, leaving one hand free for other duties. It was thus the first weapon that could be used on horseback or while steering a boat or performing other duties.

Before the close of the fourteenth century, fire-sticks had been invented. These were simply long metal barrels that would receive a charge of powder and a lead ball. At the closed end they terminated in one or two prongs that could be driven into a rough billet of wood. As in the case of the early pistols, they were drilled at the inner and upper part of the barrel with a touchhole to receive a priming charge of powder and were fired with a match. When the weapon was about to be discharged, the marksman placed the billet of wood under his right armpit and clamped the end between his body and the inner side of his upper arm with all the power that he could command. Then he had to swing his body to aim the gun and apply the match with his left hand.

After a time it occurred to somebody that the wood block might be dropped at an angle and permanently attached to the barrel. This permitted the gun to be fired from the shoulder and the first crude muskets made their appearance. As in the case of the pistol, they were first fired by matchlocks then flintlocks and went through other developments.

Crude as these devices were, they were probably the greatest single determining factor in the spread of European people about the world. In their conquest and colonization of great areas in North, Central and South America, the Spaniards were assisted by the use of horses. It is doubtful, however, if the use of horses alone would have made them victorious over the Indians, for the natives often outnumbered them many times over. It was the use of firearms joined with the use of horses and superior ships that gave them the victory.

Between the year 1000, when the Norse made several attempts at colonization of the North American continent, and 1492, firearms were discovered and developed in Europe. The Norse discoverers of North America were just as brave and just as eager to settle in Vineland as the Iberian discoverers were to settle in Central and South America. The Spaniards and Portuguese succeeded and the Norse failed largely because the former had firearms and the latter did not. Karlsefni and his companions remained on the American continent for at least three years in a determined effort to establish a permanent colony. After several attempts to defend their settlement against the Indians the record shows that Karlsefni clearly recognized that he was outnumbered by the Indians and had few advantages in the matter of weapons. Under such conditions the attempt at colonization was doomed to failure, and he reluctantly loaded his ships and sailed back to Greenland.

The Spanish conquerors brought to America horses, firearms and a new religion. What they took back was gold and food. They were well repaid. The gold and silver that came out of Mexico and Peru were romantic and spectacular. There was such a hoard of treasure as the world had not seen for a long time! It seemed easy to get and inexhaustible.

News about the riches of Spain and the treasure in the New World spread throughout Europe; in fact, from the point of view of Spanish safety, there was too much treasure and it was too well advertised.

It was not long, however, before it aroused the envies of other nations. The English and the Dutch and the French too resented the Spanish successes. Privateering vessels and plain pirates moved in on the Atlantic seaway that connected Spain with her American colonies. Many Spanish vessels, bearing treasure from America, fell a prey to marauders either on the Spanish Main or on the broad Atlantic.

It is estimated that in 1521 the shipments of treasure from America to Spain had a value of £52,000. At the former rates of exchange, this would represent over a quarter of a million dollars but, of course, in terms of the present American dollar, this value would have to be multiplied several times. By 1545, a peak shipment had been reached which ran to £630,000. By the end of the sixteenth century, the value had dropped to £300,000.

Raids on the Spanish coast and the Spanish vessels became so frequent that the Spanish had to organize protective measures. Arrangements had already been made so that all trade from and to the Spanish colonies in America had to pass through the single port of Seville. On the American coast all shipments came and went through two ports, that is to say, Vera Cruz in Mexico and Porto Bello on the Isthmus of Panama. By 1561, conditions had gotten so bad that individual sailings of ships with valuable cargoes between Spain and America or America and Spain were abandoned.

From this time on the government collected each year two fleets of vessels which sailed for the West Indies under the convoy of a fleet of warships. In the West Indies the two fleets separated, one going to Vera Cruz and the other going to Porto Bello.

These were the high old times. Naturally in the course of the year enormous treasure piled up in Porto Bello. Then there were days when the streets of the town were literally piled and paved with gold and silver ingots. Naturally also, there was a market and a fair and a roaring celebration when the fleet came in.

Despite the Spanish precautions, Drake raided Santo Domingo, Cartagena, Panama and the Pacific coast from 1577 to 1580, and even a century later, 1655-1671, Henry Morgan, plundering the Spanish ships, captured Porto Bello and Panama.

No treasure that ever came out of the New World was a small per cent as valuable as the foods that America added to the world's dietary. This, and not the wealth and art of Mexico or Peru, was the great treasure of the Indians and their great contribution to world civilization.

This is true in a quite literal sense. We may begin with a limited and a rather prosaic example. After running over figures such as those we have given above for the value of the treasure shipments from the Caribbean to Spain, Brenton, an English scholar, shows that the annual shipment of codfish from the Grand Banks to English ports exceeded even the high point of the shipment of Spanish treasure. By 1615, the English catch on the Banks was yearly in excess of £200,000. By 1640, the revenues were running to £700,000 and this continued year after year.

In 1670, the value of the American fisheries to England alone ran to £800,000. This is the real or literal statement of one phase of the matter, but in a general and philosophical sense the value of the Indian contribution to the wealth and health of the world is almost incalculable.

In the fields of many a farm edible corn and field corn have been growing in different fields. The corn has been set in little hills and the hills arranged in rows. Until they were harvested, bean vines were climbing about each hill of corn, and melons and pumpkins were set to grow between the rows.

As I write, the autumn season is upon us. The woods of New England and Long Island are glowing with autumn colors. In the fields of many a New England farm, hills of field corn and corn edible by human beings are being stacked and harvested in the fields. Between the rows of corn, pumpkins are growing and in some cases also edible beans. All these plants were developed and grown by the

Indians centuries before the Puritans landed on the New England coast and it was the friendly Indian that taught the white man this standard method of cultivation and so made possible the first celebration of Thanksgiving.

In Maine and on Long Island, valuable, not to say notorious, crops of potatoes are being harvested and the potato also was the Indian's innovation. Over and over again in the course of colonial history, white colonies were saved from privation and starvation by the Indian's skill in agriculture and in the domestication of native plants. In many other cases, lost colonies would have been saved if they had remained on friendly terms with the native inhabitants.

The culture of edible corn and of potatoes has spread around the world and they have become two of mankind's great and stable food crops. To this we must add field corn which is used not only as fodder for animals but which, when ground and otherwise processed, also is added to the human dietary.

The American Indian also domesticated and added to the world's dietary the following plants: many different varieties of edible beans (including the lima bean), the sweet potato, the cassava (manioc), pumpkins, squashes and gourds in great variety, melons, grapes from several stocks of native American vines, the cacao tree which yields cocoa and chocolate. Among the trees and plants that yield drugs he knew about cinchona that yields quinine and the coca plant that produces cocaine and he also utilized for his own purposes the alkaloid of the peyote. He cultivated and used the fiber of native cotton and spun yarn and rope from a number of other fiber yielding plants.

One would suppose that the sum of these contributions was sufficient to have satisfied even the Indian and to have rendered the rest of the world forever grateful to him. The Indian, however, was inventive and generous to an unprecedented degree. On top of everything else, he domesticated several different varieties of tobacco and invented the solace and luxury of smoking.

In the cultivation and utilization of plants the Indian exhibited a talent that amounts almost to genius. He knew about drainage, irrigation and the need for fertilizers. It is possible also that he knew something about the value of rotating crops though this latter knowledge was important only in the areas of sizable settled communities. Elsewhere there was plenty of land available and most Indian tribes were mobile even where they were not nomadic.

The discovery of America benefited the world's food supplies in two important ways. First, it contributed the many different food plants listed above which later were adapted to cultivation in soils and climates of many different parts of the world. In the second place, it provided vast tracts of land and a variety of different climates suitable to the cultivation of plants that were already known to the Europeans. Among the plants that took on a new lease of life in the New World were sugar and coffee.

It all began a long time ago. In its broadest sense, the New World, the modern world, may be contrasted with the Old World that Europe knew in the Middle Ages and early Renaissance. This New World emerged and took shape in a remarkably brief time, considering the length of human history.

Three developments of fundamental importance to human history, developments that shaped the modern world, took place in the century between 1450 and 1550. They not only followed each other in rapid succession, they seem also to be related as cause and effect. These are the three developments:

1. Firearms were developed—firearms that could be transported and that would operate with some effectiveness.
2. The Great Age of Discovery and Exploration took place. This more than doubled the area of the world known to Europeans.
3. The potential food supply and the variety of food available to Europeans was enormously increased and living room was increased manyfold.

To be on the safe side we have named a century of development, but so far as geographic knowledge is concerned the bulk of the discoveries were crowded into the fifty years that followed Columbus' first voyage.

Naturally it took time for these inventions and discoveries to produce their full effects in the course and direction of human history. First, they produced in Europe an opportunity for relief and readjustment such as followed the Black Death, only of a larger, more lasting and more positive nature. Then they set the stage for the Industrial Revolution and the great wave of expansion of European peoples that accompanied it.

In 1650 the population of Europe numbered about 100,000,000. By 1937 the people of Europe plus the people of European descent in other parts of the world increased to 720,000,000. That is over sevenfold. By contrast, the rest of the world, during the same period, had increased only fourfold. By contrast also in the 300 years that preceded 1650, the population of Europe had grown very slowly indeed.

This may be expressed in another way. Before the great expansion, Europeans made up about 18 per cent of the world's population; after it, 35 per cent.

Respecting the growth of the white race, one authority supplies the following figures: in 1750, 175,000,000; in 1929 (that is less than 200 years later), 675,000,000.

One measure of growth may be made in terms of the use of language. Between 1800 and the present, the English-speaking people have increased eightfold. In the beginning they represented one-eighth of the people of European descent—now one quarter.

In an important way these changes were due to the exploration and settlement of the North American continent, some details of which are presented in the next chapter.

Chapter 11

TO THEIR NEW HOMES

K ARLSEFNI and his company were the first—the first of
the millions that were to follow. The first to find the new land good
and love it; the first to build homes and beget children here; the first
to be turned back—to lose the new life where others later won it.
What they lacked was neither purpose nor organization nor courage,
but powder and guns. The year was 1010 or a little earlier.

Years went by—nobody knows how many—before the fishing fleets
from various countries in Europe began coming each summer to
the Grand Banks of Newfoundland. No doubt they came ashore at
various times for a place to dry and pack their fish and to obtain
wood and water, but there is no evidence that they attempted a
permanent settlement.

Then in the early part of the sixteenth century the Spaniards
moved into the southern part of North America from the Caribbean
and from Mexico. They were determined men in armor and they
came in many ships with horses and guns and other weapons. Yet
many wandered, fought and died or failed and sailed away before permanent homes were built, children raised to manhood and towns
established in America.

We shall see now how many different peoples from the beginning
contributed to the pattern of American culture and how the ways by
which they crossed the Atlantic often determined where they were
to settle in America.

In 1512, Juan Ponce de Leon was governor of Puerto Rico. Probably his discovery of Florida would have been forgotten had he not also admitted that he was looking for a Fountain of Eternal Youth which had been described to him by the Indians. He had been with Columbus on his second voyage and was, in fact, already an old man according to the standard of the time. Being ambitious as well as old, he was anxious to believe the stories of the Indians regarding lands beyond Puerto Rico and the health-giving fountain.

On the first voyage he sailed through the Bahama Islands and discovered and named Florida. He went to Spain to report his discovery and was named governor of Bimini and of Florida. In 1521, with two vessels, he made another voyage to Florida. He found neither gold nor a Fountain of Youth; indeed, he met his death in a battle against hostile Indians.

Before Juan Ponce de Leon died, the western shore of Florida had also been discovered; in fact, Alvarez de Pineda followed the gulf coast all the way from Florida to Panuco (Tampico) in Mexico and back again. During this voyage he discovered the Mississippi River to which he gave the name Rio del Espiritu Santo.

The climate of Florida seemed warm and inviting, the soil rich and the vegetation luxurious, but Florida continued to prove a death trap to many ambitious European expeditions.

In 1528 Pánfilo de Narvaez made an ambitious attempt to colonize Florida and also to reach the Carolinas where a colony had recently failed. Before he even reached the coast of Florida he had lost two ships and sixty men in a hurricane and others had deserted. Against the advice of wiser men, Narvaez attempted a march through Florida. His fleet waited a year for him and then sailed home. In the meantime, Narvaez's march through Florida proved a disaster before a few survivors reached Apalachee Bay. What was left of the Narvaez party built five shaky boats and tried to escape by sailing westward to Mexico. Narvaez and most of the boats were lost.

One ship under the direction of a wise, resourceful and courageous individual named Alvarez Nuñez Cabeza De Vaca was wrecked on the Texas coast. After six years of captivity and wandering among the Indian tribes he and three companion survivors succeeded in making their way into Mexico. In the process of reaching the Mexican settlements Cabeza De Vaca almost completed the first crossing of the American continent, but there were still no permanent settlements north of Mexico.

There was one other survivor of Narvaez's expedition. His name was Juan Ortiz and he was a captive of the Indians in Florida. After twelve years he lived like an Indian, moved like an Indian, spoke like an Indian and dressed like an Indian; that is to say, he mostly went naked but he was still alive in Florida to greet the next Spanish disaster. This was the expedition of Hernando De Soto, who landed near the present city of Tampa in 1539.

De Soto started out with 600 men and many horses loaded on seven vessels and he went fighting and bullying his way northward through Florida into Georgia. They made a loop through North and South Carolina and returned southward in the region of the Tombigbee and Alabama Rivers. The name of the region was reported as Mauilla from which the name "Mobile" may later have been derived. By this time De Soto's men were hostile to his leadership and to his plans so much so that he did not dare to approach the gulf with his main force. In addition, he had to fight a battle against the Indians who had assembled in great number.

It is reported that De Soto lost eighteen men killed and 150 wounded but that the use of firearms and the burning of villages accounted for the destruction of somewhere between 2,000 and 3,000 Indians. De Soto moved in a northwesterly direction fighting Indians all the way and in 1541 reached the Mississippi River in the neighborhood of the Chickasaw Bluffs. He crossed the river and in a miserable march northward during the winter lost 250 more men. After further futile wandering he reached the mouth of the Red River in 1542 and died there in the spring of the year.

A few hundred survivors under the leadership of Luis Moscoso built boats and finally made the passage to the Spanish settlements in Mexico. By this time much had been learned and reported about the North American continent but there was still no settlement.

We have seen already that the attempt of Luis de Cancer to establish a benevolent colony in Florida following the theories of Las Casas came to grief and was abandoned in 1549. Between 1559 and 1561, attempts to establish settlements in Pensacola and in the Carolinas also met with failure.

In the meantime, the French were aroused and were anxious to establish colonies in many parts of America. In 1562 French Huguenots under the leadership of Jean Ribaut failed in an attempt to establish a settlement named Port Royal in South Carolina but another French leader, René de Laudonnière, founded Fort Caroline on the St. Johns River in Florida and Ribaut returned with a new expedition. The intention was to establish bases from which the French could harass the treasure ships sailing from Mexico to Spain.

The French kept control of this fort for exactly a year, then the Spaniards under Menéndez de Avilés took the fort and massacred all the French settlers. They held the fort for two years and then the French came back under Chevalier de Gourgues, took the fort back and in turn put all the Spaniards to death.

Despite the loss of Fort Caroline, Menéndez, supported by Jesuits and Franciscan missionaries, undertook widespread colonization that ranged from Florida all the way up the east coast as far as Virginia. All of the colonies established north of Florida either failed or were captured by English settlers in the succession of colonial wars but St. Augustine in Florida, which Menéndez founded in 1565, and many of the other posts and settlements in Florida had a continuing existence and Spanish families continued to live in Florida and to survive the whole succession of colonial wars.

In the meantime, the Spaniards were also moving into western territories of North America. From 1540 to 1542, while De Soto was making his futile march through the southern states to the Mississippi River, Francisco Vásquez de Coronado was making a march in the west. He went through parts of Arizona, New Mexico, Texas, Oklahoma and Kansas before he turned back. One of his lieutenants, Garcia Lopez de Cárdenas reached the Grand Canyon of Colorado. While Coronado was returning from his march, Juan Rodríguez de Cabrillo sailed up the Pacific coast from Mexico to Oregon and back. These were strictly exploring expeditions and no settlements resulted from them.

It was not until the closing years of the sixteenth century and the opening years of the seventeenth that Juan de Oñate succeeded in establishing settlements in New Mexico and in re-examining a wide belt of territory from Kansas to the Gulf of California. Santa Fe in New Mexico was established a little later. The western settlements of the Spaniards date from about this time though the settlers in New Mexico suffered disastrously when the Indians revolted in 1680 and the country was not reconquered and pacified until the last years of the century. A serious attempt of the Spaniards to occupy and hold Texas dated from about 1720 and the occupation of California from San Diego to San Francisco came in the years from 1769 to 1776.

In most of these territories the Spanish settlers remained. Their descendants became an important part of the population of America and their ways of life contributed a pattern to the fabric of American civilization. Churches, schools and missions have survived from the time of early Spanish occupation in each of these territories. The laws of Florida, Texas, New Mexico, California and a number of other states have been influenced strongly by Spanish law and custom. This, of course, is particularly true with respect to the laws governing the ownership and use of land and the matter of water rights. The methods of organizing labor and of working on plantations and ranches was strongly influenced by Mexican customs and this was particularly true of the organization of the early cattle ranchers. The clothing, equipment, method and even language of the American cowboy were in many ways based on Spanish models. The Spaniards began the cultivation in these areas of many agricultural crops and they are responsible for the founding of the citrus fruit industries in both Florida and California.

What the Spanish settlers had to contend with was not only the development of the land and the struggles with the Indians but also the wars with English and French colonists. There was a period when the greatest dread was the French. We have had an example of the character of this hostility in the case of Fort Caroline but similar battles developed in many other parts of the continent.

As we have seen already, Champlain, following Cartier, moved into America through the St. Lawrence Valley. By 1613 he had penetrated 100 miles beyond Ottawa and by 1615 he had reached Georgian Bay, thus opening up the route into the American interior country that the fur traders were to use so consistently. From this date on the French explorers and missionaries began their systematic penetration of the American West.

While these northern developments were going on, the French were not by any means ignoring the southern approaches to the continent. By 1660 the French were well established in the West Indies and had occupied Martinique, Guadeloupe, Tortuga, Grenada and a whole chain of other islands.

In 1627 Richelieu well expressed the range and extent of French ambition in America when he organized the Company of the Hundred Associates. The purpose of this company was to colonize New France. It was given control of all the lands between Florida and the Arctic Circle. To show that they were ready to test Richelieu's extensive claims, the British captured Acadia and Quebec in 1628, but these were restored under a treaty of 1632.

The French methods of exploration and of dealing with the Indians were markedly different from those of the Spanish. The Spaniards sought to intimidate the Indians, to make servants of them and sometimes slaves. If there was any delay or show of resistance they fought their way from point to point.

The French were more flexible. They had a facility with languages and they sought to learn from the Indian. They used the Indians as guides and were quite prepared to accept them as allies and companions in the forests. It was not that the French were unprepared or unwilling to fight in an extremity but they preferred to exhaust other methods first. This friendly approach to the Indian paid off in two ways. It accounted for the rapidity of the travel of French explorers on long expeditions and for a long period it also added military strength to the French occupation forces.

As early as 1634 Champlain sent out Nicolet, who reached Sault Ste. Marie and who traveled along upper Michigan and reached Green Bay. Radisson was at the western end of Lake Superior by 1659 and it was not long before a mission was permanently established in this region. In 1673 the missionary Fathers Joliet and Marquette traveled down the Mississippi Valley as far as the mouth of the Arkansas.

Their work was completed by La Salle, who started from posts that the French had occupied on the Great Lakes and traveled down the Mississippi until he reached its mouth in the year 1682. He claimed the whole valley in the name of the king of France and determined to establish a French colony at the mouth of the river.

With this in mind he recruited 400 men in France, but on his return to America missed the mouth of the river and landed on the Texas coast instead. After futile attempts to reach the river, La Salle was murdered by his companions and later the colonists were attacked by Indians and completely wiped out.

Nonetheless, the French were determined to protect the mouth of the river and to have bases on the gulf coast. This was the territory they intended to defend against the expansion of the Spanish and possible occupation by the English. With this in mind, Iberville established colonies in Louisiana and at Biloxi. Mobile was founded in 1710 and New Orleans in 1718. While the French hold on the lower Mississippi was being developed, the forts, settlements and missionary posts on the Great Lakes were also being strengthened. Cadillac founded the city of Detroit in 1701.

Thus, the French sought to drive a wedge between the Spanish settlements in the west and the Spanish settlements in Florida and to hem in the English settlers and the Dutch that had founded colonies on the Atlantic seaboard. The French, of course, made a large and permanent contribution to the population of the country in ports of the central Gulf coast and in Louisiana. This area and particularly the city of New Orleans has continued to be the heart and center of the French impact on American life but, of course, the effects of French speech and culture were not limited to this area.

French influences continued strongly all the way up and down the Mississippi Valley even after the time of the Louisiana Purchase in 1804. Something as fundamental as the geographic structure of the country entered into this situation and this the analytical French mind was quick to discern.

Before the days of highways and railroads, the Mississippi River and its tributaries constituted the transportation system of the whole heart of the continent. Once the early settlers crossed the Alleghenies and the Appalachians, they were inevitably dependent upon some phase of the Mississippi River drainage. Their movement westward followed the flow of the Ohio and the Tennessee or one of the other Mississippi tributaries.

The results of their forestry operations, their hunting, their trapping, their agriculture were all carried on the Mississippi River to the port of New Orleans where they were sold or shipped to other markets. The settlers themselves often accompanied their goods down the river and, after they were disposed of, proceeded by sailing vessel to one of the Atlantic ports and then went over the mountains homeward again. Many of the settlers made such trips repeatedly and thus the influence of the French settlement in Louisiana—its language, its customs, its cookery, its amusements, its methods of doing business— became a part of the experience of whole generations of settlers in the central West.

The French settlers in eastern Canada have, as we all know, maintained their own character and integrity right down to the present time. They have profoundly affected the history of Canada and the development of its government. In addition, the hostility between the French settlers and the English settlers expressed through the French and Indian Wars was an important ingredient of United States history during the colonial period.

In times of peace French Canadian settlers and influences have also penetrated into upper New York State and the upper tier of New England. It began when French lumbermen crossed the border and found employment in lumbering operations in Maine, New Hampshire and Vermont. When the New England states turned from lumbering and agriculture to manufactures, many French Canadian families came to settle in the mill towns and have remained an important element of the population of many New England manufacturing cities.

The history of English settlements in America has been often told, is well known, and does not need detailed repetition here. It is, however, a part of the story that not only touches the Atlantic but arises in the Atlantic and that cannot be omitted.

The first concerted efforts to establish English colonies in America took place between 1583 and 1588 and were directed by Sir Walter Raleigh and others. Raleigh, seeking, according to interpretation, either to "honor" or to "flatter" his queen called the land "Virginia." It was not, however, the present Virginia of the United States but a part of the North Carolina coast, and to reach it ships from England followed conventional and well-established courses such as they would use to bring them to Florida, the West Indies, or even the Spanish Main. Only at the end of the passage the ships swung farther north to avoid Spanish hostility. Thus, these passages were made south of the Gulf Stream and in part were able to utilize the favorable northeast trades. This general pattern for the outward course was followed even when the first permanent colony was finally established at Jamestown on May 14, 1607. It is clear that ships returning from Virginia to England had the benefit of prevailing westerly winds and the assistance of the Gulf Stream. With time and experience the navigators became aware of this advantage.

The *Mayflower* voyagers who started for America in 1620 met very different conditions. Their general purpose was to sail for "Virginia" and it is not explicit from the records as written why they went so far astray. They were making the passage for the first time and could not know or state the problems they were confronting. Knowing what we know now, it seems possible, or even probable, that a combination of southwesterly winds, which can be powerful in fall and winter, and the set of the Gulf Stream (North Atlantic Drift), kept edging them north of their intended course. This was important to the *Mayflower* voyagers for during the first winter half of the total colony died. What mattered to history, however, was the fact that once Massachusetts (which until 1819 included what is now the state of Maine) and later the Dutch-English settlement of New Amsterdam (New York) had been established, the English had to learn to navigate to and from England keeping north of the Gulf Stream.

On the passage from America to England the aid of the Gulf Stream and the North Atlantic Drift which the southern colonies enjoyed was generally balanced by the steadiness and power of the westerlies in latitude forty which aided the northern colonies. On the passage from England westward, the ships of the northern colonies had to battle prevailing westerly winds. This was partly offset by the fact that the southern colonies' ships had to travel far south to reach the trades or risk being becalmed in the Sargasso Sea if they sought a shorter course.

What mattered was that they learned to use different and divided courses and methods of navigation. Coastwise travel between the colonies was frowned on by England and there were long periods of history during which overland travel was incredibly slow from our point of view. It was then easier and faster to reach England by ship from either New York or Virginia than it was to reach either colony from the other overland. It was a potent and surprising surge of feeling of common interests that brought the colonies together for the Revolution. Long after the United States came into being the southern states sent their agricultural products to England by staying in or south of the Gulf Stream, while the northern states sent their products and manufactures to the mother-country by staying north of it. How the invention of a new type of ocean service broke up the old oceanic routes and diverted passengers and cargo to the north is presented in the chapter on the packets. It is quite probable that the resulting competition between northern and southern routes of transatlantic communication added to a long-standing division of cultural interests contributed its quota to the causes of the Civil War.

After the English, the Spanish and the French, the Dutch settlers exercised a most important influence on the development of America. Following up the voyage of Henry Hudson, the Dutch sent an expedition to Manhattan Island in 1612. This expedition was financed by Dutch merchants and its purpose was the establishment of trade. Its leaders were Christianson and Block. Captain Block not only came to Manhattan but also explored the coast and discovered the island that still bears his name. A post was established on Manhattan Island in 1613 and in the succeeding year Fort Nassau (also later referred to as Fort Orange) was established near Albany.

In the next ten years numerous posts were established in New York State and along the New England coast and an extensive fur trade was developed. Peter Minuit became the director of the Dutch West India Company in 1626 and purchased Manhattan Island from the Indians and founded the settlement of New Amsterdam. The Dutch settlements were not restricted to New York or New England—settlements were also established in New Jersey, Delaware and Pennsylvania. The Dutch empire on the American continent was not of long duration. New Amsterdam and Fort Orange were surrendered to the English in 1664. Dutch control over New York, Albany and New Jersey was briefly re-established during the war between England and Holland in 1673 but this was terminated in the peace of 1674.

The Dutch influence on American life was, of course, more profound than this political history suggests. The Dutch families in Manhattan and on Long Island remained in possession of their lands and of their other interests. They continued to be a most important element in the communities long after the English took over. Both because of their numbers and their abilities they continued to shape the history and customs of New York City and New York State.

The Dutch were also indirectly responsible for another strain in the pattern of American development. A Dutchman by the name of William Usselinex withdrew from the Dutch West India Company and began to interest King Gustavus Adolphus of Sweden in the possibility of a Swedish colony in America. The intention was to establish a settlement on the Delaware. Usselinex failed in several attempts to organize such an enterprise but two other Dutchmen, Samuel Blommaert and Peter Minuit, continued to encourage this venture. As a result the New Sweden Company was organized in 1637. Two Swedish vessels with colonists arrived on the Delaware in 1638 and established the colony of Fort Christina. The colony was successful but it aroused the hostility of Peter Stuyvesant, the governor of New Netherland. The West India Company, acting on his complaint, assumed control over New Sweden in 1655.

This almost completes the list of nations that tried to establish political control in the North American continent but it by no means completes the list of nations whose colonists came in large numbers and thus began establishing lines of travel and communication across the Atlantic that have persisted and have knit from shore to shore a fabric of common interests.

From the very beginning the joint process of settling and populating the North American continent had an international character. Captain Newport was in command of the vessel that established the colony at Jamestown in 1607. The very next year, on his second voyage, he brought to the colony Germans and Poles to the number of eight. These men were skilled in various trades and industries such as the making of glass, metals, tar, etc. Thus, migrants from nations that were later to contribute important elements in our industrial population were already represented in the first colony at its founding.

The peak of the Polish migration to America was long deferred but the Germans continued to arrive in most of the colonies in increasing numbers. The Delaware River and the port of Philadelphia formed an attractive haven for the early colonial vessels. The climate and the country seemed to prove inviting and congenial to the central Europeans such as the Germans and the Swiss. The so-called middle colonies such as Pennsylvania, New Jersey and Delaware had been first colonized by mixed populations which included the English, the Dutch, the Swedes, and these were now joined by the Germans.

In this part of the country each nation followed its own customs in laying out farms and in cultivating different products. Thus, from the beginning, there was a diversity in production and methods of cultivation and also in agriculture and some of the patterns then established have persisted even to the present time.

William Penn was granted the territory west of the Delaware between New York and Maryland in 1681 and Philadelphia was established in the same year. This colony was established as a refuge for oppressed Quakers who gathered here from many different quarters. Along with them came settlers from many other nations also in search of freedom. These included the Scotch, the Irish, the French and, of course, the Germans. Between 1683 and 1750, waves of immigrants came from Germany and Switzerland.

Between 1700 and the time of the Revolution at least 100,000 Germans came from the Palatinate and other lands of the Rhine Valley to Pennsylvania. Here they formed settlements of their own and became designated as the "Pennsylvania Dutch." At the time of the Revolution they composed about one-third of the Pennsylvania population. Another third of the population was accounted for by immigrants from northern Ireland.

The Germans, however, did not confine themselves to the middle colonies. A first wave of German-Swiss immigration hit New York in 1683. The conditions under which they could obtain holdings of land under the Dutch system did not appeal to them as advantageous so they began to move westward through the Mohawk Valley. Here they found themselves in company with Scotch-Irish settlers who had come in through New England.

The first movement of settlers to the west and southwest began before the Revolution and by this time what were to become the great channels of westward movement had been already marked out. There was the Mohawk Valley, later supplemented by the Erie Canal which was already being used by the Germans and the Scotch-Irish. There was the Ohio Valley. There were the valleys of the Allegheny Mountains and the Blue Ridge and the other mountains of the Appalachian system. Settlers starting to move into these mountains soon got caught in the valleys and began following them in great concentric arcs that led them to the south and west.

Beginning in 1760, many newcomers to this country moved into these mountainous sections and, once started, followed them into Kentucky and Tennessee and to the uplands of Georgia. Some of these settlers came from Germany and some from Sweden but the bulk of them came from Ireland. The descendants of this wave of pioneer settlers made their names an important part of the American historical record. They included Daniel Boone, David Crockett, Calhoun, Jackson, Polk, Houston and Lincoln.

To trace out the whole complicated pattern of the ethnic settlement of the American continent would prove to be a fascinating task but would take us far afield from Atlantic history. The three channels that we have set forth above are, however, important to us because what happened on the Atlantic in general determined the pattern of western movement of the settlers after they arrived on American shores. Thus, those who arrived in the ports south of Baltimore, when they moved westward, got into the Piedmont and finally into the Appalachian system and thus their movement tended to be deflected to the southwest. Those who came into Baltimore, Wilmington, Chester and Philadelphia tended to move into western Pennsylvania where they had a choice. They could either follow the mountain and valley again to the south and west or, having crossed the mountains, they could roll down the Allegheny, the Monongahela, and the Ohio.

Ships that stayed north of the Gulf Stream throughout their Atlantic course came into New York and the harbors of the New England coast. Their westward movement carried them into the Mohawk-Erie system and so west along the lakes. Thus, it is interesting to observe that German families from two entirely different sources participated in the settlement of Ohio, one group coming from Pennsylvania to make up an important cultural and industrial element of the city of Cincinnati and another group settling in Erie, Ashtabula, Cleveland, Sandusky, having passed through the valley of the Mohawk. Once having started, successive waves of migration carried them to St. Louis in the south and Milwaukee in the north. Migrants arriving in Canada by way of the St. Lawrence either proceeded westward through the lakes or along the route marked out by the early fur traders.

In all of this it is interesting to observe that there is a tendency for migration both on sea and on land to follow bands of latitude. The migrants that came to northern ports in general continued their movement in the same band of latitude by utilizing natural features of the continent that would help their progress. I would not interpret this to mean that their movement was rigidly determined by geographical circumstances.

It may be quite as real to point out that such movement may have persisted because it gave the settlers a natural chance to select lands, crops and methods of cultivation and to develop industries that were somehow akin to their knowledge and experience in the home country. We have already seen how the German population moved, keeping in general to types of territory that they knew how to cultivate and to industries with which they had had previous experience. On the other hand, the Scandinavian migrants have found Michigan, Wisconsin, Minnesota congenial to them and here have participated in the development of agricultural and dairying industries. Even such a small group as the Icelanders, who have come to America in relatively small numbers and at quite different periods, have somehow elected to settle in the Dakotas and across the border in Canada.

The process of settlement by a combination of geographical circumstance and cultural interest has gone on in many forms in most states of the union throughout the history of the continent. The pattern is very complicated and it is new as well as old. For example, in quite recent times there has grown up in Tarpon Springs, in Florida, a colony of Greek sponge fishermen. Their methods of conducting the industry are modern and mechanized but many of the traits of their personal and community lives are clearly of Mediterranean origin, modified here and there by American practice.

The historic map of America is indeed a monument to the settlers' divided interest. The Spanish found a New World but they did not call it a New World, they called it Hispaniola, or New Spain or New Grenada or New Leòn.

The French and the Dutch settlers were not oppressed minorities so it is easy to see why they should have called their colonies New France and New Amsterdam. They were content, even eager, to recreate in the new country what they had left at home. The case of the Pilgrims was different. They were a minority that felt cramped and abused yet the first colony they established was Plymouth and their efforts and that of later settlers resulted in the development of New England.

As time went on people came to this country from many parts of the world and in increasing numbers. As time went on they were no longer called "pilgrims" or "pioneers" but "immigrants." Often they came from the same countries and for the same reasons that brought our original settlers. Comments on how and when they came will be found in the various chapters dealing with the types of ships that brought them: packets, clippers, steamships. In time the pattern of their movements becomes very complicated—but wherever they came from, however they traveled, wherever they finally settled they brought with them interests and attachments to their old homes.

One of the results of these interests and attachments was to build up a web of transatlantic travel and trade. The ships that brought the Puritan settlers to the coast of New England returned with letters and messages to families and friends at home. The success of one small settlement encouraged the development of another one and, in time, built up a stream of new colonists and of pioneers. Even when the Puritans developed austerities and restrictions of their own, even when they rejected members of the colony that they regarded as undesirable, the result was simply to enlarge the area of colonization. Roger Williams established Providence Plantation and Anne Hutchinson, Rhode Island and these in turn developed their own contacts with the mother country.

In later chapters we shall see how the development of different types of ships affected the volume and direction of American colonization and settlement.

All of these special groups mentioned, and many more that we have not had the time or space to enumerate, each carried out across the Atlantic their own type of sailing pilgrimage. The ocean was a part of their declaration of independence from all that they found irksome and oppressive in the life of Europe. It was the ocean that gave them their first opportunity for freedom. It was not an impediment to them—it was a highway that was kept open to millions of people over a long period of time. The movement of these national, religious, racial and cultural groups has illustrated over and over again the essential and important fact that it is easier to cross an ocean than to travel a few miles across a European political, religious, economic or linguistic barrier.

Chapter 12

SHIPS AND CARGOES

FROM the very beginning the North American continent was explored, colonized and settled by a wide variety of racial, religious and national groups of settlers coming from Europe. The preceding chapter has summarized the growth of a part of the story of migration and settlement. At first only five or six distinct groups were involved in the process of colonization but later there grew to be scores of distinct interests and finally hundreds.

Now a curious paradox developed. Most of these colonists and settlers came to North America because they were dissatisfied with conditions in Europe. Many of them came with the avowed purpose of separating themselves from European ties. All of them intended to take up new residences, to build new homes, to make their lives and fortunes in a new land and to develop the resources of a continent. No doubt they felt that they had turned their backs upon Europe and upon the Atlantic Ocean which they had recently crossed in peril and discomfort.

Such a separation, however, was seldom realized. It is difficult to forget a whole continent and almost impossible to ignore an ocean. Family ties and interests persist even after all the farewells of final parting have been said. Interests of language, literature, religious and political beliefs, methods of education, styles in architecture, furniture and domestic equipment, even trivial matters like fashions in clothing kept the new Americans interested in the place of their European origin.

Usually the very ships that carried out the settlers returned to their European ports bearing from the settlers letters to families and friends. Two subjects appeared over and over in such letters. One subject was that of the needs of the new colony and colonists, things that might be sent to make the new land more homelike and manageable. The other subject dealt with the opportunities that the new land provided and often also involved the suggestion that further colonists were needed and welcome and that some friend or relative might also make the westward crossing.

Thus, communication between the shores of America and Europe continued to grow in volume and diversity. The number of ships sailing the Atlantic increased rapidly in number and also in the diversity of cargoes they carried. At first they were only European ships sailing back and forth and most of the goods and all of the people were flowing from Europe to America, but it was not long before vessels built in the colonies also made the trip to Europe carrying raw materials and even manufactured products from America to Europe. The colonists were not cut off from Europe and their passage across the Atlantic became neither trackless nor forgotten; it was rather as though the wake made by their ships continued to shine and to mark upon the sea a channel for many later vessels to follow.

As early as 1608 a vessel sailed from Massachusetts with local products for the English market. In the same year a vessel also left the Virginia colony for England with a mixed cargo that included wood products such as clapboards and wainscoting and also tar and pitch, iron ore, glass, etc.

It is interesting to note that at this early time eight Poles and Germans had already been sent out to the colony because of the skills that they possessed in handling glass and metals and in other manufactures. It was expected from the first that the Virginia colony would develop and supply manufactured articles but naturally the early English colonies had great difficulty in producing articles that would pass into European trade. Also, while colonial manufacture was desirable from the point of view of the colonizing company, it was not looked upon with favor by other merchants or by the government. It was not until the Virginia colonists began raising, curing and shipping tobacco that the economic welfare of the colony was assured.

The first profitable trade of the New England colonies was in furs which they secured from the Indians and in wood products—boards for the construction of houses, woods suitable for the building of furniture, staves for barrels and casks, masts for vessels and naval stores; codfish and other food fishes were, of course, also an important product of the colonies.

Whaling was also an early American industry. It developed first in Massachusetts Bay and then spread to Nantucket and Long Island. Long before the American Revolution, American whale ships were sailing to English ports to dispose of their products. The colonies did make early and heroic efforts at manufacture, first, to meet their own needs and second, to produce goods which could be sent to England in exchange for the goods which they could not produce themselves.

The preceding chapter mentioned a number of the groups that went into the composition of the North American population. Each of these groups did two things. It maintained its own integrity and a set of common interests that has continued to give it a recognizable unity but each has also added elements to the general culture of the states of the United States or the provinces of Canada.

These national or cultural characteristics have added interest and richness to the life of the continent. These contributions range all the way from our concepts of laws and liberty and other abstract matters such as our attitude toward education and science, to the fields of architecture and the decorative arts and finally down to such everyday matters as our favorite foods, our methods of cooking and our ways of arranging and decorating a home.

Nearly every one of the groups that have gone into the making of the American population have also left abiding contacts with the Old World that have continued to influence such matters as the way of doing business, trade and transport across the Atlantic. Even the groups that left Europe in protest of conditions that they believed to be intolerable were still bound by racial, religious, linguistic as well as by family interest to the old country. Even in protest, revolt and flight, man is seldom able to divorce himself from long-standing interests and associations.

Every group of colonists in America began sending back to Europe articles of trade. These reflected the characteristics of the new coast and of the country beyond but they also reflected the activities and interests of the colonists. Accident and stress of circumstances affected some of the very early shipments made from America to Europe but soon each colony began to develop characteristic products.

The Spanish settlers, of course, came to the Caribbean and to the southern shores of North America in search of gold and silver. The easiest way of acquiring the precious metals was to take it from the Indians, but when the Indians' supply began to diminish the Spanish settlers developed mining as one of their most important industries. Of course, there were hardly enough gold and silver mines to go around even in America and there was a crying need of other products. Ranching and farming colonies grew to have an importance almost equal to that of the mine regions. Products from the Spanish colonies included hides, corn, sugar, cocoa, vanilla, cochineal, etc.

Sailors from Brittany and the other coasts of France were among the earliest and most persistent of the fishermen to discover and utilize the Grand Banks of Nova Scotia and Newfoundland. When the French began to establish permanent settlements along the St. Lawrence and elsewhere in Canada, fishing was rapidly supplanted by a new interest and adventure; this was the fur trade. Compared with fishing, the fur trade proved a highly profitable enterprise. While fur-bearing animals ran in abundance along all the streams and in all the forests of Canada, the Indians were already successful in trapping animals and improved their natural ability under French direction. The French had a natural ability for dealing with the Indian. They were able to benefit by Indian experience and knowledge and methods of travel; in fact, the French explorers, traders and trappers were soon extending and speeding up the Indian's own routes and methods of travel. The French settlers' passionate preoccupation with the fur trade did much to account for the slow rate of development of other parts of their economy and other articles of export.

The Dutch, also, established at New Amsterdam a thriving and rapidly expanding trade in American furs. The West India Company, which established the Dutch colonies in this country, was particularly interested in the quick profits which the fur trade provided and, therefore, encouraged the settlers in this enterprise. However, the leaders in the colonies themselves had marked out large and extensive landholdings along the Hudson, the Delaware and in other areas. On these holdings they were anxious to establish many and diversified agricultural enterprises. The large estates grew and provided products which could be sent to the European markets along with furs but there was a continuing difference of view and conflict of interest between the "patroons" and the West India Company.

In the case of the English colony at Jamestown, in Virginia, we have seen already how Captain Newport's ship, on the second trip to the colony, brought skilled workers to establish industries. This was in 1608 when the vessel returned with dressed timber such as wainscoting and clapboards but the cargo also included extracted materials such as pitch and tar and raw materials like iron ore. A glass works was established in Jamestown in 1609 and the first iron works in Virginia commenced operation in 1619. Laudable efforts were made to establish a variety of industries in Virginia. It turned out, however, that the only cargo sent back to England which found a ready and profitable market was tobacco.

Tobacco grew wild in Virginia as elsewhere but careful cultivation of the plant was first undertaken by John Rolph in 1612. Tobacco had been coming into Europe from the West Indies for over a century but the use of tobacco was growing and the supply from this quarter was not sufficient to meet the increasing demand. Rolph's experiment showed that the soil and climate of Virginia were ideally suited to produce a superior tobacco.

Officially, both King James and Governor Dale tried to discourage the preoccupation of the Virginia colonists with the growing of tobacco but when the colonists found out that an acre of tobacco would yield six times as much revenue as an acre of corn or other grain, the expansion of the tobacco industry in Virginia was inevitable despite any official taxes and other impediments imposed upon it. At about this time tobacco was occasionally sold in London at the high rate of $12 a pound. Of course, Virginia agriculture and industry did furnish the English market with other articles of trade but tobacco long continued to be the cornerstone of prosperity in this colony. The intent in Virginia was to develop industries with diversified products but Virginia became largely an agricultural region, specializing in tobacco.

The Plymouth and other New England colonies reversed this process. It was thought at the beginning that they would establish plantations and would prosper on agriculture but the soil and climate of New England were not hospitable to the rapid development of prosperous agriculture. The colonists who could develop their farms so that they could be maintained on a self-sustaining basis were relatively fortunate and in time they learned to live well. When it came to products that they could use and trade with England and other countries, they had to look beyond agriculture.

The waters of the rivers, of the bays and of the banks were fortunately continually alive with fish. They traveled in such great schools that some of the captains reported that their vessels were "pestered" by the codfish. The development of fisheries was one of the early economic assets of the colony and also here, as in other colonies, the settlers in what is now Maine and Massachusetts engaged in the fur trade. However, while Massachusetts was still a colony, there were clear indications that its eventual prosperity must depend upon the development of diversified products, upon manufacture and successful trade. This is illustrated by what happened in the utilization of New England's great resources of forests and in the development of wood products.

In the seventeenth century England was building up her power at sea. She had the greatest need of materials for the manufacture of ships. In order to prevent drawing too heavily on her own forestry resources she was utilizing imports from Sweden and other north European countries with forested areas but she did not like her dependence on these sources. The forests of North America, therefore, had for her the greatest value as a source of timber for the construction of houses and of ships. The colonists, on the other hand, were anxious to clear some of the forested areas to permit the erection of homes and the development of farms.

England would have liked to have had the bulky raw timber delivered on her shores so that she could proceed with the manufacture, but at that time and in the ships then available, the transportation across the Atlantic was hardly possible and in any event would have been fantastically expensive. It was inevitable then that the colonies should have been encouraged in processing and fabricating some of their own products for export.

As early as 1621 the ship *Fortune* loaded at Plymouth with clapboards and beaver skins. As early as 1635 a sawmill was erected near Portsmouth, New Hampshire and soon thereafter grist mills and sawmills began to appear in many of the settlements. The richness of the New England forests was soon being demonstrated by the development of diversified products. Pine, cedar and spruce provided lumber for shipbuilding; red oak and white oak and other hardwoods were converted into materials for the manufacture of casks and barrels; cedar provided house frames and shingles; cherry, birch, maple and walnut were used for furniture and gunstocks.

The forests also supplied abundant fuel and thus made possible the development of other industries such as the smelting of iron, the manufacture of glass, of bricks, of pottery and the production of potash.

It soon became apparent to the colonists that while it was expedient and profitable to supply England with naval stores and materials for shipbuilding, it was still more profitable to build their own vessels. As early as 1614 Captain John Smith, on the coast of Maine, built seven boats for a fishing expedition. The Plymouth colony began the construction of ships as early as 1624 but the first sizable ship built in Massachusetts was the *Blessing of the Bay* which was built for Governor Winthrop at Mystic in 1631. In 1641 a bark of fifty tons was launched and a few years later it was reported that the colonists were able to build ships of one, two and even four hundred tons. By 1676 the New England shipyards were turning out as many as thirty ships a year, built for the English market. By this time one-third of all the tonnage sailing under the British flag had been built in America.

Cheapness of construction was an important factor in the rapid growth of the New England shipbuilding industry. In colonial times the costs of construction in New England ran to about $34 a ton, the costs in Europe for a comparable vessel would run between half again as much and twice as much.

Of course the New England colonists built ships for their own use as well as for sale to England. In addition to a great number of smaller vessels built for the fishing industry there were larger ships used for general trade. As early as 1745 vessels of the latter class numbered at least 1,000 and by 1775 this had increased to 2,000.

The construction of ships for use in England was also stimulated by the fact that New England was short on adequate currency and long on lumber and labor for the construction of ships. Consequently, the English merchants, having brought to the New England market woolens, clothing and other manufactured articles and disposed of them, found it profitable to order a ship built to their account. This they would load with naval stores, with furs, with rum or with other New England products. They would then sail for England where the ship as well as the cargo was disposed of at a handsome profit.

On two occasions, namely, during the Revolution and during the War of 1812, the young nation's merchant ships on the high seas suffered serious losses and its mercantile trade was disrupted, but on each occasion American naval vessels and American vessels that sailed as privateers or with letters of marque gave a good account of themselves. Thus, even in the test of war, American shipbuilders gained confidence in their ability to design and build new types of naval craft and American captains and seamen learned how to carry the fight into the enemies' waters. At the conclusion of the wars this confidence spread also to the merchant seamen.

We often hear or read references to the so-called "triangular trade" as though there was only one such triangle and as though everyone knew exactly where it lay and what was traded over it. This is very misleading because there were in fact a number of different triangles in use and over a period of time the exact routes and products of each triangle would vary.

For America, the classic example and the one usually intended in the references was the one that had its points or angles in New England, West Africa, the West Indies. From New England, rum and "trade goods" were carried to Africa and traded for slaves; the slaves were carried to the West Indies and sold and some of the proceeds invested in sugar and molasses; these were carried to Providence, Newport, Medford, Newburyport, Boston, and converted into rum which was loaded for Africa and so on round again. The trip from Africa to the West Indies was known as the "Middle Passage." It was the most nauseous and dangerous but also the most profitable—yielding a profit of 200 per cent when it was well executed whereas the other legs of the journey produced a mere 100 per cent.

This triangular trade had grown up out of a simpler affair. Originally New England traders in colonial times thought themselves fortunate enough if they could dodge England's restrictions and the French and Spanish letters of marque and the pirates, making a simple voyage to the West Indies and back. Up to the end of the eighteenth century the trip to Africa was simply a side trip from the West Indies made to the Slave Coast and back. After 1698 the colonists were formally admitted to the trade and the triangle developed.

But the triangle varied; not only did the voyage begin in many different ports in America, it ran at various times to various parts of the African coast and it landed in the west again wherever business was brisk and the trade could be completed with relative safety. This might be in Cuba or Barbados or some other West Indian island but it might also be as far north as an American port or as far south as Brazil.

We must remember that this was only the colonists' triangle, which became the American triangle; the British had already established and legalized a different triangle, Spain another and so on. Besides, slavery triangles existed in many trade voyages. After all, the

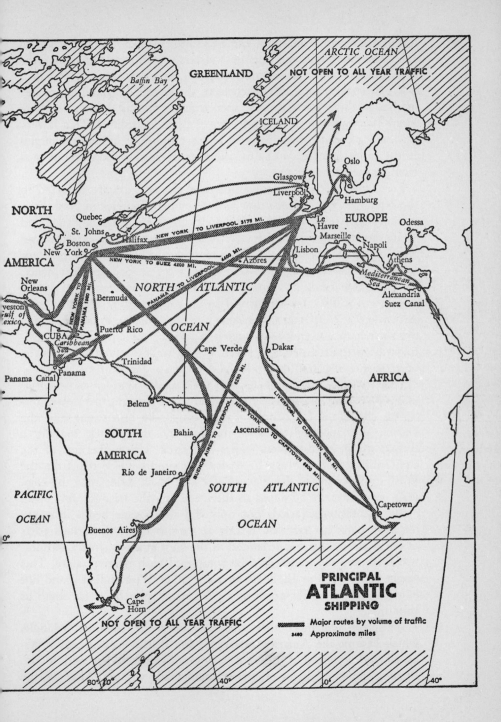

PRINCIPAL
ATLANTIC
SHIPPING

▬▬▬ Major routes by volume of traffic
2480 Approximate miles

triangle was simply an advantageous way of doing business—adding extra profit to what would otherwise be a two-way transaction.

When the *Columbia* and other early American vessels sailed from Boston to the American Northwest with manufactured articles and supplies which they traded for furs, which they bartered in China for tea and silks, which they sold in Boston, they were establishing what was technically a "triangular trade" even though their course traced out on a chart or globe might look like a warped pretzel.

The chapter on the whalers and the slavers shows in two special cases the rapid and far-reaching effects of the United States' power to recuperate. Other chapters show how the "regular traders" and the packet ships carried to Europe tobacco, cotton and other great staple products of American agriculture. As far as export freight was concerned, cotton was the special cargo that helped to sustain the development of coastwise and transatlantic packets.

As the Midwest opened up corn, wheat and other grains began to make up cargoes for the European markets. Then came shipments of cattle, of refrigerated and processed meats, ores and processed metals, special American machinery developments such as agricultural machinery, sewing machines, etc., and finally many classes of mass manufactured articles.

As far as imports were concerned, these have always reflected the diversified origin of the American population—a persistent belief in the excellence of certain Old World products as well as enduring preferences. The bands of association by blood and tradition that stretched across the Atlantic from colonial times on were reflected in trade. The trade continued from one era and generation to another.

Thus even after New Amsterdam became New York there continued to be a market there for Dutch products such as tiles and potteries, furniture, silverware, fabrics and laces, cheeses and other food products, chocolate and candies.

To this day, England supplies cloth and men's clothing, shoes, saddles and other fine leather goods, cutlery and special steel products and special machineries, fine linens and cottons, furniture, glassware and china.

Germany supplies surgical and scientific instruments, drugs and chemicals and toilet articles, optical goods and photographic equipment, special and precision machinery, printing and art reproductions, toys.

France sends silks, laces and other textiles, women's clothing and fashions, all kinds of equipment for ladies' wear such as hats and hosiery, gloves, perfumes, etc., special foods and wines, etc.

Switzerland sends clocks, watches and watch machinery, precision machine tools, toys and music boxes, etc., cheeses and chocolates, etc.

The list could be extended to many countries and many products. Of course over the centuries changes have taken place. In the beginning America and Canada shipped abroad raw materials and bulk agricultural products. In exchange the Western nations bought from Europe nearly all their finished or processed or manufactured products. As the American countries grew they set up their own processing and manufacturing plants and did an increasing amount of work on their own materials. This was often crude work but avoided shipping charges and duties and sold at reasonable prices compared with imported articles. Gradually American manufactures supplanted many foreign imports, a process that was encouraged and speeded up at times of hostility, crisis or war—which was often enough. In the nineteenth century America in part reversed the previous theories of trade by taking a lead in the quantity production of low-cost manufactured articles that could compete in world trade.

By the first quarter of the twentieth century a view or theory had grown among economists and historians that Atlantic trade and travel was, for the most part, made up of east and west passages following recognized bands of latitude and that this condition was more or less inevitable and likely to continue. Furthermore, it was supposed that this trade was competitive in character in most stages such as raw materials, processed goods and manufactures.

Now in mid-century their views require revision, at least with respect to their absolute and irrevocable character. East and west transatlantic trade is as brisk and lively as ever and probably necessary to the health and welfare of both shores. It has not fallen apart but to it there has been added, year by year since the close of World War II, an increasing Atlantic trade between North America and the Caribbean and North America and South America. Trade flows in both directions but is not quite equal. In this trade the northern countries supply manufactured goods of all kinds and the southern countries send raw materials or raw or easily processed agricultural products. There is variability from year to year, but in favorable years, if the north and south trade of the Pacific ports is added to that of the Atlantic ports, the total in volume and value begins to rival transatlantic trade between Europe and America. Thus a new dimension and a new pattern have been added to the fabric of Atlantic trade.

Part Three

MODERN HISTORY

Chapter 13

THE WHALERS

THE whale is the largest animal in the world and hunting the whale has been one of the largest and grimmest of human enterprises. It has been said that war consisted of long periods of dreary boredom punctuated by some hours of intense activity and heartbreaking fear. The same statement would apply to whaling. The men who manned the whaling vessels spent weeks, months and years in heavy work, slow sailing and dreary waiting. People often assume that the curse of whaling was the danger and the loss of life involved. The study of whaling logs makes it clear that the whalemen themselves accepted the hard work, the danger, the dirt, but what chiefly wore down their spirit was the long waiting and the boredom.

The danger was one of the compensations. It was the challenge and the excitement that held men to the chase, year after year. Of compensation, in terms of money, the whalemen saw very little. The whaling ships created prosperity for hundreds of ports on both sides of the Atlantic. They made fortunes for the owners and the operators, for the merchants and the shipyards and for a few captains, but very little of the money trickled down to the mates and the boat steerers and the crew. What little came their way easily slipped through the greasy fingers of the men who fought the whale and reduced him to so many tons of bone and barrels of oil.

Whaling was hunting on a grand scale and even men who are poor and ragged and battered by fortune may have courage and imagination and be stirred by great ventures. Whaling had its romantic aspects. One of these was the vast scale on which whaling, of necessity, had to be carried out. Those who signed on the crew list of a whaler never knew how long a voyage was going to last or where it was going to end. The whaleship was on a chase that followed the whales wherever they might lead. It stayed at sea either until the holds were full of oil or until the last pint of murky water had been issued and the last crumb of moldy biscuit consumed. A single whaling voyage might take the vessel from the Arctic to the Antarctic and extend for several years. Under such conditions the whaling ship in itself became a highly specialized and very intricate little world. This little world was made up of the officers and crew, the ship and its equipment. For long periods of time—perhaps for years—this ship would be moving about the vast oceans, cut off from contact with all the rest of the world and all of organized society. It would be entirely dependent upon its own ingenuity and its own resources. The ship, therefore, had to be stocked with all the food supplies that officers and crew would need for long periods of time; with all the weapons, tools and equipment needed for capturing the largest and most powerful animal in the world. In addition to that, it had to be a traveling factory for processing the whales it captured and reducing them to commercial products such as oils, greases, waxes, whalebone, ambergris and ivory. On top of all this, the vessel had to be equipped also to keep itself in operating condition; to build its casks for the storage of oil; to repair its boats; to replace broken spars; to renew running and standing rigging; to mend or replace its sails.

The whaler had to face all the dangers of ordinary ocean travel—hazards of rocks and reefs and unexpected shoals; of calms, of storms, of hurricanes. In addition it had some special and augmented risks of its own. One type of whale congregated at the margin of the Arctic and Antarctic ice. Here was the blind uncertainty of fog and the crushing uproar of berg and floe. Another type of whale traveled the warm waters of the vast Pacific. Here were reefs and shoals and savage natives. At any time and at any place the whaler had to be prepared to hunt the whale even if the chase carried it into unlighted, unknown, unvisited waters. In addition to this, week by week and month by month the men had to face and conquer the great whale himself.

Whaling is not only a very widespread, dangerous and specialized business, it is also a very old one. One of the earliest literary references to whaling occurs in a record of a lengthy Arctic voyage of an old

Norse sea captain. The story was originally told to King Alfred of England and was later reported by Hakluyt in Queen Elizabeth's time. In English the name of the voyager is given as "Othere"—in Norse, probably "Ottar." While describing the voyage, Othere said that in his own country, Helgeland, in northern Norway, the taking of walrus and whales was an important industry. The purpose of taking the walrus was to secure ivory, which had a very high price, and also the hides of the animals which were valued because they could be made into cables for ships. The walrus he refers to as "whale horse" —its length being no greater than seven ells—that is to say, with a length of about ten or twelve feet. The walrus, he says, is scarce.

He refers then to a common kind of whale, forty or fifty ells in length. This would be about seventy-five feet in length. He says that he was "one of six" who, in the space of three days, killed three score whales. Unfortunately, the record does not make it clear how they operated or by what method the whales were killed. Six men, in later ages, formed a normal crew for a whaleboat; but it is hard to believe that a single whaleboat could capture sixty whales in three days' time. It seems more likely that he meant that he was one of six captains, or leaders of boats, each with a crew. The meaning would then be that in the three-day period each averaged a take of ten whales.

How long before Othere's day some form of whaling may have commenced we do not know. Both the Eskimo and the natives of the northwest Pacific coast were known to have chased and captured some of the smaller species of whale, but when they began we do not know.

As far as Europe is concerned, other nations were not far behind the Norse. On the coast of Flanders ships were hunting whales about the same time as Othere was catching them off northern Norway. The English had ships out in the time of Alfric in the eleventh century. A type of moderate-sized whale has the name Biscayensis, because it was formerly caught in the Bay of Biscay. Basque fishermen began hunting it there in the thirteenth century. As whales of this type became exhausted, the Basque vessels moved farther and farther into the Atlantic and, by the end of the fourteenth century, they were hunting the same kind of whales off Newfoundland. Somewhat later they were whaling in Greenland.

In the sixteenth century there seems to have been a steady market in Europe for oil and other products derived from the whale. Every time an explorer discovered such waters or coastlines as attracted the whale, it also attracted European whalers. William Barents, sailing from Holland in the summer of 1596, while renewing his voyages to the north also discovered Bear Island. He also sailed to Spitsbergen, giving it that name. At the time, he supposed that Spitsbergen was part of Greenland. Though he was wrong in this supposition, he was right in believing that there was good hunting in this part of the world. From Barents' time on, the Dutch began building large fleets of ships which hunted whale, seal and furred animals in these waters.

Throughout the seventeenth and eighteenth centuries the Dutch whaling industry was both large and profitable. They built a town in Spitsbergen solely for the use of their whale fleet. Its name was "Smeerenberg" or, as we would say, "Blubbertown."

At the height of the industry as many as 1,000 whaling ships would touch here in the course of a season. Though the Dutch made extensive use of Spitsbergen, Barents was not the first to have been there. By the end of the twelfth century the Icelanders had already been in these waters. As early as 1557 the English had organized the Muscovy Company to carry on exploration, hunting and trade in the northern part of the world. It was on behalf of the Muscovy Company that Hudson made his trip in 1607 which stimulated the growth of British whaling. In Spitsbergen waters the English and the Dutch were soon joined by the Danes and the Basques. Whaling by European ships off the west coast of Greenland and in the Davis Straits, having been started by the Basques in the fifteenth century, had reached large proportions in the eighteenth century when as many as 350 ships would visit these waters during the season. The first ship from America came to these waters in 1750.

By this time whaling in America already had a history over one hundred years old. The colonists in Massachusetts began hunting the whale in local waters as early as 1630 and, from then on, it continued to be a prosperous business—first for the colony and then for the state.

Naturally these first ventures involved small ships and confined themselves to the taking of blackfish and the smaller kinds of whale that were often seen along the shore until they had been fished out. As whales became increasingly difficult to find alongshore, larger vessels were built and longer voyages undertaken.

In time New Bedford and Nantucket were among the foremost whaling ports of the world. Many other ports along the American coast soon joined in and regularly participated first in local whaling and then in the world-wide hunt. In Connecticut there was Mystic, Stonington, New London and many other ports. Whaling began on

Long Island as early as 1640 and Southampton, Cold Spring Harbor, Huntington, Greenport and other towns began sending out vessels.

It is claimed that a brigantine named the *Happy Return* sailed from Boston in command of Captain Timotheus Vanderuen in 1688 and was the first American ship to undertake a cruise after whales. Until ships began to sail in deep waters the whales that they captured were all of the smaller species, as we have already noted in the cases of the Flemish and Basque fishermen, the early Norse whalers and others.

Any reader of history knows that local tradition is not always to be trusted. The local story about the first catch of sperm whale goes like this. In 1712 Christopher Hussey of Nantucket was out after whales around the shores of the island. He was blown offshore by a strong gale from the west and, when this abated, he was at sea and surrounded by a large school of sperm whales. When he returned to Nantucket his little ship had one large sperm whale in tow. The story is at least accurate as to time, for deep-sea cruises for large whales began to leave the New England and Long Island coast early in the eighteenth century. The big whales that were the most sought after during the eighteenth and nineteenth centuries, when whaling was at its height, were found either in the Arctic or Antarctic, or in the warmer waters of the great oceans.

The chief of the cold water whales was the right whale. The reason he was given this name was that he was equipped with special organs that made him more valuable to the hunter than any other whale. The material that he furnished which was so priceless to organized society was called "whalebone." Also, in the markets ashore, it was known as "whale-fin."

Like most of the other names that are attached to whaling, the term itself is erroneous and misleading—just as the term "fisheries" is misleading and also the term black "fish." The whales, of course, are not fish at all. They are mammals like a horse or a cow or a human being. They are very specialized mammals that, in the course of adapting themselves to living in the oceans, have undergone a number of strange evolutionary changes. One of these changes is the disappearance from the outside of the animal of any structures that could be called legs, but a dissection of a whale would reveal relatively small bones that represented rudimentary legs. Another change was in the enormous size of the whale's mouth and the peculiar structure of the whale's head.

This brings us back to the matter of whalebone. The right whale has no teeth and doesn't need any. Instead, he has this material called "whalebone" which is a special development of the palate or roof of the whale's upper jaw. From this spot a great fringe of long plates grows down into the cavity of the right whale's mouth. These plates were made up of a material like cartilage with long bundles of fibers growing through it. The fibers frayed out all around the sides and margins of each plate. The purpose of this arrangement is to surround the whale's mouth with a sort of screen of fibers that acts like a sieve or filter. The lower jaw of the right whale is shaped like a great scoop. In feeding, the whale swims along at the surface of the water scooping up a great mouthful of it. When he works his jaw and tongue the water is forced out between the plates and fringes of the whalebone and the food for the whale is deposited in the fibrous network.

It seems strange that great creatures like the right whale, and another whale very similar to it called the bowhead, which are the largest among all living creatures, could live on animals that are so small as almost to require a microscope for their identification. The tiny creatures that nourish these great whales float at the surface of the sea in enormous numbers. They are known to the whalemen as "brit" and to the scientists as "plankton." Plankton, in unbelievably large volume, develop rapidly in northern waters, particularly along the margin of the ice fields. The presence of these little animals in sea water tends to change its color so that northern waters rich in plankton are very often green rather than blue. Sometimes the growth of plankton is so rapid that great stretches of the sea take on a brown or reddish look. In Greenland waters there are two kinds of plankton, both important to whales: *Euphausiids,* these are tiny crustaceans; and *Calanus finmarchicus,* this is a copepod.

Studies have been made that show that there is a regular proportion established between the number of plankton present in waters and the number of whales that can be caught in any one season. How many plankton that must be and how fast they must develop can be illustrated by the following observation: the stomach of a single whale has revealed the presence of 1,200 liters (or about 1,050 quarts) of this whale food.

Inasmuch as the Greenland whaling fishery, in the days of its prime, used to include hundreds of ships and inasmuch as each ship expected to take hundreds of whales, to supply thousands of barrels of oil, the richness of the plankton beds in these waters is difficult to comprehend.

There is another way of picturing the enormous amount of food required. This way is to concentrate on the energy expended by a single whale in just going about his day-by-day business. In order to breathe and to oxidize his food so that he can build up fat and muscle, the whale requires thirty-eight liters (or thirty-three quarts) of oxygen each minute of his existence. This is only an average figure. Whales take into their systems enormous quantities of air which they gradually use up as they swim at the surface or under water. The whale is an animal and has no gills such as are possessed by fish for taking oxygen from sea water. When the oxygen from the air that the whale has taken into his lungs becomes exhausted, he must rise to the surface to breathe again. Whales do their breathing through nostrils or blow holes on the upper surface of their body or near the highest part of the animal when it is afloat in the water. Since the whale is a warm-blooded animal, since he often is swimming in quite cold water, and since, also, the air in his system has been under great pressure, when he breathes he sends up a vapory mist that can be seen at a considerable distance. This the old whalemen called "blowing." The whale never spurts water though many an artist who has never been among whales makes it appear as though this were the case. The thirty-eight liters of air per minute that the whale takes into his system must produce a great amount of power. Scientists who have given some time to the study of whales assert that the whale customarily travels at around ten knots. In order to propel his great bulk through the water at this speed he must develop forty-seven horsepower. This we may think of as the horsepower at "cruising speed." It is the only statement regarding horsepower for whales that I can find. Obviously it is not a measure of what the whale can do when he really puts his heart and back into it.

When the right whale races across the ocean with a boat in tow, or when a sperm whale dives or does some of the other powerful and unexpected things that whales are always doing, they must be expending energy at a greater horsepower rating than that suggested by the scientists.

It was the whalebone that made the right whale "right" but why was whalebone itself right or valuable? The answer to that is the ladies.

The various shapes in which ladies felt it necessary to appear in the past centuries were very different from the shapes in which they have elected to cheer our eyes today, but the requirements of fashion then were just as changeable and just as exacting. The ladies counted on one kind of whale, the right whale, to keep them in trim. They counted on whale oil from several kinds of whale to provide illumination for the lamps of the chandeliers and wall sconces. If the light of the lamps was too strong they turned to the clear light of the candles made from the spermaceti of the sperm whale, and it was this whale who supplied the ambergris that served as a carrier for the ladies' perfume.

In the days of whaling metals like steel were rigid, heavy and limited in their application. Plastics were nonexistent and there were no synthetic fabrics like lastex and nylon. The one thing the ladies could count on which they knew to be durable, flexible and relatively light was whalebone.

Whalebone went into corsets but it also went into shaped materials for collars and cuffs—framework to give shape to sleeves or the brim of a hat or into a score of other places that needed attention. It was used for the ribs of sunshades, parasols and umbrellas and, no doubt, had other uses too that it is difficult now to reconstruct.

Whalebone brought fantastic prices. In the beginning, a ton of good Greenland whalebone cost $700. In the 1850's, about the time when the industry was fully developed and competition was extraordinarily active, whalebone brought only $25. Oddly enough, the highest price ever paid for whalebone was about $2,000 a ton. This price was reached because whaling had declined rapidly and, at the same time, people did not know how to get along without it.

The best quality of whalebone was always supplied by the right whale of Labrador waters though many other fisheries in the Arctic and Antarctic were also diligently developed. The price of these developments in Greenland and elsewhere was paid by ships lost and lives lost throughout the whole period of the whaling industry and was colossal. It would take a whole chapter to even suggest the form of losses in the whaling industry. But fortunately there is no need for such an extended treatment. The following incidents that come readily to hand illustrate what could happen.

In the year 1835 the British had been for some time exploring the Arctic shores and waters of Canada and had also been engaged in the Greenland–Davis Straits fisheries. Hull was one of the most important of the British whaling ports. In December of that year thirty-four shipowners of that port sent a memorial to the admiralty asking assistance. One of the whalers, the *Alfred,* had come into the port of Hull and reported that eleven ships had been beset (that is, frozen in) at Davis Straits by a sudden and early descent of winter. The 600 men aboard were caught with little chance of escaping. The value represented by these ships and the products they had aboard was approximately £60,000. It was no new thing for a few ships to be caught in the ice. Almost every year some ships suffered in this fashion but eleven ships was a number large enough to create local and even national interest. James Clarke Ross, a distinguished Arctic explorer, volunteered his services and, with the help of the admiralty and a popular subscription, attempted to carry out a rescue operation. He became commander of a vessel from Whitby named the *Cove.* He encountered extremely bad weather and his attempts at rescue were not notably successful. Some ships were wrecked but fortunately a number of them drifted out of the ice and were able to make their way to England.

As a sort of footnote, the record also shows that in the year 1836 six whalers were again caught in the ice. This time there were only 300 men aboard and this time the admiralty declined to fit out a relief expedition. Probably, again, some of these vessels eventually drifted out of the ice and returned home and, probably also, some of them were abandoned.

It was not simply the Greenland waters that brought accident and disaster to whalers, nor was the hazard of being frozen in the ice restricted to Atlantic waters. Ships from the United States Atlantic coast were the pioneers in developing the Arctic fisheries in the Bering Sea and the Bering Straits and along the Arctic shores of Alaska. In 1876 twenty vessels were abandoned and destroyed in the Arctic ice but the greatest catastrophe of all, judged by loss of vessels, came in 1871 when a fleet of thirty-two vessels was caught in the ice and had to be abandoned. The officers, crews, wives and families aboard who were shipwrecked and stranded numbered over 1,200 people. While the big whaling ships could not be moved, it was fortunate that the whaleboats were able to find a way around or over the ice. Fortunately also, seven American ships had remained clear of the ice a little less than 100 miles distant. After some days of traveling through high winds and high seas, the whaleboats managed to reach the ice-free ships, and out of the 1,200 persons, not a man, woman or child was lost.

It is worth noting where the ships that were lost and abandoned in the ice sailed from, for it provides a little picture of this part of the whaling industry. Twenty-two of the vessels came from New Bedford; two from New London; two from Martha's Vineyard; three from San Francisco and four from Honolulu.

These are a few of the large-scale collective accidents that happened to whaling vessels. They represent one type of danger in whaling. The other kind of danger or disaster was that which happened to individual whalemen or to the crews of whaleboats when they were away from the ship and engaged in harpooning a whale.

The things that whales could do to men and men could do to whales is almost endless. When a man who may be six feet in height stands up in the bow of a boat less than thirty feet long to lean over and thrust the long and painful shaft of an iron into the hide of a powerful animal that could be anything up to 100 feet long, a rapid succession of strange events could take place. Every whale is dangerous but different types of whale are dangerous in different ways. The danger spot in the right whale was in his tail or flukes. His mouth was relatively harmless. The danger spot in the sperm whale was in his long, punishing jaw, armed with enormous ivory teeth. The right whale could see to either side but could not look forward. Consequently he was always attacked and harpooned head-on. The sperm whale could see ahead of him but was not very conscious of what went on behind him so was always attacked and harpooned from the rear. The greatest danger from the right whale was that he would twist himself around and batter the whaleboat into kindling wood with one swish of his great tail. The great danger from the sperm whale was that, when struck, he might decide to "sound," that is, to dive deep into the water and keep going as far and as fast as possible. Sometimes sounding whales carried down the whaleboat and its entire crew before anyone had the power or the presence of mind to cut the ropes. Another method of response of a whale to having a long barbed iron thrust into his hide was to start with great determination and great speed for some point beyond the horizon. On these occasions the boat steerer had his hands full, for the rate of speed was terrific—the sharp prow of the whaleboat cutting through the water and throwing a wave of white spray to either side. A long and fast tow of this kind was referred to by the old-time whalers as a "Nantucket sleigh ride."

If the whale tired himself out in long straightaway charges, the boat crew was relatively lucky, but whales had countless other tricks. Sometimes the whale would swim in circles and the crew of the whaleboat would have to keep their boat on an even keel. Some whales, particularly sperm whales, would dive. The problem then was one of time and of how much line the sounding whale took with him.

Whale line was coiled into tubs to keep it neat and handy for use. A full tub of ⅔-inch manila whale line would be as long as 220 fathoms and some tubs held as much as 300 fathoms. The ends of the line were always arranged so that another tub full of line could be added, and sometimes several boats contributed their tubs of line to take care of one sounding whale. One log book records that once, in the Pacific, a sperm whale sounding ran out with four tubs of line joined end to end (7,200 feet) and was still going strong when the resources of all the whaleboats were exhausted, and the crew sat dumfounded as the last bight of the line flipped over the gunwales and disappeared.

Even if a whale did not circle or did not dive, even if it ran a true compass course, the result to the whalemen was not always a huge success. Often whaleboats were carried out of sight of the parent ship. Sometimes, after killing a whale, they had to wait hours or days before being picked up. Sometimes they were never picked up, and instead, had to make their way over thousands of miles of water before reaching an island or a seacoast. On a number of occasions whales appear to have pulled boat crews across the horizon and into oblivion.

To have a whale overturn a boat or send it high in the air with a flip of its flukes was a common occurrence. Occasionally a whale would charge a boat head-on, splintering the boat and scattering the crew in all directions. The sperm whale occasionally got a boat between its jaws and mashed it to pieces, unfortunate members of the crew also being mashed. On at least one occasion a whale chewed a boat into two distinct halves, grabbed the mate in his huge jaws and sounded. Other members of the crew, clinging to the wreckage, thought this would be the end of the matter. Presently the whale bobbed up again and spit the mate out into the mutilated bow of the whaleboat. The whaler was stunned and badly battered but, after a recovery period of several weeks, was hunting again from a new boat.

The whale was a large and tough adversary. He was capable of not only knocking to pieces the light and frail whaleboats sent out to capture him but also of creating trouble for whale ships and for other ships too. A number of ships were sunk and lost because they had the misfortune to run into a whale, unintentionally, some dark night.

In 1640 a ship, while running before a gale, stove a hole in her side by running onto a whale. The same thing happened in 1796 to the ship *Harmony* which hit a whale off the coast of Brazil and sank with all its cargo, but the crew escaped in the boats.

In 1859, the ship *Herald of the Morning* came into Hampton Roads, in Virginia, leaking badly, having struck a whale off Cape Horn.

In 1807 the ship *Union* of Nantucket was twelve days out on a passage in the direction of Brazil and was sailing along comfortably at seven knots when there was a collision so great that those aboard believed that they had run on a rock. When the rock moved and swam away they knew that they had hit a whale. This was at ten o'clock at night. By midnight the ship was sinking so that it was no longer of any use to work the pumps. By this time a storm had blown up and a high sea was running. The sails of the boats were blown away. After that, two of the boats were lashed together. These boats, after eight days, finally reached the island of Flores in the Azores, having traveled 600 miles.

Strange accidents happened in the whale fisheries. In 1802 Peter Paddock was in command of the ship *Lion.* He threw an iron into a whale which escaped. Thirteen years later, when he was captain of the *Lady Adams,* cruising thousands of miles away in a different part of the Pacific, he captured the same whale—with the *Lion's* iron still embedded in its hide.

This was a coincidence without particular meaning. For example, on more than one occasion whales were taken in Arctic waters near the Alaskan shore having in them irons marked with the names of ships which never hunted in the Pacific but confined their activities to Davis Straits and west Greenland waters.

This showed, therefore, that there was such a thing as a northwest passage between the Atlantic and Pacific—at least a passage big enough for the navigation of a right whale and probably, therefore, big enough to take a small ship.

A number of cases are known of "fighting whales," who built up reputations for ferocity. Melville's Moby Dick is not entirely a fictitious animal. Sometimes whales killed men and smashed a succession of boats before being finally captured.

Though it may seem odd that a big ship should run down a whale, it is still more extraordinary that a whale should run down a ship, but accidents of this kind did, indeed, happen. On November 20th, 1819, the ship *Essex,* George Pollard, Jr., captain, came among a school of whales. The chief mate's boat was stove in by the flukes of a whale that had been struck. In the meanwhile, the captain's and second mate's boats were fast to another whale. The chief mate, in charge of the ship, had headed the vessel in the direction of the captain's boat when, suddenly, a whale of about 85 feet in length shot from the water quite near to the ship and charged directly at the *Essex* and struck her on the bows on one side. The whale was stunned but, after resting a few moments, it recovered and swam away. While the whale recovered, the ship did not, for some of the planks of the ship had been displaced and the vessel was leaking rapidly. Still, repairs might have been made had not the whale reappeared and charged again. By this time the vessel was turned over on her beam-ends and all that was left for the mate and crew to do was to launch the other boats and pile in. While nothing could be done to repair the vessel, it took several days before it finally foundered. During this time the officers and crew made some repairs to their whaleboats and took aboard all the supplies and equipment they could salvage. The coast of Peru was 3,000 miles away. It took them five days to reach a deserted island. One of the boats became separated from the other two. During the 2,500 mile row to Juan Fernandez Island, many of the men died of hunger and thirst. Those who died were eaten by the survivors. The first boat was picked up by an English brig called the *Indian* and three survivors were taken aboard. The survivors, therefore, had been in the whaleboat from November 23rd until February 17th—that is, eighty-six days. The captain's boat was not picked up until five days later—that is, ninety-one days. The captain and one man were the sole survivors.

In 1858 the *Ann Alexander* of New Bedford, John S. DeBlois the captain, on August 24th attempted to capture a whale which smashed two of its whaleboats. The men from these wrecked whaleboats succeeded in reaching the ship. One boat was still aboard when the whale appeared and charged at the *Alexander*. The hole made in the ship near the keel was so large that the vessel started to sink. The men aboard barely had time to toss a few things into a boat and to escape from the ship before it sank. The whaleboats were in poor condition and food and water were scarce. Fortunately, the survivors were picked up by the ship *Nantucket* of Nantucket within two days. Five months after the wreck of the *Alexander* a whale was captured by a ship from New Bedford called the *Rebecca Simms*. This whale had two irons in its body carrying the name of the *Alexander*. What positively identified the whale as the one that had sunk the ship was the fact that large pieces of the ship's timbers and planks were still embedded in the whale's hide.

In 1901 the barque *Cathleen* was attacked by a wounded whale. The hole created by the attack was so large that the ship began to sink at once, leaving barely enough time for the captain and his wife and the crew to get into three of the whaleboats. Fortunately, the vessel was in the Atlantic, not far from the West Indies. One boat arrived at Dominica, another at Barbados and the third was picked up by a ship. There are other cases.

I have heard critics, who otherwise liked Melville's great classic of whaling, *Moby Dick,* argue that the closing scene, in which Moby Dick attacks and sinks the *Pequod* is too incredible to be an artistic success. Yet the cases cited above show that this was not an unlikely occurrence. In fact, it seems to me that there is no episode among all those mentioned by Melville that is not already recorded in the log books of some actual voyage.

The whalers of Europe and America added many shores and islands to our geographies. In the eighteenth and nineteenth centuries whaling vessels from the Atlantic coast of the United States made the most remote parts of the world familiar with the strength of American ships and the courage and resourcefulness of American seamen.

At the beginning of the nineteenth century American whalers were literally operating both in the Arctic and the Antarctic. In 1778 Cook sailed through the Bering Straits and explored the Arctic coasts from Icy Point in America to Cape North in Siberia. It was not long afterward that American whalers from the New England coast were chasing the whale on these waters. As early as 1820 the whale fisheries of the North Pacific had reached considerable proportions. From this time on lost and shipwrecked American whalers had the misfortune to arrive in Japanese waters. The best treatment they could expect was humiliation, and from here on it ranged into unspeakable brutality. In fact, it was the effort to rescue the stranded whalers and to reach an agreement with Japan for a more humane treatment that accounted for many repeated attempts to visit Japan and establish diplomatic contact with that country. As early as 1837 an American ship, the *Morrison*, was bombarded from two different ports. Efforts continued, however, and culminated in Commodore N. C. Perry's successful negotiations in 1854.

In the meantime, on the other side of the Arctic, an English whaler named William Scorsby, in 1806 reached a record farthest north in the Spitsbergen region, and his son, William Scorsby, Jr., published an account of the Arctic regions which became a classic on this subject and, two years later, made the first extensive investigations on the east coast of Greenland.

In Antarctic waters we have seen already that an American whaling and sealing expedition from Stonington, Connecticut, had its ships in the South Shetland Islands in 1820. At this time N. B. Palmer not only reported the Antarctic land mass but also visited it in his tiny sloop *Hero*. The next season, Palmer, as captain of a larger vessel, the sloop *James Monroe,* carried out an extensive cruise along the Antarctic shores.

In 1823 James Weddell took a whaling vessel into the Weddell Sea area of the Antarctic. About this time also, a number of discoveries in the Antarctic are accounted for by the enterprise and foresight of a firm operating a number of whaling vessels. Captain Enderby instructed the captains of all of his ships, whenever they could do so, to push their operations southward and to report their discoveries. Under this policy Captain Biscoe discovered two islands—Biscoe and Adelaide. He also discovered a part of the continent to which he gave the name Enderby Land. A coast adjacent to Enderby Land was added by Captain Kemp and Balenny added small islands.

In the 1890's whaling ships were operating in the Antarctic under the ownership of an old Norwegian whaler named Sven Foyen who had developed a whaling gun. In 1893 one of his captains, C. A. Larsen, in the *Jason,* discovered and named the Foyen coast in Greenland; King Oscar Land; Mt. Chasen and Robertson Island. In 1895 Captain Leonard Kristiansen, operating another Foyen whaler, the *Antarctic,* touched at Cape Adair, and the captain, together with Carsten Borchgrevink and H. J. Hull, made the first landing on the Antarctic continent. The same Borchgrevink, then in the *Southern Cross,* in 1898-1900 led the first party to spend a winter on the Antarctic continent.

So much for the cold-water whalers. The warm-water, or sperm whale, fisheries scattered American ships in both the Atlantic and the Pacific. In the Pacific many islands both large and small were first seen and reported by vessels from the Atlantic coast of America. Captain Edmund Fanning came from Stonington, Connecticut, and thus grew up with N. B. Palmer. He provided an account of Palmer's discoveries in the Antarctic. His own contribution, however, was discovering Fanning Island in the South Pacific in 1798. Wake, Howland, Baker Islands and Kingman Reef are among those that were discovered this way. Some of the information collected by captains on lonely whaling voyages was very useful to us in our late war in the Pacific.

An old friend of mine, Andy Furuseth of the Seaman's Union, once said: "Ships are the tools of seamen." The truth of his remark was never better illustrated than in the matter of the whaleboat and its equipment. These were the developments of seamen. No prescription by law, made at a distance, could have produced them. They were the natural evolutionary products of a life-and-death struggle. They were produced on the spot by alert and ingenious men whose very existence depended upon the precision and effectiveness of the tools and functions that they worked out for themselves.

As long as the whale had to be hunted—and the whole fabric of society ashore for some centuries assumed and accepted the existence of all the products derived from whale hunting—organs and functions that whalemen evolved for themselves were the best compromise possible between the urge for personal survival and the need for getting the job done. From both points of view, the solutions to the problem that the whalemen themselves arrived at were so successful that an attempt at interference by legislation would not only have lessened the capacity to get the job done but also have increased the hazards of the chase.

Just as legislation would have been of no avail, so would individual invention, at best, have been of dubious assistance. The successful solutions were the product of group activity and teamwork. Here was a case where a test under laboratory conditions was impossible. Every instrument and its function had to be tested not only in the field of battle but actually at the firing line. A good and clear diagram of a whaleboat and its equipment in place will do something to reveal the intricate character of the equipment required to approach and harpoon a whale, but it requires more than this to understand the way in which it was used—the carefully worked out operations of the six-man crew, each of whom had a predetermined series of operations to perform, which varied according to a number of different situations that might arise during the progress of the chase.

The best way to arrive at some understanding of these matters is to visit a marine museum such as the one at Mystic, Connecticut, or the Whaling Museum at New Bedford. Here, whaleboats and their equipment can be studied in detail. The New Bedford Museum includes a model of a whaling ship done to one-half natural size and

Mystic is fortunate in having preserved the *Thomas W. Morgan*—an actual example of a characteristic American whaling vessel. Since a visit to these museums is not possible for all of us, it is fortunate that the marine artist, Gordon Grant, a great many years ago, for his own amusement constructed a model of an American whaleboat and its equipment. It was unusually accurate and unusually complete and, of course, in Mr. Grant's hands it was not only a technical success but also a work of art. Later Mr. Grant not only published his plans and instructions but also made arrangements to provide materials for the construction of a similar model, so that today models of whaleboats are fairly common.

This brings up an interesting point. This model represents a standard practice in the classic period of American whaling. Only one model is required since there was just one acceptable way of arranging and operating a whaleboat and few, if any, variations were tolerated. Many thousands of whaleboats were in use each year and every whaleboat was similarly equipped and similarly operated. Each one of the many items of equipment had its appointed place and its methods of use. This, alone, made it possible to organize the many crews needed and to undertake the endless renewal of boats and of supplies and equipment that was required in the conduct of the cruises. Here was an almost perfect standardization of parts and of function in a nonmachine industry. This made interchangeability possible. Once trained, a boat steerer or a tub oarsman could feel at home in any whaleboat of any ship in a fleet. At his post he would find identical tools in identical places.

It is interesting to observe that the whaleboat, though much smaller in size, had almost exactly the same lines and very much the same type of construction as the classic Viking ship. This is very nicely brought out in Mr. Stanley Rogers' publication *The Sailing Ship—A Study in Beauty*. It is possible that the similarity between the modern whaleboat and the ancient Viking ship is accounted for by the fact that they both used oars and also sail and that they operated under similar conditions and sometimes in identical waters, but the whaleboat had a very ancient history and it is just as likely that there was a more direct connection; that the size, the design and the general construction of the whaleboat changed very little throughout whaling history. The boat in which Othere hunted whales off northern Norway in the ninth century probably looked very much like the whaleboat that was used by the last American whalers in the far Pacific only a few decades ago. Othere's boat was probably the ancestor of the one that you can see in the museums today.

The classic type of whaling began to decline after the middle of the nineteenth century. Costs rose, prices declined, cheap kerosene or coal oil came in to replace whale oil and paraffin candles replaced spermaceti candles.

Whaling has not entirely ceased but it has become a highly mechanized industry requiring enormous capital. Permanent whaling stations have been established in Antarctic waters. Great powered steamers have been built that are good examples of floating factories. They are attended by a score of smaller steamers who do the actual hunting. Some of the factory steamers are contrived so that they can swallow up a whale in a great mouth built into the bows of the vessel. In the hold of the factory vessel a number of divided operations provide that every ounce of the whale that can yield a few cents' worth of value shall be utilized.

Was whaling more a business or more a sport? I do not know the answer to that question though I am sure it had some features of both. Whether played for gain or for game it was grim. Nearly every dangerous trade that I know of has, at some time, been practiced by one or more amateurs. I can think of no case of an amateur whaleman. The genial and learned Dr. Robert Cushman Murphy of the American Museum came as near as anyone has ever come to being an amateur whaler. He made a whaling voyage but he did so in pursuit of his profession of being an ornithologist and naturalist. Whatever his rating, he has, in recently publishing his *Log Book for Grace,* provided us with a fascinating account of a young man's experiences on one of the last of the old whaling ships.

American whaling began in the time of the first colonists but extended into our own day. It provided America with one of its first industries and materials for international trade. American whaling was based on old and general Atlantic patterns but after 1743, when the Massachusetts whalemen began to install furnaces and trypots in their vessels, longer cruises and larger vessels ensued and the characteristic American whaler took form. These whalers appearing in London opened up trade not only in whale oil but in many other commodities also. Nearly all whalers, European as well as American, were built in Atlantic ports even though they were to operate in the Arctic, Antarctic or Pacific fisheries. The whalers discovered countless islands in the Pacific, a few of which have been claimed by America and utilized, and whalers early carried the American flag and American prestige around the world.

Chapter 14

THE SLAVERS

SLAVERY had an important place in the development of Atlantic travel and Atlantic history. Today we may wince a little at having to make such an admission but we can somewhat temper our regret by recollecting that until one hundred and fifty years ago, slavery, in some form or other, was an accepted fact in most parts of the world. It had existed for a long time; it was sometimes regretted by moralists and philosophers but more usually accepted by others as an inherent part of social organization. It was part of an Old World tradition and when transferred to the New World it was accepted as long as it seemed to have economic and social utility. For centuries the slave trade from Africa to America was the subject of official recognition and regulation and a subject of negotiation in diplomatic exchanges between governments. Until the opening of the nineteenth century it was energetically pursued by respected citizens of many countries on both sides of the Atlantic.

Whatever its moral results, the physical and practical results of slavery were far-reaching. It was started in a modest and genteel way by the Portuguese and first seriously developed by the Spaniards in the West Indies. It was, together with fishing and whaling, one of the few employments open to the men and vessels of the British-American colonies. In the beginning, slaving was often undertaken as a side line or combined with other trade but gradually it became a separate venture and tended to develop a special type of vessel.

Slavery affected not only the countries and states employing slave labor but also Atlantic areas like England and New England that were deeply involved in the slave trade.

The rapid development of the New World was in a considerable measure due to slavery and whole industries were founded on it such as mining and sugar in the West Indies; cotton, tobacco, indigo and rice in the southern colonies and states. Slavery added an important and permanent element to the population of the New World notably in the West Indies, in Brazil and the United States. Altogether the slave trade and the slave ships played an important part in Atlantic history and some aspects of their operations, though interesting, are not well understood.

At the time slavery grew up as an operating system, social contrasts between slavery and freedom were not as sharp as they are today. There did not then exist in any country large bodies of free and mobile labor composed of men and women who enjoyed a great measure of economic independence and all the rights of nationality, citizenship and suffrage. The contrast to be drawn was not that between the absolute slave and the absolute free laborer but between a slave and whole class of people who enjoyed various grades of relative freedom all the way from that of slave to that of independent employer.

In the colonial period all the nations that sent colonists to the New World were still strongly marked by feudal traditions and practices. In varying measure this was true of Spain, Portugal, France, England and Holland. It was assumed and accepted that the leaders of the colonial enterprises would become the large landholders and as such would exercise economic privileges and also a measure of political and social control over those who helped them in the development of the properties whether slaves, indentured servants, peons or laborers for hire.

A large number of those who came as colonists to American shores came as indentured servants with few possessions save the clothes on their backs and with no independent financial resources. They signed an agreement with an individual master or with a colonizing company under which in exchange for their transportation and for their maintenance they were, for a variable period of time that might run up to seven years, to perform labor for the other party to the contract. But an independent and enterprising indentured servant by performing extra services or by other means might be able to shorten his term of service and buy his freedom. In any event, he became free and independent on the termination of the contract. The fact remains that many American colonists were very far removed from freedom as we understand it today when they set foot on American soil.

Quite apart from the matter of indentured service there was also the matter of apprenticeship. All the trades were highly organized and were in the hands of master craftsmen, and all of those who were learning a trade were bound, for a period of years, to perform services for the master craftsman in exchange for education and training. Many colonists came to America bound to a master craftsman for a period of years by the rules and conditions of the craft.

Thus in many ways the distinction between slavery and other forms of service was originally not as clear-cut as we suppose today. As time went on and men won new political and economic liberty in America, the separation between slave and freeman became greater and sharper.

We have already noted some of the origins of the transatlantic slave trade. Its seeds were planted when the ships of Henry the Navigator began bringing back to Portugal occasional slaves from the West African coast. The first permanent Portuguese stations in Africa were set up south of Cape Verde in 1482 and in the succeeding years and from this time on a modest trade in slaves became an accepted part of the Portuguese development of West Africa. The Portuguese trade never reached any very large proportions.

From the literature and art of the period it did appear that no wholesale abuses attended this traffic and that a considerable proportion of the early slaves returned to Europe from Africa passed into personal or domestic service. They were apparently regarded as curiosities and as such enjoyed a number of rights and prerogatives.

Slavery of this European type was not destined for any great measure of success and could have gone on for years with no world-shaking consequences. The fact was that Europe, in the fifteenth century, was plentifully supplied with labor and that as a consequence labor of all classes was still relatively cheap. In fact, Europe was in a better position to export labor than to import.

What accounted for the rapid and spectacular development of Negro slavery was the discovery of the vast regions of agricultural lands in the West Indies and the American continents. Slavery would have had a slower growth and have been more restricted if the Spaniards and the other conquerors and colonists had made better use of the natives that already populated those territories. This was particularly true in the West Indies and in Central America that had a large Indian population.

This Indian population disappeared in a remarkably brief time following the arrival of the Europeans. It disappeared for a variety of causes. In part it was wiped out in warfare; in part it was eliminated by torture and by the system of slave labor imposed by the conquerors; in great measure it was eliminated by disease. The Indians had built up no immunity to many diseases that had long been endemic in Europe so that many of the ills that we regard as childhood diseases produced in the native populations all the ravages of a plague. When forced labor on plantations and living under congested conditions in stockades and compounds was substituted for their natural outdoor life, they became a prey to these diseases and died by the hundreds of thousands.

Columbus on his first voyage to the Caribbean islands captured Indians and took them back to Spain. Later some shiploads of Indians were sent as slaves to Spain. This was shortsighted. Quite apart from the resistance that it aroused in Queen Isabella, it was doomed to failure. The settlement and labor system employed by the Spanish in the West Indies was so destructive of Indian life that in the first quarter of the sixteenth century, as the writings of Las Casas show, the native population of many of the islands had all but disappeared. There was a shortage of labor to continue the operation of the mines, the workshops and the plantations that the Spaniards had established.

In the face of this labor shortage there was soon a demand for Negro slaves from Africa and the trade was developed first by the Spaniards in the West Indies and later, progressively, in other areas. The Portuguese in the colonization and development of Brazil encountered somewhat similar conditions, made many of the same mistakes and resorted to the same solution—Negro slavery.

The first Negro slaves were brought into Hispaniola in 1501. At this time the Indians were still being used as slave labor so that there was a period in the West Indies marked both by Indian slavery and Negro slavery. The colonization system had been so brutal, the disappearance of the Indian population so alarming, and the appeals of Las Casas and other missionaries to the court in Spain had been so persistent that there was built up a strong tendency to reform. New laws respecting the colonial system and particularly the treatment of the Indians were passed in 1542 and 1543. In theory at least these did away with Indian slavery though they were difficult to enforce and abuses continued. However, from this time on the position of the surviving Indians in the West Indies and elsewhere began to improve. In the West Indies this improvement was partly due to the fact that Negro slaves, in increasing number, were arriving in the colonies.

Apparenty Negro slavery in North America began in 1619. In that year a Dutch privateering vessel landed at the Jamestown colony in Virginia and sold its cargo of slaves to the settlers. From this time on there was a gradual but steady increase in the use of Negro slaves in the English colonies of the south. In Virginia the discovery and development of tobacco as a prime commercial crop accounted for the increasing use of slave labor. They were employed in clearing the land, in cultivating and in moving the crop preparatory to shipment.

Tobacco is a crop that soon exhausts the soil and this was particularly true in the methods of cultivation that were then employed. This, in addition to the naturally increasing demand for tobacco in the English and other European markets, brought about the necessity for continually clearing new lands and increasing the area under cultivation. Negroes were in demand to carry out the heavier part of this labor. As long as the tobacco market was good and lands were available and white labor scarce, slave labor was readily resorted to.

Virginia was the best tobacco country and prospered on this single crop. In fact, the rapid development of this crop and the furor for its cultivation that seized the colonists accounted for neglect in the establishment of other industries and manufactures which had been one of the prime motives of the Virginia company in establishing the colony. Other southern colonies had difficulty in discovering profitable enterprises. The great plantations which were soon established in Virginia did not extend into North Carolina. This region was divided into smaller farms and many of them were taken up by indentured servants that had won their freedom. They raised cattle and other domestic animals, cultivated some tobacco and corn. The general situation of the colony did not lend itself to the employment of slave labor.

South Carolina, on the other hand, furnished a different situation. The cultivation of rice had been introduced into Virginia in 1647 but production was not large and this crop was soon replaced by tobacco. When rice was introduced into the low swampy lands that lay along the South Carolina coast it did well and large yields resulted. The long hot summers brought the crop to full maturity.

While the crop thrived under these conditions, the white settlers suffered. They either could not or would not adapt themselves to the heavy work entailed in rice cultivation in the hot and humid surroundings. Negro labor, however, was more resistant to the conditions and large plantations, utilizing slave labor, developed rapidly. Indigo formed a second commercial crop in South Carolina. The success of this crop was almost wholly dependent on experiments carried out by Miss Eliza Lucas and the industry did well until the period of the Revolution. In 1775 the exported crop ran to over a million pounds.

Despite the fact that Virginia and South Carolina provided situations suitable for the employment of Negro slave labor, the slave trade was slow to develop during the colonial period and was not popular. Before 1700 some 25,000 slaves had been imported into all the colonies. It is estimated that in the period between 1700 and 1750 the annual introduction of slaves from Africa ran between 15,000 and 20,000. The institution, however, was increasing before the period of the Revolution for in the year 1771 the British ships alone brought to this country 47,000 slaves and by this time American built and operated ships from New England were also engaged in the trade and doing an aggressive business.

The system operated in this way. A vessel from one of the New England ports would load with rum and trade goods which were carried to the slave coast in Africa. Here the cargo was disposed of at various slave-trading posts along the coast and a cargo of slaves put into the holds of the vessels. The ship then sailed as rapidly as wind and weather permitted to one of the ports of the West Indies. The ports of the West Indies served as the prime center of the international slave trade. Here the slaves were usually disposed of, though many of the slaves so transported might later be shipped to the North American colonies.

A portion of the large revenue resulting from the sale of slaves was expended in the purchase of sugar, molasses and other West Indian semi-tropical products. The remainder of the proceeds from the sale of slaves was carried home in the form of gold and silver and negotiable coins. The vessel then sailed for its New England port. Here the cargo was disposed of, again at a handsome profit. In New England the molasses was converted into rum and the cycle was complete.

This trade was enormously successful since a profitable transaction was effected at the end of each leg of the voyage. The most difficult,

disagreeable and risky part of the voyage was that between the West
African port and the port in the West Indies, and on account of its
position in the cycle this became known as "The Middle Passage."
In the early days of the slave trade, the Middle Passage was made
without too much difficulty and with what might be regarded as normal difficulties and risks. As we have already noted, for a long time
the general efforts to suppress the trade merely increased its severity.

At any time, however, the Middle Passage was a gruesome affair.
The hold of the vessel was completely cleaned out and tables or
benches were erected as close together as possible running the full
length of the vessel. Bolts and shackles were fitted into the sides of
the vessels and at convenient places along the tables. The slaves were
brought aboard the ship chained together in long lines. Still in long
lines, they were made to lie down upon the benches and chained into
place. Here they remained through most of the voyage. Occasionally one of the chains would be brought on deck for light or air and
for inspection, but if the weather was bad or difficulties arose these
occasions were infrequent. As the voyage progressed conditions in
the hold became more noisome and the conditions of the slaves dete-
riorated.

One of the risks referred to was the possibility that one of the
slaves might escape from his shackles and then be able to free some
of his fellows with resultant riot and bloodshed.

The great risk was that of infection and disease. No proper care
or medical attention was given to the slaves. Anyone, however, who
is familiar with naval history will understand that medical and surgical care at sea was either lacking or extremely crude even as applied
to the white crews and white officers of naval vessels.

The only precaution taken in the case of the slaves was that of an
occasional inspection made by the captain or mates who weeded out
slaves who in their judgment showed signs of illness.

These were immediately thrown overboard. Some form of sickness
usually developed in the course of the voyage and epidemics were
frequent.

The resulting loss of an important part of the cargo was one of
the inherent risks of the trade. It accounted in part for the steady
increase in the costs of slaves. Here again we might suppose that the
risks involved in loss of part of the cargo through sickness would
have led the operators of the vessels to provide better conditions for
the crew, but such a conclusion was not in the spirit of the times.
On the contrary, the slavers argued that because they were likely to

lose a part of their slave cargo it was expedient to overload the vessel in the hope of arriving in the West Indies with something like a full complement even after those who had died of disease and suffering had been thrown overboard.

Even in the colonial period there was a good deal of resistance and resentment directed against the slave system. By 1760 there were somewhat less than 400,000 slaves in the North American colonies and the colonial legislators became alarmed at the rapid increase of the Negro population. They imposed taxes on the traffic which were intended to prohibit it or at least restrict it, but commercial interests on both sides of the Atlantic had found the trade so profitable that they succeeded in having these measures vetoed and nullified in England.

This was not the first time that England had taken a strong position in supporting the slave traffic. Up to 1698 the Royal African Company of England had had a monopoly on all slaves imported into the North American colonies. She had also successfully invaded the slave traffic between West Africa and the Spanish American colonies. Her position was made a part of the Treaty of Utrecht of 1713. Under this agreement the English enjoyed, for a period of thirty years, the exclusive right of bringing Negroes into the Spanish possessions. This agreement, known as the *Asiento,* permitted them to import 4,000 Negroes a year and also to keep a ship stationed at Porto Bello. The *Asiento* was confirmed in the Treaty of Seville in 1729.

Before the Revolution opposition to the slave traffic was fairly strong in the southern colonies where the slaves were most numerous. The tobacco trade was no longer at its height and it became apparent that the inefficiencies of the slave labor system were exhausting the soil, also that there was a kind of marginal competition between slave labor and free white labor. After the Revolution many important citizens in the south followed the lead of Washington and Jefferson in freeing their slaves and in directing public attention to the dangers of this institution.

It is quite possible that at this time a gradual solution to the problem of slavery might have been arrived at had it not been for the invention of the cotton gin by Eli Whitney in 1793.

Forms of cotton were native in the American continents. The fiber had been spun into thread and woven into cloth with a great degree of skill by the Incas and had been used in lesser degree by other American tribes. The production of cotton cloth had been developed in England on a small scale as a home industry and attempts had been made to raise and manufacture cotton in the American colonies, but up to the close of the eighteenth century, the total production and use of cotton had been small owing to the difficulty of separating the seeds from the fiber by hand process and the further difficulty of producing the thread by hand-spinning methods.

In the closing decades of the century the introduction of power machinery in England for the weaving and spinning of cotton gave a great impetus to the industry and an enormously increased demand for the raw material. At the same time the southern colonies in America needed a new cash crop as a substitute for or supplement to tobacco. Thus, they turned to cotton but found a great handicap in the difficulty of ginning or cleaning the fiber from the seed.

So-called "Sea-Island" cotton was introduced from the Bahamas in 1786 and did well in the Atlantic lowlands. It partly met the situation because it had a long staple and was easier to clean and handle. Production of long-staple cotton was restricted to the seacoast. Whitney's machine made the use of short-staple cotton, which would grow in the interior, economically profitable. Even in its early crude forms, one of Whitney's machines operated by water power or by a horse could perform the same work that formerly required fifty men. Within a few years cotton became the greatest commercial crop of the south and the greatest single export of the United States. Beginning in Georgia and South Carolina, cotton culture spread into North Carolina and Virginia, then it began a westward march crossing the mountains into Tennessee. By 1850 Alabama had supplanted Georgia as the leading cotton state and a decade later it was Mississippi, Alabama and Louisiana that raised over half of the total crop.

Cotton, of course, was the ideal crop for slave labor and the development of the cotton industry changed the whole social attitude in the South toward the institution of slavery. The number of slaves in 1790 was about 1,700,000 and by 1860 it had increased to around 4,000,000. At the time the cotton gin was introduced the average price for an able-bodied slave was about $300. Before twenty years ran out this price had doubled; by 1830 the price was $800; by 1850, $1,200, and in 1860 the prices ranged from $1,400 to $2,000.

In 1807 the British government, by decree, abolished slavery in its colonies and possessions and also moved against the slave trade on the high seas, but enforcement was lax. In 1808 the United States made it illegal to import slaves into its territories, but this provision was also commonly evaded. Wilberforce, the English abolitionist, led an agitation which in 1833 led to the passage of an act outlawing the international slave trade and after this efforts of enforcement were rapidly intensified. Lincoln's Emancipation Proclamation came in 1863 and in 1865 the Thirteenth Amendment was ratified.

As the abolition movement increased its activity and the period of the Civil War approached, efforts to suppress the importation of slaves from Africa grew more determined. The operation of slave vessels became more and more difficult and hazardous. The slavers disguised their ships and in order to avoid detection carried false cargoes and false manifests and also in many cases ran under false colors. They kept their cargoes concealed below decks and sailed on roundabout courses.

The slave cargoes were treated with increasing brutality and carelessness. In part this was due to the fact that only brutal and desperate men could be found to command the vessels engaged in the trade. In part it may have been due to the fact that the traders and captains, knowing that their activities were illegal and despised, and feeling a sense of guilt about the whole business, found an outlet for their feelings in abusing their helpless cargo.

In any event, when an illegal slaver was being chased and was about to be captured, it was common practice to bring the slaves on deck in their chains, to weight them still further and throw the whole cargo overboard so that when the slaver was captured there was no evidence of its activities left and no witnesses to describe what had taken place on board. The details of the management of the slave crews in the later days of the trade are so brutal as to forbid their inclusion in a volume such as this one designed for general circulation.

The gradual suppression of the international slave trade tended to increase the price of slaves in the domestic market. The domestic trade, however, continued active and brisk right up to the time of the Civil War. As the production of cotton moved westward the active use of slaves in the border states and in the states of the Atlantic seaboard declined, but they continued to be interested in the maintenance of slavery because they found a profitable market for their excess slaves in Texas and in the other newer states of the West. This was the background that made the Fugitive Slave Law, the repeal of the Missouri Compromise and the Kansas-Nebraska Act dangerous and explosive issues.

The greatest economic benefit of the slave system was reaped not by the owners and operators of slaves but by those who dealt in the slave traffic. These were the prosperous and respectable British merchants and operators and later those of the New England coast and other American ports. They were the power behind the slave trade and to them went the lion's share of its profits. Later, when the human and economic costs of the system became apparent and when it became unpopular, their descendants were leaders in the movement for reform. The whirligig of time brings in its changes.

* * * *

The term "slave coast" was very generally and very loosely used. It meant different places at different times. In a general sense it extended all the way from the port of Dakar in Senegal to Cape St. Martha in Angola or Portuguese East Africa in the south.

Beginning in the fourteenth century with the arrival of the Portuguese trading vessels, slave ships from various nationalities carried on the trade for a period of approximately 400 years. The first slave shipments were secured from the northern ports of this vast coastline. As the supply of slaves that could be easily secured in one part of the coast became exhausted, newer ports and stations were established farther south and so, over a period of time, the trade moved southward around the bulge of Africa and into the Bight of Benin and later to the Congo region and to Angola.

This did not mean, however, that the older stations were abandoned. Even after they had passed the peak of their volume of trade they were still used as collecting centers, as places of internment and storage of the slave captives and as trading centers.

Native traders from tribes along the coast picked up the tricks of the trade and in turn became traders, securing their captives from tribes farther in the interior. Thus, with the passage of time, raiding and trading parties penetrated farther and farther into the hinterland of Africa. These native expeditions were equipped, armed and trained by white traders.

A good deal has been written about slave ships and it is sometimes supposed that this referred to a particular type of vessel. This, however, was not the case as must be apparent even from the foregoing condensed and abbreviated account of the slave traffic.

The first slave ships were the vessels of exploration that Henry the Navigator sent to the West African coast. Later Portuguese commercial vessels of the fourteenth and fifteenth centuries carried some slaves to Europe but they were not vessels especially designed for the slave trade. Along with some slaves, they carried back to Europe mixed cargoes that included ivory, hides, nuts and oils and other tropical products.

English vessels of many different types occasionally were employed in the transportation of slaves on the Atlantic but again they were not particularly designed for this traffic. Whatever the type of hull and of rig, they were usually produced and first used for the transportation of regular cargoes and gradually drifted into the business of "blackbirding." The same was true of the New England vessels that participated in the triangular trade. In this case it is plain that since the vessels carried other cargoes on at least two of the legs of the voyage, a general purpose ship was quite satisfactory for the operation. Ships, barks, brigs and schooners were all occasionally employed on these voyages.

Throughout most of the years of the slave trade any seaworthy vessel that had an ample carrying capacity in her hold was regarded as satisfactory for the trade and little effort was made to attain speed on the passage. As time went on, however, it became apparent that a rapid crossing from Africa to the West Indies was desirable since this decreased the time during which the slave cargo had to be fed and cared for and also decreased the likelihood of the spread of contagious disease. As efforts to suppress the slave trade increased, the need for a speedy passage became obvious. It became necessary for the slaver to outrun, outsail and outmaneuver any vessel that might be sent to overtake and capture it. In the closing days of the trade the remaining slavers went to great lengths to secure fast and weatherly vessels.

In the early part of the nineteenth century, the so-called "Baltimore Clippers" found special favor with the slavers and were often bought for this traffic. Their holds were of rather extreme design and had a limited carrying capacity and this in turn led to extreme overcrowding of the slave cargo, but they in part overcame this defect by making some notably fast passages from Africa to the West Indies. Diagrams are still in existence showing how the cargo was disposed in vessels of this type.

For the most part, these were small fast vessels with hull lines unusually fine and sharp for their time and still capable of carrying a large spread of canvas. They were rigged as brigs, brigantines, hermaphrodite brigs and schooners. The Baltimore Clippers seemed to have developed out of the vessels that were used during the War of 1812 and they appear to have been used for privateering and other purposes where speed and handiness was desirable in a vessel.

Mr. Howard I. Chappelle, in his *History of American Sailing Ships* shows that at least some of the Baltimore Clippers were built as slave ships and he believes that the conditions of the trade had an influence on their design. At Page 156 he provides the plans of such a vessel.

As we have already noted, the Baltimore vessels came into use at the time when efforts were being made to enforce decrees and laws against the slave trade. Thus, there was a premium on sail-carrying capacity and speed to avoid capture. There was also a premium on being able to work to windward on a chase and this accounted for the use of the fore-and-aft elements in the sail plan and particularly for the preference for the schooner rig.

Here a word of explanation is needed for the modern reader. Our present-day schooners carry the fore-and-aft principle even to the topsails; that is to say, their topsails are set between the topmast and the gaff. Thus they lie in the same plain as the mainsail and the fore-sail and are managed as a unit in tacking or in jibbing.

The term "schooner" as it was used in the years, say, 1815 to 1860, designated a ship that we should call today a topsail schooner. That is to say, on both the main- and the foremast it carried yards on which a varying number of topsails were set. They were managed as square sails. This was desirable or even necessary because the vessels were usually operating in the trades with winds coming from some quarter abaft the beam, a condition under which square sails are relatively most effective.

The West African slave ports were mostly small and this, as well as the need to escape detection, made a small vessel desirable. The water-line length of these vessels was not much in excess of 100 feet. Many of the ports were also at the mouths of rivers where shoals and sand bars are frequent so that the shallow draft of the Baltimore vessels was also an advantage.

Some of the risks of the trade were inherent in the character of the Atlantic Ocean between the African coast and the western continents. Everything considered, the passage should have been an easy one. Sailing from any of the ports north of the equator, the vessel, once it left the African shore, could usually maneuver its way into the favorable influences of the northeast trades and the North Equatorial Current.

Most of the slavers, particularly in the later days of the trade, though rather small vessels, usually made fast and satisfactory passages. *Kinkajou,* a schooner with a seventy-foot water line in which

I made a voyage over the route of the Middle Passage from Dakar to the West Indies, was probably smaller than any of the vessels carrying slaves. We found the sailing conditions fast and agreeable though we found the trade winds stronger and the seas more lively than we had expected. Incidentally, on this voyage we took our departure from Goree Island, a small island south of the port of Dakar on which stand black, tall-walled buildings that were used as fortress and barracoons in the days of the slave trade.

Ships leaving a West African port south of the equator or near it could correspondingly seek the southeast trades and the South Equatorial Current and this would have been a particularly favorable course for slavers bound for Brazil. As the charts show, the passage from the south end of the slave coast to Cuba, another market and distributing point for the slave trade, could also be made with ease provided that the vessel kept to the southeast trades until it began to approach the eastern shore of South America. Here there is a point in the Atlantic at which the South Equatorial Current is diverted northward and crosses the equator and thus would assist the vessel throughout the latter portion of its voyage to Cuba.

The shortest possible passage from land to land would be that from Dakar to the extreme eastern ports in Brazil. This, however, would involve crossing the equator and the belt of fitful winds and calms called the doldrums. Here was the greatest risk in this part of the Atlantic. Vessels running out of the trades and getting into the doldrums might encounter weeks of calms or baffling intermittent winds.

As long as a vessel is in the belt where the trade wind is blowing even though it is in low latitudes, conditions are comfortable, but life aboard a sailing vessel that is becalmed in the doldrums or elsewhere in the tropics would provide the slavers and the slaves with the foretaste of hell. The deck planking begins to shrivel, any metal work about the ship gets so hot that it will blister fingers laid upon it, even an awning or the shadow of a sail gives little protection from the scorching sun.

There is no breeze and thus no circulation of air below decks is possible. The air vibrates as though it were being heated in a furnace. Even though there is no wind, the ship is not still. Big swells keep sweeping across the sea and the vessel is in constant movement. Even though it is flat calm, some sail is usually carried in the wild hope that some breeze or stir of air will help to carry the vessel out of the iron grip of the calm, but the sails hang idle. There is no pressure of wind to steady the vessel and the yards or the gaff and boom swing and sway and slap in ceaseless noisy idleness. Under such conditions a week is an eternity. With the passage of time, water in the casks gets putrid as well as hot, stores rot or become exhausted, disease and death mount.

The doldrums were not the only hazard. Close to the African coast it is possible for a sailing vessel to utilize land and sea breezes that alternate around the clock but between the coast and the trade-wind belts there was often an area of alternating calms and storms. There was also the matter of hurricanes which in the warm weather months originate in the westerly section of the trade-wind belts. Slaving vessels are known to have run into hurricanes but on the whole this risk was not as great as would appear. Hurricanes at the time that they originate in these areas have very high rotary wind speed but they are tightly knit and compact. They do not spread over a large area as they do after they have recurved and come into more northerly sections of the Atlantic. Thus, it is usually possible to avoid this kind of storm.

At the time of the Civil War there were less than 4,000,000 Negroes in the United States. The presence of millions of colored people in the population of the United States has always been and continues to be a political and social problem but it is continually improving and is less acute today than at any time in the past. Census figures show that today Negroes make up less than one-tenth of the total population. This is a lower proportion than prevailed in the active days of slavery and in the intervening period. The peak was reached in 1790 when the Negroes made up 19 per cent of the total population. At this time there were common expressions of fear over the rapid growth of the Negro population. However, from that time on the proportion began to decline. Concentration was reflected in the fact that at this time in South Carolina the ratio of Negroes to whites was two to one.

It is now almost a century since slavery was abolished in the United States and it has generally disappeared in the Western World. Even at its height, American slavery involved less than 4,000,000 people. In the meantime the Old World has developed new forms of political and economic slavery. The slave-labor—prison-camp systems that existed in Hitler's Germany and that exist today in Communist countries exceed in numbers and rival in barbarity anything the world saw even in the most exuberant days of Negro slavery.

Chapter 15

THE PACKETS

NEW YORK in 1815, at the close of the war, was hardly distinguishable from other American seaports. In fact, New York had certain disadvantages from the point of view of sailing-ship operation. Before the days of powerful artificial lights and enormous buildings entrance to the harbor was not easy to detect; and the low-lying beaches of Rockaway and Sandy Hook were a constant hazard waiting to trap and destroy any poorly navigated ship. Should the harbor entrance be missed, there was no alternate refuge or harbor entrance able to accommodate even the small ocean vessels of those days in all the whole 100 miles of Long Island's south shore or the longer New Jersey shore from New York City to Cape May.

Trading ships came and went to New York as they did to many other American harbors, but the advantage of New York and the deep-water harbor was obscured by the dangers. Entrance to the harbor through Long Island Sound and Hell Gate was even more dangerous and quite impractical until the days of reliable steam power.

Then in a few years three basic ideas altered the history of the whole Atlantic seaboard and led to the development of the world's largest port and metropolitan area. Two of these ideas involved man's use of certain natural resources—one of them was a sheer invention of management.

Before the Revolution, Benjamin Franklin observed that American whalers consistently made better time in passages to and from Europe than even the government ships that carried the mails. This was remarkable, for the whaling vessels were not designed to be fast sailers. Franklin discovered that the whalers had learned to use the Gulf Stream, sailing with it when they went eastward and keeping north of its northern edge on their return, and this way they benefited by the current in one direction and avoided its retarding effects in the other direction. With the war approaching Franklin kept this information to himself—afterward he imparted it as information that would benefit American traders. Franklin produced one of the first descriptions of the Gulf Stream together with a chart embodying his ideas of its course. At a later date Maury repeatedly expressed the idea that the utilization of the Gulf Stream by vessels operating out of New York gave them a distinct advantage over those sailing from Charleston or other southern ports in establishing trade with northern Europe. The Gulf Stream assisted them with its current; it provided fair weather and warmer waters; it set a boundary that could be used in navigation. Those who followed the Gulf Stream were induced in a natural way to sail a great circle course rather than a compass course.

The second idea that utilized natural resources was Clinton's development of the Erie Canal, which was begun in 1817. The Hudson Valley opened up a natural highway into a large hinterland, but this was greatly extended and the Erie Canal opened the pathway into the heart of a developing continent.

The idea referred to as a sheer management invention was the "packet" ship. There were two separate applications of this invention, both of which centered in New York. The first application was the development of "packet" service to the southern or cotton ports, such as Savannah, Charleston and New Orleans. The combined services gave New York an outstanding advantage as the great trading port of the Atlantic seaboard. R. G. Albion, who has studied the history of the port of New York, says the packet service was even more responsible than the Erie Canal in establishing New York's leadership.

In the beginning the packet was not so much a type of vessel as she was an idea of management. To make this clear, we will suppose that you have been living in Hartford, Connecticut in the summer of 1816. Your father, who came from England when he was a young man, died in the midst of the recent war, and now you have received an invitation from your uncle, who lives near Oxford, to visit him because he is aging rapidly, and there are some items in the family estate that should be settled before his death. You also have a notion that your own business could be profitably extended by the importation of English woolens, giving a further reason for this trip.

With appropriate letters both for your business and private affairs, and with "bag and baggage" you proceed by stagecoach to New York to arrange for your departure. The charges at the hotel are a little larger than you had expected or provided for, so you are anxious that this should be at as early a date as possible. With this in mind you scan the newspaper columns headed "Marine Intelligence," which deals with the arrival and the anticipated departure from the port of merchant vessels. The paper is dated September 13, 1816, and in an adjacent column this advertisement attracts your eye: The Superior Ship *Minerva*. As there is great difficulty in procuring freight, the ship will positively be dispatched on the 15th of September "cargo or no cargo." That sounds definite and businesslike, so you proceed at once to the agent and arrange for your passage and pay your fare. Your evening is occupied with saying farewell to your friends and making arrangements to get your baggage to the ship. On the following day, however, the agent announces that the departure of the *Minerva* in "consequent of present unfavorable weather is unavoidably detained until the 25th instant." Thunderstruck, you ask: "Why such a long delay?" and "How does the agent know that the weather may not improve in less than a ten-day period?" It develops that the ship is still able to accommodate a cargo of 130 bales of cotton or some other commodity. In the meantime, other ships are sailing, but you have paid your passage and protestations to the agent are of no avail.

In the meantime, that hotel bill is running on. It is September 18th before the *Minerva* is cleared at the custom house: Then there is a fog so that your departure actually takes place on October 3rd. By this time, weeks have elapsed in frustration and idleness; weeks marked by rumors and by the necessity of having to keep in touch with the agent in anticipation of the promised departure.

No doubt you have had extremely bad luck; but no matter which ship you had chosen, you would not have avoided the possibility of uncertainty and delay. In your situation you would have naturally avoided the trading vessels that were designated as "transient." This was the politer nineteenth-century designation that today we would call a "tramp." The "transient" vessel had no established trade route or regular port of call. She operated in accordance with anticipated demands for shipping space, the prospect of securing passengers and the convenience of her operators. "Transient" vessels were not necessarily inferior ships, but they were irregular in operation and on one voyage might sail from New York to Liverpool but on the next one from New York to Havana. In fact, they might cover the three points in a triangular voyage.

The other class of vessel was so-called "regular traders." These confined their activities to a particular route, such as the passage from New York to Liverpool or from New York to London. The term "regular" applied to the destination of the vessel, but not necessarily to the time of her departure or of her arrival.

The term "packet" was also applied to vessels. It was apparently intended to suggest that a vessel was not only a regular trader but also prompt in her departure and fast at sea; but in practice, the term was so often misapplied that it lost its meaning. The honored meaning was won back for a distinct class of ships that earned the designation the hard way.

The New York *Evening Post* of October 27, 1817, carried an advertisement that differed from any other shipping notice that had ever appeared up to that time. It announced that a line of American packets would operate between New York and Liverpool. Four ships were mentioned: the ship *Amity,* John Stanton, master; the *Courier,* William Bowne, master; the *Pacific,* John Williams, master; and the *James Monroe,* whose master was not listed. The announcement further said that the *Monroe* was to sail from New York on the 5th of January, 1818, while the *Courier* was to sail from Liverpool on the first, and that similar sailings were to take place on the first and fifth of each succeeding month. The backers of this enterprise were: Issac Wright & Son, Francis Thompson, Benjamin Marshal and Jeremiah Thompson. On the morning of the 5th of January a snowstorm was raging over New York; but promptly at 10:00 o'clock, Captain James Watkinson, who had assumed command of the *Monroe,* gave orders that the vessel's lines were to be cast off the dock, and when the sails were trimmed she slipped into the river. At that time she had on board a rather limited cargo but a scheduled one. She had on board eight male passengers who had paid forty guineas (about $200) apiece for passage which included bedding, food and wines, and she also carried mail. Thus, the *Monroe* began the first scheduled transatlantic sailing from New York of a vessel performing a combination of services which included the carrying of passengers, of mails and of freight.

New Year's Day in Liverpool did not witness the scheduled departure of the *Courier*. In fact, it was the 4th of January before Captain Bowne was able to leave the dock and take his vessel down the river Mersey. Possibly the idea of a scheduled departure did not seem so important over 3,000 miles away from the home offices of this new type of ocean service. Yet the delay should not be attributed to any negligence on the part of the captain. The departure from Liverpool had to be made from a dock. The Mersey is notorious for the great rise and fall of its tides, and head winds from the west could constitute an additional reason for delay. In any event, the departure of the *Courier* from Liverpool was still ahead of that of the *Monroe* from New York, and thus constituted the first sailing of a transatlantic liner. When the vessel departed her hold was filled with a large cargo of British woolens and other manufactures consigned to the owners of the line and many other merchants. She carried in her cabins a Mr. and Mrs. Irving and four other men passengers. To this Mrs. Irving, therefore, goes the distinction of being the first woman passenger on a transatlantic liner.

The men who organized this service had already for some time been business associates. They were textile importers who had become joint owners of the *Pacific* in 1815 and in the succeeding years they had also jointly participated in the building of other vessels. Jeremiah Thompson has been credited with the idea and initiative of operating the vessels as a line and on schedule. The four vessels were similar in appearance and construction to the regular traders of their day. What set them apart from all other vessels was their method of operation. In time there developed the type of vessel and a method of sound and durable construction that might be recognized as the distinguishing marks of packet ships. At the beginning all that the eye could see was that each of the vessels carried at the top of the mainmast a round black ball, and that when the sails were set the fore-topsail was marked with an enormous circular black spot. This distinguishing mark became known to all seamen and travelers, and the organization was known as the Black Ball Line. They remained in business for a period of sixty years, though during the latter years of its operation the character of its business was much changed by the competition with clipper ships and steamers.

The Black Ball Line held the field of operation alone, building up business and prestige through the regularity and effectiveness of its operations until January of 1822. Then, the firm of Byrnes Trinble & Co. of New York entered the field with a line of four ships to be operated on the Black Ball method, with monthly sailings from New

York to Liverpool. Their first vessel to leave New York, the *Meteor*, under command of Captain Nathan Cobb, carried a large red star on her fore-topsail. This, therefore, became known as the Second Line or the Red Star Line. The Black Ball responded by doubling its services.

On July 30th of the same year a fourth line was announced by Fish & Grinnel which later became Grinnel, Minturn & Co. The reason for its being known as the Fourth Line was that the additional fleet of the Black Ball Line was considered to constitute an independent service. The flag of the Grinnel, Minturn was a blue swallowtail, and the Fourth Line was, therefore, popularly known as the Swallowtail Line. Beginning in the autumn of 1844 the lines had sorted out their services so that a Black Ball vessel left New York on the 1st of each month, a Swallowtail left on the 8th, another Black Baller the 16th, and a Red Star on the 24th. This arrangement continued for the next sixteen years.

It took only four years of operation for the new method of ship management to establish itself. In fact, the development might have come even more rapidly had it not been for a temporary financial depression. The Black Ball kept rigidly to its schedule and through reliability in operation secured the best of the business: the carrying of news, the transport of specie and financial papers, fine freight and important passengers in a hurry. When competition came it came with a rush, but the line was so well established in public confidence that it could afford to meet the competition by its own expansion and it continued a busy life as long as the basic idea of the sailing packet filled a useful place in maritime history.

Very interesting is the fact that, in the midst of competition, the lines arrived so rapidly at a sensible arrangement for providing service and distributing the business. Noteworthy also is the length of time during which the arrangement persisted. That the idea of a scheduled line operation was badly needed was proved by its rapid growth. During the next forty years the principle was extended to operation between other ports in America and other ports in Europe. It was extended also to coastwise shipping in the United States with lines operating to all the ports of the Atlantic seaboard including the gulf ports of Mobile and New Orleans. It was the combination of foreign and domestic service that gave New York the early leadership which was never seriously challenged. The pattern has, in fact, been repeated and accentuated in steamship operation and even travel by air.

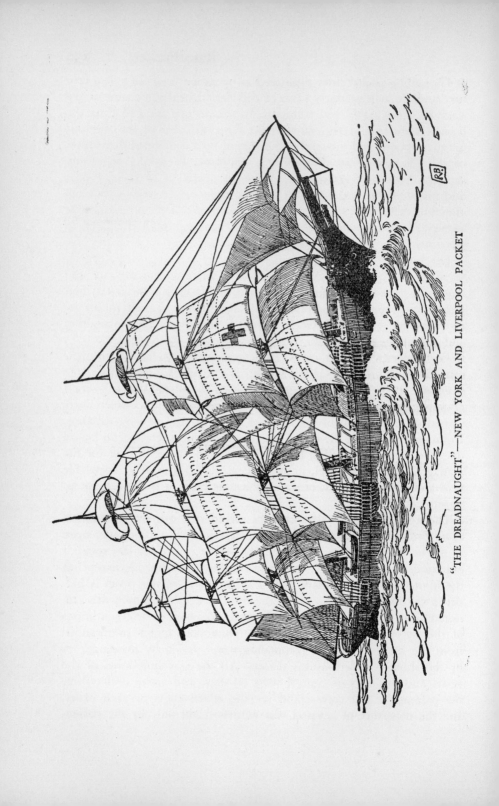

"THE DREADNAUGHT"—NEW YORK AND LIVERPOOL PACKET

The sailing packet liner continued in operation for over half a century and for at least thirty years of this period held the center of the stage of ocean travel and transport. It was an operation that set the highest standards of performance for the organizers of the services; for the captains and the crews; and this in turn demanded the utmost of ship designers and the building shipyards. From the beginning captains had an interest in the financial operation of their vessels, and many of them became part owners, either in the vessels they operated or in the line as a whole. Eventually some of them became sole owners of vessels which they themselves operated, or participated in the organization of new lines.

The builders of ships also had occasionally had a participating interest in line operations. Mates grew to be captains and captains and mates that grew up in the service of one line later transferred their interest to those of a competing line; for there was a premium set on knowledge and skill. Ships were sold from one line to another and sometimes carried with them the services of the captain.

To be a captain of a transatlantic packet in the heyday of their operation was to stand at the height of the profession so far as the maritime services were concerned. It also involved holding a position of public prominence, for in those days the eyes of the world were turned on the records of the lines, of the ships and of their captains. In those days, before the use of telegraph and cable service and before the invention of the radio, the captain was solely responsible for the management of his vessel, its passengers, its cargo and its crew. He held and carried with success a responsibility that it is difficult for us to reconstruct.

There is another fact that must be considered: namely, that almost every event of a captain's professional services in his career was open to public inspection. In a steamer, the whole control of the vessel is exercised from the bridge, and here no one dares intrude except on the invitation of the captain. The motive power of the vessel is hidden away in the engine rooms; the lines of communication are protected from inspection. All this is totally opposed to the conditions of the operation of a vessel in sail. Here the captain commanded from the quarterdeck, his commands were carried by messenger or by the shouted orders of his officers. All the traveling force of the vessel and the lines of control were on deck and above deck where the passengers and crew could see the effectiveness of each order, and the departure of a vessel was witnessed not only by the passengers but also by the friends that had come to see them off, and often by a large company that crowded the docks and the shores.

The smartness with which a crew prepared a vessel for sailing and set sail, the skill, or the lack of it, of the captains and officers in maneuvering her out of a dock through a harbor crowded with all manner of ships were matters of public knowledge and of public comment. It was intelligent comment too, for in those days Americans were natural seamen and built and operated the world's finest and fastest ships. They knew about the records of captains and vessels as much as "fans" know about the standings in the baseball leagues and the batting averages of individual players. Even after the ship had left a harbor and was well at sea, the captain had more than his normal lot of business and of professional duties to attend to, for he lived in daily, almost hourly contact with his passengers, who usually constituted the most important section of the community. Leaders in all professions and in business and social life appeared on the sailing lists. The captain presided at the head of the dinner table and in more ways than one was the life of the party.

Naturally, under such circumstances, there was an intense process of selection going on. The packet captains that served with honorable records were men of both professional and cultural distinction. Repeatedly, noted travelers left written comments on the captain's range of education, his interest, and his qualities of personal distinction.

Included in this group were such men as N. B. Palmer of Stonington, Connecticut, who in his youth had taken a small vessel to the Antarctic and made the first discovery of the section of the Antarctic coast that now bears his name. Palmer served as captain both in the Black Ball and the Dramatic Lines. Later he commanded the clipper *Houqua,* and when he retired from active command at sea performed distinguished business services ashore.

C. H. Marshal and his four brothers were successful ship masters. He had his original training at sea in a Nantucket whaler. After serving as a captain in a number of the Black Ball ships he retired from sea to become part owner and principal operator of the Black Ball Line and later organized C. H. Marshal & Company. He built up a large operating company and a fortune and performed many distinguished public services.

Captain Joseph C. Delano, of New Bedford, Massachusetts, a brother of Warren Delano, the great-grandfather of Franklin D. Roosevelt, commanded ships in the Swallowtail Line, Liverpool service.

But he was in Swallowtail London in the 1830's when he established the westbound speed record of fifteen days, eighteen hours from Portsmouth to Sandy Hook. When he retired to a business life ashore he became one of the original directors of the Wamsutta Cotton Mills.

Captain William H. Allen, Bridgeport, Connecticut, commanded several Liverpool Red Star Liners from 1840 to 1860 and then retired to serve as an officer of an insurance company. He lived in Brooklyn and served as a trustee in the Brooklyn City Hospital.

Nathan Cobb, of Stonington, Connecticut, commanded the first Liverpool Red Star Liner. After his retirement from the line he became the owner and operator of his own ships. After operating in the interest of the Black Ball Line, he became part owner in the line and later participated with Marshal in reorganizing the line. He was owner of a coastal steamer and organizer of a project to establish an ocean steamship service. Throughout his long life he was financially interested in many packet and steamship lines.

On occasion wealthy travelers individually, or all the cabin passengers banded together, would make a gift to the captain presented with a testimonial to his skill on the completion of what they regarded as a particularly noteworthy crossing.

The captain, who had to be courteous in dealing with passengers, had also to be a forceful driver in handling tough crews. Operating a sail ship on the stormy North Atlantic winter and summer was rough and dangerous work in itself. All the rigor and risk was multiplied when every crossing of every packet was at least an effort to keep to schedule, and frequently also an attempt to break the record. The endurance of the crew was tested as severely as the skill of the captain. In the beginning there were many experienced seamen to draw on and the packets attracted them. As competition increased and the volume of transatlantic shipping rose, the relative number of skilled seamen fell even though the absolute number increased.

Often packets sailed and made fine passages with depleted and inexperienced crews. The process of making records usually involved also the process of taking some landlubbers aboard and making seamen of them before the voyage was over. The process had to be fast and could not afford to be gentle because many lives and fortunes might depend on the outcome.

In the nineteenth century all sailors were tough—they had to be to survive; the packet sailors were tougher than the others—also because they had to be. This at least is their reputation.

The experienced sailors who usually made up a small nucleus of a transatlantic liner crew became known as "packet rats." Both ashore and afloat they enjoyed the reputation of being tough and often disorderly. They were often denounced by their captains and were either envied or scorned by other seamen. They performed the most difficult and dangerous work and got the most punishment and abuse. It is certain that they themselves habitually complained; that they were always difficult to handle and sometimes mutinous; yet, year after year, they made possible the best marine services that the world had ever seen. There is a good deal to indicate that they took a kind of fierce pride in the very difficulty of their job and, as we would say, in their capacity to "take it." Like a "sand hog" in construction work and the "topper" in the lumber camp, they constituted a special group in a dangerous trade.

Captain Samuels asserts that a Captain Bryer was murdered by his crew, but Dr. Albion's researches do not confirm this story. In fact, they throw a good deal of doubt upon it. On the other hand, protests and occasional mutiny would take place on the packet ships, though there was less of this than the literature of the time would have us believe. If there was trouble aboard it was apt to occur at the time of sailing or shortly thereafter. This was the time when a number of those aboard would be new to their tasks and before the organization of the crew had fallen into place. In addition, the sailors usually came aboard full of liquor or recovering from the effects of some. This is illustrated in one of the most picturesque of the mutinies—a mutiny that was quelled by one small woman.

In 1832 William G. Hackstaff was a proud and happy man. He was in command of the *Sheffield*, of the Red Star Line, and had just married an attractive and accomplished girl twenty years old. In those days, the wives and families of ship captains often accompanied them on their cruise. On the day of sailing from Liverpool, the *Sheffield* was moved out into the Mersey River with the crew and a passenger list of men and the captain's bride aboard. He was detained ashore, apparently completing the ship's business. It was then that the mutiny started. The rebellious crew overran the ship. The terrified passengers ran to their cabins and locked themselves in. Mrs. Hackstaff went to her captain's cabin and got his pair of pistols. With a pistol in each hand, she went on deck. She faced the crew and said that she would shoot down the first man that came aft. She held them at bay until the captain arrived, when the ringleaders were put in irons and sent ashore. From this strenuous and heroic honeymoon, Captain and

Mrs. Hackstaff went on to live out together a busy and successful lifetime.

The packet service made just as strenuous demands upon the vessel as it did upon the officers and the crews. In the beginning there was nothing except her insignia and her method of operation to distinguish a packet from any one of the better "regular traders"; in fact, they were the same ships. But as time went on, the designers and the shipyards of New York and New England began to specialize in a type of vessel whose design and construction were particularly suited to the scheduled North Atlantic service in which they were to sail. The chief demand was for strength and the ability to keep sailing even through the stormy North Atlantic winter weather. The second demand was for carrying ability which could be devoted to fine freight, to heavy freight if this proved to be necessary and to the carrying of passengers both of the cabin and steerage class. The packet, therefore, had strong lines; she was built with relatively flat floors and full lines amidships. The hull of the packet was about four times as long as it was wide. A good deal of pains were taken to refine the lines aft so that the vessel would leave a clean wake, and it was here that some concession was made in the interest of speed. In general, however, throughout the packet, the emphasis of the design was on durability, regularity of performance, and carrying capacity; or to borrow a phrase from the aircraft designer, "payload." Even before the clipper emerged, designers and builders knew enough to create faster vessels; but they would not have performed as well, voyage by voyage and year by year.

The packets were all three-masted, full-rigged ships with the conventional sail plan that their name implies. They were vessels with two decks. This gave them a hold for the storage of heavy cargo. The space between decks was used for the living quarters of officers and passengers aft; a special storage space for fine and fragile cargo in the midships section; and the forecastle for the crew was in the bows. The early packets were flush deck so that there was no visible deck structure. They had an almost flat sheer line, and were finished with waist-high bulwarks. This gave them a trim appearance, especially contrasted with earlier vessels that had a number of built-up decks forward and aft.

The strength of the packet was largely protected by control of materials during the course of its construction. It was heavily timbered and all the different woods that were used in its construction were carefully selected and repeatedly inspected. Making for strength, too, was a feature of construction that was not used in ordinary vessels of the period. They were given inner sheathing or "ceiling," and the space between the planks making up this structure was caulked with oakum; just as were the outer planks of the vessel. This served to keep the interior dry and clean, and it also added to the strength of the vessel's fabric. Repeatedly, packet ships survived groundings or strandings that would have totally wrecked the ordinary ship of the period.

This kind of construction showed also in the service records. The *Virginian* of the Swallowtail Liverpool service sailed regularly for fifteen years. The *Sully* and the *François I* both operated for nineteen years. The *Liverpool* continued on the Liverpool or London run for thirty-seven years.

In all the years of its history, the packet stayed true to type. Even at the end it would have been recognizable to the observer as the same kind of ship that it was in the beginning. It did, however, undergo a great increase in size, as well as a few structural changes. With the passage of time the length of the vessel increased in proportion to the beam. Structures on deck were permitted and in some cases packets were built with accommodations for passengers removed from " 'tween decks" and put in the deckhouse. Some three-deck packets were also built. What chiefly marked the later packets from the earlier ones was the matter of size. The packets of the early lines averaged about 350 tons. By the time the packet had settled into a particular type of vessel, its size was increasing from 500 to 800 tons. Toward the end of the period, when the Dramatic Line was operating under the management of Edward Knight Collins, he built the *Roscius,* which had exceeded a thousand tons.

The packets may have been sturdy and businesslike in their construction; but from the start, they tried to balance this with comfort and elegance in the part of the vessel devoted to carrying cabin passengers.

The newspapers on both sides of the Atlantic referred to the cabin quarters of the ships as "large" and "elegant." They noted the fine mahogany tables in the gentlemen's dining saloon, the sofas and rich draperies, the shaded lights, the fine silk curtains, etc. As each new packet came into service, some additional effort had been made to make the traveler more comfortable, or at least more impressed with the money that had been spent on his surroundings. The same standard of luxury that was applied to living accommodations was applied also to the food, wines and liquors supplied for the customers. Four meals a day were served, each of which strove to preserve the full content complexity and service that distinguished fashionable eating habits ashore. In order that there might be fresh food throughout the trip a section of the deck was given over to a barnyard fully stocked with ducks, geese, chickens, pigs and even a cow for fresh milk.

An Irish actor named Tyrone Power, who traveled in a Black Ball liner in the 30's, provides a detailed description of the living quarters, the foods and the drinks so liberally provided, all of which came for thirty guineas. Mr. Power seems to have been very nimble at getting about; for he offers a description of the ladies' boudoir including the observation that, "between the lights, this snuggery affords a tolerable convenience for a little flirtation."

The list of people who traveled on packets would include most of the famous people of the time: Charles Dickens, P. T. Barnum traveling with Tom Thumb the Great, Carl Schurz, and scores of others. The artist and inventor S. F. B. Morse was traveling with Captain W. W. Pell in the *Sully* when a dinner-table conversation turned to the matter of recent experiments in electromagnetism. At the table Morse expressed his belief that an electrical circuit could be used for the transmission of messages, and before the trip was out he had invented the telegraph and filled a notebook with sketches of possible instruments.

The age of elegance and distinction in the packets for a long time survived the competition of the early steam vessels. Steamers were already operating between New York and Albany and between New York and ports on the Sound when the first packets commenced their regular services. The first packets were, in fact, occasionally towed through harbor ice by steam, paddle-wheeled tugs. For forty years after that packets kept their hold on transatlantic services. The early steamers were irregular in operation. They sometimes went astray and not infrequently were wrecked. It was only in 1848 when the Cunard Line commenced operation from New York and adopted the packet plan of operating on regular schedules that the packets themselves finally lost their best customers.

In the beginning the packets carried more cabin passengers than they did immigrants in the steerage, but at the end the largest packets were devoted to the carrying of new settlers to American shores. For example: in 1848, three ships of the Swallowtail Line, operating from Liverpool, brought in a total of 5,773 steerage passengers.

When the first packet, the *Courier,* sailed from Liverpool to New

York in 1818, she had seven steerage passengers. This seems a very trivial beginning for what was later to develop into the great wave of the nineteenth-century immigration. At the beginning, the packet lines were indifferent about transporting immigrants. Their chief business was the handling of news dispatches, specie and commercial paper, fine freights and cabin passengers. Too much accommodation for steerage passengers interfered with the space available for freight. From the financial point of view the carrying of steerage passengers was of marginal assistance.

During the forty years of packet prosperity there was a slow but steady increase in the number of steerage passengers per voyage. With the arrival of the clippers and the steamers and the intense competition which they created, the interest of the operating packet lines in immigrant service increased in proportion as their previous business declined.

We must remember that in 1820 the population of New York City was only 152,056 and the population of the United States was only 9,638,453 so that even a modest but steady flow of immigrants would have a great effect on population balances. As a matter of fact, in 1826 the packets brought into the port of New York from Liverpool less than 300 steerage passengers whereas the irregular "regular traders" brought in 2,000, but the number of packet steerage passengers was to increase enormously before the packets went out of business. The packet *Hottinguer,* in 1845, for example, carried 397 immigrants, that is roughly 400 on a single voyage and about 100 more than the total that all the packets carried in 1826.

Havre liners, almost from the beginning, served as an outlet for a large number of Swiss and German immigrants but few French. The Robinson Line was organized to provide immigration service but this was not a real packet line so much as a collection of traders and transients chartered to sail on scheduled dates. By the 40's and 50's there were a number of special companies operating immigrant service.

When the transatlantic steamers began regular operation to New York their first effect was to make inroads on the cabin passengers of the packets. The early steamers did not provide for steerage passage and so for a time the packets and other sailing vessels carried the bulk of American immigration.

The immigrants of this period constituted an important contribution to the working population of America. Human history and physical geography conspired to produce an intense transport service between New York and the English coast. The packet service operated chiefly between New York and Liverpool served first to select the kind of immigrants that came to this country in that period. It also influenced the way they distributed themselves on arrival in this country. The Liverpool to New York run was naturally a convenience to those living in Ireland over the period of the great exodus of the last century.

New York, however, was not the only port affected. Several packet lines operated out of Boston to Liverpool including the one organized by Enoch Train, operating the large, fine packets designed and built by Donald McKay. These combined packet services to Boston laid the foundation for the large concentration of Irish found in Boston and the surrounding area.

Packet services from the port of Havre, likewise, carried to New York another wave of migrants. Though the port of departure was French, the French contributed relatively few passengers to this group—the greater number being made up of Germans and a considerable number of Swiss immigrants.

For their position of leadership in the world trade, the packet service paid a price in death and disaster. One out of every six packet ships was wrecked. When we consider the dangerous and stormy character of the winter North Atlantic, the difficult shores and the poor aids to navigation, the desire to depart on time and keep to schedule—this was not a bad record. In other terms it meant that there were only twenty-two wrecks out of 6,000 packet crossings or in the language of modern air lines, one death for every 500,000 passenger miles.

In 1822 the Black Ball packet, *Liverpool,* was launched on June 15; she sailed on July 16 in command of Captain William Lee, Jr. On the 25th of July she struck a fog and an iceberg almost at the same time. Within two hours the thirty-six persons who made up captain, crew and passengers had abandoned the ship in boats, finding space even for the mailbags. In seven days they had sailed to St. Johns, Newfoundland without loss of life.

During the winter of 1826 the packet *Crisis* sailed from England for the westward passage and was never heard from again. At the end of 1844 the *United States* of the Red Star Line and the *England* of the Black Ball Line sailed within five days of each other. Other ships reported encountering terrific storms during that Christmas season but neither of the vessels reached port and neither was ever reported.

One of the most dramatic disasters came early. In April of 1822 the fine fast packet *Albion* was making a fast passage with a distinguished international company aboard, including Count Lefevbre-

Desnouettes, and a party of other French travelers aboard. She ran
into a fierce gale just after she had passed Bishop's Rock Light off
the southwest corner of Ireland. She lost her canvas and her mast during the night and drove hard on the rocks of the Old Head of Kinsale.
Captain John Williams and his officers and the Count had been swept
overboard. Early in the morning an Irish fisherman passing over the
cliffs saw five dead bodies laid out on the quarterdeck and beside
them living men and women imploring rescue. But the winds and
waves were still raging and rescue was impossible. Only eight survivors out of fifty-four persons on board were able finally to struggle
up the cliffs to safety and the kindly assistance of farmers and fishermen. At the foot of the cliff, boxes of money and commercial papers,
escaping from burst mailbags, littered the rocks and the narrow
beach. There were bodies too from the wreck. One of them, a French
lady, extremely beautiful and entirely naked, seemed only asleep
when a country boy from near Ballinspittle found her. He took off
his coat and covered her and walked off through the mist that was
rising from the breaking surf.

By the 50's, the steamers had deprived the packets of a good part
of their most profitable business and the clipper ships, by making
longer voyages at higher rates of speed, stole from them their popular
interest and romantic appeal. Before they went, aside from carrying
the major ocean service of the world for a period of almost half a century, the packets had made other prominent contributions to the life
of America and the life of the ocean. They had built up generations
trained to the tradition and to the service of the sea. They had served
as the training field for mates and captains some of whom, like
Palmer and Waterman, were to become captains of the first clippers.
They likewise trained and gave employment to designers like Griffiths and McKay who designed and developed the clippers. They
established the standard of speed, of regularity and of luxury in transatlantic passenger service which set the pattern for steamship operation.

Chapter 16

SEAMAN'S OCEAN—
LT. M. F. MAURY, USN

IN VIEW of all the progress we have made since, it is extraordinary to think that a little over a hundred years ago, say about 1840, we had almost no organized, scientific information about the oceans. There had accumulated a considerable number of observations about the behavior of the ocean and the weather, but these observations were obscured rather than explained by a great amount of traditional belief, abstruse theory, hearsay evidences and even superstition. What was totally lacking was a systematic method for collecting the facts, for assembling them and for having a fresh look at their meaning. There did not exist anywhere a scientific institution devoted solely to the study of the sea. To be sure we had charts that showed, with an approach to accuracy, the outlines of the land and water in the better-known and more frequently traveled parts of the world. There were sounding and navigation marks for the frequented harbors and a peppering of soundings for depths up to the hundred-fathom line offshore.

A few soundings to bottom had been taken here and there in the open ocean but the methods of securing these soundings were sketchy and many of them were quite inaccurate. Celestial navigation had been well developed but the methods were involved and cumbersome. Then, as now, it was easy to get a noon observation for latitude but longitude was still a problem. Longitude depended on the use of chronometers for neither telegraph nor radio had then been used for time signals.

Naval officers and some skilled navigators would do well with the problems of latitude but many skippers and mates were so uncertain of their longitude results that they would sail until they reached the proper latitude and then close with the shore by sailing along the parallel of latitude. This was called "running down your easting" or "your westing" as the case might be.

This device became embedded in the story about an old New England skipper who was asked how he managed to find his way to Jamaica. His answer was, "South until the butter melts and then turn west."

There existed handbooks for ship's officers, and these contained directions for sailing based on hearsay evidence and some practical experience. Some scientists had worked on problems connected with the sea. A French mathematician named Lagrange had developed a theory and formula about ocean waves. Both he and Newton had presented theories of the tides. Hardly anything was known about a systematic organization of the winds or a structure of ocean currents and drifts. These were all interesting beginnings, but however valuable each might be as a fragment, they were not related. They were parts of a machine that had not yet been invented.

The man who changed all this was an American named Matthew Fontaine Maury. When his work began he was an obscure midshipman in the United States Navy. In his life work, he laid the foundation for two separate sciences—meteorology, the science of the weather, and oceanography, the science of the sea. Since he was an American it was natural that a great part of his researches were conducted in the Atlantic Ocean and that his discoveries began to reveal the nature of the Atlantic.

Maury spent his boyhood in Franklin, Tennessee. His family were fine people but not wealthy and he was one of a large number of children. He went to sea to get an education and this the sea and his own genius provided in a generous measure. His father was opposed to the venture and he had no aid from his family. By teaching at the local school he earned enough money to make a down payment on the purchase of a horse to carry him to Washington.

He went directly to Sam Houston, then a congressman from Tennessee, and with his aid secured an appointment in the navy. At the time, there was no naval academy at Annapolis; in fact, years later, it was Maury's writings and arguments that helped to bring about the creation of that institution. He simply was assigned as a midshipman and began a cruise around the world in a frigate, the USS *Vincennes*. During the cruise (1829-1830) the older officers drilled him in navigation and the elements of naval conduct but he had to drill himself in the elements of his fine and yet broad education.

In 1831 Maury, still a midshipman, serving in the *Falmouth* off the west coast of South America, was assigned to act as sailing master and ordered to bring the vessel home. Maury, with his usual thirst for knowledge and hunger for excellence, began combing through all the records he could put his hands on. He wanted to know what kind of treatment he could expect from the winds and the currents of the sea and what courses he should follow to bring his ship home in the least time. He found that the information he sought did not exist. There was only guess and gamble. This experience started him collecting his own information and he began a cycle of thinking that later was to produce both practical and theoretical results.

In 1839 Maury had been fourteen years in naval service, twelve of which had been spent at sea in a variety of vessels and he had only recently been promoted from midshipman to lieutenant. While returning from a brief shore leave to survey a vessel to which he had been assigned, the stagecoach in which he was traveling overturned, fracturing his thigh and dislocating his knee. Important results followed from this accident. To supplement his income he published a series of articles dealing with improvements in the naval service.

He also had the time to complete and publish a textbook on navigation which received wide and favorable recognition. In 1843 he was assigned as superintendent of the Depot of Charts and Instruments at Washington. After some years of persuasion he induced the Congress to improve the quality of instruments provided. In 1847 an appropriation of $10,000 permitted the purchase of an electrochronograph. Under his leadership an inactive small office gradually developed into the Naval or National Observatory and was so designated.

In the meantime he began a systematic study of thousands of old log books that were under his care. What had previously been a mere depository of outworn records he converted into research material of the greatest value. His object was, by the use of these materials, to build up a composite and comprehensible picture of the winds and currents of the various oceans. With this knowledge in hand he foresaw the time when practical charts and sailing directions would be issued which would cut down the period of ship passages from port to port.

He did not rest content with his study of past records. Though he had little authority and no funds for such an undertaking, Maury devised standard methods for recording information on winds and currents and these he incorporated in standard log books which he induced captains of merchant vessels to use voluntarily by promising them that eventually they would get better charts and sailing instructions.

For purposes of such study Maury created charts that divided the ocean up into 5° squares of latitude and longitude. He recognized sixteen compass directions or points. By the use of appropriate symbols he could make entries showing for each square how often the wind blew from each of the points, how hard it blew. . . . There was provision also for recording the direction and speed of the current, the temperature of the water, state of the barometer and other pertinent facts. He made one chart of this character for each of the months of the year. Thus, he was able to show any important seasonal variations of the ocean's character.

At first he had few direct observations to guide him; but, by combing the observations of many ships over a long period of time, he was able to draw charts which, for the first time in history, presented a picture of the winds, weathers and the currents of the ocean. Taken together, the charts showed how the ocean could be expected to behave at any particular time and place.

To be sure, these were pictures of probabilities, but they were probabilities based on a great number of cases. It turned out that the ocean is sufficiently consistent so that the probabilities reveal its true character.

By 1847 Maury had published *Wind and Current Charts of the North Atlantic Ocean*. In a few years of ceaseless work he had shaped the foundations of the two new sciences—oceanography and meteorology.

Maury's prodigious efforts produced a prodigious success. The first edition of the *North Atlantic Charts* was instantly purchased and put to use and a whole succession of subsequent and improved editions were absorbed as fast as they could be brought off the presses. Maury's collaborators and those who followed his methods were soon outsailing all their competitors. Maury's charts and methods proved useful to all types of ships and on all ocean passages but there were certain circumstances that gave an added and spectacular value to his work. One circumstance was that in the year following the first publication of the charts, gold was discovered in the state of California. The rush to the Pacific coast was on. The other was that the design of ships was changing in the interest of speed and shorter passages. The clipper ship was replacing the old packet. It offered a special opportunity to test Maury's methods and to benefit by them.

An example of the benefits that came to early collaborators of Maury is the case of the barque *W. H. D. C. Wright* of Baltimore. The first year after the publication of his charts, that is in 1848, she made a voyage to Rio and back. Previously this had required fifty-five days between the Virginia capes and Rio and the same time for the return passage. Now, using Maury's charts and instructions, the time was thirty-six days out and forty days home.

Likewise, when Maury dealt with passage between English and American ports and Australia, he shattered records and precedents. The custom was that ships bound from London or New York to Australia would head directly for the Cape of Good Hope; on the return voyage they would work their way back by the same route. Maury pointed out that if the ships would sail south at once (which they would in any case have to do to pass either Cape Horn or the Cape of Good Hope) they would get in the brave westerly winds that blow continually about the world below the capes. So a trip to Australia became a trip around the world which turned out also to be "the shortest way home." The original time of 120 days was reduced by one-fifth for English vessels and by one-third for American vessels.

The usual time allowed before Maury's publications for a passage between the Atlantic and Pacific coasts of the United States was 180 days. As early as 1851 President Fillmore, in his annual message to the Congress, reported that the use of Maury's charts and sailing directions had reduced by forty days the average time of such a passage round the Horn. Fillmore's announcement was only a beginning; for decades times of passage fell and records tumbled. Soon passages only a little over 100 days were common and records under 100 days were established. In fact before 1851 ended the clipper ship *Flying Cloud*, following Maury's directions, exceeded even the President's predictions by sailing from New York to San Francisco in 89 days 21 hours.

She was a new and extreme ship. What part of her record should be assigned to McKay's genius in design and what part to Maury's genius in navigation would be difficult to determine. The fact remains that merchants, shipowners, captains and governments credited Maury with contributing to the success of the new clippers. In the case of already existing ships the time savings were almost entirely due to Maury methods.

It was soon evident that a saving in days and hours of passage time due to a better knowledge of the sea translated themselves into dollars and cents in the account books of shipowners and merchants. The saving to the operators of American ships sailing out of Atlantic and Pacific ports was calculated at $2,250,000 each year. But America was not the only or even the chief nation to benefit. Soon after the charts and directions for the Indian Ocean had been issued, it was calculated that the annual savings to British vessels operating in that ocean ran to $1,000,000 and the general saving to all British vessels using Maury methods on any ocean $10,000,000 annually. No wonder recognitions, honors and rewards came to Maury from all the civilized world.

So far as the general public was concerned, the practical results of Maury's study of the oceans overshadowed all other considerations. Maury himself was not overcome by the acclaim and honors that now began to crowd upon him. He seems to have regarded them as a fortunate but inevitable result of the pursuit of proper methods and broad interests. It is clear that they never dulled his interest in basic and theoretical studies. He was the leader in organizing the first international conference for the systematic studies of the oceans which took place in Brussels in 1853.

Also in 1853 he published *Physical Geography of the Sea,* and in the same year published a "Letter Concerning Lanes for Steamers." This letter proposed the establishment, for reasons of both safety and efficiency, of a sort of double-track railroad across the Atlantic. Each lane was approximately twenty miles in width with a broad area intervening between them, the southern lane for those westbound. The lanes he proposed were based on an analysis of the abstracts of logs covering over 46,000 days of observation. With the passage of years there have been some modifications in the lanes that Maury established but his basic concept, method and principles are still in effect today.

Maury's interests and capacity for leadership were not confined to the sea. Like other inventive minds, he saw natural connections between his main interest and other phases of knowledge and practice. He was the first to advocate the establishment of a national weather bureau to be operated for the benefit of American farmers. The bill was not passed but after many years, when the Weather Bureau was established, it followed the ideas that he had originally proposed. He proposed the establishment of a railway or a canal across the Isthmus of Panama. It was Maury's indefatigable scientific work in the study of the ocean extending over many years that made it possible for Cyrus Field, after repeated failure, to finally lay the first transatlantic cable.

Maury's work first made the scientific world conscious of how the methods of science could be applied to the study of the oceans and the skies. Even a condensed outline of his work helps us to a feeling of greater intimacy with the ocean. *The Physical Geography of the Sea,* published in America in 1855, was the first systematic book on oceanography and also on meteorology. Even a limited acquaintance with the book would show anyone that Maury was describing the ocean as an organized system of winds and currents. He starts off with a description of the Gulf Stream, describing its origin, its course in the western Atlantic and its behavior in the northern and the eastern part of the Atlantic. He described its depth and its relationship to surrounding water. He described the effect of the Gulf Stream on the climate of England and the continent and described at length the bearing it had on the management of ships upon the sea and its effect on trade; contrasting, for example, the trade growth of the ports of South Carolina with that of New York. He referred to the effect that this current had on the feedings of sea life including that of whales. In other chapters he described such matters as measurements of the temperature of water at different depths, the taking of soundings in connection with which he printed the first bathymetric chart of the North Atlantic and a score of other matters that were systematically treated for the first time. It is quite evident that from the point of view of modern knowledge Maury occasionally made an error and occasionally drew wrong conclusions. This is not surprising. What is surprising is that he was so often right. Surprising also is the volume and the scope of his work.

Occasionally a modern writer on oceanography is tempted to refer to him as having an interest only in the study of weather and the study of surface currents in the ocean. Such comments must be based on a very superficial acquaintance with Maury's work. He was interested in multiple measures of salinity and of temperature and of measures taken at depth no less than on the surface. He valued such measures quite as much as measures of surface currents and his writing showed that he understood their theoretical importance. He issued instructions for securing such measures. He was guilty of no lack of interest or of insight. It was under Maury's direction that the first series of deep-sea soundings in the open ocean was consistently carried out. Up to Maury's time soundings were taken by dropping overboard a cannon ball fastened to a hemp cord; the shot was usually lost together with the cord; the method was uncertain and soundings were infrequent.

While Maury was in charge of the Naval Observatory, Lieutenant John Mercer Brooke invented a simple but practical deep-sea sounding apparatus. It was under Maury's direction that this apparatus was put into use by O. H. Berryman on the *Dolphin*, and that in 1853 a complete set of soundings was built up between Nova Scotia and Ireland which permitted Maury to construct an orographic map and an underwater profile. It was with the apparatus also that the first satisfactory samples of ocean bottom were secured. Maury sent the samples to Professor J. W. Bailey of West Point for analysis. This analysis demonstrated for the first time that the bottom of the open ocean was not simply composed of mud or silt but of undisturbed and unbroken, though minute, shells of tiny marine organisms. Deposits of this kind were later given the name of ooze, but Maury's seem to have been the first samples procured and examined.

We have already referred to the fact that the first international meeting to bring about a co-operative study of the sea was organized under Maury's direction and took place in 1853 at Brussels. Scientists interested in the study of the sea were officially present representing a number of the most important governments of Europe. Before these meetings adjourned most of the government representatives had agreed to a form of scientific log which was to be carried and to be used on all the naval vessels of each subscribing country and had agreed to the conventions for the presentation of such records even in time of war.

Maury's essential genius rested in the fact that he was able to view the ocean in a manner both scientific and philosophic. He began with the practical needs of a young midshipman serving as a sailing master of a small naval vessel. As we have seen, it took him years to assemble the facts and he had to invent the scientific methods for handling and presenting them. His patience and his scientific attitude are well recorded in the following passage: "To keep the mind unbiased by theories and speculations; never to have any wish that an investigation would result in this view in preference to that, and never to attempt by premature speculation to anticipate the results of the investigation, but always to trust to the observations."

Once he had the facts he was able to put them together into a comprehensive and eloquent picture of the structure and behavior of the ocean of water on the surface of which man sails and carries on his commerce and the ocean of the air at the base of which man dwells. On the scientific side he first demonstrated that each has a structure which could be made comprehensible to the human mind, and on the practical side that patient study could make each serviceable to human welfare.

Maury's lifework is surprising not only because he made discoveries in so many different fields but also because in each of these fields he upset traditional beliefs and provided new ways of looking at the world.

Before Maury died he had received honors and rewards for his work not only from his own country but also from most of the other countries about the shores of the Atlantic. I am sure that no recognition Maury received in his lifetime would have had for him a greater value than the one that comes each month of the year showing that his work is still alive. Every pilot chart issued by the United States Hydrographic Office carries this special notice: "Founded upon the researches made in the early part of the nineteenth century, by Matthew Fontaine Maury, while serving as a Lieutenant in the United States Navy."

You may investigate many lines of human activity and in few of them will you ever find an extensive contribution like Maury's that has had a continuous useful life for over a hundred years, and seldom has a man earned so appropriate and so enduring a monument.

* * * *

The two related sciences that Maury began—meteorology and oceanography—both needed two essential things: many co-operative workers and international organization. Maury himself took the first steps to secure the workers and the organization for it was at his suggestion that delegates from many nations meet in Brussels in 1853 to constitute the first international conference on the study of the sea. Maury also sought international agreement and action when he published his letter concerning lanes for steamers crossing the Atlantic in 1855.

So much for theoretical organization. In practical ways ships of many nations helped Maury to build up his charts, and English and American ships both worked to build up the tables of Atlantic soundings that were required for the laying of the transatlantic telegraph cable.

The American Civil War absorbed the interest of the world and sank many ships and burdened the remaining ships so that there was little progress in the study of the sea for a number of years. However by 1873, the year of Maury's death, Sir C. Wyville Thomson was able to publish *The Depths of the Sea* based on cruises of two British ships, *Porcupine* and *Lightning*.

This introduced the decades of great and basic explorations of the sea. One of the most productive of these was the voyage of H. M. S. *Challenger*. This voyage officially commenced in the year 1872 and continued until 1876. The commander was Sir George Nares with Sir Wyville Thomson, Sir John Murray and many scientists working on many different phases of oceanography and marine biology.

It would burden this book to even list the scientific accomplishments of this one expedition but we can form an impression of its importance from the fact that publication of the results began in the year 1880 and continued for fifteen years until 1895. By this time no less than fifty large and full volumes had been published. Many of these had interest only for the scientist and the trained specialist but many also opened up for all men new worlds beneath the waves. People saw for the first time the great variety of the strange creatures that lived under pressure in the depths of the sea, and learned also about the variety and distribution of the sediments that lie on the bottom of the ocean. Sir John Murray, who edited the scientific results, was himself interested in the sediments that compose the ocean floor, and it is said that following his *Challenger* reports his position was so important and well established that he had an opportunity to examine all samples of ocean bottom brought up from great depths until his death in the year 1914.

Other nations were not far behind the British in sending their own research vessels to sea for extended cruises. Thus the U. S. Coast and Geodetic survey vessel *Blake* was at sea in the years 1877-1880 and the results were reported in two volumes by no less a scientist than Alexander Agassiz. The Germans sent out S. M. S. *Gazelle* 1874-1876, results published in five volumes. The Russians, the Swedes, the Danes, the Norwegians were sending out their own research vessels only a few years later. All of this work was useful. Naturally the students of different countries had different interests and they went out on many different errands with varied ships and varied equipment. There were vast oceans and great depths to explore; duplication of effort was unlikely to occur; would have been difficult to secure even if planned and desired; and would have had a value if secured.

In time questions of overlapping interests, of economy of effort, of neglected opportunities did arise, and in 1902 an international meeting was held in Stockholm which resulted in the creation of an international Council for the Study of the Sea with permanent headquarters in Copenhagen.

At the same time that the great research expeditions were sailing the high seas research was also commencing in special centers alongshore. As early as 1872 Dr. Anton Dohrn, a German biologist, established at Naples one of the first and one of the most famous stations for marine biology. Before the century closed even a prince had become a devotee of marine science. This was Prince Albert I of Monaco who equipped his fine steam yacht as a research vessel and made a number of cruises in her. Ashore he built and equipped a station for marine biology, an aquarium and a marine museum. In 1919 the International Hydrographic Bureau was also established in Monaco. Over the years many different types of institutions have grown up in Europe. Some pursue purely scientific interests, others have practical and economic purposes such as the improvement of fisheries or the cultivation of oysters. In fact, the separation of practical and scientific is not as sharp as it sounds, for the abstract work of the scientist often turns out to have a practical application and the problems of the fisheries research stations have sometimes provided materials for development by the scientists.

On this side of the Atlantic shore stations had a growth very similar to those of Europe both in character and time. In 1880 C. O. Whitman, a biologist from Harvard, went to Woods Hole in the summer and there gave instruction in marine biology. Thus at one stroke he not only laid the foundation for the great Institute of Marine Biology at Woods Hole but also anticipated the summer school or summer session which has become an important feature of so many American universities. A fisheries laboratory has also been added to Woods Hole and a fully equipped oceanographic institute with its own seagoing research vessels.

Oceanographic departments for teaching and research have grown up in a number of American universities. Yale University has the Bingham Foundation for Oceanography and Columbia carries out its activities as part of the Lamont Observatory of Geology.

On the west coast the steps in development that we have seen on the Atlantic shore were repeated. It started with a personal interest. When Edward W. Scripps was compelled by ill health to give up some of his most strenuous activities in the newspaper business he settled on the west coast in California. There he became interested in the life of the sea and supported a small study group in marine biology. This was later moved to La Jolla and became the Scripps Institute of Biological Research. In turn as interest in basic problems grew this became the Scripps Institution of Oceanography, now a part of the University of California. The University of Washington also maintains oceanographic laboratories.

As in other sciences, institutions in oceanography sometimes become famous for their work in some specialty. Thus the U. S. Coast and Geodetic Survey while carrying on all of its many regular duties has devoted special attention to studies of the tides and its staff have invented and built special machines for the analysis or computation of tidal movement. In England at Liverpool comparable work is carried out by a special organization, The Tidal Institute.

Invention and ingenuity are an inseparable part of oceanography. Two examples will serve to illustrate this fact. Back in the last century the Scandinavian oceanographers were much concerned with the nature of ocean currents. This work culminated in a theory of currents formulated by Bjerknes which recognized that sea water was not everywhere the same but differed in temperature and salinity (saltiness) at different places and depths. The differences were essential in accounting for the behavior of the currents. But no one could prove the theory or apply it because there were no known ways of taking samples of water and temperatures of water accurately at different depths.

Then about 1900 Fridtjof Nansen, who was an ocean scientist as well as a great explorer and humanitarian, invented the reversible water bottle. Briefly put, this was an open tube having valves at both ends. Nansen attached numbers of the tube to a stout wire at selected distances by a special device. Then he lowered the wire with its tubes —valves open—into the sea. When all the bottles were in place at different depths he fastened a small but heavy weight, called a "messenger," about the wire and let it fall. The messenger striking the upper fastening of the first bottle released it. The bottle swung down with the lower fastening as a pivot, reversing its position on the wire and closing the valves, thus taking on a sample of water at that depth. The swinging of the first bottle also released a second messenger which reversed the second bottle and so on. A reversible thermometer attached to the bottle recorded the local water temperature at the time of reversal. In this way accurate measures of salinity and temperature at many different depths could be secured with one lowering of the wire. The theory was demonstrated and practical applications developed.

Again, the science of submarine geology that had begun with Sir John Murray's samples of ocean bottom developed very slowly because no one had developed a method of getting really thick sections of the ocean bottom, and most methods merely scratched the surface. Then in 1936 an American scientist, C. S. Piggott, invented the submarine gun. The heavy weapon loaded with an explosive charge was lowered till it was hanging just over the ocean floor. Then when it was fired it shot a long open tube into the ocean bed and when drawn up often provided a core many feet in depth. Since most deep ocean deposits accumulate slowly this could provide a clue to a long period in earth and ocean history. These are but samples. Many submarine problems remain unsolved awaiting a new generation of inventors.

Chapter 17

THE CLIPPERS

SHE was a lady and no commoner; she was large yet tall and graceful; she had an oppulent charm yet was swift and sure in movement; she was expensively dressed and equipped from head to heel; she was an exacting mistress rather than a faithful housewife; it cost a fortune merely to keep her alive yet she had little domestic value; restless, she traveled far and fast, always on gallant and sometimes on dubious errands; everywhere she went she stirred men's admiration; upon her they lavished their greatest talents and efforts; sometimes she tossed a sudden fortune into a man's hand but quite as often she broke his heart; she was jealously pursued by envious rivals and she died young, but while she lived she was the toast of the town, the poetry of an age—she was the Yankee Clipper.

She came along to meet certain basic needs that the men of her time were discovering. She was indeed created to meet them and the needs were these: the need for speed; the need to cover enormous distances in large ventures; the need for beauty and elegance.

In the years between 1840 and 1850 people began to be conscious of the value of time; they began to want things done in a hurry. This feeling was most frequently expressed in the United States which had, for a generation, been growing rapidly both in population and settled area. There was a general expansion of industrial and mercantile enterprise.

In England, for instance, machine manufacturers had begun to assume an increasingly important place in the life of the nation. This involved a greater demand for materials such as American cotton and Australian wool as well as new markets for the finished products. China and other parts of the Far East were new and rich sources of trade both for American and European merchants. The sense of speed and timing arose from the fact that many of the articles of trade were produced in seasonal cycles and tended to reach their distant markets also in cycles. Such crops were fruits and grains but especially tea, cotton, wool. There was thus a special profit for the ship and trader who first reached the market with the new crop and thus relieved any shortages built up during the unproductive period. There were other factors working on the mercantile world to increase the sense of urgency. From the early packets of 1820 to 1840 ships were getting larger; they cost more to build. The operator had more money tied up in each unit and each carried a larger cargo which affected the shippers. Slow passages meant slow returns on the investments.

These were the economic factors; but there were other incentives to speed. Steam had come into use for transportation on land and water early in the century. It was a long time—1840—before a locomotive could beat the thirty-five miles per hour that represented the speed of a race horse and it took half a century or more to develop steamers that had the speed, the range, the reliability, the safety and the economy of the ships in sail. Still, steam was there as a threat, a challenge, a promise.

As far as North Atlantic travel was concerned, the old packet lines met the challenge by hard driving and by gradually increasing the size of the ships. They contributed to the sense of speed. They had not in the beginning tried for speed; their purposes were scheduled reliability and cargo-carrying capacity and steady year-by-year profits. But schedules meant speed and a safe margin for turn-around in port; competition meant speed; passengers meant speed.

The packets contributed to the interest in speed but packet line owners for the most part insisted on building ships that followed the general traditions of packet architecture. There is a curious point here. It was not the Atlantic packet operators that stimulated the creation of the early clippers or provided the incentives for their development. After the clipper ship emerged a few were used in the Atlantic packet lines. The first ships to look like clippers came into being and found their opportunities in a different kind of service and later the characteristic clipper sailed from an Atlantic port to some port on the other side of the world—California, Honolulu, the East Indies, China, Australia or where you will.

In a way the clipper was the daughter of the packet. They had a certain resemblance, but the beauty and distinction of the clipper form depended essentially on the way in which her lines were slender and sweet just where those of the packet were full and complacent.

However much they differed in appearance and behavior, it was still a case where the younger generation benefited by the work the older generation had accomplished. The earliest clippers were designed by men who also designed packets and were built in the yards that built the packets and were often commanded by men who had received their trainings in the packet lines. It follows, therefore, that both the packet and the clipper were American developments. At the time that each of them emerged, each burst upon the shipmasters of the world, including the British, as a new and surprising development.

No one can say with any certainty just when the first clipper was built. Experts have spent years writing about the clipper ships and have not yet come to an agreement. There had been a growing opinion that faster ships could be built. There were men waiting with novel ideas of design; what they needed was an opportunity to try them out. When the opportunity arrived, in the booming years of the 40's and 50's these ideas emerged in practice. Designers borrowed freely from each other—new features of design and rig were blended; the lines of a new type of ship structure flowed together and the clipper was born.

The name "clipper" was old. Just as the term "packet" was used loosely before the packet line services were invented, so the term "clipper" had been applied loosely to a variety of ships before the vessel that we now know as a clipper came into existence. It was used for any vessel that was supposed to have speed, or as the language of that time had it, "to go along at a good clip." The name appeared particularly in connection with a number of vessels built in Baltimore and referred to as Baltimore Clippers. The basic ideas of the Baltimore shipbuilders seem to have been derived from small French vessels of the eighteenth century, but these grew up and went through a number of changes along the shores of the Chesapeake. The Baltimore vessels specialized in speed; they were relatively small and light and thus formed a sharp contrast with the New York packets which specialized in strength, reliability and cargo carrying capacity. The Baltimore vessels had light, pointed bows, whereas the packets were round and full forward. The Baltimore vessels were apt to employ a V-shaped cross section below water. The packets already tended to use flat floors with little dead rise. The Baltimore vessels, operating from a river, kept to a fairly shallow draft particularly in the forward section of the vessel. Their maximum depth was aft so that they were built with what is technically known as aft-drag. This, of course, was balanced by a sail plan that brought the largest areas of canvas aft. The masts were not stepped perpendicular to the water line or to the deck of the vessel, but were sloped backward or given a rake.

Some of the Baltimore vessels had hollow water lines at the bow and this was one of the features that characterized the clipper design. Most of the Baltimore vessels were two-masted and thus in a technical sense they were not ships; they were schooners or topsail schooners, brigs or brigantines; but a few of them were rigged as small ships.

The ship *Ann McKim* was built by Isaac McKim in Baltimore in 1833. She was unusually large for a Baltimore vessel, running to 493 tons. For her times she had an unusually large bow and a slight concavity in her water lines. She preserved a certain amount of after-drag. The *Ann McKim* is sometimes referred to as the first clipper ship. Even if we reject this view, she certainly foreshadowed many of the features that were more completely developed in the characteristic clipper models and it is generally agreed that she had an influence on at least two of the New York designers who later built the great clippers.

In 1837 she was purchased by the firm of Howland & Aspinwall, who were outstanding merchants in the China trade. This firm ordered only a few ships built to their account. It had long been their practice to buy packets after they had served for a period of time on the transatlantic line and proved their qualities, and then employ them in lengthy voyages to China. The *Ann McKim* proved one of the fastest of such vessels and it is supposed that on some occasion when she was drawn up in one of the New York yards for overhaul, she stimulated the thinking of men like Capt. N. B. Palmer, John Willis Griffiths and Donald McKay.

N. B. Palmer of Stonington, Connecticut, was an accomplished, practical and many-sided man. As a young man he had served in sailing vessels that were operating in Antarctic waters and it was in 1821, when he was twenty-two years old and in command of a tiny sloop, that he discovered the coasts of the Antarctic that bear his name. After he had turned north from this discovery he was overtaken in the night by fog and calm. In the early hours of the morning he was surprised to hear the sound of a ship's bell for he supposed his vessel was alone in the thousands of miles of icy Antarctic waters. Dawn revealed to him the ship of Admiral F. G. Bellinghausen who for two years had been in command of a Russian Antarctic expedition. Bellinghausen entertained Palmer on board his vessel and in due course reported Palmer's independent discovery of the Antarctic coast that still bears his name.

For some years Palmer commanded the packet *Huntsville* operating out of New Orleans. Because they had to carry large weights and also traveled over shoals in entering the mouth of the Mississippi, these packets were built with flat floors and little dead rise. According to the shipbuilding theory of the day, this should have decreased their speed in sailing, yet Palmer found that in the *Huntsville* he could consistently complete faster passages than other packet vessels. He became a champion of the flat-floor principle of construction. In 1837 E. K. Collins organized the Dramatic Line of Liverpool packets and he credited Palmer with having persuaded him to embody the flat-floor principle in the construction of his large, elegant and speedy ships. In 1840 Palmer became a captain in the China trade. On one of his passages back from China he had with him as a passenger Charles Porter Low of the firm of A. A. Low & Brother, China traders and the owners of the vessel that Palmer commanded. Palmer had carved a model of a vessel that incorporated the flat-floor principle with hollow water lines in the bow and other features that Palmer believed would produce a speedy vessel without sacrificing cargo capacity. Mr. Low was so impressed with Palmer's work that as soon as they landed in New York Palmer was introduced to the senior partner, A. A. Low, and an order was immediately placed for the ship *Houqua*. This vessel of 600 tons is believed to have been based on Palmer's wooden model and was an early and successful example of the clipper ship. Palmer was her captain on a run from New York to Canton that was completed in ninety-five days. He also had an influence in the design of the clippers *Samuel Russell* and *Oriental*.

Palmer seems to have felt that the very fast and successful passages that he made with these ships demonstrated the value of the clipper design. He retired from the sea in 1850. The old seamen would have said that Captain Palmer "swallowed the anchor" in 1850; that is to say he gave up his command at sea and went ashore to live. This did not end his period of usefulness; he continued as a superintendent for the Lows and in other ways led a busy life for an additional quarter of a century.

Reference to Palmer's career brings to mind another famous ship commander of the period because for a part of the time they followed parallel courses and were, in a sense, rivals. This was Captain Robert H. Waterman, also known as Bully Waterman or "The Killer." In the 30's, when Palmer was serving in the New Orleans packets and in the Dramatic Line to Liverpool, Waterman was commanding the Black Ball Line. In the 40's, both of them appeared as commanders in the clippers operating to China; in fact at one time Waterman, then in the employ of Howland & Aspinwall, commanded the old packet *Natchez* which was a sister ship of Palmer's *Huntsville*. In 1843 Waterman drove this old vessel from China to New York in a ninety-two-day passage which was very near to a record for that time. In the same ship in 1845 he brought the record down to seventy-eight days. This prompted Howland & Aspinwall to order a new ship for his command. This was the *Sea Witch*, designed by Griffiths, one of the most beautiful and fastest of the clippers. In 1849 Waterman brought the *Sea Witch* from China to New York in an all-time record of seventy-four days and fourteen hours. The next year Waterman in the *Sea Witch* took eighty-five days for the China run and Palmer in the *Oriental* beat him home in eighty-one days.

Waterman then began operating on the run to California, and it was in this service that he earned the reputation for brutality and hard driving that has always been attached to his name. On one occasion his arrival in San Francisco provoked a riot and almost a lynching. In this case, however, the charges of brutality that were made against him were proved to be without foundation. They seem to have had their origin in the stories of a few of his crew who were drunk two days after his arrival in San Francisco and to have been fanned into a public conflagration by an inflammatory newspaper article. The accusations against Waterman were disproved at a trial on evidence supplied by the testimony both of passengers and seamen from his ship. However that may be, Waterman was a rival of Palmer's only in the sense that they both commanded record-breaking vessels, but he never exhibited any of Palmer's great abilities in other fields.

Before Waterman and Palmer were racing each other across the broad Pacific other designers and builders were making independent contributions to the development of the clipper. That the lines of the *Houqua* first found expression in Palmer's little carved wooden model is not unusual. In fact that is the way in which shipbuilders worked in those days. Up to the 1840's there were no commercial marine architects other than those that may have been employed in the design of naval vessels. William Webb, Isaac Webb, Bell and Brown and the others who built the packets apparently served both as architects and as builders. It was customary for them to work from a model, the lines being taken off the model and reduced to drawings after the model had been completed. Two young men served their apprenticeship in different yards of the early builders and are said to have been acquainted with each other even in those days. One of these was John Willis Griffiths and the other Donald McKay, and both were destined to achieve world-wide fame as the designers of the clippers.

John W. Griffiths, in the 1840's, was one of the first men to establish himself as an individual marine architect and to have a vessel identified as the product of his design. The opportunity came to him in 1843 when the firm of Howland & Aspinwall departed from their usual practice and ordered him to design a fast vessel to be put into their China tea trade service. They did not insist that this vessel should conform to the prevailing standards of marine architecture as expressed in the packets; apparently it was their intention to give the young designer a free hand. Griffiths produced the *Rainbow,* which was definitely a clipper ship and one of the earliest examples of this type of vessel. In fact as she began to take form some of her features were so novel to the eyes of the shipping men of her time that she was an object of comment even before she was launched. Certain misgivings seemed also to have arisen in the minds of Howland & Aspinwall for it is said that conferences between the designer and the owners accounted for delay in her construction so that she was not launched until 1845. Her form made it clear that Griffiths won the arguments. She was 750 tons; for her day she was unusually long and sharp in the bows with hollow water lines. This caused one of the water-side wits to remark that she looked as though she had her bows "turned inside out." The theory had been that a ship that was to carry a heavy press of sail had to have full bows to preserve her buoyancy forward and to keep her from burying her nose in every wave. Griffiths reversed this theory, keeping her bows keen and sharp for entry into the water under all normal sailing conditions. He provided the additional buoyancy needed by widening and flaring her bows outward above the water line; thus the deeper her bows entered the water the greater was the area for her support. She had a greater length in proportion to her beam than was customary at the time, a long straight keel and the flat floors that were also characteristic of Palmer's model. The water line was carried farther aft than was customary.

All of these features Griffiths could defend with arguments. He was one of the first theoretical designers and he had benefited considerably by study, and whereas the usual builder worked by practical experience and rule-of-thumb methods, Griffiths not only read scientific works which he thought had a bearing on his subject but also had conducted some experiments of his own working with models in a tank.

The *Rainbow* did all that was expected of her. Though Captain Land, who was driving her to the limit, lost some spars and sail, she completed her run out in something over seventy-nine days. The most unusual part of her performance was that she completed a round trip including the time in port in seven months and seventeen days and returned a handsome profit for the voyage. This was the same season that Waterman drove the old *Natchez* from Macao to New York in seventy-eight days.

Had social history pursued a normal course, the clipper design that was proving its merit in the China trade might well have experienced a slow and steady evolution. What it might have been we shall never know for history seldom moves steadily. Almost simultaneously a series of events developed that greatly accelerated and enhanced clipper development. First there was a boom in all normal trade; next gold was discovered in '48 in California and the gold rush was on for a number of years. The California fever had hardly abated when gold was discovered in Australia, and this brought on another fever of shipbuilding.

One of the results of this extraordinary set of occurrences was that ideas in ship design that had formerly lain idle or gone begging were instantly in great demand.

Among the men who had ideas for sale was S. H. Pook, a young man who had recently set himself up as a consulting architect. The Lows went to him and in 1850 he produced the extreme clipper *Surprise*. He had shoved her tonnage up to 1,006 tons and no sooner was she launched when she went roaring around the Cape to establish a record of ninety-six days to California. This beat by just one day the passage that the *Sea Witch* had recently completed.

The last and greatest of the clipper ship designers and builders was the extraordinary genius Donald McKay. McKay was one of the sons in a large Nova Scotia family. He went to school for a while, but like many another able and cultured man, the best education he received was that which he provided for himself. It was supposed that he would become interested in the management of the family farms, but he and his brother Lauchlan were more interested in the ships that came and went in the harbors and when they were still boys they built themselves their first little ship. Then Donald came to New York and apprenticed himself to Isaac Webb, whose yard on the East River built some of the best packets. McKay was a little over sixteen years old when he and his father signed the papers of apprenticeship. Under the terms of the agreement McKay was to work for Webb for a period of four and a half years and to be on call at any time, day or night. He was to receive $2.50 per week as well as $40 per year for his general expenses. McKay agreed to work faithfully and to be on call at all times, day or night. He gave assurance that he would not "contract matrimony, nor haunt Ale Houses, Taverns, Dance Halls or Play Houses." He was also to avoid card playing and other forms of gambling and so forth. Webb agreed to teach him "the mystery and trade of a ship's carpenter."

McKay proved himself industrious and intelligent and seems to have won the affection as well as the approval of Isaac Webb. Their relationship and contract was terminated by mutual agreement when McKay had an opportunity to assume a good position with the yard of Brown & Bell in 1832, and about this time he contracted matrimony appropriately enough with a Miss Albenia Boole, the daughter of a prosperous shipbuilding family, with ideas and knowledge of her own regarding ship construction.

In these years McKay was immersed in shipbuilding. All of the shipyards that built the packets stood side by side—a long stretch of the East River opposite the Navy Yard, and occupying about a mile of the waterfront. Here the young man acquired not only his intense interest in and knowledge of ship design but also the latest and most systematic methods of yard operation. He also laid here the foundations of his reputation as a man of unusual talents, and he formed friendships with Griffiths and others that were to last him a lifetime.

McKay wisely felt that he would have better opportunities for advancement in another community. He moved first to Newburyport and then to East Boston and shortly associated himself in the organization of the independent shipbuilding firm of Currier & McKay. They built some vessels together but the partnership was not one of long duration, and McKay was soon in business for himself.

During this period McKay produced the *Delia Walker,* which was engaged in trade with South America. The owner of this vessel, Dennis Condry, was both impressed with McKay and with the excellent record of his ship. By chance Condry returned from England in a packet vessel that was also carrying Enoch Train, who was then engaged in organizing his line of White Diamond packets to operate between Boston and Liverpool. As a result of conversations between these two travelers Train, on arrival in Boston, went up to Newburyport to meet McKay. This resulted in McKay's receiving the contract to design a fleet of four packets for Train's service. It resulted also in McKay's moving his yard from Newburyport to Boston.

Below is a brief list of a few of the vessels that McKay designed and built in a period of approximately ten years. McKay was responsible for many more than these vessels but this list illustrates certain things. It shows in the first place what a large volume of business developed in sailing vessels just at the time when some observers in the 40's were predicting that the sailing ship was finished and that the steamers would absorb all their business. In the second place it illustrates how rapidly McKay's ideas developed and the size of his vessels along with them. In 1842 he began with the *Courier* of only 380 tons; by 1853 he had already completed the *Great Republic,* 4,555 tons, which was certainly the largest and would probably have been the fastest clipper ship ever built had it not met with a tragic accident.

PACKETS

Name	Tonnage	Year
Courier	380	1842
New World	1,414	1846
Staffordshire	1,817	1851
Star of the Empire	2,050	1853
Chariot of Fame	2,050	1853

CLIPPERS

Name	Tonnage	Year
Stag Hound	1,534	1850
Flying Cloud	1,783	1851
Sovereign of the Sea	2,421	1852
Great Republic	4,555	1853

We must remember that McKay was only one of the clipper ship builders. It is said that practically all of the North Atlantic packet ships were built in New York over a period of thirty years and that there were only 150 of them. To contrast with this it is said that over 300 clipper ships were built in the yards of New England and New York in a ten-year period. It is quite possible that this figure is too high, for the clipper enjoyed enormous popularity and undoubtedly many vessels were called clippers that did not deserve this distinction. Even if allowances are made, this is a record of enormous activity. There was never any question about Donald McKay's ships deserving the title of clipper. He brought the whole movement to its logical culmination and built the fastest sailing vessels of all time. The first of these was the *Stag Hound* in 1850. The tonnage of the *Stag Hound* was 1,534; more than twice the tonnage of Griffiths' *Rainbow* built only five years earlier. In several other ways she differed both from the *Rainbow* and from the ships that McKay himself later designed. She had a sharp entrance and a concavity at the water lines but she avoided the flair in the upper part of the bows which Griffiths thought so necessary, and she also was built with considerable dead rise rather than with the flat floors that Griffiths and Palmer had both felt to be so important. She certainly illustrates the fact that McKay, working alone in Boston, wanted to develop his own line of attack and work out his own ideas, and it would be in keeping with his character also that he did not want to encroach on the work of his friendly rivals in New York. The lines of clipper development, however, were each year becoming more clearly established and so achieving an inevitable organic unity.

This is clearly illustrated and expressed in the *Flying Cloud,* the *Sovereign of the Sea, Lightning* and the *Great Republic* that came along in rapid succession from McKay's yard. The way in which McKay worked on his various ships illustrates both his integrity and his independence. He now had a prosperous business and was constructing a number of vessels to order, and when he wished to develop a particularly novel or striking vessel he did so on his own initiative and at his own cost. The case of the *Flying Cloud* illustrates the success of McKay's ships as business ventures. This vessel was ordered by Enoch Train and therefore was to be a distinctive Boston venture. While she was building, however, news of her unusually attractive design spread to New York. She was inspected by the Lows who made a handsome offer to Train and she was sold at a profit before she was launched. In the meantime McKay's first clipper, the *Stag Hound,* had made an eleven months' voyage which had brought the following results: it had paid for the building cost; it had paid for the operating cost and had returned an $80,000 profit. The case of the *Sovereign of the Seas* is one that illustrates McKay's aggressive independence. He wanted a free hand in building an unusually large and novel vessel. He was now employing relatively flat floors and a full clipper bow. In this case he was striving for an increased carrying capacity and also expressing his belief that increase in water-line length would bring an increase in speed, so he lengthened her midship section and the ratio of her length to breadth was in itself a novelty.

Lauchlan McKay was placed in command of his brother's ship and her first cruise to California and the Hawaiian Islands proved both her speed and her economic value. It was on March 17, 1853, while in the South Pacific running for Cape Horn, that she established several world's records. For a number of hours she was logged at nineteen knots, a speed of about twenty-two land miles per hour. It was also at this time that she was the first vessel to travel more than 400 miles in a twenty-four-hour period. Laing has shown that there have been only thirteen occasions in world history when a sailing vessel has traveled more than 400 miles in a twenty-four-hour run. All of these records have been established by clipper ships built in New England. Twelve of them were established by vessels that Donald McKay designed and built. S. H. Pook, with the *Redjacket* at 413 miles, is the only other designer to hold such a record.

Flying Cloud, Great Republic, Donald McKay and *Sovereign of the Seas* bettered the mark on two occasions; the *Lightning* on three and the *James Baines* four times. The greatest day's sailing of all was recorded for McKay's ship the *Lightning* that covered 436 miles in a single day's sailing. This record was not beaten by any steam vessel for a period of twenty-five years.

In 1853 McKay felt that his position was sufficiently secure and his ideas of design sufficiently stabilized so that he could undertake a great venture. He designed and built the *Great Republic.* Her tonnage when completed was 4,555; she was 335 feet long, had a 53-foot beam and a depth of 38 feet. She had four decks with eight-foot headroom between each deck; she carried four masts with full rig on the first three, the height of the foremast was 200 feet from deck to trucks. The fact that it required over 16,000 square yards of canvas to provide sails for this vessel gives some idea of her lordly proportions. She carried a crew of 100 men and 30 boys and even this much crew would have been unable to handle her enormous yards and her great area of canvas, so McKay had installed on her the first steam winches to assist in raising the yards and trimming sail and in the handling of cargo.

The *Great Republic* was successfully launched and partly loaded with a cargo in Boston and then proceeded to New York to pick up the remainder of her cargo. Again Lauchlan McKay was in command. She attracted so much interest that a modest charge was made to those that wished to inspect her and she had so many visitors that a handsome return was realized, all of which was devoted to seamen's charities. In the meantime McKay personally carried the entire cost of the building of the vessel and of her operation.

When she was ready to sail, but still at her berth in New York, a fire broke out in the city. The wind that was blowing at the time carried sparks from the burning buildings ashore to the new ship; she caught fire and during a single night burned to the water line. The vessel was insured and McKay recovered a part of his investment, but nonetheless it represented to him both a financial loss and the defeat of a great plan. When McKay came from Boston to inspect the remains, many of his friends and advisers urged him to rebuild the vessel, but this seemed against his better judgment. The vessel was bought and raised by the Lows and N. B. Palmer was put in charge of her reconstruction. As she was rebuilt one deck was eliminated and the rig of her sails considerably cut down. Even so, in the rebuilt state her tonnage was 3,357 and she was still a noble vessel and a fast one. Even in her altered form she was one of the few vessels that turned in a run of over 400 miles a day. There seems little doubt that if she had sailed the high seas as McKay designed and built her she would have been the fastest as well as the greatest sailing vessel of all time. It is difficult to contemplate the story of the *Great Republic* without a feeling of loss and regret that this supreme expression of man's ability to use the winds in the interests of commerce and human intercourse never had a chance to fulfill its usefulness.

The loss of the *Great Republic* might well have terminated the career of an ordinary man, but it only stimulated Donald McKay to renewed activity. He returned to his Boston yard and crowded into the next few years the building of more ships with a larger aggregate tonnage (17,313 tons) than at any other period during his career. By this time the fame of the American clipper services had spread to all the parts of the world. Among other things a ship operator from Liverpool by the name of James Baines came to McKay with orders for a line of clipper ships to operate in the Australian trade, and the series of handsome ships that McKay produced proceeded to establish good business, prosperous runs and record passages in an entirely new section of the world.

Some of McKay's best ships were produced in this period. When *Lightning* was launched McKay invited representatives of Baines to sail with him on the first trip to England. They replied that they were extremely busy and had planned therefore to sail with the Cunard steamer out of Boston. Possibly this offended McKay, certainly it stimulated him. He sailed with *Lightning* from New York the same day that the Cunarder sailed from Boston. *Lightning* passed the steamer on the way over and was in Liverpool the same day that the Cunarder arrived in Cork in Ireland.

This great ship went on to break many records and to establish also a record of prosperous operation for her owners, but what was memorable about her was not only her speed but her beauty. The feeling which the vessel created has never been better expressed than in the words of a rival designer.

> No timid hand or hesitating brain gave form and dimension to the *Lightning*. Very great stability; acute extremities; full, short midship body; comparatively small dead rise, and the longest end forward are points in the excellence of this ship.
>
> John Willis Griffiths
> *Monthly Nautical Magazine*
> August 1855

This tells us not only about the quality of the vessel but also about the character of the man that built the great ships.

These were the great years. It was exciting enough when a ship like the *Lightning* showed that she could hold her own against a steamer, but what chiefly moved the people was the duels between vessels sailing in the same trade and often the fleets that sometimes left port on a single tide. Four American ships in the China trade passed Java Head together and this started a race in the open ocean to New York. These were the *Samuel Russell,* the *N. B. Palmer,* the *Wild Pigeon* and the *Joshua Bates.* This meant that they were traveling 12,000 miles to their port of destination. The *Palmer* came in two days ahead; the *Russell* and the *Wild Pigeon* practically sailed together the entire way and came in neck and neck.

Another list shows that between October 11 and November 17,

1852 fourteen American ships sailed from New York for ports in China. One of these was an extremely small vessel and one vessel was overloaded. Despite this, the average time of all vessels was only 112 days and two of the vessels completed the passage in ninety-four days.

The records are full of the beautiful, the incredible and the tragic, but here are the stories of four ships that were on passages around the Horn at about the same time, their records supplied in *Cutler's Year by Year Analysis of the Activity of the Clippers*.

1856 was a stormy year about the Horn. Captain Phineas Winsor, trying to reach San Francisco with his heavily laden clipper *Rapid* found it so. He had made a good run down the Atlantic, but the nearer he got to the Horn the worse the weather became, building up into a crescendo of gales from the west. Week after week he tried to battle his way westward while the great graybacks swept his deck and the ice accumulated on his spars and sails. Every week of struggle and every mile gained for the vessel to the westward was paid for with infinite fatigue, with sickness and with death. At the end, out of a total crew of twenty-four aboard when he sailed, ten were dead, ten were helpless with sickness and fatigue, while the captain, his mates and four men tried desperately to work the ship. At this point, after months of struggle, he had to give up and run for Rio to refit and reman. At one point he was within signal distance of another clipper that was taking up the struggle just when he was preparing to abandon it. Winsor thought it was the *Intrepid* under Captain Gardener but it was proved later that at the time Gardener, who had sailed on July 1st, was many miles away. It might have been *Neptune's Car* that had also sailed on July 1st and which should have been under the command of Captain Joshua Patten, a young and brilliant officer, but *Neptune's Car* was having her own troubles in addition to the endless heavy weather.

Captain Patten had been taken ill with some fever that affected his brain. He was in the cabin with his hearing and sight gone, incapable of responding to any signal. Before he had been taken ill the mate had made trouble and was now in chains. The person who commanded *Neptune's Car* through these bitter days was Patten's wife, nineteen years of age, but trained to the sea and already proving her competence as a navigator. She divided her time between supplying care and comfort to her sick husband and shoving her big ship forward against the western gales. She did it so successfully that she brought her ship into San Francisco ten days before Gardener got there with the *Intrepid,* and long before Winsor was able to complete his run in the *Rapid.* Mrs. Patten was acclaimed by the newspapers and rewarded with a purse raised by public subscription, but Captain Patten was dead in his thirtieth year.

The clipper captains were often selected for their youth and strength, but despite this many of them were the victims of the winds and the seas, and some also like Captain Patten were struck down by illness. Captain Higham was just as young and just as hopeful as Patten when he succeeded to the command of the *N. B. Palmer* but his health began to fail and before he could turn her bows homeward he had developed some fever and a persistent cough. Maybe he realized all the time how ill he was but if this was so he never let it interfere with his navigation of the vessel and he drove her to the best of his ability and the last ounce of his strength. He came into New York to tie the record from Shanghai of eighty-two days. A few days later he died of tuberculosis at his home in Brooklyn.

The men of the last century turned out great ships; and the ships turned out great men. Together they carried a new age around the world. The arts, the sciences and the inventions were making great strides throughout the nineteenth century. Manufacturing and industry were supplying new goods in increasing volume; trade and communication was pushing out into all parts of the world; year by year it needed new conveyances to keep the different parts of the world in touch with each other.

The clipper ship came when she was needed and because she was needed. The application of steam to the propulsion of vessels had literally been discussed and experimented with for more than a hundred years, but until well beyond the middle of the century was inadequate to the task of handling the world's affairs. It was only slowly that steam vessels grew up to be able to handle any important part of the world's business with volume and dispatch and safety. These were the responsibility first of the packet and later of the clipper. They were primarily the responsibility of the United States of America where these services to mankind were developed. They were one of America's most important contributions to the organized life of the world.

The great ships appealed to so many different aspects of our human character that when anyone starts thinking about them some special interest or enthusiasm is likely to appropriate the center of the stage. The artist has put on canvas the beautiful lines of their hulls and the rhythmic masses of their canvas in strong swift motion; the poet saw them as a vehicle of romance or a symbol of man's fate; the designer and engineer saw in them an extreme and successful effort to get maximum efficiency out of all the available kinds of wind; the merchant and operator saw them as fast carriers bowling home heavily laden with fat profits. All men praised them, but each for a different reason.

Perhaps the time has come now when we can see their essential contribution. They were the culmination of 2,000 years of human effort expended on producing the perfect sailing vessel. For the services they had to perform and the conditions they had to meet, the clipper ships came near to realizing an abstract ideal of beauty and service. In the middle of the nineteenth century technological progress was taking tremendous strides and going forward with great speed yet the sailing ships, decade by decade, were outstripping technology. In speed, in volume, in safety and in beauty they supplied services to trade and travel that exceeded anything that steam and steel were able to provide.

In terms of social history they carried hundreds of thousands of migrants from Europe to America, and from the eastern seaboard of the United States to its Pacific frontiers, and they carried English pioneers to Australia and New Zealand.

The decade of the clipper ships was also the period of great immigration into the United States. In the year 1852 immigration hit an all-time high. In the decade 1851 to 1860 over two and one-half million people entered the United States. Compared with the then existing population of the country, this is a larger proportion of immigrants than came at any other time. Proportionately, it exceeds even the period 1900 to 1910 when great superliners were trying to outdo each other in carrying immigrants. Practically all of the new arrivals in 1850 to 1860 came to America in sailing vessels. There were, in fact, no steamers to carry them. Even a decade later—that is, in 1870 —steam vessels of all kinds made up less than 12½ per cent of the world's shipping. As late as 1880 steam was only up to 25 per cent. The migrants came in the sailing traders, the packets and the clippers. Thus, at a formative period in world history, the sailing vessels speeded the settlement of continents; they first brought together, in rapid transportation, the nations of a new and expanding world.

Chapter 18

FORE-AND-AFT

THE packets and the clippers were types of vessels that had a special use at a particular era. They did their jobs, earned their pay and their fame and then disappeared in the spindrift of time to the haven where all good ships gather.

They provide nice and neat chapters in the story of the Atlantic. Not so the fore-and-afters for "fore-and-aft" describes a method and principle of hanging and using sail. This principle is closely tied up with the ability of a vessel to sail into the wind. Its use is very old and it may have had an independent origin in other oceans but its full development is essentially an Atlantic story. The principle emerges in many vessels and at many times; in early Dutch vessels, large and small; in the first English yachts; in American river boats; in New England schooners and Baltimore Clippers; in Banks fishermen and West Indian traders; in the great timber and cargo schooners of the early twentieth century; in modern ocean racers. Today there are still many sailing ships afloat on the Atlantic and practically all of them are fore-and-afters.

Following their development, our chapter takes us back and forward in time and moves freely about an ocean.

It was a long time before mariners of any nation developed in their vessels the ability to work into the wind by sail alone and without assistance from oars or any other propulsive device. This ability is closely related to the use of the fore-and-aft sail as a component of the rig of the vessel.

The above sentences seek to state a complicated matter simply but exactly. They recognize that in general there are two broad classes of sailing vessel. The first class is those we call "square-riggers" which are chiefly driven by square or quadrilateral areas of canvas, hung from yards. The yards in turn are hung from the mast in such a way that they usually form a right angle with the mast and also a right angle with the center line of the ship.

In this class the yards are hung and rigged so that they may be swung about to some degree and thus the yards and the sails they carry may be made to diminish the angle between themselves and the center line of the ship from bow to stern. Owing to the rigging which is necessary to support the mast and to other factors, there is a strict limit to the amount of this movement. The sails and yards are most out of their normal position when the angle above referred to is reduced.

The second general class is that of the "fore-and-aft" vessels. Here the chief sails are stretched between the lower spar, called the boom, and the upper or raised spar called the gaff, the inner or forward ends of which are attached to the mast. The forward edge or luff end of the sail is likewise held to the mast by hoops or other devices.

In this case the booms and gaffs and the sails stretched between them are in their most normal and natural position when they lie along the center line of the vessel from bow to stern or form a slight angle with it. They are rigged so that they are free to move in an arc so that the force of wind coming from aft may carry them out so that they may, more or less, increase the angle with the center line and approach the normal setting of a square sail, but in this case they are farthest from their natural position.

There are other types of sail called staysails which are set on ropes or wires which run from one mast to another or from the mast to the bowsprit or to some other part of the vessel. Sails that are set in the very forward part of the vessel on stays that run between the foremast and the stem of the vessel or the fore-topmast and the bowsprit, bear the special name of jibs. For general purposes, the jibs belong to the class of staysail. From what has been said above, it will be evident that jibs and staysails may be chiefly classified as fore-and-aft sails.

The chief characteristic and value of the fore-and-aft vessel is that she enjoys a superiority over the square-rigged vessel in working to windward. Some readers will be quick to point out that many square-rigged vessels, particularly those in the later days of the sailing ships such as the packets and the clippers, had an ability to work to windward. This was demonstrated repeatedly in their ability to negotiate passages from Europe to America against the prevailing westerlies and likewise their ability to beat around the Horn from the Atlantic to the Pacific against another and severer belt of westerlies. My statement has been phrased, therefore, so that it does not deny these undoubted accomplishments. It only says that the fore-and-aft vessel is greatly superior in this particular ability. This is balanced by the fact that the square-rigged vessel enjoys advantages in sailing with favoring or following winds. Since it is customary even today for vessels sailing in deep waters and on long passages to seek out well-known courses where winds and weather are generally favorable, this is no mean advantage.

There is another special point of some importance. The so-called fore-and-aft rigged vessels do not, as a rule, confine themselves to the setting of fore-and-aft sails. They usually supplement their main equipment with spinnakers, balloon jibs, raffees or other sails that serve the same purpose as square sails. Likewise, for some centuries, there have been few so-called square-riggers that are entirely dependent upon square sail.

The spinnaker, which is set on the aftermast of even a square-rigged ship is in all respects a fore-and-aft sail like the mainsail of a schooner and the staysails and jibs are, in effect, fore-and-aft sail. This we have tried to recognize in saying that the fore-and-aft sails of the square-rigger have been an important component in its ability to work to windward.

Nobody knows just where or when vessels were first built that had the capacity to work to windward. None of the classic vessels of the Mediterranean up to the time of Christ appear to have had this ability. The galleys used for transport and for war carried sail which was used when the winds were favorable. When the winds were unfavorable, this sail was furled. Then the ship was either driven by oars or anchored or it sought refuge in a harbor.

In the Mediterranean no improvements in this respect were made for many centuries; in fact, the galleys of the Venetians and the Genoese, at the time of the Renaissance, while they were larger and better built than the classic models, showed little improvement over them when it came to sailing. The Romans, in the later days of the empire, built large sailing ships to carry cargoes of grain from

Egypt. These vessels were well built and carried a large sail area but neither the setting of the sail nor the shape of the hull, which was like the bottom of a bowl and which had no keel, would have permitted the ship to work to windward.

Toward the middle of the first century B.C., when Caesar was on his way to the conquest of Britain, he came upon vessels of the Veneti. He says that his own ships, driven by oars, could usually overtake the ships of the Veneti. Then, using knives set on long poles, they would cut the rigging of the northern ships and so disable them and board them. He also says that when the wind was blowing and when the Veneti turned their ships in the direction of the wind, they were able to escape.

Mr. Charles E. Gibson recently pointed out in *The Story of the Ship* that this might indicate that these vessels were able to work to windward. It is at least probable that they were better in this respect than the Roman vessels but we have little other information on the ships of the Veneti and this leaves the matter rather in the field of inference and literary interpretation. In fact, the whole matter of the historic origin of this ability, even after much research and speculation, is left in doubt. This is quite a common situation in matters relating to the history of ships.

Of all the thousands of inventions and developments that have contributed to the effectiveness of sailing vessels, practically none are the invention and work of a single man who can be named as the originator and very few can even be assigned as the work of a single people at a single time. It seems more than probable that the art and science of sailing to windward was independently discovered and developed by different people at different times.

In the Pacific I have sailed on proas and outrigger canoes. These vessels are driven by sail of a triangular shape; that is, the shape of a large slice of pie. Two of the edges of the sail are lashed to spars and the spars are lashed together at their forward ends which, in turn, are fastened near the bow of the canoe. The sail is raised by a single rope (halyard) running from its middle point or point of balance of the upper spar to the top of the mast. This approximates the form of sail that is known in the Mediterranean and in other parts of Europe as a lateen sail and can be swung to have the effect of a fore-and-aft sail.

In cases where these canoes are given a deep hull form or employ timbers which act as keels and where they are steered with long sweeps which have great directive power, they can be maneuvered to windward by sailing on very long tacks. The long tacks are necessary because the process of changing the direction in which the vessel is sailing, or tacking, is very cumbersome with this rig and time and distance are wasted in the maneuver. Still, the fact remains that they can work to windward.

An examination of ship models collected from all over the Pacific shows that a number of native sailing boats probably had this ability. Where the rig and the ability originated we do not know, though a number of different points of origin have been suggested, including the ships of early India.

The term "lateen" that we have used above takes its origin from the fact that Mediterranean sailors, descended from Latin stocks, employed rigs of this type on a variety of vessels. Some of these vessels, having deep hulls or keels, would appear to have had weatherly qualities.

In historic time rigs of vessels adhering in general to the lateen type have been widely distributed all the way from the east coast of Africa through the Gulf of Aden, the Red Sea, the Egyptian coast to the shores of Tripoli and Morocco in the West. They are, thus, characteristic of the Islamic and other Eastern people. It seems probable, therefore, that they were introduced to the Mediterranean at the time of Islamic expansion and conquest and were later adopted and adapted by the people of Portugal, Spain and southern France for their fishing vessels. It is possible but not clearly demonstrated that the Islamic people in turn may have derived their practice from East Indian sources.

An independent origin of the fore-and-aft rig and of the devices of hull construction that make it possible to work to windward seems to have taken place in the North Sea. The European shores of the North Sea are shallow and are marked by many estuaries, bars and banks. This situation appears to have encouraged the Flemish, Dutch and north German people, at an early historic period, in experimenting with many different sizes of vessels employing different hull forms and rigs to meet the different conditions encountered.

Early representations of Dutch vessels are among the first to show a consistent use of fore-and-aft sails for the mainsail of the vessel. The head or upper margin of the sail was carried on a permanent but movable gaff. To be sure, these gaffs were relatively short and the top of the sail, therefore, relatively narrow, but they represent a definite development in this type of rig.

Obviously the short gaff can differ in either one of two directions.

It can be extended to give the longer gaff of the later sailing vessels or it can be diminished leading in the direction of the jib-headed or so-called Bermuda rig.

On account of the many shoals encountered in this coast the Dutch vessels employed neither keel nor a deep form of hull. To off-set this disadvantage and to give lateral resistance they developed an adjunct to the hull called lee boards. These were large strong structures having the shape of a paddle. Two of them were employed on each vessel. The upper or smaller end of the board was mounted on a pivot fitted at the side of the vessel amidships so that the large end of the board could either be hauled up, clear of the water, and fastened in place or lowered into the water to serve as a sort of supplementary keel. They derived their name from the fact that when the vessel was sailing into the wind the board on the windward side of the vessel was raised and the board on the leeward side extended into the water.

By a curious event in history, ships of Dutch design and Dutch methods of sailing were adopted by English seamen and the first English private yacht or pleasure vessel was of Dutch origin. It came about this way.

Charles II, with his followers, was in Holland on May 8, 1660, when the announcement came that he had been restored to the throne. The Dutch at once put at his disposal a small but fast and handy vessel of a type called a jacht. She was single-masted, carried a large fore-and-aft mainsail that was set on a fixed gaff and was loose-footed, with topsail and jibs. This vessel was apparently used as a dispatch boat and she was gayly painted and had a comfortable and elaborately decorated cabin.

King Charles was greatly pleased with her and enjoyed his passage in her sailing to meet the British vessel, *Naseby,* which, in the meantime, had been sent from England to bear him back to the throne. In fact, Charles' enthusiasm was such that he wished to acquire the vessel for his own use. The Dutch responded by promising him a vessel of this type. They at once set to work and built him a vessel which was later christened the *Mary*. The *Mary* was fifty-one and a half feet in length, had a beam of nineteen feet, carried eight guns and a crew of twenty men. The best artisans of Holland were employed in furnishing her cabin and the leading artists contributed to her decorations. She was sent to England as a royal gift in 1660 where the king used her as the first yacht.

With the *Mary* as a start the British began building a number of pleasure vessels. In a few years the king ordered from Peter Pet,* a member of a great family which enjoyed a great reputation as designers and builders of ships, a yacht called the *Jenny,* while Christopher Pet constructed another vessel called the *Anne* for the Duke of York. These two ships were sailed by their owners in a royal race won by the king.

Dutch influence in the design and management of ships reached the American continent through several different channels. Most roundabout and difficult to demonstrate is the fact that by the time the English colonies were well established English ships owed something to the contacts that had grown up between England and Holland, both through trade and desire of peace and through warfare. The American colonists, when they began to build vessels, naturally followed English models and utilized all they could of the maritime knowledge of the country.

One of the first ships of any importance constructed in the present territory of the United States was a Dutch vessel, built by Captain Adrian Block (also spelled Adrien Blok) on the banks of the East River in Manhattan. Captain Block had sailed to America in a ship called the *Tyger* which had been lost. *Onrust,* or as we would say, *Restless,* which he built as a replacement, had a thirty-eight-foot keel, was forty-four feet six inches overall and had an eleven-foot beam. This was the ship in which Block sailed to the island that bears his name and in which he explored the shores of Connecticut, Narragansett Bay and the Cape Cod area. She was the forerunner of a considerable shipbuilding industry developed by the Dutch for coastwise service between their various settlements and for use along the Hudson River to Fort Orange or Albany; in particular, a sloop developed for use on the Hudson which had a long and useful life. As late as 1825 a whole series of views of the river shows the presence of ships of this type throughout its navigable course, with the Dutch influence clearly discernible in the form of the hull and in the rig, the mainsail having a particularly narrow head attached to a short gaff.

This development of a particular type of vessel on the Hudson River was not exceptional. On the contrary, it was quite characteristic of most of the important rivers and sections of the coast. Each of these developed, for its own use and particular conditions, a vessel

* or Pett, usage varies.

or set of vessels that gave its waters a characteristic appearance and atmosphere and that added to the richness of American maritime history.

The vessels of the Connecticut were different from the vessels of the Hudson. There were other local types in Narragansett Bay, in the Cape Cod area and the major rivers of the Maine coast. Some of these types had a long history and survived even into the present times. To mention only a few, there was on the Chesapeake, the "sharpie" and "bugeye," the Cape Cod sailing "dories" and the Cape Cod "cats"; the "friendship sloop" from Friendship in Maine. Many of them were created to do special kinds of work; the friendship sloop, for example, was much used by the lobstermen.

The Great South Bay in Long Island was formerly a vast natural oyster bed and for generations did its best to satisfy New York's inexhaustible hunger for these wonderful bivalves. Here, the oystermen developed a characteristic schooner for their work. These were small but very stoutly built schooners. Their strength was required to accommodate the great weights of the catch and also to permit them to sail in the open Atlantic on the run to the market in New York. While operating in the bay, they could have gotten along very well with small and light sail area but the run to New York again accounted for their being equipped with a very substantial complement of all regular and some special sails. It was naturally desirable to reach the market on time and to return to the beds with as little wasted time as possible, so they were smart sailors. The shallow draft was compensated by the use of a large and heavy centerboard.

What was probably the last sound survivor of this fleet was purchased by a discerning yachtsman, Mr. Henry Anderson, and presented to a boys' school in Florida. This was the well-known schooner *Hickory* and I had the pleasure of sailing on it for a number of years. The characteristics that made her a good Great South Bay oyster boat also made her an exceptional good vessel for the Biscayne Bay area and for exploring the sounds, the cuts and the banks of the Florida keys.

Just as Dutch influence accounted for the Hudson River sloop, Swedes no doubt influenced the early vessels that were built on the Delaware at New Sweden and at other points.

Other New World centers of Dutch shipbuilding were in the West Indies. Here at Aruba, Curaçao and other islands the Dutch developed their own vessels, schooners as well as other types. Even the strange island of Saba, in the West Indies, stands as a continuing monument to the Dutchmen's love of the sea and passion for ship-building. This island is little more than a truncated cone of lava rock jutting out of the sea. Its top is green with tropic vegetation but its sides are no more than black cliffs. There is no harbor and scarcely even a beach to land on.

Nothing daunted, the Dutch inhabitants of this island built siz-able schooners at the top of the cliffs and then launched them by lowering them into the water. In Trinidad I anchored my ship near such a vessel and had an opportunity to inspect her. She sailed under the proud title, *The Dutch Princess of Saba.*

The building and use of schooners for trade among the islands of the West Indies was once enormous and is still lively. Even in colo-nial times there developed a large trade by schooners as well as by other vessels sailing between New England and the West Indies. How far the general type of West Indian schooners were influenced by Dutch tradition seems to be uncertain and whether the New Eng-land schooners influenced the development of the West Indies types or the other way about is also an unsettled matter.

Though hampered by political restrictions and interrupted by wars, this trade had a long history. It seems likely that the two centers of schooner development lying at either end of these trade routes must have had some influence on each other and led to the exchange of ideas of construction and design. From observation and casual study I would judge that this was the case but I have not succeeded in finding a comprehensive discussion of this matter in literature.

The American schooner was certainly developed in a New Eng-land port at an early date and had a very wide use.

Respecting the origin of the New England schooner there is an oft-repeated story which runs to the effect that there was a definite time and place at which this vessel emerged. It goes on to say that Andrew Robinson was the first to build such a vessel in 1745 at Gloucester, Massachusetts. When she was launched she took the water cleanly and scudded across it. A spectator is supposed to have cried out, "See how she scoones"; scoon, apparently, meaning to skip or scud as when a boy shies a flat stone over a smooth surface of water. The builder is supposed to have replied, "A schooner let her be."

This may have happened or it may be a folk tale; in any event the inference is misleading. There is little doubt that both the name schooner and the type of vessel to which it applied had their origin in Dutch shipbuilding practice.

Another center of development was in Baltimore and other ports on the Chesapeake. The ships developed in this area had sharp bows, a smooth entry and generally fast and graceful lines. They set value on speed rather than cargo-carrying capacity and acquired the name of Baltimore Clippers.

The schooner rig was one of a number of rigs employed on this hull form. Vessels of this type were widely used during the Revolution as privateers or letters of marque and also as blockade runners. After the War of 1812 they were developed for a variety of uses one of which, as we have already seen, was in the slave trade. They had a long life; in fact the type has never really disappeared.

When the slave trade was disrupted this type of schooner, with some modifications, was widely used as a vessel for pilots, as a ship for the revenue service and in other special employments. Chappelle points out that these schooners appear finally to have emerged as the pattern for the schooners built in New England and employed in the fisheries on the Grand Banks of Newfoundland. These vessels have become famous not only for their qualities of utility and seaworthiness but also for their trim yachtlike lines, their ability to beat to windward and their great turn of speed under sail.

A special and somewhat extreme development of the characteristic American schooner was embodied in the famous yacht *America*. George Steers, who designed the vessel, somewhat exaggerated the principles that were already embodied in the hull of fast American schooners, but she was still recognizable as a variant of this type rather than as a completely independent creation. By the standards of her time, or of any time, her sail plan was extreme, involving very large sail areas in the mainsail and the jib. The masts were set so as to give them a very decided rake. The great length of the main boom was balanced by an extremely long bowsprit.

In 1851 the *America* sailed from Sandy Hook to Havre in twenty-one days. During that season she outsailed most of the English yachts and captured the king of England's cup in a match race around the Isle of Wight. European seamen were already familiar with the superior speed of American packets and clippers. The *America* demonstrated this superiority in a new and unsuspected field.

That season's sport not only initiated the custom of international yacht racing which has persisted from then until recent times, but also set the conditions under which such races were to be carried out. It can be reasonably argued that these conditions, notably the necessity for the transatlantic crossings of the challenging vessel, imposed an unequal burden on the challenger.

From a disinterested point of view, however, the significant thing was not in the defeats or in the victories but in the succession of wonderful ships that participated in these events for so many years. The validity of the whole enterprise is exemplified in the remarkable evolutions of hull form and of sail plan that were tried, tested and demonstrated in these races.

In the years while the *America* was demonstrating the advantages of the fore-and-aft rig for speedy yachts, the square rig was at its apex of popularity and utility in the field of cargo carriers, as exemplified in the clipper ships and clipper barks. It continued in operation until the Civil War and after that survived in a long period of gradually declining usefulness. Before the Civil War America was the leading and most rapidly developing maritime nation in the world. The war terminated American ship construction and brought the wholesale destruction of fine vessels already built.

During the critical years when steam was developing so that it might later replace sail, America was falling behind. After the war it took some years for the nation to reawaken her interests in ship construction and operation and to revive the hope that some fair share of her foreign commerce should be carried in ships flying the American flag.

By this time the procession had passed by. The era of major clipper ship activity was becoming a part of history. The Suez Canal was in operation. Transatlantic passenger and freight service was progressively, year by year, traveling in the bottoms of the Cunard steamships subsidized by the British government and then into the transatlantic lines subsidized by the Germans, the French and other nations.

All this affected the design and development of sailing vessels. Competition was increasingly intense; construction costs and the wages of seamen were continually rising. Having lost most of the passenger traffic, America was seeking to retain some of its business in transatlantic freight. The extreme clipper was not the type of vessel for this time or for this service. Ships and barks were still being built but their hulls were no longer of clipper design. Smart service, at extreme speed, was no longer the watchword but rather cargo-carrying ability, so fuller and heavier hulls were in demand. It became evident also that the square rig required large crews.

By various stages the fore-and-aft rig began to supplant the square rig. There were more barkantines and fewer barks, more brigantines and fewer brigs. The very large massive cargo-carrying schooner underwent a period of development. Traditionally the schooner had been a two-masted vessel but these heavy cargo carriers soon departed from that model and began adding supplementary masts as fast as the trade could absorb them so there came to be three-four-five-six- and even seven-masted schooners. The rig of these giant centipedes was not particularly attractive and had nothing in common with the beauty and symmetry of the two-masted Banks fishery schooner. In fact the hull of the giant cargo schooner was not derived from the traditional small schooner. It seems to have begun where the late modified packets left off and went on from there to the point where a cross section of the hull began to look very much like the hull of a freight steamer.

These sailing freighters were developed for use on long coastwise hauls but they also crossed the oceans in international trade. They carried cargoes of corn, wheat and other grains and also raw materials like wood and coal and bulky manufactured articles like steel shapes and steel rails.

The cargo schooner seems to have reached the apex of its development in about 1902 with the launching on the Fore River in Massachusetts of the *Thomas W. Lawson*. This was a steel-hulled seven-masted schooner, 403 feet in length. The same general conditions that finally eliminated from the sea the ships and the barks have also brought about the disappearance of the transatlantic schooner. The coastwise schooner had a longer life. Until recent years we used to see along our coast lumber schooners from Maine and coal schooners from the Delaware, but these also have disappeared. The beautiful "Banks Fisherman" is still occasionally seen in use but is now rapidly being displaced by uglier auxiliary vessels and so-called "power schooners."

The schooner survives as a fast and fine pleasure boat or yacht. Notable examples of this class that still linger in memory are the schooner *Dauntless* that in 1887 made the crossing of the Atlantic from Bay Ridge to Queenstown in sixteen days. In 1890, at the beginning of a trip around the world, the same vessel sailed from Newport to the Old Head of Kinsale in twenty-three days. In 1905 the schooner *Atlantic* crossed the ocean and won the cup offered by the German kaiser. She was a vessel of 207 tons; her length on the water line was 135 feet; her beam 29 feet; her draft 16 feet 6 inches. She crossed the

Atlantic in 12 days, 4 hours and 1 minute, a distance of 3,013 miles; her average time for the crossing was 10.4 knots.

In 1928, Mr. Bell's fine schooner the *Elena* led the large class of ocean racers across the Atlantic to Santander in Spain to win the cup offered by the king of Spain. As late as 1929 I sailed in Cowes races with Mr. F. T. B. Davis on his fine schooner *Westward*. In 1910 she was designed and built by Herreshoff for Alexander Smith Cochran. She was 135 feet overall; 96 feet on the water line; carried 12,000 square feet of canvas before Mr. Davis had her and under his management she had added to her canvas. Her trucks swept the air 150 feet above her deck and her keel was 17 feet deep in the tides. Despite her heavy handicap, we were still able to win races in the "J" class.

In their turn, the big gaff-rigged schooners have been disappearing but they are being replaced by smaller vessels, mostly Marconi-rigged ketches, yawls and sloops. The sport of long-distance ocean racing on the Atlantic seems to have taken a new lease on life. Year by year the Fastnet race in England and the Bermuda race in this country are drawing an increasing number of entries. Furthermore, considering their water-line length, the small ocean racers have turned in records of some remarkable transatlantic crossings. In 1926 *Landfall* crossed the Atlantic in nineteen days and in that same year *Dorade* made the passage in seventeen days.

As we have seen, for hundreds of years fore-and-aft sails had an important place in the equipment and operation of square-rigged vessels. In general as time went on there was a tendency to add more fore-and-aft sail such as spinnaker, staysails, jibs to the basic square-sail plan. This led to the practice of equipping one or more masts of a vessel with all fore-and-aft sail while leaving the other mast or masts in square sail. Thus the "ship" when altered in this way became the "bark" and then the "barkentine"; the "brig" became the "brigantine" and then the topsail schooner the extreme form when square sail was only in use on the fore-topmast.

Small ships and boats entirely equipped with fore-and-aft sail have followed a different pattern and served a different purpose. They originated in shallow waters and in narrow waters for handling local passengers and small cargoes in coastwise trade. They are adapted for this work by their special virtues such as: ease of handling, ability to work to windward, small crew requirement.

For thousands of years they worked along the Mediterranean and the Atlantic coast of Europe, their myriad small hulls with their small burdens aggregating an incredibly large total tonnage. It was they that in the great ports assembled the cargoes that made the large and more spectacular ocean vessels needed and useful. For centuries they performed similar services for the many islands of the Caribbean and the Atlantic shores of North and South America.

The huge cargo schooners of the type of the *Thomas W. Lawson* and the *Roger P. Frye* did not seem to be the small schooner grown large but rather the last and ultimate stage of the big square-riggers shedding their square sails in favor of fore-and-aft sails. In any event they won a brief usage in the last days of the large ocean sailing vessel.

The small fore-and-afters survive in many parts of the world as useful carriers of passengers and cargo though their places are more and more usurped by motorships and motorboats. On every Atlantic coast they survive as yachts and pleasure boats, for no motor can provide an equal measure of quiet ease or of sportsmanship or of beauty. They will continue to survive as long as sane men dwell in a reasonable society. Finally it is interesting to observe that when the small fore-and-afters undertake long ocean passages they feel the need for, and tend to add, square sails or elements that act like the square sails which were so essential to the big sailing ships of the past.

Chapter 19

THE COMING OF STEAM AND STEEL

WHEN the nineteenth century began, steam-propelled boats were already in existence. When it ended sailing vessels were still in use on many of the oceans, but during the century there took place a shift from an age of sail to an age of steam and other mechanical methods of propulsion. The progress from one kind of vessel to another was not orderly. It was, in fact, full of curious, illogical and unanticipated changes. The evolution from the full-rigged sailing ship to the purely power-driven steamer produced countless variations and combinations of the two alternative methods of crossing an ocean. Some were ingenious and effective, some fantastic or monstrous. In the interests of clarity and order we may note that the use of steam power to drive ships did go through certain stages of development. In the beginning the steam engine was thought of as being a device that could propel a small vessel on quiet waters such as lakes, rivers and canals; then as a tug, a vessel that could assist a sailing ship in getting in and out of harbors; then, more by necessity than by intention, some of the steam vessels made short, singular voyages on seas and even the open ocean. In many of these activities the ship driven by steam also employed sail. When steam finally went to sea it did so simply as an aid to the sailing vessel, and the period of this service lasted for the better part of the century. This point is worth special notice for it is not today clearly understood.

Toward the middle of the century there were vessels crossing the

Atlantic that were called "steamboats," "steamships" or "steam liners." This leaves us with the impression that they were entirely dependent on steam power, but this is not the case. A good deal has been written about the competition between sail and steam that is supposed to have taken place in the middle of the last century and this has led to a good deal of misunderstanding. There was not a clear-cut competition between a full-rigged sailing ship on one hand and a pure steamer on the other. The competition was actually between the sailing ship and another form of sailing ship that also carried power machinery. Gradually as the steam engine improved in reliability and efficiency she was able to count more and more on her motive power until finally she used her sails only in case of engine failure, exhaustion of her fuel supply or other emergency. It was only in the last quarter of the century that the steamers gave up the practice of also carrying sail. Finally, toward the end of the century, two new forms of propulsion of ocean vessels came into existence simultaneously; one was a new form of steam engine called the turbine and the other was the Diesel engine.

Logically and technologically the steam engine and the metal hull ship should go together, but this is one of the cases where history violated logic. The steam engine came into common use long before metal hulls were thought practical for the ocean. The use of coal fires and of steam in wooden hulls accounted for many fires at sea and great loss of life. Iron hulls were used in fresh water within the first quarter of the century, but the fact that iron is subject to destructive corrosion in salt water accounted for a long delay in their use at sea. In fact these are the changes that happened to seagoing ships in the twentieth century. Brief as they are they do provide an orderly pattern. That is perhaps their trouble, they suggest an order that is much more logical than the events with which they dealt.

For one thing there were not clear-cut periods in which these changes took place. For example there was not a point before which ocean vessels were built of wood and after which they were built of metal, nor a point before which vessels were driven by paddle wheels and after which they were driven by propellers. In the first case there were many transitional stages between the all-wood hull and the all-metal hull, in the second case some of the very earliest steamboats were driven by propellers, then there was a long period in which the propeller was abandoned in favor of paddle wheels only to be rediscovered at a later time. Metal hulls were used for large sailing ships at the same time that wooden hulls were still being used for very large steam vessels and so on through a whole series of unexpected combinations. One aspect of this history is so curious as to deserve a special mention in this place.

The packet liners commenced operation in the year 1818. They were small old-fashioned trading vessels. In that bitter winter there were often gales driving up the Mersey River at Liverpool and ice flows clogged the harbor of New York. On their earliest trips, the *Courier,* the *James Monroe* and the other ships that made up the Black Ball Service were frequently towed down the river at Liverpool or assisted up the harbor at New York by early and strange looking little steamers serving as tugs. Thus we see that a practical steam vessel was already in existence before the great Age of Sail began. It was after this that the whaling fleets of America and Europe reached their maximum development; it was after this that the packets went through their sixty years of evolution; it was long after this that the clipper ships crowned the Age of Sail. All the changes in the sailing vessel that took place between the Roman cargo ship to the trader of 1818 were not as great as those that separated the trader of 1818 from the great clipper ships and that were crowded into the sixty years or so after the steamship had already become a reality.

Before you can have a steamship you must have a steam engine. The first use of steam is usually attributed to a Greek author named Hero of Alexandria, who left a manuscript of about 200 B.C. which described and drew a device called an aeolipyle. This consisted of a hemispherical copper kettle set over a wood fire. The steam generated was led through copper pipes to a round ball which was left free to rotate. The steam, escaping from two bent tubes, caused the ball to spin. This first steam device therefore represents the principle of turbine or jet propulsion rather than the expansion of steam within a cylinder producing reciprocating motion. Hero's engine seems to have been used simply for amusement or instruction—an early forerunner of a Rube Goldberg device—a machine for doing nothing with 100 per cent efficiency.

The next references to steam were as ponderous and practical as Hero's machine was light and frivolous. After the Renaissance in Europe the idea of a practical steam engine stirred the imagination of a number of people. It is said that as early as 1543 Blasco de Garay of Barcelona proposed the plan of a steam-driven ship. It is not clear what kind of an engine he had in mind. It was almost two centuries later before Denis Papin, in 1707, made a steamboat run on the Fulda River in Germany. It is doubtful if his boat would have had any practical success, but it at least succeeded in convincing the canal bargemen that it was a threat to their occupation. They destroyed Papin's steamer.

Patents for steamers or steam tugs in England were sought by John Allen in 1712 and by Jonathan Hulls in 1736, but no ships seem to have been developed under these patents. In 1783 a French steamer, designed by the Marquis d'Abbans, ran for a few minutes on the Saône River, and one year later an American inventor named Rumsey, on the Potomac, made a steam engine operate a water pump which in turn moved a vessel by jet propulsion. Rumsey gave up in America but before ten years had elapsed he had succeeded in England in moving another vessel at the rate of four miles an hour on the Thames.

John Fitch, an adventurous and inventive American, devised and built the first steamboat that ever carried freight and paying passengers. In 1788 he designed and built a steam engine and mounted it in a boat that looked very much like a straight-sided barge. The steam engine operated a whole series of paddles that dipped into the water on either side of the barge and thus propelled the ship. This strange craft actually traveled on the Delaware River between Philadelphia and Trenton. Two years later Fitch built another steamship that was driven by a stern paddle wheel. This vessel operated for a season between Trenton, Philadelphia and Wilmington and is said to have traveled as fast as eight miles an hour on the river. It carried passengers, but not enough of them and when the trade failed Fitch's backers deserted him. Fitch went to France in search of the support which he had failed to find in America, but France was busy with her own problems. By 1796 Fitch was back in New York operating on Collect Pond a "Yawl Boat" in which a steam engine drove paddle wheels and also a screw propeller. Again, though Fitch succeeded in driving his boat, he did not succeed in getting support. In 1817 a committee of the New York Legislature said of Fulton's steamboat that it was "in substance the invention patented by John Fitch in 1791." As not infrequently happens, the public recognition and the official political opinion came too late for Fitch had committed suicide in Bardstown, Kentucky in 1798.

One of the people who saw Fitch's steamboat of 1787 in operation was Colonel John Stevens. By 1802 he had developed a good and practical steamer. This vessel was remarkable in that it was driven by a screw propeller whereas most of the vessels both before and after this time employed some kind of paddle wheel. In 1804 he had

THE "CLERMONT"

another steamboat which again had unusual features. He had discovered that a single screw caused his vessel to turn, so in the vessel of 1804 he used a twin screw drive. He also carried a steam pressure of fifty pounds per square inch. Stevens was ahead of his time. Despite the fact that his vessels operated effectively, paddle wheels became the fashion and it was not until 1836 that the Swedish-American inventor Ericsson reintroduced the idea of the screw propeller and brought it into some practical use.

In the same year that Stevens produced his first steamer in America, a paddle tug named the *Charlotte Dundas* was built in Scotland and operated on the Forth and Clyde Canal. It succeeded in drawing two loaded barges, and in six hours of travel covered 19½ miles.

So far all the steam vessels had succeeded simply in demonstrating that an engine could be made to propel some kind of a vessel. Nobody yet had demonstrated that such a vessel was capable of regular and profitable operation. This was left for an American named Robert Fulton.

Fulton did not invent the steamboat, but he and his partner, the American statesman Livingston, were practical businessmen. They had the foresight to secure from the New York Legislature a monopoly to operate steamboats in New York waters, and had this monopoly extended from time to time until they could produce a practical vessel. They ordered a hull built in this country and had a boiler and engine built by Boulton and Watt in Scotland. The resulting vessel was christened the *Clermont,* using the name of Livingston's estate on the Hudson. On August 9, 1807, she commenced operation between New York and Albany covering the distance of about 150 miles in thirty-two hours. Whenever the wind was favorable the *Clermont* depended on her sails as well as her engine power. The *Clermont* attracted passengers and was the first demonstration that a steamer could operate regularly and profitably.

Fulton's monopoly had one unexpected result. Stevens had built in New York waters a vessel named the *Robert L. Stevens.* Like all the ships of her time she was designed to operate on rivers and other quiet waters, but the monopoly made this impossible so that it was decided she would operate on the river from Philadelphia. Therefore in 1808, during a spell of suitable weather, she ventured to sea and made the passage from port to port.

It was not until 1815 that two Scotch steamers ventured on sea passages. Both were built in Glasgow. The *Elizabeth* made the run from Glasgow to Liverpool and the *Thames* made the run from Glasgow to London. We should know that all these early passages of a steamer were special one-way trips. In every case the vessel could wait for suitable weather and then at some risk scurry to the protected waters in which it was to begin its regular operation.

Up to this time no vessel on either side of the water had been designed for operation at sea. The bold idea of putting a steam engine in a seagoing vessel seems first to have been developed by a number of prosperous businessmen in the city of Savannah, Georgia. Their vessel, the *Savannah,* on May 24, 1819, commenced a passage to Liverpool which was completed in twenty-nine days and eleven hours. This was an important passage. It demonstrated that a vessel equipped with a steam engine and with paddle wheels could be driven across the Atlantic Ocean. It was, however, far from being a crossing of the Atlantic by a steam-driven vessel. Indeed the *Savannah* could be considered a large, fully equipped sailing vessel with the steam equipment added. Her passage across the Atlantic took more than 700 hours of travel and during this time her engines could be operated for only eighty hours. It is interesting to observe that this passage was made almost entirely in the Gulf Stream and North Atlantic Drift and these, operating on her hull during 700 hours, probably aided her progress as much as the engine did during the eighty hours of operation.

In 1822 there occurred a remarkable voyage which illustrates not only the increasing enterprise of steam vessels, but also the way in which the patterns that were set on the Atlantic Ocean were gradually extended to other parts of the world. In this year an auxiliary steamer called the *Enterprise* was built in England for the P. & O. Steamship Company. She succeeded in making the passage around the Cape of Good Hope and in getting to India. Thereafter, for many years, she continued in operation between India and the Red Sea. This made it possible for the company to send goods and passengers by vessel through the Mediterranean and then to transport them overland to the Red Sea where the *Enterprise* picked them up and continued to India. Naturally this represented a great saving of time over the passage around the cape either by sail or steam. Considering the inefficiency of the early steamers and the enormous expenditure of coal, the long trip of the *Enterprise* was a heroic adventure. The year that she started her service in the Orient there were already 140 steamers operating from British ports but nearly all of these were traveling on canals or making short runs across the Channel or the Irish Sea, or else serving as harbor tugs. Long passages were the exception, but in

1827 a ship named the *Curaçao* was built in Dover and bought by the Dutch Navy. In 1829 she made the passage between Holland and the West Indies, and thereafter for a number of years repeated this run annually. In 1831 a steamer called the *Royal William,* built in Canada, crossed the Atlantic in nineteen days.

Steamers continued to grow in size and also in number, and the developments took place in the United States quite as rapidly as they took place in England. By 1835 there were 700 steamers operating in American waters and this was twenty more than were accounted for in British waters two years later. About a third of the English steamers had engines of 100 horsepower and sixty-five of them were rated at 200 horsepower, but these were still vessels designed for coastwise operation.

In 1838 there comes into the record of ocean vessels a remarkable man, Isambard Kingdom Brunel. He was primarily a railroad engineer, but he was so much an engineer that he felt he had to take his steam experience to sea. Specifically he was an engineer for the Great Western Railroad and in order that the influence of the railroad might reach to America he began building steamers, the first one of which was naturally christened the *Great Western.* The *Great Western* was, for her time and age, a handsome vessel amply powered and her construction and her projected Atlantic service aroused interest. Another company decided to compete and bought and equipped a smaller steamer called the *Sirius.* The overloaded *Sirius* got away to sea first and the *Great Western* sailed four days later and they commenced a race to New York. Both vessels had been scheduled for an earlier sailing but had been delayed, so there was apprehension in New York regarding their fate. Apprehension was succeeded by excitement when the two vessels made port safely. They did not arrive on the same day, but within twenty-four hours of each other, the *Great Western* having made the passage in fifteen days.

The arrival of two steamers in a single port, having made the passage across the Atlantic, led many people to feel that the day of the sailing ship was drawing to its close and that the period of the steamer had arrived. This however was far from the case. The public did not yet realize how dangerous and how expensive the steamers were. They were hardly even aware of the fact that a little steamer like the *Sirius* had to carry an enormous volume of coal since her engine was so inefficient. She came staggering into New York under her own power, but by the barest margin, having burned up the sweepings of her coal pile and some of the wooden fittings and furniture of the ship. She really used her steam engine though often the crew would have given up had they not been driven by Captain Roberts, R.N., at the point of a pistol.

In 1840, despite a few apparently successful crossings of the ocean, steamers were far from being either mechanically efficient or economically profitable. The capital cost of building a sailing vessel, reckoned in British pounds, was about twenty to twenty-five per ton. The cost of building a steam vessel was twice that, and this only represented the initial outlay. Owing to the large coal consumption the cost of operating a steamer mile for mile and ton for ton was much greater; so great in fact that no steamer then or for some time thereafter could be reckoned as other than an unprofitable venture.

This was fully realized by Samuel Cunard, a Canadian-born businessman who succeeded in getting a contract to carry mail in steamers and also a subsidy from the British government. This permitted him, in the year 1840, to build the vessel *Britannia,* the first Cunarder, which succeeded in crossing the ocean in fourteen days and eight hours, and thereafter operated between England, Canada and the port of Boston. *Britannia* was rated as having a carrying capacity of 865 tons whereas her coal requirement for a passage was 640 tons. After the great race between the *Sirius* and the *Great Western* in 1838, ten years went by during which vessels with steam power came to New York occasionally and irregularly. Then in 1848 Samuel Cunard, again operating with a British subsidy, built two steamers, the *Hibernia* and the *Cambria,* and commenced regular operation of his line between New York and Liverpool. These vessels were not large and they were not record breakers. Cunard's whole emphasis was on regularity and safety.

These qualities were badly needed for the next generation was marked by new developments and ceaseless experimentation, and the experiments were often accompanied by lack of financial success and not infrequently by disaster. These experimental failures in steam and metal construction provided an incentive for the continuous development and success of the sailing ships. One of the troubles and causes of inefficiency in the steam engine was the low steam pressure in the early boilers and cylinders. We have seen already that John Stevens succeeded in completing in America one engine that carried a boiler pressure of as much as fifty pounds per square inch. This was twice as high as any of his competitors were able to achieve, but neither the materials that were available nor the skills of the mechanics were capable of continuing at this level. There was also the problem of efficiently using such steam pressure as the boilers could safely generate. The first engines introduced steam on only one side of the piston, but John Watt in Scotland soon discovered that he could increase the efficiency of his engine by introducing steam alternately on both sides of the piston, thus creating the double-acting engine which became the standard practice; but engines were still single cylinder affairs that exhausted the steam before it had been fully utilized.

As early as 1824 an American engineer by the name of John P. Allaire recognized this defect and built up the first engine with two cylinders, using the steam first in a high pressure cylinder and then passing it to a larger low pressure cylinder before it was exhausted to the condensers. While his engine was right in principle it was not a great success because he could not get a sufficiently high pressure out of his boilers. It was not until 1854 that John Elder of Birkenhead built the *Brandon,* the first effective double-expansion engine. Up to this time coal consumption had been at the rate of four or five pounds for each horsepower developed in the engine, but the record in the *Brandon* was 3¼ pounds per horsepower. Operation of this vessel made it clear that a triple-expansion engine would be an improvement on the two-cylinder engine, just as the two-cylinder engine was an improvement over the old single cylinder; but it was not until 1874 that the first triple-expansion engine was built and put into the steamer *Propontis.* In the meantime in 1857 the *Thetis* had been built, which demonstrated that boilers and cylinders could safely carry a steam pressure of 115 pounds per square inch, and that under these conditions it required a little less than two pounds of coal per horsepower. Higher steam pressures were developed only after the old-fashioned oblong boiler was replaced by the cylindrical boilers in 1862. Also adding to the strength and efficiency of boilers was the introduction of the water tube principle. The French Belleville was developed between 1880 and 1889; the Scotch Yarrow in 1889.

Another change that came in the 1850's related to the position or structure of the steam engine. Naturally the designer of a vessel wishes to keep the heavy weights of his mechanism set low in the hull to insure a low center of gravity. This was particularly desirable in the days of the large and cumbersome engines put in rather small wooden hulls. Therefore, the early steam engines had the heavy cylinders at the base of the engine with the pistons operating vertically upwards, and the connecting rods and driving mechanism above that. This was a perfectly satisfactory arrangement for driving paddle wheels which had an axis that of necessity was elevated above the water line, but it was awkward or impossible for driving a screw propeller and probably accounted for the long delay in adopting this more effective method of propulsion. Around 1850 it occurred to designers that the cylinders could be carried on a framework with the piston and connecting rod operating downward and with a shaft placed low in the hull to drive a propeller below the water line. Gradually this became the standard practice.

The first steamer driven by a screw propeller to cross the Atlantic was the *Great Britain* in 1845. She was designed and built by Brunel who had already, as we have seen, built the *Great Western,* and who made himself the pioneer and champion of large steamers. Her rated tonnage was 3,500. She was 322 feet long with a beam of 51 feet and a depth of 31 feet. She was also unusual in that she was built of iron. She was the largest steamer afloat and in 1846, carrying many important passengers, had the misfortune to run aground on the Irish coast. After this experience the passengers were happy to find passage on the famous Black Ball packet liner *Yorkshire,* commanded by Captain David G. Bailey. The *Yorkshire* then made a record crossing the Atlantic westward in sixteen days which was better than the average time of Brunel's steamer the *Great Western*. It is said that the passengers included the girls of a Viennese ballet company and though the record does not make it clear it is probable that their visit to America was connected with that of the famous Viennese ballerina Fanny Ellsler. However that may be, to celebrate the record crossing and to express their joy at seeing America, the girls put on an informal ballet on the deck of the *Yorkshire* as she came blowing into New York harbor.

In 1851 Brunel was at it again; in this year he projected the *Great Eastern,* one of the most remarkable vessels of his or of any other time. She was not ready to launch until 1857 and made her first voyage in 1858. She was 680 feet long and had a beam of 83 feet. Her displacement tonnage was 27,384. She had an engine of 1,000 horsepower driving paddle wheels, and of 1,800 horsepower driving a screw propeller. The boilers to provide this power required her to have five funnels on deck spaced out in line. Even with all this mechanical equipment she was not purely a steamer for she also stepped six masts to carry her complement of sail. She was designed to carry 200 first-class passengers, 400 second-class and 2,500 in the steerage. Her spacious accommodations were but poorly utilized at any time in her history, and from the start she was an unfortunate vessel. On account of her great length Brunel had decided that she would be launched sideways, and unfortunately she stuck on the ways before reaching the water. It took months of work before she was finally afloat, and in the meantime the company that built her had failed. Later she commenced operation but was never popular or successful. She was, however, so large and so powerful that she performed one kind of lasting service that no other vessel was able to accomplish. She was used for laying many of the transatlantic cables, which is another story. After her cable service she ran aground, and when she was finally raised she was anchored off a World's Exhibition where she wound up as a vast and vulgar entertainment showpiece that was visited by thousands.

Despite the misfortune to his vessels, Brunel was a great engineer; his essential misfortune was that he was working ahead of his time. He demonstrated the value of metal construction in hulls. Despite her grounding on the Irish shore, the *Great Britain* survived a pounding for a period of months that would have destroyed any wooden hull. She was refloated and later used, and the *Great Eastern*'s hull stood years of punishment. She was the first vessel built with a double hull to the water line. Brunel was correct in his intention to make this an important feature of safe construction. He also demonstrated the advantage of having the space provided between the hulls for use as ballast tanks.

Brunel's were not the only steamers that had an unfortunate history. Though late in its decision, the United States government decided to match the subsidies on steamship building that the British government was providing to Samuel Cunard. With such subsidies the Oceanic Steam Navigation Company, in 1847, completed the steamers *Washington* and *Hermann,* but they were never a great success. In 1848 a Line to operate between New York and Havre built the *Humboldt* and the *Franklin,* but the *Humboldt* ran aground in 1853 and the *Franklin* followed suit in 1854. In 1852 E. K. Collins, who had so successfully operated the New Orleans packets, and later with Palmer's help had built up the transatlantic Dramatic Line of packets, sold his sailing ships and commenced building a line of large and luxurious steamers. The first of these, the *Atlantic,* was rated as having a tonnage burden of 2,860 with engines of 2,000 horsepower. She crossed the Atlantic in eleven days and ten hours beating a Cunard Liner by thirty-three hours. However, in 1854 Collins' liner *Arctic* had the misfortune to run into the French steamer, the *Vesta,* in a fog with a loss of 300 lives. This tragedy no doubt had something to do with Maury's proposal of 1855 to establish international steamer lanes.

In 1856 another Collins' steamer, the *Pacific,* sailed with a full crew and a full passenger list and was never heard from again. The government withdrew its subsidy and the line failed. Other American steamers that had been operating ceased operation and by 1860 there wasn't a United States mail steamer sailing from any American port.

Transatlantic steamships were not the only ones to meet with disaster. In 1834 and to 1838 coastwise steamers were operating between New York and Charleston, South Carolina, but they were in continual trouble running to port to escape storms or held in port because of needed repairs to machinery or running aground. In 1837 the steamer *Home* broke down. About the same time a steamer operating between Baltimore and Savannah blew up and killed over 100 people. In 1873 a French steamer, the *Ville de Havre,* sank with the loss of 200 lives; a sailing vessel, the *Trimountain,* under Captain Urquhart, succeeded in saving eighty-five of the steamer's passengers.

Even when they did not meet with disaster the steamers were not necessarily faster than the best sailing vessels. In 1848, in a period of heavy storms, Captain Tinker's *Toronto* was the only vessel to come to America in a period of six weeks, but he made better time between England and New York than the Cunarder did between England and Boston. In 1853 the *Sovereign of the Seas* made better time between New York and Liverpool than the Cunarder *Canada* made from Boston to Queenstown. In 1864 the packet *Adelaide* made the passage between New York and Liverpool in twelve days and eight hours, which was better than the average passage of any of the steamers.

The steamer did not become reasonably safe for ocean crossings until it was placed within a metal hull, and it is natural to wonder why this was so long delayed. The reason is partly technical, having to do with the destruction of metals by sea water, and partly economic—a matter of the availability and cost of large quantities of metal.

As early as 1787 John Wilkins, an iron founder, had built an iron barge. In 1821 Aaron Mamby built an iron steamship and in 1825 a steamboat with a hull of iron began operation on the Shannon River in Ireland. In that same year an American Quaker by the name of John Elgar built a ship with a two-ton iron hull and a two-ton engine which he contrived himself. This vessel was named the *Codorus.* While it was unsuccessful as a commercial vessel, it did make a long cruise on the Susquehanna River.

All of these, and some other metal vessels, were to be used on fresh water and there was nothing inherently wrong with this idea, but when John Laird in 1829 built an iron hull to be operated as an ocean sailing vessel, trouble started. Everybody knew that a sheathing of copper was the only thing that could protect a hull from rapidly acquiring a coating of seaweed and barnacles and this worked very well on a wooden hull, but when Laird put a copper sheathing on an iron hull and set it afloat on salt water he had unconsciously invited the destruction of his vessel through electrolytic corrosion. It took a long time to get around again to the use of metal hulls. In the meantime iron was frequently used as a material for binding and reinforcing wooden hulls and was employed, for example, by Donald McKay in his larger clipper ships including the *Great Republic.*

In the mid-century Brunel, as we have seen, was using iron for his large steamers avoiding the use of copper and counting on paint to keep his hulls from being corroded and overgrown with marine life. In the 1860's a composite hull was frequently employed; this used iron for the framework of the vessel and wood for the planking. The wood was then covered with a copper sheathing so that the metals were separated by an insulating layer of wood. Composite construction was employed for some of the clipper ships, particularly those built in England, but iron was coming into increasing use both for sailing and steam vessels and its use was speeded up by the discovery about 1870 that paints and other compounds which were chemically hostile to the plants and animals growing in sea water could be applied to metal hulls. By 1880 steel was coming into use instead of iron.

Still, the whole transition from sail to steam and from wood to metal hulls was mixed and gradual.

For example, the *Great Eastern,* launched in 1858, was Brunel's double-hulled iron vessel. In 1859 the British admiralty launched a great warship of 6,000 tons built of wood. In 1868 a steamer called the *Japan* was launched which was 385 feet in length and was the largest wooden steamship.

At the same time that these great steamers were being built of wood some of the last of the great clipper ships were being built with composite or with metal hulls. These included vessels like the British clippers *Ariel, Taeping* and *Cutty Sark.* How confused the technology of those days was is well illustrated by the fact that in 1882 the art of freezing meat and of handling it in refrigerators was undergoing rapid development, but the first vessel to carry this kind of cargo from New Zealand to Great Britain was a sailing ship, the *Mataura.* In that same year as many as 550 sailing vessels cleared the ports of

California and Australia with cargoes of grain. In 1891 as many as seventy-seven sailing ships or sailing barks left Australia with cargoes of wool.

At the beginning of the new century, that is in 1902, there was launched one of the largest sailing vessels. She was 403 feet in length with a steel hull. This was not a square-rigged ship but a seven-masted schooner, the *Thomas W. Lawson.* Sailing vessels, both square-rigged and fore-and-afters, have continued in use right down to the present time. The transition from sails to steam has been gradual but it has been relentless. Thousands of us now living who have had the good fortune to see large square-rigged sailing ships in operation, or better yet to sail aboard them, have had an experience of beauty combined with power and utility that will be enjoyed by no future generation. It has been my good fortune to have sailed with Arthur Curtis James on his square-rigged steam auxiliary yacht *Corsair,* and to have been on a four-masted bark sailing the Pacific out of Oakland, the *Santa Clara* and to have seen the departure from that port of a number of the square-riggers that sailed in the fleet of the Alaska packers. On the east coast we can well remember vessels like the *Tusitala,* commanded by Captain Barker, which James Ferrel kept in operation for a number of years out of affection for the vessel and the vessel's friends, and the yacht *Seven Seas* and Allen Villiers' little gem, the *Conrad,* and mention of her brings to mind the fact that his many books with their photographs provide a beautiful and sympathetic record of the closing days of the square-rigged sailing vessel.

Before the last century closed two new inventions were added to the history of mechanical power at sea, and they appeared simultaneously. Experiments with engines that substituted for steam, the explosion within a cylinder of a gas created by the evaporation of a liquid fuel, were carried on for a number of years. These early developments depended upon electricity or a "hot bulb" to ignite the gases within the cylinders. The most important development in this field took place in 1893 when Dr. Diesel of Germany created an engine that ran at such high compression and high temperature (1,100°F.) that combustion of the fuel was automatic.

The other invention related to a new use of steam power. The Honorable Sir Charles A. Parsons invented the steam turbine to generate electricity on land, but a year after the Diesel engine, that is in 1894, he began working on the use of the steam turbine to drive ships. He created a small, fast hull and christened her the *Turbinia.* She was about 100 feet in length. The first turbines he provided spun propellers at a rate of 16,000 revolutions per minute. This only drove the ship at about nineteen knots, which was regarded by Parsons as a failure. He made a study of the way in which propellers were losing their grip on the water and produced as a by-product one of the first scientific papers on cavitation. By 1896 he had a new set of turbines in the *Turbinia*. These drove three shafts and each shaft had on it three propellers. The boilers provided steam pressure at 210 pounds per square inch. All of Parsons' work on this vessel had been confidential and secret.

His opportunity came in 1897 when Queen Victoria was celebrating her diamond jubilee and when vessels of the British Navy and visitors from many other nations were assembled in the waters off Cowes in the Isle of Wight. Parsons had smuggled his ship into this port and when all the vessels were lining up for the review the *Turbinia* suddenly appeared on the course. At first she was regarded as an insignificant little nuisance, then she got under way, eluding and outdistancing all patrol vessels. She flashed up the line of the parade at the unheard-of speed of thirty-four and a half knots, the equivalent of approximately forty miles per hour.

Many years later I stood in a Paris apartment looking at a model of the *Turbinia* while Parsons explained some of her technical features to me. I ventured to remark on the complexity of his problems and the enormous cost involved in their solution, and to suggest that he might have begun with a simpler demonstration.

He said it would probably have cost more in the long run. "Besides, my boy, if you believe in a principle never damage it with a poor expression, you must go the whole way. I had to startle people."

He succeeded. Among other things he startled the British Navy into an order for two turbine destroyers, the *Viper* and *Cobra,* in their day the fastest ships in the world. By 1904 the Allen Line had built two turbine liners, the *Victorian* and the *Virginian*. The *Virginian* could make twenty knots, which was about as fast as the best hour's sailing of the *Sovereign of the Seas*. The *Virginian*'s advantage was that she could hold this pace hour after hour regardless of the wind, and she succeeded in doing it hour after hour and year after year at least until 1929. Some of my readers will remember her under her new name, the *Drottningholm* of the Swedish American Line.

So in the nineteenth century the steam engine grew up and went to sea. It began as a baby—heavy but puny—its costly and feeble

horsepower barely able to move a shallow barge. It wound up before
the century closed, driving great ships to new transatlantic records,
with two new forms of propulsion pushing abreast for a race in the
twentieth century. Also in the nineteenth century, iron, composite
and steel construction appeared first in sailing vessels and then in
steamers. In the beginning forests were abundant and wood construction was cheaper than metal, in the end forests were being depleted,
wood construction was relatively more expensive and metal more
plentiful, cheaper, lighter and safer.

It is strange that with so many technical changes crowding each
one on the heels of the one ahead, the coming of steel and steam did
not in some emphatic way open up new territories or dramatically
alter the course of travel and commerce. Looking at the record it is
hard to detect any way in which the mechanical ships in the first
seventy-five years of their existence altered the direction of transportation and travel at sea. The reason seems to lie in the fact that the
sailing ships came along at a time when the need for world-wide
communication was most acute. They did their job well. The packets
regularized commerce across and about the Atlantic. The whalers
pushed into new territory in the Arctic and Antarctic and ranged the
Pacific. Following the packets, the clippers speeded up and consolidated travel to California, China, Australia and South Africa.

The first engined ships simply followed in the tracks of the sailing
vessels. To be sure the *Savannah,* on her maiden voyage, made one
bold effort to establish direct contact between the southern port and
Europe. The steamers were soon running the same courses as the
packets and clippers—New York to Liverpool, Boston to Liverpool,
New York to Le Havre, London to Australia, etc. The need for traffic
at sea was between the large ports and dense areas of population in
Europe and the growing cities in the rest of the world. Maury laid
down the courses between centers in accordance with the structure
of the ocean's currents and the ocean's winds. The wise clipper captains followed Maury and the wise steam captain followed the clippers. Gradually steam grew strong enough to avoid tacking and to
battle head winds direct. This saved time, but the general courses
were still the same. Those who appreciated time and who could afford
the high cost of steam service still lived in the big ports.

The first service of steam to ocean history was not to open new
channels of travel but to speed up and intensify the routes that already
had been established by sail. The second service was gradually to
decrease costs of freight and passenger service. Finally, in the last

quarter of the century, engine and hull settled into more or less conventional patterns and ships of convenient size designed for special purposes emerged, such as the small steamer to combine freight and passenger services to the smaller ports and the ocean tramp freighter. They never broke records, they seldom made the headlines, but they did provide useful and economical services. They carried their special services to many new small ports, and because of them many new areas opened up and were linked more or less directly with the growing fabric of world-wide trade and travel and communication.

The part that the development of the steamship played in immigration and settlement is often exaggerated. As we have seen already, a great exodus of many peoples from Europe was already taking place by the middle of the last century. Immigration into the United States had hit a high level in the decade 1845-1855 and it continued till the Civil War. Because migration and settlement in large volume came at about the same time that steamers were first reported as crossing the ocean, it is often supposed that the steamers carried the migrants. This was not true of any of the early steamers. Their accommodations were limited and expensive—too expensive, at least, for volume migration. Of the millions who came to America each year in the 50's, 60's, and 70's, the greatest volume came in sail. This was true also of the trek to California, Australia, New Zealand and other parts of the world.

The steam vessel came into its own in the last decades of the nineteenth century. The opening of the Suez Canal in 1869 greatly increased the growing advantages of power over sail for the steamers could traverse the canal under their own power whereas the towing of a sailing ship would involve management problems, delay and large sums of money. By this time, boilers had improved in strength and efficiency; effective condensers had also been developed; increasingly high steam pressure had brought about a more efficient use of fuel; the triple-expansion engine had become the recognized form of propulsion. In large vessels like the ocean liners, multiple engines and propellers began to appear.

Improvements in the power plant gradually brought about not only an increase in the size of the vessels but also changes in their form and appearance. The early steamers that had to depend quite as much on sail as they did on their engines were compromises and, like many other compromises in life, they were necessary but often grotesque. Smoke from the boilers dirtied the white canvas and clung to the running rigging and often made the operation of sailing a nightmare.

An open or suppressed feud developed between the deck officers and the "black gang," or engineering crew, and phases of this hostility have gone echoing down the ages. Some few liners appeared that retained the clipper bow and the fine lines of a good sailing vessel and that still had the advantages of engine propulsion. Then gradually the masts and sails shrank in size and in proportion; later the yards and sails were removed and stored, to be called on only in an emergency. The clipper bow was replaced by the straight stem.

It is remarkable how long the notion of using sail on steamers hung on. I can remember, as a small boy, crossing in an old liner that still carried provisions for setting sail in case of an emergency. An old seaman, who had grown up in the sailing ships, proudly showed me the spars and the sail locker that were his special responsibility.

At the end of the century the steam vessel had not only developed into the modern liner, it had also assumed a score of other useful forms. We have already referred to the small seagoing tramp. In addition, there was the small freighter that also carried passengers; there was the channel steamer; the ferry boat; the river steamer; the tanker and many other variants.

History runs its course. At the beginning of the nineteenth century the steam engine had appeared that displaced sail before the century was over. At the beginning of the twentieth century electricity, turbine, Diesel appeared at sea; they have already almost displaced the steam engine.

The century opened with a golden age—the era of speed, elegance, luxury. Goods flowed and people traveled freely across international boundaries and across the ocean. There was room for all, everything was improving, even steerage services, which now accounted for an important part of the revenues of the giant liners racing for the Blue Ribbon of the Atlantic.

Chapter 20

WORDS UNDER WATER

O NCE, after many stormy days at sea, I brought a small vessel into a foreign harbor that I had not previously visited. The light from a murky winter sun was already fading from the sky as I was casting about for an anchorage. I found a likely spot in quiet waters a little removed from the larger shipping and was about to give the order, "Let go," when my first mate pointed to a sign along the shore. Owing to fatigue, to poor light and unfamiliarity with the port, I had ignored the sign. What it actually said was this: CABLE CROSSING DO NOT ANCHOR!

Perhaps you have been in similar circumstances or have seen a similar sign from the deck of a steamer. The sign is often inconvenient and irritating to a seaman but if you have a proper respect for your own property as well as for that of the cable company the thing to do is to begin casting about for a new berth.

Even after traveling thousands of miles and living many months at sea, such a sign and a few markings on a chart may be the only visible signs you ever encounter that hint at the vast hidden empire of ocean communication that is forever flowing between the continents across the bottom of the sea.

The whole world uses the cable services. They are woven into the fabric of modern life and yet they operate so unobtrusively and so efficiently that they attract little public attention and few people bother to inquire or to see how the miracles of modern communication are performed.

It was the idea of the ocean telegraph that gave interest and additional meaning to a more profound knowledge of the depths of the sea. It was an American of titanic energy, organizing ability and persistent courage by the name of Cyrus Field who made himself the champion of the ocean telegraph development.

In 1866, when Field had made the transatlantic cable a reality, all of the leading men of the time in government and in business and in science met in New York to offer Mr. Field congratulations at a great testimonial dinner. There is a story that at this time Mr. Field said, "Maury provided the brains, the British provided the financing and I did the work." There is no concrete evidence that Field ever made this remark; he might well have said it for every element of it is true.

Matthew Fontaine Maury worked indefatigably on the oceanography and other technical aspects of the system. The British did provide the bulk of the financing and Field not only did the work but carried and overcame the burden of repeated failure extending over many years. The remark would have been misleading in the sense that the British contributed not only to the financing but also to the technical developments and that it really took the work of many lesser men also to solve all the problems.

The submarine telegraph was a development rather than an invention. By this we mean that the idea of sending a message by way of a wire resting on the bottom of the sea was essentially simple and probably occurred to a number of people in various places and times. For example, a Spanish scientist named Salva is credited with having developed the general idea of such a system of communication before the beginning of the nineteenth century. After this, it took a full half century before even a very limited cable service came into practical use. However simple the idea, scores of technical difficulties had to be overcome and an equal number of technical devices perfected before the idea could become an operating reality.

A land telegraph encounters fewer difficulties than a submarine telegraph and so it is natural that the land telegraph was invented and developed first. The strange circumstance is that the land telegraph was invented at sea. We have noted that this was on the packet ship *Sully* in the middle of the Atlantic Ocean. The dramatic circumstances were these: The *Sully* was one of the packets operating between Havre and New York and on a particular crossing in 1832 she was in the command of a very distinguished captain, William W. Pell. At this time the packets attracted all the well-known and even the famous international passengers and prided themselves on offering the fastest and best possible services. Yet the western passage was slow and tedious even under the best weather conditions. The packets, therefore, made a special effort to please their passengers by providing the best foods and wines in an elaborate dinner served in the latter part of the afternoon which became one of the features of life at sea. It was a method of occupying the time of the passengers and it was customary for such a dinner to last anywhere from two to three hours, and there was a premium set on intelligent conversation as well as on wit.

Among Captain Pell's passengers on this particular occasion were a Dr. Charles T. Jackson of Boston and Samuel Finley Breese Morse. At this time Morse already enjoyed an international reputation for he was the president of the National Academy of Design and was a painter of vivid portraits of famous people. During one dinner that was to become famous Dr. Jackson began talking about electro-magnetism, which was then a matter of popular as well as scientific interest. He described in some detail experiments with various circuits that he had recently seen carried out in Europe.

Morse listened very attentively and asked a number of questions. Then, very deliberately, he said that if at some point in the circuit system the passage of the current could be made visible, he saw no reason why such a circuit should not be used as an instantaneous method of communication. In due course the conversation and the long dinner came to an end but the ideas that had been discussed began a new and vigorous life. Morse spent the rest of the voyage brooding about the possibilities of electrical communication. Before the voyage was over he had filled a small notebook with drawings and descriptions of instruments that might have a use in a telegraph system. Before he landed in New York Morse showed this book to Captain Pell and some of the other passengers. Twelve years went by before Morse, in 1844, sent the first message over a successful and practical land telegraph system.

It is very seldom in the history of invention that we are permitted to know the exact time and circumstance at which an invention takes shape in the mind of the creator. We happen to know in this case because after Morse had completed his work Dr. Jackson brought suit against him claiming that the basic ideas of the invention were his own. At the time of the trial Captain Pell and others who were present at this famous dinner party testified on Morse's behalf and described the occurrences of the voyage.

Even after the land telegraph began its rapid growth, the submarine telegraph still required time for development. Morse in America and Wheatstone in England projected a submarine telegraph system but arrived at no practical results.

Apparently one of the first of all attempts to lay a practical underwater cable took place in New York Harbor as early as 1843 under the direction of Samuel Colt. A cable was laid from the Battery to Governors Island. The service was inaugurated and messages were sent for a period of about twenty-four hours. Then a ship anchored in the wrong place and dragged up 200 feet of the cable. Thus, at the very beginning of cable service, the first failure was due to a classic type of accident that was to make such grief for the cable companies in the future. Colt only attempted to lay a cable in the shallow water of the harbor. Naturally, the proposal to lay an ocean cable was a much more daring project.

Then there were countless difficulties to be overcome: the development of a metal wire or a combination of wires capable of conveying an electrical current over long distances without too much loss of strength along the way; the development of a wire system that would take a certain amount of strain without breaking; insulation of the cable; protection of the cable and its insulation from the destructive action of salt water and also from destruction by the ship worm (*teredo navalis*) and other marine creatures. These were only a few of the major difficulties.

Apart from the matter of the cable there were the great questions of where it was to be laid and how it was to be laid. A hundred years ago very few soundings had been taken in the open ocean that succeeded in reaching the bottom and very little was known about depth, shape or composition of the floor of the ocean. Sailing vessels were interested in soundings along the shore somewhere within the 100-fathom curve. Beyond this depth soundings had little practical value for naval and merchant vessels. Only the scientists saw any value in deep-water soundings and so the methods employed remained primitive and the number of soundings taken remained small.

It was natural that Cyrus Field, as soon as he began to think seriously of the promotion of a submarine telegraph, should turn to Matthew Fontaine Maury for advice. Maury was already the director of most of the scientific work carried out by the navy both in practical astronomy and in the study of the sea. The resources for study that

Maury had at his disposal were a very important element in providing both scientific and practical information on the development of a cable system. Of equal or even greater importance to Field was the fact that Maury was already beginning to enjoy an international reputation not only as a scientist but also as a scientist whose work had great practical importance. Up to this time Maury had devoted his attention to the study of the wind and weather systems of the ocean and the flow of ocean currents. His study of these matters on a vast scale had permitted him to construct these sets of pilot charts and sailing directions which resulted annually in the savings of millions of dollars to the ship operators on both sides of the Atlantic.

Maury now began collecting all available information on ocean depths and ocean bottom and under his direction United States naval vessels initiated a series of voyages to secure systematic soundings. When this work commenced, the methods of taking a sounding were extremely cumbersome and time consuming. It had been the custom to lower a great weight of lead on a rope and then when it appeared that bottom had been reached to make an attempt to recover the rope and weight intact. This consumed many hours of time for each sounding, the length of time being more or less dependent upon the depth of the ocean.

The great length of rope involved the set of the current, the drift of the ship, and made it difficult to determine exactly when bottom had been reached and otherwise rendered the soundings inaccurate. Maury suggested substituting a wire for the rope and using an ordinary metal shot as a substitute for the weight, the shot being attached to the wire in such a way that it would become detached when bottom had been reached. The wire could then be recovered with a fair amount of speed.

This system reduced the time required to take a sounding and greatly increased the number of soundings that could be taken in any one voyage. A further improvement was made with the invention of a simple but practical sounding machine by John Mercer Brooke in 1852. Maury at once put this machine to work and in 1853 the *Dolphin,* under command of O. H. Berryman, completed a line of soundings between Nova Scotia and Ireland.

Maury had already developed the idea that the line between Newfoundland and Ireland was not only one of the shortest that could be drawn from one side of the Atlantic to the other but also that here the ocean was relatively shallow. The Grand Banks extended a long way east of Newfoundland and even beyond the Banks there seemed to be a submarine tableland or plateau stretching away to the Irish shore. To describe this condition, Maury coined and used the phrase, "A table for a cable."

Maury's interest in the depth of the sea was of a dual character, being both scientific and practical. He served both of these interests by constructing an orographical chart of the Atlantic Ocean. This was based on inadequate information and had other imperfections but it was the first serious attempt to produce such a work. During the years the cable was being developed and laid Maury was carrying out a heavy schedule of research and administrative duties for the navy. However, in this period he also found time to send Field over 3,000 communications on the subject of the Atlantic cable such as letters, memoranda, charts, diagrams, drawings of instruments, etc. Maury with his energy and knowledge and Field with his energy and organizing ability made a lively highpowered team.

In the meantime the British were not idle. Field sought international financing for his project and as it turned out the bulk of Field's financial support came from British sources. Lord Brassey and other important financiers gave Field unusually loyal and courageous support and on a number of occasions, when a cable was lost or broken, undertook the refinancing of the enterprise.

At the same time William Thomson, who later became Lord Kelvin, independently invented another type of sounding machine which was used by a number of vessels and supplied additional information. Thus, through a combination of efforts, over a period of years, enough information was assembled to show that it was not altogether impossible to lay a cable from Ireland to Newfoundland in relatively shallow water and gradually the route for such a cable began to emerge.

Early cables failed not only because of their lack of strength but also because of their lack of insulation and other protection. Then it was discovered that gutta-percha, wound in long strips around the inner core of the cable that carried the current and the message, provided the best insulating material. This, in turn, had to be protected from shock and bruise which was done by applying layers of vegetable fiber (jute). Then the whole had to be bound together and strengthened with a long winding of galvanized iron wire. Later coatings were developed and used in the cable structure which not only were waterproof but which also repelled the voracious appetite of ship worms and other destructive creatures living along the sea's bottom. Gradually a cable structure was developed that was both strong and resistant. The early cables were subject to all kinds of interruptions and accidents but in later times cables have been taken up from extremely deep waters that had given more than forty years of uninterrupted service and whose interiors were still almost as sound and serviceable as on the day that they were first laid in the darkness and silence of the ocean depths.

The first subsurface cable was stretched across the shallow English Channel from England to France in the year 1850. It broke before service could be established and the next year a more successful cable was laid between Dover and Calais which did get into operation.

In the 1850's repeated attempts were made to lay a transatlantic cable. On several occasions storms arose and the cable parted or the end which was being laid was lost and could not be recovered. One such attempt was made in 1857 but at this time the cable was apparently too heavy and too weak to bear the strains involved in laying it at great depths. At a depth of 2,000 fathoms, that is, 12,000 feet, the cable parted.

Another, and this time a partially successful attempt to complete a transatlantic cable took place in 1858. Two vessels participated, each carrying a part of the cable. The British ship *Agamemnon* sailed from Valentia in Ireland at the same time that the American vessel *Niagara* worked eastward from Heart's Content in Newfoundland. This time a splice was made and the cable actually completed. A number of messages were transmitted, then the signals began to fail because of defective insulation. Poor business conditions and the approach of the Civil War postponed any further attempts to complete a transatlantic cable service.

As soon as the war was over the proponents of the transatlantic cable resumed their task with renewed vigor. One of the great difficulties was that of finding a ship that could carry out the work of laying a cable. Almost any ship could be equipped with reels and winches and the other devices necessary for laying or holding a cable but very few vessels of that time had sufficient cargo capacity to carry the great lengths of uninterrupted cable that were necessary to span the ocean even at a narrow part.

The need for a cable-laying ship was finally supplied by Brunel's fabulous structure, the *Great Eastern*. Our chapter on the coming of steam and steel supplies a brief description of this extraordinary vessel and we have seen there how she failed as a passenger vessel and as a carrier of ordinary cargo. Brunel's great imagination and his technical abilities led him to build a vessel that was way ahead of the maritime needs of his time.

The *Great Eastern* was of some service as a transport vessel during the Crimean War but she really came into her own as a cable-laying ship. The great halls of her living quarters and her vast holds were then, for the first time, of genuine service. She was so large that with only minor adjustments she was able to accommodate the full length of a transatlantic cable.

The *Great Eastern* commenced the fourth attempt to lay a transatlantic cable in the year 1865. When she sailed she was loaded with enough cable to stretch all the way across the Atlantic and she completed the run but the cable parted. By the time a year had passed another full length of cable had been constructed. The *Great Eastern* sailed on the fifth attempt on July 13, 1866 and reached her destination on the American side of the Atlantic on July 28; a remarkably fast passage and one that saw the inauguration of the first continuing transatlantic service.

Not quite satisfied with this accomplishment, the *Great Eastern* put to sea again and succeeded in finding, grappling and raising the two ends of the parted cable that she had deposited on the ocean bottom in the previous year. Thus, she was the first ship to successfully recover a parted cable and completed the first successful splice. By the end of the summer, Field's company had two transatlantic cables in operation.

The original cable enjoyed a monopoly until 1869 when a second cable was completed from France to America by the French Atlantic Telegraph Company.

These early cables, even when they remained in operation, had many limitations and drawbacks. In 1858 the cable could operate only at the very limited speed of sixteen letters per minute. Naturally charges were high, the cost running to $100 per message. This may be contrasted with the standard rate in recent years of twenty-five cents per word.

Despite the drawbacks these early cables performed many extremely useful services; they increased the speed and the accuracy of the transmission of international news; they increased the tempo of private business and they were extensively used by governments though, for a considerable period, the extremely high costs involved restricted their use for personal messages. The demands for services were large and very often there were delays and messages had to wait their turn for transmission. These difficulties were gradually overcome and once the success of the cable had been demonstrated the use of cable services expanded rapidly.

A great forward step which increased the rate of transmission and therefore the value of any cable was taken in 1871 with the invention of the duplex cable system. This made it possible to send messages in two opposite directions simultaneously. The duplex system was later replaced by the multiplex system and a whole succession of improvements in the pattern of cable construction permitted the transmission simultaneously of a great number of messages in each direction. The old-fashioned sending and receiving equipment has also over the years been replaced by complicated coding and decoding devices and by the use of instruments for printing out, on a continuous tape, a succession of messages. The whole process is now largely automatic from the typing of a message from one end of the line to its reception, in typed form, at the other end of the line where the tapes are cut into their component messages, mounted on an appropriate form and delivered to the addressee.

The islands of the Atlantic have naturally become an important asset to the cable companies. At Horta, in the Azores, there is an important center from which cables radiate to northern Europe, southern Europe, Africa, North America and South America. This station has been in continuous operation for many years and through a succession of wars. The station is jointly maintained by several companies and messages are relayed from one service to another. Hundreds of automatic machines are in continuous operation and the personnel which handles this enormous flow of traffic is surprisingly limited.

Some idea of the volume and importance of the cable business can be ascertained from the following brief summary of facts: In 1925 there were twenty-one cables operating across the Atlantic Ocean alone. In all parts of the world there are 3,000 separate submarine cables; these account for 300,000 miles of submarine cable. Present-day submarine cable weighs about two tons per nautical mile. However, cables have to be protected as they reach shallow water and the anchorage ashore and this, naturally, increases their weight. The shoreward end of a cable may reach a weight of thirty tons per nautical mile.

One might suppose, once a cable had been carefully laid down over the ocean floor and the two ends carefully secured at shore stations, that for a long period of time the cable would be safe and could be counted upon to remain in useful operation. This is far from being the case. The history of cable is full of accidents and mysteries. Some of the accidents are due to fairly obvious and well-known causes, other interruptions of service have been difficult to explain and some remain in the realm of mysteries.

Naturally the difficulty of laying a cable increases with the depth of the ocean, but once a cable is down the depth at which it lies seems to have little bearing on its length of life. The greatest hazards to cables occur in shallow water in the continental shelf and at the points where they reach the shore. Here they are subjected to the effects of tide and of ocean currents, to the wear and tear of storms, to damage from the anchors of ships inadvertently dropped in the wrong places.

Over many years, also, commercial fishermen have added to the worries of cable company executives. The nets and lines and anchors and other gear of fishermen have often been tangled up in the cables. A particular hazard have been the trowel nets dragged over the bottom in shallow waters such as the beam net and the net controlled by otter-boards.

Otter-boards are huge wooden planes weighted with heavy metal and metal bound. They are so heavily constructed that they can be towed over the ocean's floor by a steamer with no damage to themselves. They are attached to the towing line and to the edge of a net at an angle so that when the towing commences they do not fall in a straight line but tend to ride off at a sharp angle to either side of the center line of the vessel.

In this respect they resemble a sort of underwater kite, operating sideways. Their tendency to sheer off sideways is used to keep open the mouth of a great net which also is being dragged over the bottom of the ocean to capture sole, halibut, plaice and other flat fishes that like to lie on the bottom of banks and shallow waterways like the English Channel.

While this whole apparatus is very skillfully designed to catch fish, it is equally well adapted to getting tangled in marine cables to the annoyance and cost both of the fishermen and of the cable companies. The resulting irritations and arguments have been resounding and long-continued.

Some years ago the cable companies put their inventive heads together to solve this expensive dilemma. The result was the extraordinary and unexpected invention, the submarine plow. It should have another name for the term "submarine plow" is neither descriptive nor adequate. The device does not look like a plow and it does much more than any land plow is expected to do. The submarine plow is actually a huge structure, many tons in weight, which performs a whole series of useful operations. In use, it is lowered to the bottom and dragged along behind the cable-laying ship by special towing hawsers. The cable to be laid is threaded through the plow with a minimum of strain or tension. The plow handles the whole laying operation. As it is dragged along it first digs a deep trench in the bottom of the sea. It then deposits the cable in the trench and finally closes the trench again and buries the cable. When deep water is reached, plowing is discontinued and the submarine cable laid in the usual fashion.

Ships' anchors and fishing gear are not the only hazards suffered by the cables. At the American end near Newfoundland, cables have been subject to damage and rupture by icebergs grounding in shallow waters. Even in deep waters on the bottom of the sea cables are not entirely free from unusual accidents; submarine earthquakes and submarine volcanic activity are believed to have accounted for a succession of accidents to the cable services.

The *Great Eastern* was the first successful cable-laying ship. Of course, she disappeared from the scene a long time ago, but undoubtedly she demonstrated the advantages of creating a special type of vessel to lay and maintain submarine cables. The cable ship has developed into a special type of vessel, very ingenious in design and almost a museum of mechanical inventions. Some such ships have been built by the cable companies themselves, others have been constructed by companies that specialize in laying and maintaining cables, selling their services to the operating company. A modern cable ship called the *Dominia* is a good representative of one of the vessels in the latter kind of service. Though not an excessively large vessel, she is so well arranged and equipped that she can accommodate 3,000 miles of modern submarine cable; that is enough to reach across the Atlantic.

Such a cable ship is strictly a business undertaking. Her business purpose is to lay and maintain cable services. The cable ship is designed so that she can, if necessary, stay at sea for long periods of time and in all kinds of weather. She is equipped so that she can reach and study the ocean bottom even at great depth and under adverse conditions. The cable ships and cable companies have a commercial interest in all that pertains to oceanography and they are eager consumers of information about the sea such as is supplied by government services and private research institutions. Over the years, since the first cable was laid, the cable ships have also contributed to research by reporting their soundings and other discoveries relating to the ocean's bottom. Cable ships have reported some of the deepest soundings ever taken.

Today radio competes with the cables yet the volume of cable services keeps on growing. The longest cables have, of course, been laid in the Pacific, but the Atlantic, which carries the overwhelming bulk of ocean freight and passenger services, also carries the most complex web of cables whose strands not only race back and forth across the ocean but also spread out to Africa and South America. Indeed telephone messages in both directions that were formerly conveyed by wireless are now being sent over two new cables which opened for business in 1956.

Chapter 21

"JUST FOR THE HELL OF IT"

SOME years ago, in an Atlantic port, I met a young American who had built himself a "tabloid" cruiser. The word tabloid was then used to describe a vessel so small and compact that an active man could sail it anywhere single-handed. This little cruiser was about twenty-five feet on the water line, and he was starting off alone for the Panama Canal and beyond that for some vague destination in the South Seas. I asked him why, and his reply was, "Just for the hell of it."

This seems a good title under which to consider the adventures of some of the men and women who have sailed the Atlantic in small vessels. Both the title and the account are informal as befits the character of the people and their ships. The stories of the little vessels, their cruises, and their "captains" that make up this section have been selected for a variety of reasons. Some are here because their stories have already been told in books that can be recommended as good reading; others because their stories never have been told; others because the events are so extraordinary that they should never be forgotten.

All the stories show that the ocean can be both tough and tender in its handling of the "little fellows" that, year by year, put to sea with a kind of contemptuous daring. No doubt there are omitted here some accounts that should be included and vice versa. It would indeed require special and lengthy research to list all the small ships that have crossed the Atlantic. Hardly a year goes by but what some small vessel with a small crew or a solitary navigator slips into an American harbor and is duly heralded by the newspapers. Occasionally such a vessel comes and goes and is never noticed by the newspapers and yachting magazines.

Usually, as our title suggests, the motive of the traveler is amusement or adventure or curiosity—to find out what it is like. Sometimes it is sheer disgust with the complications of life ashore. In recent years the roster of small boats crossing has been increased by a steady stream of refugees fleeing from political tyranny—very often in inadequate or unseaworthy vessels. From time to time a gay adventure winds up in misery and disaster.

Let us begin with an example of good fun and good sense at sea that happens to be also a personal experience, leaving for later consideration the extreme examples and the wild eccentricities. In 1929 I sailed my schooner, *Kinkajou,* into Gibraltar and found at anchor there a small but beautiful little English yawl with the name *Daydream* spaced out in letters of bronze across her transom. At the moment I first saw her, a tall, dark-haired young fellow was swinging in a boatswain's chair, just under the truck of the mainmast, reeving a new set of halyards. He turned out to be John Campbell, and he and his partner, Phillip Merton, presently came aboard for pink gins and dinner. It would have been hard to find pleasanter company. Campbell was a chemical engineer and Merton had for years been secretary to Rudyard Kipling. With their savings they had bought and equipped the *Daydream* and started off to see the world. They had had a successful cruise down from the Channel ports and were bound for the West Indies and the American coasts, so we decided to sail in company.

We were together in the ports of Morocco and in the passage to Madeira and the Canaries. We parted company then, for while they sailed to the Cape Verde Islands, I went down the African coast; but we were together again in the West Indies, and so on. From time to time I would sail on the *Daydream* while one or the other of the boys would join my amateur crew on *Kinkajou.*

Daydream was a small, though not an extreme, vessel for ocean passage. She was well designed, well built, properly sailed and properly navigated. Naturally, in heavy seas she was lively, and being a deep boat with only a few feet of freeboard, she was occasionally wet; but life aboard her was generally pleasant and always safe. In all her many miles of travel she met with only one misadventure.

While making a fast passage in the trades a combination of heavy seas and heavy winds snapped her main boom. This was repaired at sea in orderly sailor fashion and she came into port at Barbados with flying colors.

Indeed, the reason for mentioning Merton and Campbell is that they serve as a good example of how intelligent amateurs can sail a small vessel across the ocean with comfort and safety. Photographs of *Daydream* appear in my book, *Atlantic Circle*.

We may think of *Daydream* as being representative of a whole class of small ships that in the hands of sensible sailors establish pleasant stories of ocean passages. Ralph Stock bought a little ship in one of the Channel ports, fitted her out as a yacht, learning seamanship and navigation as he went along. Then he and his sister sailed across the Atlantic to Panama and across the Pacific to New Zealand. The whole story is found in his book, *The Cruise of the Dream Ship*.

Arthur Hildebrand used to talk with me about ships while sitting in the Yale Club library. One day I missed him. Some years later I learned that he had gone to Scotland and bought a small yacht which he and two companions took on a cruise to the Mediterranean which lasted for several years and resulted in his charming book *Blue Water* which has become a classic of small-boat cruising. I saw Hildebrand again but very briefly, because he was in a hurry to go to Scandinavia where he was to board a small vessel and try to repeat the route of the Vikings' crossing to America. He sailed but the ship was lost on the crossing.

In 1911 Thomas Fleming Day left Providence, Rhode Island in a scrap of a yacht, twenty-five feet overall, called the *Sea Bird*. Thirty-seven days later he sailed into the harbor in Gibraltar. Considering the size of his vessel this could be regarded as a fast and skillful passage, but Day had enjoyed the trip and had not felt at all hurried. In fact, he had passed by way of the Azores and had spent five leisurely days ashore, so that his total sailing time from the United States to Gibraltar was thirty-two days.

All of the foregoing could be regarded as rather exceptional ventures in the field of yachting. The next long-distance sailor I met could not, by any stretch of imagination, be regarded as a yachtsman. The only classification that I can think of for Pidgeon is that of "inspired individualist." In his youth he had no yacht, few resources, and not too much education; but he wanted to see the world, and he thought he could master the sea. He built the *Islander* himself, following but enlarging the lines of Day's *Seabird* to thirty-four feet overall sixteen-foot nine-inch beam and five-foot draft. He taught himself navigation and sailed around the world. When I visited Pidgeon on his ship in New York I found that he was a knowledgeable sailor, modest and quiet, but full of humor when he was launched on a story. Pidgeon wrote an account of his circumnavigation, but it seemed to me inarticulate compared to his conversation. Perhaps his best stories did not fit within the covers of a book.

Once before I had found myself on the deck of a small vessel that had been around the world. This was the *Spray,* a thirty-seven-foot yawl which Captain Joshua Slocum had sailed around the world in three years and two months. Slocum had a right to his title of captain. He was a professional seaman and had actually been in command of a square-rigged ship. There is nothing reticent or inarticulate about his book, *Around the World Alone.*

Slocum was sailing about the beginning of the present century, but the record of ocean passages and small ships is as old as our nation, and one might almost believe as old as history itself. It is a matter of record, for example, that at the time when the Portuguese had hardly begun their conquests and their establishment of colonies in India a young Portuguese named Diogo Botelho seems to have been in a hurry to get home and didn't want to wait for the sailing time of the larger vessels. He took a boat seventeen feet long and sailed this from India to Africa, then around Africa by way of the Cape of Good Hope and so on to Lisbon.

The American record of small-boat sailors seems to begin with a Captain J. Cleveland of Salem, Massachusetts. In 1797 he took a forty-three-ton cutter with a sloop rig and sailed it from Havre to the Isle-de-France. He seems to have specialized in small-boat sailing; for again he took a twenty-five-ton pilot boat and sailed it from Calcutta to the Isle-de-France. Later he sailed from Canton to Formosa and from Formosa to Norfolk Sound in America. Cleveland was not a "single-hander," for it seems that he usually had several hands helping to make up the crew of his little vessels. It has been said that he sailed a fifteen-foot cutter from the Cape of Good Hope to Alaska, but this may be a mere exaggeration or legend based on the reputation that his real passages had earned him.

On the other hand there is no inherent reason why Cleveland's passage in the fifteen-foot cutter from the Cape of Good Hope to Alaska should be regarded either as impossible or improbable. The proof of this statement is that it was about Cleveland's time that another American, John Boit Jr., acquired a sixteen-foot sloop. Boit, who was nineteen years old, declared himself the captain of his small boat and proceeded to sail it around Cape Horn to Vancouver. Here he became a trader on a miniature basis that fitted his miniature vessel, but his business carried him as far as that of even the largest vessels of his time. From Vancouver he sailed to Canton and arrived safely back in an American port in the year of 1796.

In 1886 Captain J. B. Hudson and Captain Fitch embarked from New York City in an American metallic lifeboat. The lifeboat was twenty-six feet long, had a six-foot beam and a depth of two feet ten inches. They left on June 30 and, after encountering several vessels on the way across, were reported at Hastings on the south coast of England on August 15. Up to this time this was the smallest vessel to cross the Atlantic. This lifeboat, named the *Red, White and Blue,* was exhibited at the Paris Exposition of that year. She apparently recrossed the Atlantic and on July 25, 1887 she is referred to in the newspapers as the twenty-six-foot boat that had twice crossed the Atlantic—so apparently she was sailed home. What brought her into newspaper notice at this time was that during the international yacht race, while carrying a complement of newspapermen, she upset in the crowded harbor. Her honorable record does not seem to have been very effective in soothing the feelings of the dripping representatives of the press.

This seems to have been the era of eccentric ventures and absurd craft. A year later, that is in 1887, Captain John Wilkes and two other men put to sea floating on four iron cylinders that had been put together as a life raft. Presumably, they wanted to demonstrate its efficiency—their passage took them from New York to Southampton in fifty-two days.

The inventors of lifeboats, like the inventors of parachutes, seem to be seized with all but a suicidal mania for demonstrating their own equipment. Most of the stories make rather dreary reading, but there was one demonstration so inept in plan and so unlucky in execution as to constitute an epic of dogged misfortune. The story is a little out of order here but is offered as the lifeboat story to end all lifeboat stories.

In 1904 a Captain Brudel had evolved what he believed to be a new form of lifeboat. It was eighteen feet long, had an eight-foot beam and an eight-foot depth. The boat was little more than a tank or a cylinder and ballasted with wooden rubbing strakes running along her side. A hatchway with a cover gave entrance to the interior. She carried a single mast with a not very effective lug sail. Brudel christened her the *Vraad*. It is hard to imagine what inducements he offered, but somehow he persuaded a crew of three other men to sail with him. On June 27 they climbed into the dark and forbidding interior of this strange vessel and sailed from Aalesund, Norway, headed for some vague destination on the American shore.

The *Vraad* was painfully slow but at least she demonstrated her ability to remain afloat. Summer came and went without the vessel being reported. At last in the fall she appeared off the coast of Nova Scotia. She had proceeded as far as the Bay of Fundy when a winter gale came howling out of the northwest and the tank was blown out to sea again. Twice more she worked her way toward the coast and each time was caught by another storm. She was still at sea on Christmas Day—she was still at sea when the first day of 1905 rolled around, then, on January 7, she came under the beam of Eastern Point lighthouse in Gloucester Harbor.

Captain Brudel and his men had then spent 215 days in their eighteen-foot length of icy metal. They may be pardoned for being weary and confused. They did not know the harbor and apparently they did not understand the meaning of the American harbor lights so they drove their extraordinary craft high and dry on the shore. When they staggered up the beach they had at least demonstrated the capacity of the human being to stand punishment and to survive.

1867 was the year in which Wilkes sailed his life raft to England in fifty-two days. This was almost twice the amount of time that it took an ordinary sailing dory in the same year to make the passage between Gloucester and Southampton. Miller and Lawton were the crew of this dory, and the time of their passage was recorded as twenty-seven days. They seem to have set the pattern for a whole succession of ocean passages in sailing dories and other small vessels.

These were more fun, more sensible and more effective than the dreary trip of Brudel's barrel. Following Miller and Lawton, the next passage was notable in that it was made from Europe to America, which is always more difficult in our latitudes than a passage from the west to the east. The crossing is reported in Leslie's *Illustrated Newspaper* under the date July 16, 1870.

J. C. Buckley had secured a ship's lifeboat. He reconditioned her, decked her over and rigged her as a yawl. In this new condition she was christened the *City of Ragusa*. Buckley became the captain and a man named Harper became the one-man crew. They sailed from Liverpool to Boston and made the passage in ninety-eight days.

Ladies seldom permit the men to monopolize a sport, and this seems to have been quite as true in the 70's as it is today. At least it was so in the case of Mrs. Thomas Crapo, who proved herself both a resolute woman and a courageous seaman.

In 1877 Crapo, in New Bedford, had acquired a sound whaleboat at an economical figure. She was nineteen feet in length, and he saw the possibility of converting her into a comfortable little yacht. He had a lot of fun decking her over and equipping her with two masts. Each mast carried a sail on boom and gaff.

When she was completed it appeared that Mr. Crapo meant to slip away for a nice little cruise to Europe. Mrs. Crapo, an English-woman with a seagoing ancestry behind her, had a quite different view of the matter. She had no intention of letting Thomas sail alone, and she embarked with him.

They left in May, bound for England in their ship which was measured as being 1 62/100 tons. They made a memorable and stormy passage, surviving rough weather and sickness aboard. They followed the ship lanes and were reported by many different vessels who aided them by supplying occasional food and water. In forty-nine days they landed in Wales and in five days of further sailing made their way to Penzance. Later they exhibited the ship in London and were visited by members of the royal family, and on the return of the couple to New York by steamer they exhibited their glorified whaleboat in Madison Square Garden.

The American Republic was one hundred years old in 1876. To celebrate this event an American fisherman of Danish origin, named Alfred Johnson, decided to sail a dory to England. He built a dory of sixteen-foot keel, twenty feet overall. He decked her over and rigged the mast in a tabernacle so that it could be lowered. For sail he carried a mainsail and two jibs. On the bow and stern he painted her name, *Centennial,* and the name of his port, Gloucester.

He sailed on the 16th of June amid the honest skepticism of his companions. He encountered rough weather and got little sleep for the first week. Finding he was having difficulty with his compass, he put into Shag Harbor behind Cape Sable in Nova Scotia. He had twenty-five days of good sailing and then heavy weather again. On the 16th of July he was still at sea. Then a German passenger ship tried to rescue him. Johnson refused, but accepted a bottle of brandy.

In another gale, after the passenger ship had left, the lurch of the little vessel threw him against the edge of his water cask so that he was knocked unconscious, and the little vessel had to look out for itself. Fortunately, at this time he had all sail in and was riding to a sea anchor. By the time the storm blew out he was conscious again but with a feeling of a split head. But he got in his sea anchor and set sail.

He began to pick up ships and in recognition of his courageous attempt they were glad enough to give him his position so that he gave up his own navigating. But the passing vessels had their drawback too, for in 1876 many ships sailed without running lights, so Johnson was forced to stay awake all the nights and to do his sleeping in brief snatches during the daylight hours. Once, on the way over, after speaking to the brig *Maggie Gander,* in the midst of a stiff gale the dory capsized with him. After waiting in the water by the side of the dory for twenty minutes, another huge sea permitted him to right the dory. After some six hours of bailing he was able to clear his little ship of water. Then he went through four days of rain, followed by a fog, during which time he made very little progress. Much of his food had been rendered useless by the dip in the sea. Still he held on. He finally made the Welsh port of Abercastle, but he had decided that he would sail his dory into an English harbor and Abercastle did not seem to meet the specifications.

So he pushed off again and made his way to Liverpool. This time the news of his successful undertaking was spread abroad and a whole steamer full of people had come out to meet him, but he avoided the reception committee in the center of the town and went up the Mersey to a little hotel dock. This was on the 21st of August. He could have made money and publicity out of his enterprise. P. T. Barnum wanted him to exhibit, and he himself had planned to have his ship at the Centennial Exposition at Philadelphia. But he was a modest seaman and not a good businessman. He was too late for the exposition, and he turned Barnum down and went back to live as a fisherman in Gloucester.

One of the most persistent of the small-boat sailors is W. A. Andrews. His name first appears in 1888. In this year, in a small boat, the *Dark Secret,* he sailed from Boston in an attempt to reach Europe; but after sixty-eight days of adverse weather he had made only 150 miles. He was then fortunate enough to be picked up by a ship named the *Nor* and was returned to Boston.

An ordinary man who had spent over two months at sea and, in all that time, had averaged only a little over two miles of progress per day might well be discouraged with small-boat sailing. Andrews was no ordinary man, and his confidence in his seamanship was unshaken. In 1891, we find him making a bet with Josiah W. Lawlor. This involved a race across the Atlantic in two dories. Andrews christened his dory the *Mermaid,* and Lawlor chose for his the name of *Sea Serpent.*

They sailed on June 17 from Boston. They separated on their course. Andrews drifted into light airs which held him for thirty-five days. On August 4 the ship *Hafis* reported Andrews as having been in 45° 26′ N. and 41° 22′ W. on July 27. It was reported that Lawlor had had much better weather so was well ahead of him. This was proved true by a report brought to Boston on August 6 by the steamer *Queensmore* that had spoken to both dories at a time when Lawlor was some 100 miles ahead. Finally Andrews was capsized, picked up by a steamer and landed in Antwerp. By this time Lawlor had already been in England some fifteen days.

Despite three failures, Andrews was not discouraged. The spring of 1892 found him in Atlantic City preparing to sail for Spain in a wonderful ship christened the *Sapolio.* Maybe he gave it this name because it was little larger than a cake of soap—to be exact, fourteen feet six inches in length. *Sapolio* was a folding boat built of thin cedar boards, the boards being covered with canvas. From the descriptions of her existing, she seems to have been a relatively flat and shallow craft built either with a chine or hard turn in the bilges. Andrews referred to her as a "sneak-box." He admits she pounded horribly when going to windward, but he succeeded in sailing her to the Azores, which he reached in thirty-one days, and finally took her past Cape St. Vincent and into the ports of Huelva and Palos in Spain, from which Columbus had sailed on his first voyage to America.

No record of heroic small-boat ventures is complete without a reference to Captain Howard Blackburn. Since his story has been repeatedly and adequately told, the following lines will serve simply as a reminder of the accomplishments of this extraordinary man. Blackburn, a large and powerfully built man, was in the crew of a Grand Banks fishing vessel sailing out of Gloucester. The schooner was fishing on the Burgeo Bank and Blackburn and a dory mate named Welch were in a dory working with hand lines when a winter gale suddenly cut them off from the schooner. For a time they waited, hoping that the weather would moderate or that the schooner would succeed in picking them up. Finally, in desperation, they decided to row for shore. They took turns rowing until Welch finally became exhausted by the heavy weather and froze to death.

Blackburn, finding that his hands were becoming numb and that they were continually slipping from the oar, decided to let them freeze fast so that he would not again lose his grip. After five days of continuous rowing he came into a Newfoundland port. After his hands and parts of his arms had been amputated and he had otherwise recovered, he was unable to secure employment as a fisherman.

All that was left to him was to exploit his endurance and his knowledge of the sea. After learning to use his artificial arms and hands he built himself a little thirty-foot sloop, the *Great Western,* and in 1889 sailed from Gloucester, Massachusetts to Gloucester, England. In 1891 he built a smaller vessel, the *Great Republic,* a sloop twenty-five feet in length, which he sailed to Lisbon in thirty-nine days. He made another attempt in a seventeen-foot dory, the *America,* but this trip ended in failure, and Blackburn was picked up by a passing vessel. On his return he established a shop in Gloucester which he maintained for many years.

The fantastic contrivances in which men have put to sea can be almost indefinitely extended, but surely one of the strangest of all was a collapsible German rubber boat of the sort that was popular in Europe in the 20's, generally known as a faltboat—the folding boat. Captain Franz Romer had one built that was slightly larger than the ordinary two-place canoe. In 1920 he succeeded in sailing her from Spain to the Canary Islands and from there to St. Thomas and the West Indies. He was, therefore, successful in making the ocean passage in a craft that had about eighteen inches of freeboard. Compared with this, the passage from St. Thomas to Santo Domingo should have been for him only a brief outing. Unfortunately, he was caught in a hurricane and lost.

All of the stories up to the present time have dealt with boats or other contrivances that were sailed across the ocean. However strange they may appear, they hardly prepare us for the final surprise which leaves an indelible impression regarding man's relationship to the Atlantic Ocean.

In 1896 a Mr. Richard K. Fox, of New York, speculated on whether it were possible to row across the ocean. Two New Jersey fishermen of Norwegian origin, George Firbo and Frank Samuelson, decided that they would try the passage entirely under oars. They had a skiff built by a New Jersey boatbuilder named Seeman, something like a Seabright dory. The boat was eighteen feet long with a five-foot maximum beam.

They left the Battery in New York on June 6. The boat was christened the *Fox* in honor of the man who backed the plan. Once they capsized, as they were almost bound to do when the heavy weather hit them. But they had built-in tanks for buoyancy and succeeded in righting the boat and in bailing her out. They had spare oars lashed in the boat, so they were able to carry on, but they had lost all their provisions. However, five days later, on July 15, they encountered the bark *Sita*. They went aboard the *Sita* and had a hot meal, secured a few provisions and then started off again. From another bark, the *Eugene,* they later secured water, for their tanks were beginning to run dry. They were reported passing the Scilly Islands on July 31, 1896, having rowed across the Atlantic Ocean in fifty-four days.

They took passage back for New York on a steamer which encountered such terrific gales and continual head winds that she consumed all of the coal in her bunkers and used even the woodwork and partitions of the ship in an effort to keep up steam. Finally the vessel was left helpless 250 miles out in the open ocean from New York.

At this point Firbo and Samuelson volunteered to row to New York and send help. They had the *Fox* put into the water and, rowing almost continuously, made the trip in four days' time and reported the plight of the steamer.

We are now in the mid-century going through a period of clamorous nonsense, with people dashing off to sea in ill-found equipment on ill-considered adventures. When Thor Heyerdahl in 1947 drifted from South America across part of the Pacific on a large balsa raft he may have added very little to Polynesian ethnology, his announced reason for the trip, but he did add some very interesting observations on life close to the sea and he and his companions had a rousing good time. He seems to have stimulated people to less worthy drifting matches and to a belief that anything that will float will get them across the ocean. One adventurer has even put to sea in a sort of amphibious motor wagon left over from the war. Such ventures are usually announced as undertaken to "prove" something but actually prove little beyond the capacity of human endurance and the forbearance of Father Neptune. Some of these adventurers might develop into good seamen if they became familiar with the seaman's tools.

A real seaman is Mrs. Anne Davison, from Gloucestershire in England. She and her husband started across the Atlantic in their twenty-three-foot sloop *Felicity Ann*. His untimely death terminated this venture but since then she has crossed the Atlantic alone and thus become the first woman transatlantic singlehander.

These stories are interesting as examples of human courage and endurance. The reason for their inclusion in this book, however, is that they tell us a good deal about the character of the ocean. In the first place, they tell us that the North Atlantic, which enjoys the reputation of being such an impetuous body of water, can also, during the summer season, be unusually mild and kindly. Further than that, the stories here reveal some details regarding the ocean's structure.

Botelho, for example, could never have made the passage around Africa had he attempted the trip in the reverse direction. Coming from Asia, he had favorable winds and currents through most of his passage along the East African coast. After he rounded the Cape of Good Hope he again had favorable winds and currents at least as far as the Gulf of Guinea. The slowest part of this trip was then probably the passage through the doldrums, though even here there are seasons when he would have had winds abeam or abaft all the way to the Canaries.

We may also note that the sensible yachtsman, and even Romer in his rubber boat, almost invariably made successful passage to the west by sailing in the belt of the northeast trades. By comparison, the passage from the northern United States ports to England and France are a little more difficult, but have been negotiated successfully even by men rowing an open boat. The passage from northern European ports to the northern ports in America is the most difficult of all at any season of the year and accounts for the slowest passage and the greatest losses.

The chapter, as a whole, should do something to dispel the popular belief that is so tenaciously held even today, that safety at sea is largely dependent upon the size of the vessel. Nothing could be farther from the absolute truth. The safety, and even the comfort, of a vessel depend on three things and three things only: careful design, stout construction and judicious seamanship. Over and over again it has been demonstrated that in even the roughest weather a small, properly found ship will outlive a poorly designed, cheaply built or poorly managed ship, even though the large vessel may be hundreds of times the size of the small one.

The belief seems to persist that a large vessel is necessarily better designed, better built and better operated than a small one; yet any careful examination of the record will show that this is not the case. An examination over the last half century of the record of ocean liners, as well as coast-size passenger ships, will show that size is not a guarantee against misfortune. Some lines, operating in large vessels, have had a history marked by one disaster after another. There is also inherent danger in size which is often overlooked. This is the matter of accidental injury to passengers and crew. In the superliners the large dance floors, the libraries, the grand salons with their period furniture seem to be very reassuring to inexperienced travelers. They are very impressive as long as the vessel stays on an even keel, and this some of the large ships will do even in fairly stiff breezes; but once really heavy weather sets in and the superliner with her high speed begins to roll or pitch, each of these vast roomy spaces becomes a hazard to life and limb. Once the furniture comes adrift or passengers begin to stagger and fall there are almost certain to be serious casualties, because the period of the ship's motion is very long and the farther wall is very far away. Likewise, in heavy weather in the kitchens and pantries below decks the accidents to cooks and waiters, as well as to glassware and china, is terrific. With respect to accidents of this kind the smaller vessel is actually safer and more comfortable. There is always a handhold close by and usually a comfortable place to sit or lie or stand, even when work is going forward in rough weather.

Experience is always more impressive than arguments, so a reference to a personal experience in this place may be in order. The forty-ton schooner in which I used to sail the Atlantic was, of course, a large vessel when compared with the small yachts and boats whose adventures we have been following. Yet, I am sure that some of the small yachts would be just as safe at sea and almost as comfortable as *Kinkajou*. On the other hand, *Kinkajou* would be a small vessel compared with a commercial freighter or any kind of passenger ship operating on the ocean. *Kinkajou* was probably as safe at sea as the average vessel many thousands of tons larger. I had a vivid experience of this on one occasion when we were caught in a hurricane off the Bay of Biscay. *Kinkajou* survived wind speeds up to 110 miles an hour without suffering serious damage, while four large commercial vessels in the same waters and in the same storm were driven ashore or were otherwise wrecked. There are many records of lifeboats surviving at sea through storms that disabled or destroyed the larger vessel from which the lifeboat was launched.

The small-boat voyages illustrate the extreme contrasts presented by the ocean. The *Titanic,* the largest, fastest and safest ship of her time, was sunk on a calm night before she had even completed one ocean crossing; yet a little cloth-covered box less than fifteen feet long sailed across safely and two men have rowed across the Atlantic in an open boat.

Part Four

THE ATLANTIC—
TODAY AND TOMORROW

Chapter 22

SPEED, ELEGANCE AND LUXURY

W HEN did ocean travel on the Atlantic reach its peak? When were the best ships built? When was the age of speed, elegance and luxury?

The answer is not hard to find. The answer is now. It was yesterday; it is today; it will be tomorrow.

When the earliest Atlantic liners, the packets, were leaving New York before 1820 newspaper reporters were reaching for their most extravagant adjectives to describe the beauty and comfort of these ships: the fine large rooms, the elegant fittings and appointments, the generous and tasteful food. Today, almost a century and a half later, as each new liner comes into the harbor the same phrases are still used. This is no criticism of the writers; I appreciate their difficulty and share their problem.

It means that over the years ships have grown and changed so rapidly as to earn the surprise and admiration of each new generation. There have been occasions when the claims were understood by the owners and accepted by the public as hopes rather than as fulfillments. Today, however, the luxury liner fully deserves its title for in many respects the services it provided are unrivaled even ashore.

First-class living quarters on a superliner are still referred to as "cabins" supposedly out of respect for tradition. Many of them, with equal justice, could be called apartments, for they may contain sitting room, bedroom, bath, serving pantry in various combinations. They

339

will include ample closet space; they will be equipped with bureau and dressing table; with beds and not bunks, with comfortable chairs and sofas. They will not be equipped with portholes but, at the very least, casements opening on the foaming sea and in many cases they may have their own private and protected deck space.

All of the normal services of life may be assumed on the modern liner. There is a barber shop for the gentlemen; a hairdressing establishment and beauty salon for the ladies. For each there are also provided a bathing establishment, massage and hydrotherapy services. There is a tailoring establishment and valet and maid services. There is laundry service for personal linens. There are bookshops, jewelry shops, shops for ladies' dresses and accessories, shops for sporting goods and a number of other kinds of sales services. All ships are provided with mail, radio and cable services and a number of vessels carry as well a broker's service. All major ships are now adequately supplied with medical services, with dispensary and surgery and in some cases an adequate small hospital.

When it comes to sports and games, the big ship is as well equipped as the average summer resort. Only the sports that require an enormous area, like polo and golf, have to be curtailed. There are almost certain to be provision for quoits, shuffleboard, deck tennis, badminton, outdoor and sometimes indoor tennis courts, gymnasiums with all manner of equipment, some combination of indoor and outdoor swimming pools. On the larger ships, the space provided on some sports deck is usually big enough to provide for practice of most of the track and field sports; even the golf enthusiasts will usually find a putting green and sometimes a netted driving range.

It may be assumed that indoor games are adequately represented in the saloons, cardrooms, smoking room, verandas and other areas. There is always a library and librarian service scaled in general to the size of the ship and the anticipated number of passengers. All modern ships are equipped with a saloon and stage that lends itself to musical and dramatic entertainments or that can be converted to a temporary motion picture theater. Permanent theater space is provided in some of the modern liners. Some ships are equipped with chapels for religious services.

All of the major liners make a determined effort to buy the best foodstuffs and to staff their ships with really expert chefs, cooks and waiters. Their idea of a suitable cuisine is always generous and sometimes lavish. The French liner has made a special effort also to provide a varying wine card and the best of wine services and is followed, with varying degrees of success, by the other major lines. Despite the general excellence of dining services, some ships have also been provided with specialized privately operated restaurants.

It must not be supposed that every liner even in the luxury class is always equipped with all the frills and flourishes referred to in the preceding paragraphs. Certain lines and certain ships have always selected features that they felt would appeal to their clientele. Many of the features and services have found a place at sea only by trial and error over a long period of time, in fact, it is difficult to assign the ship and the time of origin of most of the special services. It is possible to do so in a few cases.

Electricity has become so essential not only to the comfort but also to the safety and control of big ships that it is interesting to note that the first successful installation of electric current and light was made on the American sail and steam auxiliary ship *Alameida* in the year 1881. The plant and installation was made by Thomas Edison and the engineer in charge was Hubert Wilson. The vessel sailed around South America to the west coast and later to the Orient.

Kaiser Wilhelm der Grosse, 14,350 tons, built in 1897, seems to have been the first ship to provide a nursery and playroom for children. The origin of the steamer swimming pool seems to be uncertain. Apparently the first outdoor swimming pools were improvised affairs. In the early part of the present century improvised pools were found on quite small vessels such as operated in the American tropics and on southerly runs to the Mediterranean. After the ship left port a different framework was erected on the main cargo hatch or on some other advantageous location. On this framework was hung a collapsible tank of rubberized canvas or otherwise waterproof fabric. When warm weather and warm waters were reached the tank was filled with salt water. The Grace Line ships, operating in and through the American tropics, have made a special feature of outdoor swimming pools and also of dining saloons with movable roofs that can be opened to the night's sky in favorable weather.

As early as the beginning of the century English ships, both Cunarders and White Star Line vessels, provided special quarters for Turkish baths and other bathing services. These were sometimes equipped with what were then called "plunges" or "swimming baths" and such installations seemed to have been the forerunners of the indoor swimming pool. By 1910 indoor pools appeared as a feature of a number of the larger and newer liners.

The first seagoing bookshop appeared on the Anchor liner *Transyl-*

vania in the early 20's. Captain David Bone of that vessel enjoyed a distinguished reputation not only as a commander but also as an author. It was for this reason that Joseph Conrad and many other distinguished figures chose his ship for ocean travel. It was natural also that Miss Ilah Niehof of New York should have found a place for the first floating bookshop on the *Transylvania*.

A de luxe restaurant under Ritz Carlton management was operating on a liner before the commencement of the First World War. The French liner, *Ile de France,* appears to be the first ship to have provided a complete guignol or marionette theater for children. The *Normandie,* also of the French Line, included in her equipment a permanent regular theater.

Naturally, luxury services required the payment of luxury prices. As the size of ships and extent and quality of services increased, the price of ocean transportation rose to keep pace with them. By the time of the First World War, the luxury liners had already enjoyed a very extensive development but they had also encountered serious problems in operation and in costs of maintenance. The big ships could usually attract enough passengers to fill their sailing lists in all classes only during the height of the summer season. In winter and other "off seasons," they often operated with a fair to poor complement of passengers.

In order partly to meet this situation, rates were reduced and it also became customary for the lines to retire their larger ships for drydock or repairs during some portion of the off season. Even in the summer season it was another kind of problem that the ships did not fully meet. There were many families on both sides of the Atlantic that could ill afford the expenses of a first-class passage on one of the big ships and that still disliked the idea of traveling second class.

The answer to this situation was the development of the single class or cabin class liner. This was a smaller type of ship, being seaworthy, well built, reasonably fast and with good general appointments and services. It admitted only one class of passengers. The first cabin class liners were built in 1914. Owing to the war, they did not come into general recognition and use for a number of years. In the 20's, following the First World War, the cabin class liners came into their own and had a very general and prosperous development and still provide important and popular services.

Another development that took place during these years and that solved the economic problems of a number of the Atlantic liners and of their operating lines was the winter cruise. Liners that otherwise would have been operating during the winter months between American and European ports with a half or even a quarter of their normal passenger sailing lists were diverted to carry out cruises to the Mediterranean, to South America or to some other warm and inviting region. At first these cruises were of limited extent and duration but as the idea demonstrated not only its value as relaxation but also as economic enterprise, the range and the importance of the cruise increased. Even world cruises became popular and profitable.

At the start, one of the factors that accounted for the rapid growth of the cruise idea was the existence of American prohibition. The number of Americans who disliked having total abstinence thrust upon them was legion. They tired of poor liquors and imitation wines. Many who in normal times enjoyed a moderate use of wines and spirits refrained from drinking at all because they feared to consume the injurious and sometimes poisonous substitutes that were sold. The cruise, whether long or short, offered a ready means of escape from prohibition America.

Possibly there was an excess of cruises during the 20's. They fell off in number but did not die even during the years of the great depression. The soundness of the cruise and the cruise ship have been demonstrated by their survival and current popularity.

The full development of luxury liner services is directly dependent upon the size of the ship. The large liners now accommodate a population that is the equivalent of a small city afloat—a very wealthy, highly selected city. Nonetheless it is governed by economic laws just as the city ashore is and it has to arrive at a certain size before it can afford to support some of the special services even though the major lines are heavily subsidized and even though some of the services have been introduced for publicity and advertising purposes rather than for utility.

It is interesting to see how the size of the Atlantic liners has grown during the last half century. The steam liner, characteristic of the nineteenth century, probably reached its best expression in two ships that were built in 1889. These were the sister ships, the *City of Paris* and the *City of New York*. Originally built for the Inman Line, these ships were long and low and racy in appearance with handsomely designed clipper bows. In appearance they were quite different from our present straight steel stiff-sided ocean mammoths. They looked more like very large elegantly appointed steam yachts. They had some of the disadvantages of the steam yachts but also such grace and beauty that they are still remembered. They passed to American ownership in the year 1893.

Quite different in character was the first of the large German liners that was built in 1897; this was the *Kaiser Wilhelm der Grosse* that reached the size of 14,350 tons. This represented a very large ship for that time though she was still short of the tonnage of the *Great Eastern* by over 4,500 tons. In fact, the tonnage of the *Great Eastern* was not equaled by the famous White Star ship *Oceanic* which was built in 1899 and was only exceeded by the *Celtic* built for the same line in the year 1900, which represented 20,000 tons. Though the *Kaiser Wilhelm* and White Star liners were built in the closing years of the nineteenth century, they do not seem to belong to that period but rather to the twentieth century with the passion for size and speed.

The year 1906 was a significant year for new Atlantic liners. The development which the Germans had started with the *Kaiser Wilhelm* they continued in ships like the *Kronprinz Wilhelm* and the *Deutschland* and capped this in 1906 with the elegant and luxurious *Kronprincessin Cecilie*. This also was the year that launched the fabulous Cunarders, *Mauretania* and *Lusitania*. These were designed as sister ships; their length was 762 feet, their beam 88 feet and they had a depth of 57 feet. Their object was to achieve great speed as well as great size. They averaged 32,000 gross tons and despite the fact that they were sister ships there were some slight differences between them because they were built in different yards. Each was equipped with four turbine engines and direct drive to four screw propellers. These ships accomplished their purposes in the sense that both of them soon hung up record crossings of the North Atlantic as we shall see in a moment.

Apparently the White Star Line had doubts about being able to compete with the new Cunarders on the basis of speed and decided instead to build vessels of record-breaking size. In 1911 this resulted in the launching of the *Olympic* and *Titanic,* each of 45,000 tons. Apparently the German lines despaired of competing on the basis of speed alone so they followed the same line of reasoning that had been adopted by the White Star Line. The Hamburg-American Line in particular adopted a policy of developing large vessels which were expected to attract the traveling public because of their size, seaworthiness and general comfort. Thus, in the years immediately preceding the outbreak of World War I, they developed the *Imperator,* of approximately 52,000 tons, the *Vaterland* of 54,000 and the *Bis-*

marck of approximately 60,000. The Germans derived little benefit from these great ships for the fortunes of war placed them in the hands of the allies and they became respectively the Cunard vessel, *Berengaria,* the United States liner, *Leviathan,* and the White Star liner, *Majestic.*

In the period between World War I and World War II the Germans, the French and the British recommenced a competition to build larger and more effective ocean greyhounds. One of the characteristics of this period has been the loss of interest in steam propulsion and the gradual acceptance of the motor or internal combustion engine for even large ships. Particularly in 1929, the North German Lloyd launched the motor vessel *Bremen* which directed attention to the motor ship by establishing new transatlantic records.

In the matter of size the British established a record with the development of the *Queen Mary* of 81,235 tons. The French Line capped this with the large and striking steamer *Normandie* of 83,423 tons. The sad end of the ill-fated and mismanaged *Normandie* is so well remembered as to require no special treatment here. The loss of the *Normandie* serves, however, as a reminder that though the French Line, in the period between the wars, succeeded in developing some handsome and luxurious vessels like the *Ile de France,* the *Patapar* and others, her vessels during this period met with a shocking succession of disasters both in port and on the high seas. The *Normandie* was exceeded by the *Queen Elizabeth* of 85,000 tons, launched in 1940. At the present writing, the *Queen Elizabeth* is and will probably for some time remain the largest and most elaborate vessel afloat.

There is a general relationship between the size of the vessel and the speed at which it travels. The large vessel had some distinct advantages in being able to operate at absolutely higher speeds without a too great relative increase in space and cost. Still, a detailed examination of the Atlantic record will show that on the one hand relatively small vessels have maintained good operating records and on the other hand that many very large ships have been built and operated without any pretense at reaching maximum speeds.

The following set of records are not complete but they do illustrate how the time required for transatlantic passages has steadily decreased over the last half century. In 1888 the *City of Paris,* established a transatlantic record of six days. In the same year the White Star liner *Teutonic* lowered the record to five days and sixteen hours. This held until 1894 when the Cunarder *Lucania* dropped it to five days, seven hours and twenty-three minutes. A really important shattering of records commenced with the launching of the *Lusitania* and the *Mauretania*. The *Lusitania* hit her stride first, dropping the record for the run from Queenstown to New York to four days and fifteen hours. The *Mauretania* began to step out in 1910, dropping the record from Queenstown to New York to four days, ten hours and forty-one minutes. Eleven years later, that is, in 1921, she made the longer run from Cherbourg to New York in five days, two hours and thirty-four minutes and three years later capped this by an eastward passage of five days, one hour and forty-nine minutes. In 1929 she established for this run a record of four days, nineteen hours and fifty-five minutes. In short, the *Mauretania* was still a record-holder twenty-two years after she was launched and in the twentieth year of her age was able to steam to the rescue of another ship at the rate of twenty-nine knots. In 1929 the North German Lloyd motor vessel *Bremen* beat the *Mauretania*'s record by making the run from Cherbourg to New York in four days, seventeen hours and forty-two minutes, which was at the rate of 28.18 knots. Later that year she reduced her record for this run by eighteen minutes and hung up her record for the eastbound passage of four days and fourteen hours.

Somewhat to everyone's surprise, the current champion is an American product. In mid-century, with support from the Federal government and technical assistance from the United States Navy, a modern liner has been built in the *United States* that is satisfactory as a passenger vessel and also so carefully planned and technically equipped that she can prove of value as a potential naval auxiliary for some time to come. The *United States* is 990 feet long with a 101½ foot beam and 53,330 gross tons, driven by four high temperature high pressure steam turbines.

When the *United States* sailed on July 3, 1952, a hundred years had passed without any American steam or motor liners holding a transatlantic record or even supplying close competion for a record. On her maiden voyage the new ship established many records, the most important of which, of course, are those for the eastward and westward crossing between Ambrose Light and Bishop's Rock. Her eastward run was three days, ten hours, forty minutes at an average speed of 35.59 knots, westward three days, twelve hours, twelve minutes— 34.51 knots.

The great liner has become one of mankind's important discoveries and technical developments. There was a natural fascination in following the growth of the liner: the increase in size, the increase in speed, the sport of watching a succession of blue ribbon records established and broken. It is equally fascinating to regard the liner in another aspect, namely, as a social institution. Thus the liner is truly at once the cause, the instrument and the result of a series of important social changes in transatlantic travel.

As we have seen in the earlier sections of this chapter as far as ocean ships were concerned there was a break with tradition in the last decade of the nineteenth century. Then various countries built and launched new ships which were much larger, more powerful and faster than the ships of the past. One of the obvious results was to increase the ease and luxury of ocean travel, but one of the underlying causes was the demand for mass transportation across the Atlantic. The glamor was for the first-class passengers on the upper deck, but the important social and economic consequences traveled below decks in the steerage.

In the last decade of the nineteenth century and the first decade of the twentieth century people were both restless and free to move. There was a long period of relative peace and prosperity. Under cover of this peace and prosperity there was increasing restlessness and tension in many European countries and in the Western Hemisphere the decades of rapid industrial expansion were creating new jobs at higher wages and the promise of an indefinitely extended prosperity. Hundreds of thousands of European families were stirred by this restlessness and made eager by these promises. They were prepared to pay what for them were high prices and to accept all manner of personal inconveniences, discomforts and sacrifices if only they could reach the New World and have a chance to establish new homes there.

The new liners were built partly to accommodate the increasing number of prosperous American families that wished to travel to Europe for sightseeing, cultural development and a general good time. Partly they were built to provide better and healthier transportation for the poor families of Europe who were coming to America to fill new jobs in American agriculture and industry.

In the decade 1891 to 1900 over three and a half million immigrants came from Europe to the United States. This was the beginning of a new wave of westward travel and it coincided with the development of a new kind of ocean vessel.

The meaning of the migration of the period 1891 to 1900 did not, however, rest in absolute numbers. The meaning was to be found in the kinds of people that were seeking passage on the new ships. In the period 1881 to 1890 the number of emigrants from Europe had been even larger by more than a million, but up to the year 1890 the number of arrivals from northern and western Europe had always been many times as great as the number coming from other countries. In other words, up to 1890 the migration to the United States had, for the most part, come from countries that were on or close to the Atlantic seaboard; they were migrants from Scotland, Ireland, England, the Rhine Valley, Switzerland, the Netherlands and Scandinavia, with relatively small increments from other parts of Europe.

Thus, up to 1890 the bulk of the new arrivals annually came from countries that in history, tradition and racial affinity were close to the people that already formed the bulk of the American population. In 1890 there was a sharp change in the character of the migrants. In the last decade of the century, for the first time in United States history, the emigrants from southern and eastern Europe exceeded those from northern and western Europe.

This was only an indication and forerunner of what was to come. In the total number of those admitted into the United States immigration hit a peak in the period 1901 to 1910 when a total of nearly nine million people were admitted. While this was a record in absolute numbers it was not so in a relative sense, that is relative to the already existing population; the highest relative rate of immigration having occurred in the 1850's. Again, the significance lay in the composition of the immigration stream. In the first decade of the twentieth century less than two million came from northern and western Europe whereas the number from eastern and southern Europe exceeded six and a quarter millions. At the same time migration from Asia to the United States also hit a peak.

This proved to be more of an invasion and a break with national tradition than even the natural hospitality of the United States and the free and easy ways of the Americans could tolerate. In the decade from 1911 to 1920 total immigration dropped by almost one-half its former volume, that is, to a little more than four and one-quarter million new entrants. This drop was partly due to the fact that travel was interrupted by some years of war but it was also due to an increasing tendency to restrict immigration as a matter of national policy. This movement was fully established in the Immigration Act of 1924 which introduced the quota system as a method of immigration control. In the decade from 1921 to 1930 immigration ran to approximately two and one-half million and in the period 1931-1940 it had dropped again to less than one-half million.

The large liner grew up in the period of unrestricted immigration as a method of providing cheap and yet safe and sanitary transatlantic passage for travelers who could afford to expend very little for their passage money. It is interesting to observe that large liners have survived and have even been built in the period when the frenzied wave of immigrant travel had begun to subside. Possibly this is a hopeful sign that even in the future large ships will continue to provide many people of varied classes with a new and healthier kind of international transatlantic travel.

It is difficult to leave the great liners without some reference to the sad fact that the newest, largest and finest ships have not infrequently met with disaster. It was so in the beginning of the liner services as our previous chapter has pointed out in the case of the Collins liners and there is also the matter of the Allen Line record. The case of the *Normandie* and the other French Line vessels, in the period between the wars, would bear some special study because quite possibly special influences were operating here.

The *Lusitania* was sunk in her youth and was an early victim of unrestrained submarine warfare. At the time of her sinking she was one of the largest and fastest liners afloat. Had she survived, it would have been interesting to see whether she could have equaled or exceeded the long and successful career of her sister ship, the *Mauretania*. In view of the speed with which the *Lusitania* was capable it came as a shock to everyone that she should have fallen a victim to the limited powers of the submarine of that period. At the time of her sinking the *Lusitania* was completing a run from New York to Liverpool. She had 1,959 persons aboard. It was 2 P.M., and the Old Head of Kinsale on the south coast of Ireland was in sight of the vessel. This was the same Head on which the famous packet, *Albion,* had been so dramatically wrecked almost a century before.

The German submarine U-20, Lt. Capt. Schweiger in command, without warning, approached to within 700 meters of the liner and discharged a torpedo into her starboard side. The mortality of the *Lusitania* was surprising. Within twenty-two minutes she had disappeared beneath the waves, carrying with her 1,198 of the passengers and crew aboard.

The *Lusitania* sank at a time when President Wilson was trying frantically to keep America out of the European War. President Wilson, in the face of this ruthless sinking involving the lives of many innocent people including American citizens, was bound to protest, but his other reaction was to deliver a speech in which he said that it was possible for a nation to be too proud to fight. The American people seem neither to have understood nor to have shared President Wilson's views. The sinking of the *Lusitania* started a chain reaction of hostility to Germany. Fanned by other sinkings and other truculent threats this served to prepare the American people for the acceptance of war.

History may not repeat itself but it certainly provides some startling parallels. World War II was also heralded by the ruthless and spectacular sinking of a ship. It was in September, 1939, that Hitler's outrages on the European continent reached such a point that war was declared between England and Hitler's Germany.

A day or so before this declaration the liner *Athenia* of the Donaldson Line had departed from Scotland for the United States, and at the time of declaration was on the high seas, carrying a capacity passenger list in all classes. Owing to the hostilities and the generally disturbed situation in Europe, many sailings from the British Isles had been canceled and passengers transferred to other vessels as in the case of the *Athenia*. Within a few hours of the declaration of war, for no known reason, a violent explosion occurred amidships in the engine room section of the *Athenia* as a result of which many of the crew were injured or killed, the engines disabled and the ship plunged into darkness.

It was soon apparent that the sinking of the vessel was inevitable and passengers and crew were ordered to take to the boats. This operation was carried out with skill and with reasonable success despite the sudden character of the disaster and the difficult situation of the ship and the fact that the abandonment was carried out at nighttime. Fortunately several vessels were within call of the *Athenia* and were able to participate in rescue operations; these included a small freighter, a large Swedish private yacht and a tanker, the *City of Flint*. Survivors were landed in Ireland, in Halifax and other ports. The sinking of the *Athenia* resulted in the loss of several hundred lives, including a large number of American citizens.

There was no inherent reason for the sudden explosion on the *Athenia* and to most observers it seemed at once reasonable to conclude that the most likely explanation of her loss was that she was a victim of a renewal of ruthless German submarine warfare. However, the Hitler propagandists got to work and immediately flooded the presses of Europe with stories that were repeated in the United

States to the effect that the English had themselves sunk the *Athenia* by torpedo or by bomb in a deliberate attempt to arouse in America a hostility to Hitler's Germany and to involve the United States in war.

It was not until the time of the War Guilt trials in Nuremberg that the whole story was pieced together. At the trial of Grand Admiral Raeder, Admiral Karl Doenitz testified that the *Athenia* had in fact been sunk by the German submarine U-30 which was then in command of First Lieutenant Lempe. It was claimed at the time of the trial that this was not an official act and that Lieutenant Lempe acted without authority in firing the torpedo. Testimony also revealed that on her return to a German port the log and other records of the U-30 had been altered and falsified in an endeavor to conceal Nazi responsibility for the *Athenia* sinking.

Wherever the ultimate responsibility rested, it seemed clear that the doctrine of ruthless warfare and the individual action of "trigger happy commanders" produced the same kind of sea atrocity in one generation as in another. Furthermore, the disaster, though its cause remained unproved, also produced some sharp reactions in the American people.

Up to this time, Hitler's depredations on the continent seemed to many Americans to be, from an American point of view, both remote and incredible. The sinking of the *Athenia* both warned and aroused them. It soon became apparent that the *Athenia* was only the first of a long series of sinkings due to Nazi submarine activity and that American lives and interests were in fact being lost and destroyed in Hitler's drive for power.

The *Lusitania* and the *Athenia* were victims of war but the *Titanic* went down in an unparalleled period of peace and prosperity. This was in April of 1912, when the *Titanic* was on her maiden voyage. She was not only the latest ship launched but also the largest, running to 46,000 tons. She had already been hailed as the biggest and safest vessel afloat, having been built with a double bottom and with many watertight compartments. She was supposed to be equipped with the very latest in devices for the detection and control of fire, leakage, etc., and also the latest navigation devices, radio, communication, davits, lifeboats and other devices for the protection of life at sea.

Nonetheless, on the night of April 14, amid calm seas, still airs and apparently good general visibility, obscured only be a light mist near the water, she struck a low-lying iceberg. The blow was not severe and even went unnoticed by some of the passengers. Nevertheless, it laid open one side of the vessel and within a few hours she had sunk beneath the waves carrying with her 1,513 of the 2,201 persons aboard. The whole world was shocked by the unanticipated features of this disaster. One of the sad features was that this maiden voyage of the largest ship afloat had attracted a highly select group of people including leaders in government, industry, finance and the arts, and nearly all of them went down with the ship.

Such losses increased the sense of surprise and shock with which news of the disaster was received on both shores of the Atlantic. It also directed attention to inadequate information and training of the passengers and crew for an emergency, inadequate provision of lifeboats and devices for launching them and other safety factors. Among the ironic circumstances attending the sinking was the fact that a vessel which might have rendered important service in rescue operations was within sight of the *Titanic* at the time of the sinking; in fact, this ship saw rockets and distress signals of the *Titanic* and failed to interpret them correctly or at least failed to operate in response to them.

Radio communication also proved defective. A ship which should have responded to the *Titanic*'s radio signals failed to do so. While equipped with radio, it carried only one operator who had closed his shack and retired for the night. The loss of the *Titanic* produced at least one useful by-product. It revived a general international interest in the matter of safety of life on the high seas and led to many improvements in equipment and operation of all classes of ocean vessels.

Progress in size, speed and luxury does not always go hand in hand with safety and care in operation. This was demonstrated anew on the night of July 25, 1956 when the Swedish motorship *Stockholm* and the Italian liner *Andrea Doria* collided forty-five miles south of Nantucket Island. In this disaster some fifty persons were lost; scores were injured. After staying afloat for eleven hours the *Andrea Doria* sank in 225 feet of water. Half of the *Andrea Doria*'s lifeboats could not be launched to save her own passengers because the ship listed and the lifeboats operated by gravity. Only favorable circumstances prevented an even greater disaster. These circumstances included light winds and relatively quiet seas, the fact that *Stockholm* though damaged could launch her boats and accommodate many of the survivors, the presence nearby of the French liner *Ile de France* and other ships which were able to join in rescue operations. Testimony offered at pre-trial hearings revealed that both ships were guilty of irregularities and particularly that both ships were operating at or near full cruising speed in fog or in the presence of fog. Both vessels were relying on radar and though both ships admitted knowing for twenty minutes that they were approaching each other and though both were moving at a combined speed of forty-five land miles per hour, neither ship signaled nor spoke to the other by radio phone or radio telegraph during this period.

A trial which was to pool all the cases and claims, which according to reports at one time totaled some $100,000,000, has been settled out of court. Even had this trial been carried through it would have had only an indirect bearing on present safety of life at sea. The only purpose of the trial would have been to assign blame for this particular accident.

Recommendations and acceptable standards regarding safety of life at sea have from time to time been set forth by international conventions. The last convention in 1948 did not give a ship equipped with radar any authority to violate or exceed existing standards of conduct. These standards require a substantial reduction of speed of all vessels in the presence of fog.

It seems obvious that it is high time for a new convention on safety of life at sea to deal with the use of radar in navigation, with lifeboats and their launching devices and a score of other problems new and old. Until new standards are set vessels operating in or near fog and maintaining high speed even though relying on radar are clearly violating existing written standards.

When safety at sea is under discussion attention naturally turns to the protection of the lives of passengers on ocean steamers. It is interesting to note, however, that one of the earliest and most effective devices for the protection of life as well as property on the high seas was applied to cargo vessels. Aside from being effective it was also economical, for it consisted of no more than some lines of paint, judiciously and conspicuously placed on the outside of the freighter's hull.

After an appalling set of losses to British freighters an English Member of Parliament, Samuel Plimsoll of Derby, introduced a bill requiring that all freighters sailing under British registry should carry a series of marks, which he devised, to show the safe limits to which the vessel might be loaded under various conditions of sailing. These ranged from a relatively deep load line or water line, permitted in the Mediterranean and other protected waters, to a more severe limitation of cargo marked WNA, that is, Winter in the North Atlantic. Plimsoll commenced his campaign in 1876 but the mark did not come into effective use until 1890. In 1885 the deaths of British seamen ran to 3,500. In 1891, after the Plimsoll mark came into use, the deaths had dropped to 1,600. Other factors as well as Plimsoll's reform may have accounted for this saving of life, but even making allowances for other factors the figures are still very striking.

Nowadays, ocean travel is at least safe, pleasant, comfortable and convenient in nearly every class and size of ship. For those that care for it and that can afford to pay the price there is in addition luxurious travel offered on the superliners. So many people use and enjoy steamer services that they are always inclined to ask, what of the future of ocean travel? Will the airplane make the ocean liner obsolete and unnecessary? Will bigger ships be built or will the big ships become obsolete and will we build smaller and faster vessels? What will ocean travel in the future be like?

These all sound like simple questions. They are indeed simple to ask but require, in each case, involved and complicated answers. The most elementary truth is that the design of ships, the building of ships and the operation of ships are combinations of art and of science. They are activities that over countless centuries have been growing and developing. They are, today, marked by a high set of technological accomplishment, inventive ability and also flexibility.

Ships are tools and we can devise ships and tools suitable and effective for a thousand different purposes. The excellence of a ship depends in part upon its technical character but mostly on its adaptability for the particular kind of service it has to perform. The general question, therefore, could be answered by a counterproposition. If you will tell me what kind of a social, political and economic life the Atlantic nations will be leading twenty-five years from now it will be possible to make some kind of a reasonable forecast of the types of vessel they will be or should be using. If Soviet power and communist ideology effectively invade the Atlantic area we may confidently expect some combination of technological deterioration and social and economic disaster. If these powers, as now appears likely, threaten the Atlantic area without achieving success, we may expect sharpening enhancement and diversity in the matter of development and use of naval and maritime equipment on the part of the Atlantic nations.

Should the Atlantic nations become an effective reality and achieve a measure of collective security, we may expect a brilliant period ahead in transatlantic transport, travel and communication. Given among these nations a reasonable preservation of individual, social and economic freedom, we may expect a brilliant future upon and about the Atlantic Ocean. Increasing technological development in all countries will increase rather than diminish the demand for transoceanic freight accompanied by an increased volume of transatlantic travel.

It is highly desirable socially, nationally and even internationally that Atlantic air services be enormously increased. At present both steamers and airlines are overtaxed in the busy seasons. Neither method of travel can take care of all the eager customers in peak season. In matter of cost, comfort, relaxation and conveniences like the transport of adequate baggage the steamers offer advantages to the traveler. In freight or express the air services handle only a small amount of specialized business. Furthermore, factors tending to increase transatlantic air services will for a considerable time in the foreseeable future have an even greater effect on water-borne travel and transportation.

There will continue to be big ship enthusiasts and little ship enthusiasts and each class will argue enthusiastically and cogently for their particular specialty. For a long time there has been discussion about the possibility of developing a small to moderate size vessel that could cross the ocean at what we must currently regard as extremely high speeds. There are many good arguments including relative safety from certain forms of attack in times of national emergency or war which speak in favor of a special effort to create such a type of vessel. Cost is one of the chief problems. Whether social, economic and national factors will arise to justify such a development is at present in doubt.

The thing that seems most likely is that ships will continue to develop in great variety and number in a great range of sizes for many special purposes. As in the past, some new and specialized form of ship will undoubtedly be developed to meet new conditions. It will be hailed as a revolutionary triumph but this will not necessarily mean that it will supplant other sizes and forms of vessels nor inhibit the later development of still other types. At the present writing engines and motors for the use of ships and other propulsive methods, including the possibility of propulsion by atomic power, are under discussion or development. The possibilities are both numerous and promising and the most reasonable expectation is that this will lead to a continued diversity in the form and size of hull for varied types of ocean service.

Chapter 23

ATLANTIC WARFARE YESTERDAY

E ACH age has produced some separate type of vessel particularly suited to its needs and each type of vessel has contributed to the structure and development of our general western culture.

The vessels have for the most part been designed for peaceful purposes, and they have served in successive periods of growth, expansion, development and creation. Undoubtedly, men have often avoided war by the simple expedient of taking to the sea in quest of more peaceful pursuits. It is equally true that the ships of peace have been able to sail on their voyages and carry out their purposes because they were preceded, accompanied and protected by the vessels that were able if necessary to engage in battle. The sea is man's servant, not his master, and if he finds that he can win his freedom and protect his integrity only by going to war, the ocean will float his supercarrier and engulf his atomic submarine quite as blithely as she will receive his freighters and liners. The peace and freedom of the seas is not automatic. It seems that it must be protected or won anew in each generation.

It is not possible to say whether ships that could go to sea were first used for peaceful purposes or for war. The very earliest representations we have of Phoenician or of Egyptian vessels show that the bow projected forward in a sort of beak or spike near the water line. We know that in the Mediterranean an old and possible original method of fighting with ships was for one to try to ram the other with its beak or rostrum. It seems likely, therefore, that the first Mediterranean ship of which we have pictures was designed so that it could be used as a fighting ship.

There seems to be a long period during which ships were built that could be used for travel and transport but that could also be used as vessels of war. A reading of Homer does not show that in his time there was any clear distinction between fighting ships and ordinary ships, but the distinction did grow up and the fighting ship of the Mediterranean became a very special type called the galley. The galleys and galley warfare lasted from 3,000 B.C. down to the battle of Lepanto in the latter part of the sixteenth century.

During this period galleys increased in size and fleets grew larger, but the basic techniques of galley fighting remained the same.

The galleys carried sails which were used in getting from one place to another when the fleets were being assembled or when the ships were sailing together in search of a suspected enemy fleet. At such time the sail could increase the speed of the ship and lighten the work of the men at the oars, but ships could not sail close to the wind and the big sail and yard were clumsy to handle. The sail was therefore struck when an engagement was in progress and the ships approached each other with all the force that the great number of rowers could impart to the hull.

The first object of a sea captain was to drive the prow of his ship into the opposing vessel amidships where it would do the maximum amount of damage.

Another maneuver was to approach a vessel, or overtake a vessel, on almost a parallel course in such a manner as to break the oars on one side of the enemy ship. In the final stages of an engagement the ships grappled, boarding took place from one to the other and hand-to-hand combat ensued. Attempts were also made to set fire to opposing vessels by igniting inflammable materials and hurling them from one ship to another. A composition employed for this purpose was known as "Greek fire."

Greek fire varied from time to time. As early as the fourth century B.C. pitch sulphur, charcoal, etc. were packed in wood containers and hurled aboard an enemy ship. By 350 A.D. naphtha or petroleum had been added. Saltpeter seems to have been a later addition. "Greek fire" or "wild fire" was known to the Crusaders. A special form known also as "sea fire" or "wet fire" is said to have been developed by Callinicus around the middle of the seventh century. This added quicklime to inflammable ingredients so that the mixture not only could be squirted but also took fire spontaneously. Thus it anticipated the liquid flame throwers of World Wars I and II.

Even including the Greek fire galley warfare seems to have had very simple and restricted methods of attack and defense. Yet for many centuries wars were lost or won, empires rose and fell on the basis of this simple repertory of maneuvers.

Galleys grew larger in size, adding more banks of oars, increasing the number of oars in each bank, increasing the length of the oars or sweeps and the number of men employed on each sweep. Often these increases in size instead of improving the speed of the vessel rendered it slow and cumbersome. Still the effort to attain speed and power went on and we even know the exact date at which a new type of vessel emerged.

Aristides and Themistocles came into power in Athens in 482 B.C. as the heads of a party hostile to the Persians. At this time the state owned mines at Laurium where a new vein of silver had just been discovered. Themistocles prevailed upon the people to devote the proceeds of this vein to the building of 200 triremes described as a newly invented type of war vessel. Aristides was ostracized for opposing this plan.

In 415-413 B.C. a single Athenian expedition against Sicily involved the use of 134 triremes. These carried a fighting force of 4,000 armed soldiers (hoplites). This figure does not of course include the galley rowers, who could be compelled to row but could not be counted on as fighters, so the total expedition was a large one.

After this the classic pattern of naval warfare in the Mediterranean was set. With minor variations the battles between Greece and Rome, the Punic Wars, the battles for power among Roman generals, the conflicts of Italy in the West with Byzantium in the East all followed the basic pattern of galley warfare. The most romantic of all galley battles took place on September 2nd, 31 B.C. when a Roman fleet of Octavian went out to meet the mixed fleet of Antony and Cleopatra in the battle of Actium. Over 200 ships were engaged on each side under the very eyes of their leaders. Possibly Octavian held an advantage in having lighter and more mobile ships but the issue was still in doubt when Cleopatra deserted the battle taking her fleet with her and Antony sailed away after her leaving his army to surrender and his fleet to destruction by fire.

The ultimate development of galley warfare came on October 7, 1571, in the battle of Lepanto fought in the narrow waters of the Corinthian Gulf in Greece. There had been an unending series of naval wars between the Spaniards and the Turks but on this occasion most of the European powers felt that they had a stake in the struggle.

The fleets of the Christian League were placed under the general command of Don Juan of Austria, a natural brother of Phillip II of Spain. Much of the financial responsibility of the naval crusade was assumed by Pope Pius V. He also supplied ships under command of Colonna. Venice's ships were commanded by Barbarigo and Veniero; Genoa's ships were commanded by Andrea Doria; the Spanish fleet was commanded by Santa Cruz. Altogether there were 208 galleys and eight large galleasses in the Christian force.

The Turkish force, led by Ali Pasha, is supposed to have numbered 300 vessels of which 250 were galleys and the rest smaller craft.

The ships crowded together and fought it out for three hours. In this time 80 Turkish galleys were sunk, 130 were captured and 40 fled. The battle was over.

The scope of such a battle is reflected in the losses. The Turks lost 25,000 killed and an unknown number of wounded and captives. The Christian fleet lost 8,000 killed and 16,000 wounded. One outcome of the battle was that 15,000 Christian galley slaves were recovered from the captured Turkish ships. This was the peak of galley warfare though it was not its end. Unfortunately the European powers failed to agree on a further plan of action and after some years Turkey revived and resumed combat. Galleys indeed, as pirates and raiders, continued to operate in the Mediterranean even till the time of the Barbary pirates in the early part of the nineteenth century. Also criminals and other unfortunates in European states were condemned to "the galleys" and so branded long after the galley had been displaced as a dominant type of warship.

Even at the time of Lepanto two novelties were present that rendered the galley obsolescent: first, the galeasses were long vessels somewhat resembling galleys but having multiple masts and sails so that they could be sailed as well as rowed during an engagement; second, cannon and gunpowder were in use.

The 15,000 Christian galley slaves who were recovered and released at Lepanto suggest an interesting reflection. Galley warfare was long continued and highly developed in the Mediterranean but never attained the same importance on the Atlantic seaboard. Galleys did from time to time travel and fight in the Atlantic, but they were never produced there on a large scale. The first effective war vessel of the North Atlantic was the "long ship" or the "dragon ship" of the Norsemen. Now the Norse ship and the simpler type of galley looked somewhat alike for both were rowed by banks of oars in battle and both had a single mast with square sail amidships used for cruising. However, the hull plan and the construction of the two ships differed and the theory of combat differed. The galley depended on a large number of slaves for motive power, and since slaves are unreliable as fighters it also had to carry a complement of fighting men. In the Norse ships, on the other hand, the rower was usually regarded as a free man capable of bearing arms. Thus though galleys went into the Atlantic and Norse ships came into the Mediterranean neither seems to have affected the design and use of the other because they represented different social theories.

Besides the Norse ships the medieval maritime nations of northern Europe had developed sailing vessels which were primarily used for travel and for transport. These were rather heavy, high-sided, bowlshaped vessels driven by sail. In the beginning sail was carried on only one mast, but as time progressed additional masts and sails were added. They were slow and clumsy but they were strong and were capable of carrying pickled and dried fish from the northern fisheries to southern Europe and returning with wine in casks and barrels. They could also carry grain, hides, wool and other wares of the time. They carried passengers because no ships were set aside or particularly designed for this purpose. There were also no vessels especially designed as warships. When England and France wished to engage in wars, as they so frequently did, cargo vessels were hastily gotten together and equipped for this purpose and fighting men were put aboard with whatever arms and equipment it was customary for them to use in battles ashore. Since it was desirable to fight from an elevation when ashore it was also thought advisable to fight from an elevation when at sea. Therefore, at the bow and stern of the vessels special platforms were erected, protected by a little crenelated battlement. In these improvised towers the fighting men took their stand. They were known as the forecastle and the aftercastle. They were found convenient for other purposes beside fighting and in time they came to be incorporated as a regular part of the structure of the ship, becoming a foredeck and a poop or quarterdeck. The name forecastle for the space under the foredeck survives to this day.

Gradually the size of the sailing vessel increased but progress was slow because such increase demanded more power to drive the larger hull. So more masts were added to take more sail before and aft of the mainmast. Then also masts were increased in heights so that topsails could be set above the regular sails or courses. Similarly the bowsprit was lengthened to take more head sail.

Mere growth in size and power did not distinguish the war vessel from the merchantman. It was the use of gunpowder and cannons that brought about a real difference in these vessels. The first cannons used on ships were simply mounted on the deck of the forecastle or aftercastle. As more and more cannon were required and as they grew in size they were placed on the main deck, and gun ports through which they could fire had to be provided. Shot and powder and crews to manage the guns also cluttered the vessel and soon it became evident that a ship which was equipped to fight a naval battle was no longer of much use for general purposes. Armed merchantmen were built and used and some of these of later time were formidable vessels such as the East Indiamen. But most armed merchantmen could only stave off a small attack or serve as raiders of smaller vessels. When guns appeared at sea a ship qualified for naval battle was of necessity a specialized warship. Obviously only a national navy could afford to build and manage such vessels.

The idea of a national navy did not have to wait for gunpowder and cannons. Even in classic times the Athenians built warships and kept them in storage at such infrequent times as they were not needed for defense or attack. In England after Wedemore in 878 Alfred built up a navy to resist the next invasion of the Danes. Later Henry VIII felt the acute need for naval protection and gave the matter his personal attention so that he appeared at yards where ships were building to encourage as well as to supervise the work of naval construction. A symbol of this interest was the battleship the *Great Harry* built at Bristol in 1514, said to have been of 1,000 tons and one of the largest vessels of her time. In 1544 Portsmouth navy yard was increased in size to provide the navy with more ships and larger ships.

Navies, however, are the children of fortune. The future may sometimes be good and may often be bad; the one certainty is that it will be irregular. Even the navy of Great Britain that grew so great and worked so hard to maintain its leadership at sea was not created overnight and was in fact very irregular in growth. While a Henry VIII or a Queen Elizabeth might nourish it, other monarchs might neglect and starve it, while the people always tend to regard it as a burden in time of peace. Pepys, who shows us so many fascinating aspects of court and civil life in the Restoration, also gives us a picture of admiralty problems.

Neglect of the navy is not, however, an exclusive prerogative of kings and kingdoms; presidents and democracies may be guilty in this regard. While a Washington and an Adams may have a just appreciation of the value of naval strength, a Jefferson and many of his successors may misunderstand and neglect the whole bothersome matter.

In the case of Queen Elizabeth the attention and encouragement which she had given to the navy and its seamen paid off handsomely in a single extended engagement.

This naval action, even though it was fought in European portions of the Atlantic and even though it took place when North America was still an unsettled wilderness, had an effect on the pattern of settlement of this continent. In a general way we may say that the relative strength of Spain and England hung in the balance in July 1588 and that the last ten days of the month settled the issue.

Spain claimed almost the entire New World but England, under Queen Elizabeth, was proving troublesome. Drake, Hawkins, Cavendish and others were taking Spanish treasure ships and looting and burning Spanish settlements—not only on the Atlantic shores but even in the Pacific. They had already made an attempt to settle in Virginia and evidently more attempts were in preparation. King Philip decided to settle the matter in a radical way by invading England.

With this in mind he assembled a fleet of 132 ships manned by about 9,000 seamen and 2,000 galley slaves. This was the Armada, but its purpose was not so much to win a sea battle as to effect a landing and to take over the land itself. It was also to bring relief to the Duke of Parma whose ports at Dunquerque and Nieuport were under blockade. With this in mind the whole operation had been placed in command of the Duke of Medina Sidonia, a soldier and a landsman, and the ships had been fortified like castles and burdened with 22,000 soldiers.

The Armada entered the Channel July 19, but despite the brisk winds the Spanish galleons were clumsy and slow, their firepower heavy but short and inaccurate. The English had assembled a mixed fleet numbering 140 ships of all types and sizes under Lord Howard who assigned separate squadrons to Drake, Hawkins and Frobisher. As the Spanish swept into the Channel the English closed in behind them keeping up wind. Lighter, faster and with cannons of longer range, the English ships hung on the flank of the Armada, sinking or cutting out one victim after another, through the Channel and into the North Sea.

Some of the Spanish did indeed seek refuge in Channel ports such as Calais and Gravelines but Drake on July 28 sent "fireships" into the harbor and fearing to be set afire the Spanish ships fled again, at least one of them running aground in their haste to escape. No rest and heavy weather—the only land of England the Armada ever touched was the sands where they grounded or rocks where they sank.

The main battle—if it can be called that—took place in the North Sea. The English ships were faster and their cannons had a longer range. Under Drake's plan they wisely used these advantages and made no attempt to board any Spanish vessel. Had they done so the sheer weight of Spanish soldiers might have been of some use. As matters stood the soldiers were merely a useless, seasick, hungry encumbrance.

In a ten-day flight the Armada rounded Scotland and Ireland and scattered in the hope of reaching home, but by that time forty ships were sunk, wrecked or captured and half the manpower of the fleet was lost. By the end of July the way to colonies in the New World lay wide open to England.

It is sometimes supposed that the mere existence of the Atlantic Ocean protected a colony or a nation from becoming involved in European wars and that when English or French or other colonists came to America they evaded war.

Colonial history seems to refute this idea. It seems more likely that if the American nations have enjoyed some freedom from warfare from time to time it has been because they have been sufficiently well armed to resist invasion by sea.

Certainly the colonists had scarcely established themselves in America before they became embroiled with each other: the French fighting the Spanish; the French fighting the English colonies; the English fighting the Dutch; etc.

Very often these seemed like scattered battles or local wars. The underlying situation, however, was that the colonists had by no means escaped from the rounds of European wars. Contact with the mother country was often slow and infrequent. The colonists often felt that they were remotely and imperfectly governed, yet the ties with the mother country persisted for centuries and while it might languish when conditions were generally normal the tie became of great importance both to the mother country and to the colonists when another country threatened to sever this connection and war impended.

Thus the seventeenth century saw two wars between Holland and England and in these general hostilities colonial settlements became involved. In 1664 Colonel Richard Nicolls seized New Netherland and rechristened New Amsterdam New York. This together with the seizure of Holland ports in West Africa led to the reopening of hostilities in 1665. From July 30, 1673, to November 9, 1674, control over New York reverted but Holland lost it permanently at the time of the Treaty of Breda which concluded the second Anglo-Dutch War. By this treaty the Dutch surrendered all claim to New Amsterdam in exchange for the inestimable privilege of retaining Surinam.

In 1689 to 1697, King William's War, in which the British colonists fought the French colonists, was simply a local phase of the general war against Louis XIV which was known in Europe as the War of the League of Augsburg. In 1702 to 1713, in America, the conflict known as Queen Anne's War was simply a phase of the War of the Spanish Succession. It was during this war that the English plundered and burned St. Augustine in Florida and that brought about the French and Indian attack on Deerfield and other similar raids. The English colonists revenged themselves by attacks in Nova Scotia and the St. Lawrence. Though these were only partially successful, the Treaty of Utrecht of 1713 recognized England's claims in Hudson Bay and the possession of Newfoundland and Acadia.

King George's War of 1743 to 1748 was likewise the American aspect of the War of Austrian Succession. The most memorable part of this conflict was the attack on the strong fortress of Louisburg on Cape Breton Island. This was carried out largely by the people of Massachusetts, supported also by Connecticut, Rhode Island and New Hampshire. The land forces, under Colonel William Pepperell of Maine, numbered over 4,000 soldiers and the fleet, under Captain Tyng of Massachusetts, contained nearly 100 vessels. With such a force the fall of Louisburg was inevitable.

It was a futile victory for in this war, as in others, when the treaty makers finally met they were moved chiefly by the consideration of the balance of powers in Europe and very little by the outcome of military and naval campaigns in far-off America. The Treaty of Aix-la-Chapelle in 1748 restored Louisburg to the French.

France's continual involvement in European war always involved her at the same time in a war between the colonies in America and finally brought about the loss of her overseas empire which she had worked so hard to establish. The French and Indian War, which raged in America from 1755 to 1763, was the American aspect of the Seven Years' War in Europe. Again Louisburg became the object of attack in 1758.

The young commanders, Amherst and Wolfe, led a force of 12,000 troops and a naval force in command of Boscawen was made up of forty warships, manned by 8,000 sailors. This time the fall of Louisburg opened up the way for the successful attack on Quebec and the St. Lawrence in the succeeding year. The Treaty of Paris of 1763 left Britain with the following claims recognized: Acadia, which became Nova Scotia, Cape Breton, large parts of Canada, all the part of Louisiana lying east of the Mississippi River. By this treaty, England, also in exchange for restoring Havana, gained from Spain all of Florida.

All these wars that involved the American colonies of the European powers as well as the later wars that involved the United States had certain features in common. It will be well to summarize these here. This will avoid the need of raising the same points repeatedly in connection with each new war or set of battles. Also we have to-day certain ideas that do not apply to most of Atlantic history; in fact, they prevent an understanding of events.

First, then, is the fact that the wars fought around and across the Atlantic have been fought over the control of Atlantic trade. The sinking or capture of trading vessels, the impressment of seamen or other violent interference with trade have usually been the immediate causes of the outbreak or declaration of war. It is often supposed that the Civil War was a purely domestic quarrel and that it was entirely fought and decided by large armies meeting in a long series of land battles. Yet we shall see presently how control of the international cotton trade was an essential element in the war; that the economy of Europe, particularly of England, was violently affected by the struggle; that England paid a large idemnity for getting involved and that naval battles and blockade of the southern ports were crucial in determining the outcome of the war.

The declaration of war was a formality often postponed or dispensed with. In general, the distinction between war and peace at sea has not been sharply drawn. The expectation that there is always a sharp break between war and peace is a modern idea, so also is the complete separation between naval vessels and merchantmen.

Very often trading vessels have gone armed at least for self-protection from pirates, hostile natives, privateers, commerce raiders, etc. Private armed vessels with crews trained in combat carried special commissions from their various countries. They were known as privateers and their special function was to attack and capture merchantmen of an unfriendly or hostile power. The captured vessel and its cargo were known as prizes and could be sold in a neutral port, the proceeds being divided in various ways between the owner, the officers and sometimes the crew. The commission was important because without it a privateer looked very much like a pirate and piracy was frowned on. Letters of marque and reprisal were issued to armed merchantmen under which the captains were authorized to mix raiding, warfare and commerce in such proportions as seemed to them artistic and convenient.

The privateers were an important and quasi-permanent feature of international commerce on the high seas, for there was usually some war going on and even in times of relative peace new hostilities were rapidly developing or old hostilities were slow in dissolving.

Some people seem to believe that the convoy system was discovered and developed at the time of World War I. It is at least as old as the Greeks and the Romans and it was widely used in the seventeenth and eighteenth centuries as a standard defense against privateers. Spain used it to get her gold and silver home from Panama. France and Holland ran convoys from the West Indies. England was so perpetually dependent on her colonies and possessions that she ran convoys in all directions—from the West Indies, from various points on the American coast, from the Mediterranean and Baltic Seas.

During the American Revolution the United States did create an official navy but it was small, unevenly officered and relatively ineffective. It was the privateers and the irregular sea fighters that troubled the British and kept American resistence alive until effective help finally came from France and other allies. As many men served in the privateers as in the Continental Army at its largest and often the ratio was 4 to 1.

It was George Washington who first armed ships to send against England and his first efforts, though feeble, were nonetheless effective. In September 1775 he was in command of the colonial militia before Boston and desperately lacking arms and military supplies. The quickest, though perhaps not the safest way to acquire the arms and stores that he needed, was to take them from the British. As a first step he ordered a Captain Broughton of the army and a detachment of soldiers to man and arm a schooner, *Hannah*. On her first cruise *Hannah* took several prizes and captured from them a small supply of arms and munitions for Washington's militia. The general had no authority to acquire ships or send them to sea, yet he finally had at least six ships in his unofficial navy and they kept a trickle of captured arms flowing his way. At the end of November Captain John Manly in the little *Lee* captured the brigantine *Nancy* and took among other supplies 100,000 flints, 2,000 muskets and a large brass mortar.

Then the Congress began to take an interest in naval affairs drawn forward by Washington's success and pushed from behind by the fact that Admiral Graves had already on October 17th burned Falmouth (where Portland, Maine now stands) and threatened other ports. In October, *Alfred* and *Columbus* were to be bought and fitted out. In November a marine corps was created. On December 13 the building of thirteen frigates was authorized, $100,000 having already been appropriated to purchase four men of war, and before the year closed a list of eighteen officers to command these vessels had been drawn up. Of this list only Nicholas Biddle and John Paul Jones could be regarded as competent naval commanders establishing in the newborn navy an heroic tradition. The other officers of the navy were generally outnumbered and also outfought so that at the close of the Revolution, the U. S. Navy consisted of only two ships left afloat, *Alliance* and *Hague,* which were promptly sold by Congress.

It was the privateers and the raiders who carried the war to England. By 1781 449 American privateers were at sea and 300 or so were still afloat at the end of the war. England had lost to privateers nearly 2,000 vessels—the losses involving £18,000,000 and 12,000 seamen captured. In 1780 the *Pickering,* the Salem letter-of-marque, set some sort of all-time record even for a privateer. Under her Captain Jonathan Haraden of Gloucester, age thirty-five, with a crew of forty-five men and boys she sailed for Spain. She was armed with only fourteen six-pounders yet she captured a British privateer *Golden Eagle*—twenty-two guns. She lost *Golden Eagle* when a British forty-two-gun privateer with crew of 140 men suddenly emerged from Bilbao but the next day Haraden outmaneuvered *Achilles* and re-

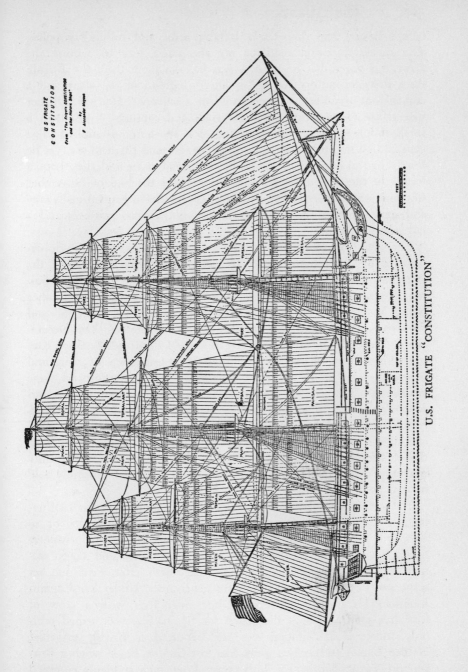

U.S. FRIGATE "CONSTITUTION"

captured *Golden Eagle*. On the return journey he encountered three merchantmen which he attacked one after the other. One of these had twelve guns and the other two each fourteen guns. On a later cruise he fought and captured a heavily armed brig with full crew— a king's packet.

At the end of the war the privateers were reconverted presumably to legal and peaceful pursuits—though some of them might have become slavers or smugglers. With no navy and no privateers it was only good fortune and a lot of heavy uphill shipbuilding and crew raising that brought the United States through the battles with the French and the 1812 War with England. Jefferson was a learned man interested in many fields but devoid of any sense about the sea. He evolved ideas on seaboard defense that were childishly naïve. Fortunately Adams was able to create a navy and one of the best bits of good fortune was the selection in 1794 of Joshua Humphreys as naval constructor. It was he who designed and built the great frigates *Constitution, Constellation, Congress, Chesapeake, President, United States.*

These were a new type of vessel; they were smaller than line-of-battle ships, which America could ill afford, but they were also much faster; they were also, however, larger, faster and better armed than any British frigate so that they gave a new meaning to that word. American gunnery was another asset. Just as in naval construction the object was to build a few ships of very excellent qualities, so in gunnery the aim was to increase range and accuracy rather than to depend on the mere weight of projected metal. The new ships outsailed and outshot the traditional British vessels that were ponderous and impressive but were slow on their feet and with a short reach. England had forgotten the lesson she taught Spain in Elizabeth's day and had to learn it again from new states.

Of course the United States could not successfully meet an English fleet in battle either at the time of the Revolution or in the War of 1812. What she did do successfully was to send out her best ships and fighters in the hope of winning an individual duel or small engagement against one or a very few British ships or French ships. Thus we had such battles as John Paul Jones in *Bon Homme Richard* vs *Serapis*, Truxtun in *Constellation* against *L'Insurgente*, etc. A full scale naval battle was quite another matter. It was one of the marks of Washington's great capacity and insight that he knew it was futile for him to attempt to win a major land victory until he could also counter the great English strength at sea. The purpose of the alliance with France, negotiated in 1778, so far as Washington was concerned was to win the support of a strong French fleet so that a joint land and sea attack could be made on some strong point held by Britain, preferably New York. This failed to materialize and Washington waited three years and sent a special mission to France before he achieved the support of the superior fleet under Admiral Comte de Grasse. Even though the army of Rochambeau arrived in 1780 Washington delayed the grand attack until de Grasse was off the Virginia Capes and Cornwallis at Yorktown was doomed.

The traditional form of naval battle up to the end of the eighteenth century was for the two fleets of ships involved to approach each other in some broad expanse of water where the vessels could maneuver freely. The vessels approached each other in long lines, either following each other in a formation known as "line ahead" or sailing parallel courses in a formation known as "line abreast." Thus the important vessels of any navy came to be known as "line-of-battle ships" or, more briefly, as "ships of the line."

Such a ship of the line was an enormous structure with multiple decks each deck fitted with ports and implemented with appropriate types of guns. The number of guns in fact was used as a rough rating of a ship's size and capacity. Thus a frigate might be rated as forty-four guns; a ship of the line sixty. Obviously, to carry those sixty guns together with shot, powder and stores a vessel had to be constructed with great strength and weight. To drive this massive structure through the water required three masts, each made from the section of a tree of great girth, straightness and strength; each mast fitted with full array of large and heavy sails. Such ships were dignified and impressive, whether seen in a harbor or moving up the channel in battle formation. In an actual engagement when a ship was maneuvering to bring its broadside to bear on an enemy, where speed and nimbleness represented the difference between life and death for captain and crew, they would appear painfully unwieldy and sluggish. The design of a successful sailing warship involved a thousand nice adjustments and compromises between the desire for strength and firepower and the desire for maneuverability.

The character of the ships dictated the character of the formalized naval battle. The commander of the fleet wanted his vessels in one kind of line or another so that he could as far as possible keep track of their positions and performance and prepare and issue sets of orders and commands that all could carry out in concert. Also stragglers or ships out of position offered a notable target for concentrated enemy attack. In wearing or in coming about each ship required ample space for its operations, which determined the distance between the vessels of the line. The commander also wished ample sea room for the parade and maneuver of his fleet as a whole, and no one wished his movements restricted by capes and shoals, and in particular nobody wished to be caught on a lee shore.

In theory a classic naval battle had a set and rather formalized appearance in which one line of battleships met another line of battleships in a martial encounter in which good gunnery and good seamanship were the determining factors. In practice, the battle often broke up into a series of duels between opposing vessels. Also in practice, as the battle progressed the commander's control over the operations of the fleet as a whole diminished in the excitement of battle, and much was left to the courage and ingenuity of the captain of each ship. In time the most intelligent commanders observed that the fleet that early in the battle was fortunate enough to win a slight advantage in the duels between individual ships was apt to multiply this advantage as the battle progressed. Thus, without expressing it so formally, commanders were learning by experience that concentration of firepower was one of the determining factors in this type of naval engagement.

There was no doubt that in the latter part of the eighteenth century the British had already on a number of occasions demonstrated their superiority over the French with whom they were so often engaged in battle, yet it also became clear that their losses suddenly became alarmingly high at a time when they were engaged in brushes and skirmishes rather than in full-scale naval battles. What was happening was that the French, conscious of their defects and weaknesses, had evolved a new set of naval tactics. About 1870 they developed a new form of naval battle—a defensive one. At the start this had the appearance of the beginning of an old-style set naval battle. The English would be advancing their ships, usually in a line-abreast formation. The French would be awaiting them in a line ahead. In this case, however, the French would intentionally select the lee gage, usually considered a disadvantage, but instead of engaging in the set battle the French would deliver their broadsides against the leading British ships. They would then bear away to leeward, reform their line and await the renewal of the British attack when they would repeat the operation. Thus they were able repeat-

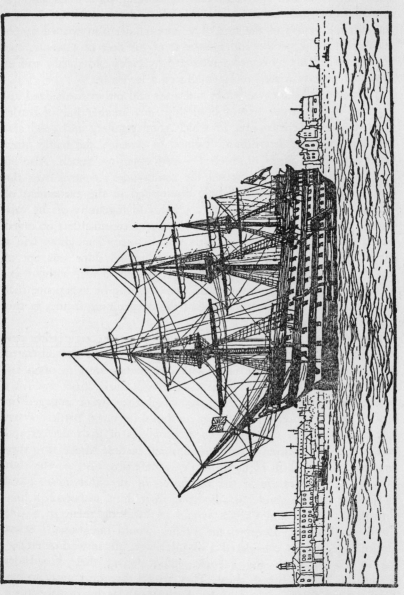

H.M.S. VICTORY

edly to subject the leading British ships to raking fire, and to concentrate their firepower on a small portion of the English fleet.

F. W. Lanchester has pointed out that this was probably the beginning of the recognition by the defensive side of the value of firepower in a naval operation. Possibly a similar recognition affected the tactics of offense some two years later. Lanchester does not know whether it was by design or by accident that Admiral Rodney in the Battle of the Saints in 1792 departed from the usual form of battle by cutting through the line of the enemy in concentrating his attack on the center and rear ships. However this form of attack originated, its value was soon recognized and it became a form of operation that was customary with the British and recognized by the French. The French Admiral Villeneuve anticipated that Nelson would employ a plan somewhat similar to this in the Battle of Trafalgar.

Nelson on October 9 wrote a memorandum on the battle. He assumed a combined French and Spanish fleet of forty-six, his own fleet could number no more than forty. He believed that the enemy would travel with a favorable wind in single line ahead formation. His plan was to divide his ships into two lines of sixteen ships and one line of eight ships. The first line of sixteen ships was to engage the rear twelve enemy ships. The second line of sixteen was to engage the next eleven enemy ships, the final short line of eight was to concentrate on the next three or four ships of the enemy's van at all cost to prevent the van from returning to the main scene of battle which they would already have passed. Such a return on the part of the van would in any case be laborious and time-consuming. During this time while they were tacking back, Nelson hoped to establish his superiority and win a victory.

It should be noted that in this plan each of Nelson's three columns outnumbered the section of enemy ships it was to attack. F. W. Lanchester, who formulated and published a mathematical formula for a measure of military or naval strength which he called the "N^2 Law" cites this plan of Nelson as an almost perfect example of a tactical plan based on the concentration of power which the law implies.

Briefly put Lanchester says that a just mathematical measure of relative strength of two forces such as "Reds" and "Blues" is not to be arrived at simply by counting noses. Assuming for the moment that one Red unit was about equal in value to one Blue unit, then NR^2 or the "number of reds squared" contrasted with NB^2 would give a measure of military superiority. Assuming that there were some difference in the military value of Red and Blue units this could be expressed as a value C for Reds and K for Blues; the formula then reads:

$$CR^2 = KB^2$$

In other words, "The fighting strength of a force is proportional to the square of its numerical strength multiplied by the fighting value of its individual units."

Apply this to Nelson's battle plan for Trafalgar and see how much he gained by splitting the enemy exactly in half.

It is interesting to note that this simple formula of Lanchester's was rediscovered during World War II and served as an impetus in creating an Applied Mathematic Branch and thus in stimulating the growth of a large and complicated science of military mathematics.

In practice, both Nelson and the combined fleet had fewer ships than were contemplated in the memorandum. The combined fleet still had an initial superiority in number and Nelson's attack, though simplified, involved the same principle of an initial division of the enemy. Though Nelson died during the battle, his fleet won one of the greatest and most complete naval victories.

Between 1816 and the Civil War there was on the Atlantic an age of rapid and profound development. The packet and the clipper evolved and sail reached the peak of use and development, steam power was introduced at sea, the propeller came to supplement and then supplant the paddle wheel, iron was used for armor and construction—but in all this the U. S. Navy played a small part. As usual, in time of peace, the navy suffered reduction and congressional neglect.

Belatedly in 1841, owing to fortunate political support, steam and screw found a place in the navy's *Princeton,* and in 1842 *Missouri* and *Mississippi,* the first United States steam warships, were completed. Three years later George Bancroft, as secretary of the navy, secured from the army Fort Severn at Annapolis for use as an academy for the training of naval officers.

The navy came to life not only in the matter of training and theory but also in far-flung practical activity. Texas came into the Union as the twenty-eighth state in 1845 but there was a restless uncertainty about what was to be the fate of large sections of the southwest and California, vast regions claimed by Mexico but thinly settled and loosely held. In 1846 a small Pacific squadron under Commodore John Drake Sloat, later under Captain Robert F. Stockton, assisted by land forces raised by Major Fremont, occupied Monterey, San Diego, San Francisco and finally secured Los Angeles in 1847.

In the Atlantic the navy was also kept busy. Land fighting had been going on in the large vague area along and beyond the Rio Grande without notable result. Then the fleet under Commodore Matthew Calbraith Perry was called on to transport a large force to Vera Cruz to take that port by a naval action and support the troops on their way to Mexico City. As a preliminary step the navy took Tampico and Panuco. Then the land force was transported to Vera Cruz and on March 9 12,000 troops were landed three miles south of the city. After four days of shelling by smaller naval vessels and by shore batteries landed from the larger ships and by army batteries, the city surrendered on March 29, 1847. Other ports in Mexico and Yucatan were taken by the navy to cut off any flow of arms to the Mexican forces. Mexico City, attacked by army and marine troops, was taken in September and the peace of Guadelupe–Hidalgo was signed on February 2, 1848 under which the northern boundary of Mexico was fixed at the Rio Grande and California, Nevada, Utah, Arizona (parts) New Mexico, Colorado and Wyoming becoming United States territory.

The newly acquired territories in the west kindled considerable interest in men's minds even in the Atlantic seaboard states and this broke into flash fire when gold was discovered in California. This gave that added impetus that made the Fifties the flashing culmination of America's rapid development as the world's foremost maritime nation. That sweep carried America forward until almost without realizing it she was in a depression and on the eve of civil war.

There is a general belief held particularly in the United States that ironclad vessels appeared for the first time during the American Civil War and that the duel between the *Monitor* and the *Merrimac* was notable because it was the first engagement fought by this type of vessel. As a matter of fact it was during the Crimean War that ironclad vessels were first developed and first demonstrated their effectiveness in battle.

In 1853 Czar Nicholas assembled his men in ships for a campaign against Turkey with the object of capturing Constantinople. This did not at all appeal to England and France who promptly came to Turkey's assistance. The first naval engagement was that of Sinope during which the Russians, using newly developed shell guns, practically wiped out the wooden navy of the Turks, destroying ten vessels out of a fleet of eleven. The three allies had to accept the fact that the new firepower converted wooden vessels into mere fire traps and rendered them obsolete.

To meet this situation Napoleon III immediately commenced the construction of a fleet of armored vessels in the shipyards of France. These vessels could be sailed but their masts were dismountable and they were also supplied with auxiliary steam power. The decks of the ships were protected with thin plates of iron while iron plates four inches thick protected the vessel's sides.

A fleet of five ships was built by the French, three of which participated in the operation at Kinburg at the mouth of the Dnieper River. Though these three ships received hundreds of hits from the shore batteries, their plates were merely grooved and dented and no ship suffered any serious damage while their firepower was such that the Russians surrendered after three hours of fighting.

The British had already ordered the construction of four armor-clad vessels and after the battle at Kinburg the French set seriously to work to supply themselves with an armor-clad navy. This was six years before the Confederates hung armor plates on the old *Merrimac* and Ericsson constructed the *Monitor.*

When the Civil War broke, the Federal government enjoyed the immediate advantage of holding and utilizing the bulk of the United States Navy which then consisted of some ninety warships, forty-two of which were in commission, twenty-seven of which could be commissioned and twenty-one of which were judged to be unserviceable. Gideon Welles, Lincoln's secretary of the navy, soon had seventy-six vessels in commission. To this number he added 136 vessels which were purchased and fifty-two vessels built in government and private yards. By 1865 200 vessels had been constructed, seventy-four of them ironclads.

Most of the navy yards were also in Northern hands. Out of ten navy yards, only Norfolk and Pensacola were available to the South. Norfolk was wrecked and dismantled before it was abandoned by the Federal government and Pensacola was largely a yard for repair rather than construction.

Stephen Russell Mallory assumed command of the Confederate Navy and he was ably supported by many skilled and highly qualified naval commanders such as Buchanan, Maury, Semmes, Catesby Jones and John M. Brooke. There were, however, only a few old inadequate vessels for these splendid officers to command.

The Confederacy, throughout the war, did its best to buy and build vessels but under great handicaps, for the South was largely an agricultural area with few developed industrial resources. The Federal Navy commenced at once an effort to establish a blockade of the Southern ports. The South encouraged blockade runners and many different ships, both of American and foreign origin, were put into operation as blockade runners. Privateering was also a method natural and serviceable to the hard-pressed South. The South had a third naval hope or ambition: this was to create a small but effective fleet of armor-plated vessels.

The United States Navy had been dilatory and inert in its whole attitude on ironclad vessels. Robert L. Stevens had originally submitted to the navy and to Congress plans for an ironclad vessel shortly after the War of 1812, but thirty years passed before he was finally able to commence construction and he died before his proposed ship could be brought to completion. Farragut had applied for permission to observe and study naval operations during the Crimean War but had been officially denied this opportunity.

The Southern commanders, Porter and Brooke, saw an opportunity of beating the Northern wooden navy by creating and employing ironclad vessels, and with this in mind they proposed the plan of armoring and utilizing the *Merrimac.* The *Merrimac* had originally been built in 1855 in Charlestown, Massachusetts and was then a forty-gun steam frigate of rather novel type. She had been wrecked, scuttled and sunk at the time that the Federal government abandoned the Norfolk navy yard.

The plan of Porter and Brooke called for raising this vessel, cutting her down to the water line and erecting on her new deck a sloping structure to house two broadsides of four guns each and two rifled guns firing forward and two aft; the whole ship to be covered with a double thickness of two-inch iron plates laid over and fastened to a massive wooden structure. This amor-clad floating battery the Southerners christened *Virginia,* but she has still always been known to history as the *Merrimac.*

Every effort was made to complete this vessel as rapidly as possible for there were rumors abroad that the North was bringing to completion the strange structure developed by Ericsson called the *Monitor.* After feverish work *Merrimac* was ready to proceed into battle on March 8, 1862, and early in the morning she moved into Chesapeake Bay.

The *USS Congress* first saw her proceeding under a cloud of smoke at 8:30 A.M. The *Merrimac* led a little group of five small Confederate warcraft. Arrayed against them were five large Federal vessels. In addition to the *Congress* of fifty guns, there was also the fifty-gun *St.*

Lawrence, the thirty-gun *Cumberland* and the *Minnesota* and *Roanoke,* steamers of forty-six guns each. In addition, a Federal gunboat, the *Zouave,* dashed up to the *Merrimac* to look at her and to fire a thirty-two powder at her.

At about 1 o'clock the Federal ships began firing broadsides at the *Merrimac* and these were augmented by the fire from the forts ashore, but the shots seemed to simply bounce off the *Merrimac*'s armor plate without producing any visible damage. It was not until after two o'clock that the *Merrimac* opened fire on the *Congress* and the *Cumberland.* One shot from the *Merrimac* disposed of a whole gun crew on the *Cumberland* and discharged a broadside that took great affect on the *Congress.*

Later, *Merrimac* rammed *Cumberland* and in this operation *Merrimac* lost her iron ram but left such a hole in *Cumberland*'s side that the Northern vessel began to sink immediately. *Cumberland* refused to strike her flag and surrender despite the fact that she was in a helpless condition and was kept under fire until she finally rested on the bottom of the bay.

Buchanan, in command of *Merrimac,* was then able to devote his attention to *Congress,* which had run aground during the engagement. *Congress* was shelled so severely that she was forced to surrender. At the time of the surrender *Congress* had already caught fire. Before the surrender could be carried out the flames had spread so rapidly that sixty of the wounded aboard could not be rescued from the fire.

Buchanan was wounded and command of the *Merrimac* passed to Lieutenant Catesby Jones. The rapid fall of the tide was all that prevented *Merrimac* from taking a further toll of the remains of the Northern fleet which was now seeking the protection of the guns of Fortress Monroe. In that day's battle, at the cost of very slight damage with two men killed and eight wounded, *Merrimac* had disposed of two large ships and had inflicted a loss of 257 men killed or drowned.

It was plain that *Merrimac* could dispose of an ordinary wooden naval vessel almost at will and in Washington there was excited and apprehensive discussion at the White House concerning the possibility of *Merrimac*'s making her way up the Potomac and shelling the capital.

The hope and faith of the North for a defense against the *Merrimac* seemed to reside in a strange new vessel that had recently been christened *Monitor. Monitor* had been invented and designed by John Ericsson, who had come from Sweden by way of England. In addition to designing the *Monitor* Ericsson was one of the first to have developed a practical screw propeller and was also the inventor and developer of a series of hot-air engines.

Construction of the *Monitor* had begun in October of 1861 and been carried forward with great haste. *Monitor* was 172 feet long, had a beam of forty-one feet and a draft of ten feet. Her iron deck was raised only a foot or so above her water line. Set upon this deck was a rotating iron turret mounting two heavy guns of eleven-inch diameter.

At the very hour that Buchanan, on the *Merrimac,* was disposing of the *Cumberland* and the *Congress, Monitor* with a crew of fifty-eight volunteers under command of John L. Worden was making a slow passage between New York and Hampton Roads and taking a terrible beating from heavy weather. She arrived in the Chesapeake just in time to hear the last of the gunfire of the engagement of March 8 and to see the bay still illuminated by the burning *Congress.*

Monitor was forced to take up a position in the bay and had no opportunity to permit her tired crew to rest or to make repairs on the ship's machinery that had suffered from the storm during the passage from New York. When the sun came up on March 9 *Monitor* presented a strange sight and promptly became the target first of Southern abuse and then of the guns of the *Merrimac.* She was at once called the "cheesebox on a raft" and Catesby Jones brought the *Merrimac* out to dispose of her as rapidly as possible.

Monitor, however, presented a poor target. Even *Merrimac*'s broadsides only skipped off *Monitor*'s low deck or glanced off the sides of the revolving turret. She sustained some damage and Captain Worden was injured when a pilothouse or conning tower was hit, but otherwise *Monitor* came through the engagement very well. On the other hand, even *Monitor*'s heavy guns were not able to inflict any damage on *Merrimac.*

Exasperated at their inability to damage each other by gunfire, the commanders of the two ironclads finally commenced a ramming match. This also was inconclusive and no serious damage was inflicted on either vessel. *Merrimac* finally withdrew.

The general results of the battle have been often debated. Even though the duel between the *Monitor* and the *Merrimac* might be regarded as indecisive, the engagement had the effect of a Northern victory. It was clear that *Monitor* could at least stand up to *Merrimac,* could neutralize the effectiveness of her operations and prevent her from inflicting any further damage on the Northern fleet.

Thereafter *Merrimac* confined her operations to a patrol of the James River, thus protecting the approach to Richmond. At the same time *Monitor* was performing similar duties with respect to the Potomac and the approaches to Washington. Later in the war *Merrimac* was scuttled and sunk. After this an attempt was made to move *Monitor* but she went down with all hands in a gale off Cape Hatteras. Together, the two famous ironclads did much to demonstrate the futility of the old-fashioned wooden warship and the value of protective armor and of steam propulsion.

The naval war then settled down into a long and systematic attempt of the Northern navy to establish a complete blockade of the Southern ports and the desperate effort on the part of the Confederacy to nullify this blockade. The establishment of such a blockade is a long and tedious undertaking and in this case, as in others, demanded an enormous fleet of ships and a tremendous complement of men. Lincoln proclaimed the blockade in April of '61 with a supplementary proclamation covering the coasts of Virginia and North Carolina in May of the same year. In theory the blockade, therefore, extended from the Virginia capes to Mexico at the Rio Grande, thus covering a coastline of over 3,500 miles.

At the beginning the North did not have enough ships to make the blockade truly effective, therefore, from the point of view of international law, there was doubt about its legality. Europe was deeply involved in the success or failure of this blockade for European countries including Britain, France, Holland and Spain had built up enormous trade with the Southern states. For example, in the year 1860 Britain alone bought $20,000,000 worth of Southern tobacco and on this collected import duties of $21,000,000. France and Holland absorbed comparable amounts and even Spain accounted for $5,000,000. Southern cotton sold in England in the amount of $150,000,000 and a large population was employed in England in the spinning and manufacture of this cotton.

The outbreak of the Civil War was, therefore, of great importance to a number of European nations and it initiated in Europe a long-drawn-out conflict of interests. For a time there was uncertainty as to where Great Britain's sympathies rested and what part, if any, she would play in the conflict. The South believed that the products and materials which she supplied to Great Britain were of such economic value that Britain might take steps to protect her trade and manufactures and might even recognize the Confederacy as a free and independent nation.

The Northern states recognized that in establishing the blockade they inevitably ran the risk of creating a certain amount of hostility in England. The North believed, however, that in the long run Britain would recognize that the termination of the war in a Northern victory would constitute the quickest and soundest condition for the removal of the blockade and the restoration of international commerce. In the long run Lincoln's confidence in Britain was justified but there were some years of uncertainty and of wavering allegiances. These created the conditions for a number of extraordinary adventures on the high seas.

A Northern fleet operating in the Gulf of Mexico under command of Admiral David G. Farragut was one of the chief instruments for enforcing and extending the theory and practice of the blockade. Farragut first showed his audacity and skill by breaking a boom which the Confederates had fastened across the main mouth of the Mississippi River and then led his squadron past two forts without stopping to capture them and proceeded at once to fight his way up the ninety miles of river that separated him from New Orleans at the same time that the city was being attacked by a land force under General B. F. Butler. This was a first and most important step in the establishment of the blockade.

The intention here was not only to deprive the South of the important port of New Orleans but also to cut off the equipment and supplies that were reaching the South from the states west of the Mississippi River and from Mexico. This was a most important action, but as late as 1864 the South had in Mobile, Savannah, Charleston and Wilmington four important ports through which she was able to send out on the blockade runners some proportion of her customary exports and through which she received in exchange supplies and manufactured articles. Farragut's impetuous attack on Mobile made in the summer of 1864, like the taking of New Orleans, was another important step in the establishment of an ironclad blockade.

The South made two important and valiant attempts to nullify the blockade and to offset the North's great superiority in naval and maritime strength. The first of these efforts consisted in building up a fleet of blockade running vessels and in establishing blockade running as a systematic combination of business and warfare. The Southern blockade runners began operations as a sincere effort to continue the trade of the South and to supply the Confederacy with needed war equipment and military supplies.

In the early years of the war evasion of the blockade was relatively

FARRAGUT'S FLAG-SHIP THE "HARTFORD"

easy and a considerable amount of goods flowed into all the Southern ports. European goods reached the gulf ports of Mobile and New Orleans by way of Cuba and Mexico and the Atlantic ports by way of Nassau in the Bahamas and Bermuda. The capture of New Orleans and later of Mobile threw an additional burden on the remaining Southern ports of Wilmington, Charleston and Savannah.

By this time the risks of blockade running had increased, the price of goods in Southern markets had skyrocketed and the blockade running business had proved enormously profitable to the operators. The companies operating the blockade running ships prospered and degenerated at the same time. There was a tendency to replace cumbersome and military cargoes with luxuries that were light and easily handled and that brought fantastic prices like these: salt, at Nassau, sold for $7.50 a ton and coffee at $2.40 a ton; in Richmond, Virginia, the salt sold for $1,700 and the coffee for $5,500; at one time a pound of tea became worth $500 in the Southern market. One of the blockade runners specialized in supplying corsets for the Southern belles. These he bought in Nassau at a cost of one shilling each and found a market for them in Charleston at twelve shillings each.

In England special vessels were financed, constructed and manned for this business. They were built with very little freeboard to avoid detection and also had to be shallow draft. In order to be able to carry a cargo and also to travel at high speed they were built with extremely long and fine lines and it is said that they were able to reach a speed of seventeen knots.

Such a vessel was able to make a rapid trip between Nassau and one of the Southern ports, Wilmington for example. The operation of such a vessel might bring the owner a monthly profit of $90,000 in gold. A few successful trips were enough to pay for the entire cost of the vessel. The captain of the vessel could earn $5,000 a month and even a seaman was paid $100 gold per month and given an additional bonus of $50 for each successful trip.

This fantastic business was terminated as one Southern port after another was blockaded and captured by combined naval and land operations. Savannah was blockaded by a squadron under command of Dahlgreen and fell to Sherman in December of '64. Wilmington, which was important because it served as the port for the capital at Richmond, fell to a combined sea and land operation in January of '65 and Charleston, the last Southern port, was captured in February of '65. After this the South was without useful ports, the blockade was complete and the results of the operations on land inevitable.

Before the South lost all her harbors she had initiated another kind of warfare on the high seas. This was carried out by a group of ships known as the commerce raiders. These ships were constructed in England for the Confederacy on the order of Captain James D. Bulloch and included the *Florida, Alabama* and *Shenandoah*. Of these *Alabama* had the most notable career. She was 220 feet in length, 32-foot beam, 1,040 tons burden, was rigged as a barkentine but also carried steam auxiliary power. She was commanded by Captain Ralph Semmes and was commissioned in the Azores in August of 1862.

She began by taking prizes from the New England whaling fleet that was then present in the Azores. In October she took sixteen prizes on the Grand Banks among the grain ships and other vessels operating between New England and Europe. Then she turned her attention to Southern waters and captured the steamer *Ariel,* making a passage between Panama and New York. For this vessel she claimed a ransom of $261,000. Next, in the Gulf of Mexico, she provoked the gunboat *Hatteras* into chasing her. After *Hatteras* was thus separated from the blockading fleet, she was attacked and sunk.

On her way to the Brazilian coast *Alabama* took other prizes and justified her trip to the Cape of Good Hope in capturing and sinking some twenty-four vessels. Her trip to the China Sea was not equally successful and she returned to Cherbourg, France, in June of 1864. This was her first and last mistake. The American minister in Paris, hearing of her arrival, immediately informed Captain John A. Winslow of the steam corvette *Kearsarge* which was then lying in the Dutch port of Flushing. Winslow at once took his ship to Cherbourg, set up a watch outside the harbor and challenged Semmes to come out and fight.

The vessels were very similar in size and construction, the *Kearsarge* being perhaps a shade larger. Any real advantage she possessed over the Southern vessel resided in a concealed protection of chain armor and in a highly trained naval crew. On Sunday, June 19, these two vessels fought a duel in the waters between Cherbourg and Dover while the population of Dover thronged the cliffs and the French lined the cliffs and breakwaters as though they had come to watch a football game. Front row seats, however, were claimed by the family and friends of the owner of the British yacht *Greyhound* who took his ship into the Channel to get a better view. The view included something like an hour of fighting during which *Kearsarge* outmaneuvered and outshot the *Alabama* until Semmes was forced to haul down his flag and surrender.

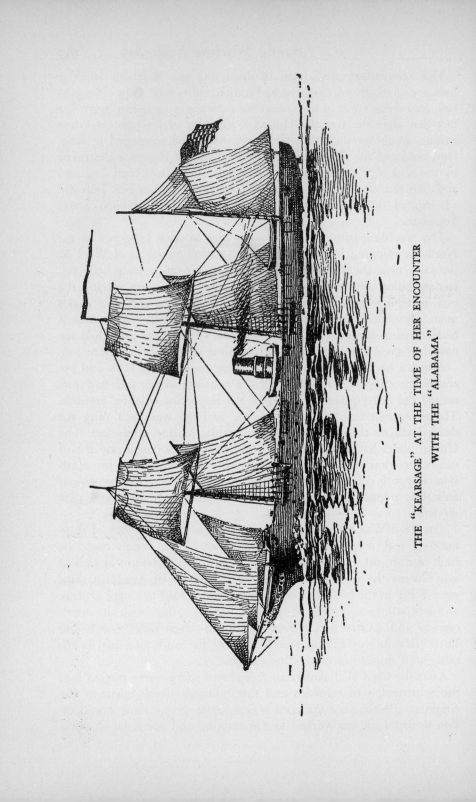

THE "KEARSAGE" AT THE TIME OF HER ENCOUNTER WITH THE "ALABAMA"

The *Shenandoah* specialized in disrupting the Northern whaling industry of which she captured and burned thirty-four ships. The general destructive effect of the commerce raiders can be judged from the fact that after the war the United States filed claims against Great Britain on the grounds that the vessels built and purchased in England rendered the British liable for the value of the ships destroyed by the raiders. The claims stated that 258 vessels had been captured and that their value was nearly $18,000,000. The Geneva Tribunal adjudicated the claim directing England to pay the United States $15,000,000.

The preceding paragraphs give some idea of what happened to the Northern shipping industry during the period of the Civil War. At the same time the losses of the Southern states ran to over 1,500 vessels including almost 300 steamers. The Northern states, during the war, had built up a navy of 671 ships, 9,000 officers and over 50,000 men. Through maintenance of the blockade and other operations it had played a decisive part in the outcome of the war, but while the navy had grown strong American maritime supremacy had been lost.

America had developed the transatlantic packets, had built and operated the clippers, had perfected the whaling vessel and had pioneered the development of many of the important whaling grounds. The depression that preceded the war and the war itself rang the death knell on these and other characteristic marine enterprises. The United States had also played its part in the development and use of steam for transatlantic freight and passenger services and for coastwise shipping. Here, again the depression and the war first slowed and then stopped American efforts to develop new ships and new services.

The Civil War came just at the time when the technology of shipbuilding had developed to the point where ocean vessels could be built of iron instead of wood and could be driven by steam as well as sail. During the years of the war, while hundreds of American ships were going to the bottom or were being sold abroad to escape capture and reprisal, the shipyards of Great Britain were busy with the development and construction of iron-hull steam-driven cargo vessels and liners. Britain was able to absorb most of the trade that had previously been shipped in American bottoms.

After the Civil War American capital and energy were poured into the construction of railroads and the industrial development of the continent. By the time America was ready to give serious consideration to merchant marine and to the building and operation of ocean vessels the cost of materials and the wages of American shipwrights and sailors had risen to such a point that she was unable to compete on a sound economic basis with foreign-built, foreign-operated vessels.

In two World Wars the United States has demonstrated that it has the materials and the technical skills to create a great navy and simultaneously to build and operate a serviceable merchant marine. At such time the safety of the nation is paramount and costs are of secondary importance, but in times of peace, when the economic factors are all-important, America has let her merchant marine languish.

The decline in America's maritime position after the Civil War was matched by her decline in naval strength. At the end of the war America had ships aplenty and some of them had taught lessons to the naval students of Europe, but both lessons and ships were repugnant to Congress and the voters behind Congress. The existence of many old ships blinded the nation to the need for any new ones. Expensive repairs were succeeded by extensive reconstructions until the ships became priceless antiques; polyglot crews and well-trained Annapolis officers frittered and fretted in elaborate idleness; the most terrible and resounding battles in which the navy engaged were those fought in the bureaus and offices between the deck officers who wished to continue the use of sail, which they understood, and the engineers who longed for a modern navy in steam and steel.

The stagnation, apathy and graft in naval repairs continued to the 80's, at which time matters were so bad that reports of boards of naval officers at last won the ear of Congress. The legislative hearing was sharpened by the fact that a current war between Peru and Bolivia on one side and Chile on the other had not only proved the value of an active navy but also demonstrated that Chilean ships were better than any in the United States Navy. Timidly and reluctantly reconstruction commenced in 1883 and was stepped up in 1885 so that the navy showed some awakening strength to support its interests in Samoa in 1889 and in Hawaii in the 1890's. There was need for all the speed in building and skill in operation the navy could muster for in 1895 Britain and Venezuela were in dispute over the boundary of British Guiana and President Cleveland was ready to invoke the Monroe Doctrine should Britain refuse arbitration.

That she did not refuse must have been due to some mixture of motives such as convenience, forbearance, preoccupation with other interests and not to any American show of strength, for even with then-current increases and improvements the United States Navy would have been about as dangerous to a British fleet as the attack of a small dog upon an elephant. It was fortunate that the next quarrel America took up was with a distracted and declining power.

America took up this quarrel in the first place because a nuisance was being committed at her doorstep. For a long time the fire of revolt against Spanish rule had flared up here and there in Cuba and then died or been extinguished but it broke into flame in 1896. Not even the repressive and cruel measures instituted by General Weyler in command of the Spanish troops could dampen the flames this time. Weyler's method was to make war not only on the rebel troops but also the civilian population, which he began to shut up in large concentration camps where they starved and died of disease in great numbers. In those days at the turn of the century Weyler's methods were not so well known and widely employed as they have since become. Instead of putting out the fire Weyler scattered sparks that began to burn brightly in America where sympathy and support for the Cubans developed rapidly. After American protest Weyler was recalled in 1897 but the revolt went on and, with mounting hostility toward Spain, the navy kept growing in an atmosphere of tension and expectancy.

In February, 1898, the USS *Maine* exploded while she was at anchor at Havana Harbor with a loss of 260 lives. After an American naval inquiry had been conducted it was reported that the explosion was due to a submarine mine. This conclusion was anticipated by the American press and public and the clamor for war increased to such a point that on April 11 McKinley recommended intervention in Cuba to the Congress, asked for authority; a joint resolution was signed on April 20 and war was formally declared on the 25th.

Toward the end of the month it was known that a small Spanish fleet of four armored cruisers and three torpedo-boat destroyers under Admiral Cervera had left the Cape Verde Islands. Nothing further was learned about the course and destination of this fleet. The United States populace then living had had little or no experience with war and the excitement and alarm which spread along the Atlantic seaboard was incommensurate either with the size of the Spanish fleet or any particular place along the Atlantic coast being hit by its shells. On May 12 the alarm subsided as rapidly as it had arisen for then Cervera was reported off Martinique.

In the meantime the army had taken San Juan Hill on July 1. Theodore Roosevelt, who had appeared as the assistant secretary of the navy during the year leading up to the Spanish War, had thrown down his pen in Washington and, doing a "quick change" that would have delighted the heart of any vaudeville performer, appeared as a colonel of a cavalry regiment in britches, puttees and the felt hat with its broad brim pinned up on one side which was the distinguishing mark of the "Rough Riders," which working at a furious pace he had assembled and transported just in time to participate in the attack on San Juan. The Spanish army in Cuba capitulated on July 17.

In the meantime, Roosevelt, when he was still in the assistant secretary's office, had succeeded in having Commodore Dewey assigned to a Pacific squadron and instructed to proceed to Hong Kong where he would be handy in the event that hostilities with Spain did arise. Dewey carried confidential instructions that in the event of such hostilities he was to proceed at once to Manila. Thus it happened on April 27 a telegram from navy secretary Long reached Dewey on the China coast. On the morning of the 30th he entered Manila Bay under cover of darkness where a small Spanish fleet under Admiral Montojo lay at anchor.

At dawn the Spaniards began an irregular and inaccurate fire in the direction of the American fleet. This proved a futile gesture since the American ships outnumbered the Spaniards and since their guns had a longer range. After Dewey had made several trips up and down the harbor the Spanish fleet had virtually disappeared. A little after midday the Spaniards ashore hoisted a white flag as token of surrender.

Despite the naval victory Dewey was unable to land and take full possession of the port and city until news of his victory had reached Washington and reinforcements of 10,000 troops had been transported across the Pacific. Dewey hung on in Manila until August when the reinforcements arrived. Being then in a hopeless position, Manila agreed to occupation and capitulation which were carried out on August 13.

A peace protocol had been filed in Washington on August 12. Thus, the United States, with a cost of one man killed and one man wounded in the Atlantic and of eight men wounded in Manila, had won two naval battles and come into possession of an overseas empire. She had done this with a navy that, judged by world standards, was small and inferior and with gunnery that was highly inaccurate except as compared with Spanish gunnery. Still, in the course of a century she had grown from a handful of states on the eastern seaboard into a nation that stretched from coast to coast with stations under her control across the Pacific terminating in her new possession—the

Philippines. Her navy was undoubtedly destined for further growth and it was clear that she had become one of the world powers.

In a general way the end of the century marked also the end on the Atlantic of the simpler and older style of naval warfare where single ships or squadrons or fleets, within view of each other, maneuvered for position and sighted guns at each other and exchanged fire from ship to ship—the last of naval warfare fought almost entirely on the surface of the sea. For the new century a new type of warfare would emerge when men in search of victory dove in black waters or soared into blue air; when naval warfare was under way to becoming in an increasing measure unseen, indirect, elusive, mechanical, remote and at the same time all-enveloping.

As the century closed America had fought the most recent battles in the Atlantic but she was far from either possessing or exerting a naval power commensurate with her size. Her weakness lay not only in the size and character of her navy but in the lack of an adequate merchant marine. During the Spanish hostilities the United States had been saved by the good fortune of being able to acquire rapidly, though at enormous cost, sufficient ships to transport and supply her armies, for the merchant marine was quite inadequate to this task. England, France, Russia and now Germany not only had the merchant vessels to carry the bulk of the Atlantic trade but they also were building the fleets to hold their commerce secure.

As early as 1889 England had set the pace in naval armament and she passed the Naval Defense Act under which she declared her intention of having a navy that would be as strong as that of her two nearest rivals. This has been referred to as the Two-Power Standard. At the time, the two powers greatest in strength were France and Russia. Though the balance might shift, England spoke and behaved as though she intended to maintain this ratio.

At the close of the century trade flowed fast and freely, travel was easy and popular, there was an air of busy prosperity and expectancy. Whatever insiders may have felt, the race for naval supremacy was treated by the press and the public as though it were the friendly rivalry of college football teams.

Chapter 24

FLYING THE ATLANTIC

R EGULAR and practical flight across the Atlantic is only a few years old but the general idea of navigating in the air is very old indeed. The travel of human beings in the air began on both sides of the Atlantic at about the time that the United States became a nation. In those years France and the United States were in close touch with each other and shared many ideas and enthusiasms; travel through the air was one of them. The first flights by balloon were made in France but the first American flights came only a few years later.

Americans were even more hopeful and enthusiastic about travel by air than the French because they felt it might become of practical and even national importance. Washington, Franklin, and many other prominent Americans were interested in the early balloon flights because they were interested in all forms of transportation. Water transportation had developed rapidly and the coasts, seaports, bays, rivers, lakes of America were already full of ships, but transportation over the land was in a very backward state. Roads were primitive, rough and dangerous. Land travel was uncomfortable, painfully slow and expensive.

The original states had an enormous coastline and back of the coastline lay a whole continent waiting for development. Better and more rapid transportation was needed to knit the states together—it might even be an important factor in determining whether the American experiment in a new form of government was to succeed or fail. Travel by air was welcome indeed if it could make some contribution to the general problem of transportation.

It was in June of 1783 that the first balloon took to the air and remained suspended for a period of about ten minutes. This was at the town of Annonay, forty miles from the city of Lyons. Two brothers, named Montgolfier, were responsible not only for the general idea of balloons but also for the construction of the first examples. Their ideas were very crude—they had simply observed that smoke inevitably rose into the air. They argued, therefore, that if smoke could be confined in some container it would at least lift the container into the air and possibly also carry some load. However crude their theory, their practice was admirable. They were able and willing to experiment. They were following their father's business of manufacturing paper and were quite prosperous. Moreover, one of the paper mills gave them a place where they could experiment in secret.

They discovered that a light paper bag, if placed over a fire, or as they would put it, if filled with smoke, would rise to the ceiling. As their balloons got bigger, they discovered that paper was not always strong enough so they tried bags combining linen and paper. Finally a globular linen envelope, 105 feet in circumference, made the ascent outdoors in June 1783.

Their next experiment was with a silk balloon that rose to 6,000 feet and traveled a mile and a half. This flight first attracted and then repelled an audience—the crowd, having no explanation for the behavior of the balloon, fled in terror. By August popular interest in the balloons had developed to such a point that the Montgolfier brothers staged a demonstration flight before King Louis XVI and Queen Marie Antoinette at Versailles. Up to this time nobody had traveled in a balloon and no one knew whether a living creature could survive a flight. On this occasion a sheep, a duck and a rooster made the ascent and survived.

This made it seem possible that a human being might survive a trip into the air and it was suggested that the king might offer a pardon to one or several condemned criminals who would volunteer to make a flight in a balloon. This idea was spiritedly rejected by one of the king's officers, Jean Pilâtre de Rozier, who thought that it was absurd that a criminal should have the honor of having made the first human flight. He proposed to make the ascent himself.

His first flight was made in a captive balloon, that is, one that rose in the air but was still attached to the earth by a mooring rope. It was also a "fire balloon," that is, it carried its own source of "smoke" with it. There was a grate for the fire and de Rozier was supplied with wood and other fuel to keep the fire going. When the fuel ran out the flight was over. After several such trial ascensions de Rozier made a free flight on the 21st of November, 1783, which was given wide publicity and in which he was joined by a companion, the Marquis d'Arlandes. They landed successfully but both of them were smoky black.

In the meantime the scientists began to take an interest in the balloons and the idea began to grow that there were less smoky ways of making a balloon rise. The Academy of Sciences suggested that it was not the smoke that made the balloon rise but hot air, therefore that a gas lighter than the general atmosphere would do the same thing.

Professor J. A. C. Charles of the University of Paris set to work to make a balloon and fill it with hydrogen which Cavendish had discovered in 1776 and at that time named inflammable air. Charles' balloon was made of silk and coated with an elastic varnish to keep in the gas. This balloon flew without passengers, is said to have reached a height of 3,000 feet and to have traveled at least fifteen miles. Before the close of the year Professor Charles and an assistant made a flight in another hydrogen balloon which lasted an hour and forty minutes and carried them nearly thirty miles.

By January of 1785 the first American air traveler appeared on the scene. This was an American physician named John Jeffreys who financed a French balloonist named Jean Pierre François Blanchard. Their conveyance was a hydrogen balloon which Blanchard had built. The balloon was inflated at Dover and in it they crossed the English Channel and landed safely in France. Jeffreys and Blanchard were, therefore, the first to cross even a small arm of the ocean by air.

Jeffreys was not the only United States citizen to exhibit an active interest in air travel; in fact, he continued his trip to Paris so that he might deliver in person a letter which he carried written by George Washington and addressed to Benjamin Franklin. In the States the Philosophical Society of Philadelphia was taking both a theoretical and also a practical interest in air travel and actively promoting some flights. In one of these the aeronaut was carried aloft by a whole cluster of small hydrogen-filled balloons. These he punctured, one by one, when he wanted to reach the ground.

The first important balloon ascension in the United States, however, was that made from the city of Philadelphia by Blanchard in

1793. President Washington was apparently still actively interested in air navigation for on this occasion he not only issued a safe conduct to Blanchard, dated January 9, but also went out to join the crowd watching the balloon make its departure.

Air transportation, which stirred the interest of Franklin and Washington, went beyond the mere ability to raise a human being in the air and to keep him floating there. Transportation implies the ability to get from a present spot, called the point of departure, to some other selected or desirable spot called the destination. The balloon was an exciting beginning which could, after all, get a man into the air and, with good luck and good management, it could keep him there. It could even move him to another position on the earth's surface and deposit him back on the ground. However, once the traveler was in the air he was at the mercy of the winds and had little or no control over the direction of his travel and even a very limited control over the length of his flight. This was hardly transportation. It is not surprising, therefore, that the idea of controlling the movement of a balloon or airship was almost as old as the balloon itself.

The year after the first hot-air balloons were sent aloft, that is as early as 1784, the Robert brothers created a hydrogen balloon which they intended to propel through the air. With this in mind, they gave the balloon a shape something like that of an American football, suspended six men under it in a long car and equipped them with aerial oars or fans with which they were supposed to row the ship through the air. Thus there grew up at the very beginning two methods of air travel and two kinds of air traveler whose interests differed one from the other. There were the free balloonists who wanted to rise high or go far even if this involved being more or less at the mercy of the wind. On the other hand, there were the guided-airship people who were content with quite limited flights and slow progress provided they could exercise some control over the airship that carried them.

For a long time the balloonists had the best of it and received the chief public acclaim, while it was very uncertain whether the controlled airship would ever be practical or even possible. The balloons began to make long flights. In 1836 three Englishmen, namely, Robert Holland, Monck Mason and Charles Green, ordered a great balloon built in which they took their departure from London on November 7. They not only crossed the Channel but traveled to a point in Nassau, approximately 500 miles away. Their balloon was thereafter referred to as the *Great Nassau Balloon*. Charles Green, who was the leader of this flight, was also the inventor of the guide rope or trailing rope which had a considerable vogue among balloonists.

Later, bigger balloons were built and went on longer flights. In 1859 an American by the name of John Wise built a large balloon in which he left St. Louis, landing at Henderson in New York, covering a distance of 1,120 miles. This record was not beaten until Count Henri de la Vaulx rose from Paris and traveled to Korosticheff, a point in Russia, 1,193 miles away.

From the point of view of distance covered such balloon ascensions were impressive. Even into the twentieth century balloons were popular and widely used. They were used for entertainment and spectacle on such occasions as exhibitions and county fairs. Frequently the daring balloonists returned to earth by parachute. National and international balloon races became annual events. Balloons were also used for serious scientific study of the atmosphere and the cumulative records of the balloonists added considerably to our knowledge of the weather and of the behavior of the upper air in periods of winds and also of calms.

In fact, the first proposal to cross the Atlantic by air contemplated the use of a balloon and not of an airship. In 1873 a New York publication named the *Daily Graphic* publicly proposed such a crossing and John Wise, who had already made his long flight from St. Louis, announced himself as willing to make the attempt and prepared a balloon for this purpose. There is room for skepticism regarding the complete sincerity of this proposed crossing. At least on this occasion Wise not only didn't see the ocean, he didn't even rise from the ground. His huge balloon appears to have been made of very weak materials for it tore open while it was being inflated.

An entirely honest and serious attempt to reach the North Pole was made as late as 1896. The originator and director of the enterprise was a Major S. A. Andrée, who had had some experience both in ballooning and also in Arctic travel. He was accompanied by Nils Strindberg and Knut Fraenkel in a balloon called the *Eagle*. Their departure was made from Danes Island, Spitsbergen, on July 11. Messages which they dropped in buoys were recovered but later it became apparent that the balloon and its three occupants had disappeared. Thirty-three years later, that is in 1930, remains of the expedition were discovered on White Island. Journals and diaries were recovered which showed that the flight had lasted three days and reached 83 degrees north. Even photographs of the expedition were recovered and developed.

The airship which could be controlled in flight was clearly a more advanced and valuable idea but it was one that was destined for slow development since it really depended upon the availability of adequate mechanical power. As early as 1852 Henri Giffard equipped an airship with mechanical power. The only practical source of power available to him at that time was the steam engine, and he actually contrived and mounted in his ship a boiler and engine that supplied approximately three horsepower and drove an air propeller at 110 revolutions per minute.

Considering the power obtained, the engine was very heavy indeed, yet the gas bag was able to sustain the load and Giffard was able to demonstrate that with this limited power he was able to control the motion of the ship and even to direct it on a curved course. This was a wonderful effort for its time. It did demonstrate that power was important but it also demonstrated that for use in the air the power had to be greater and the weight less. It turned out later that the internal combustion motor, operating on gasoline, was the first practical and effective source of power for use in airships and later in airplanes. Before this was demonstrated many proposals were made and many experiments carried out.

It is said that in 1872 a Frenchman named Dupuy de Lôme tried to drive an airship by the use of electric batteries and that later he also employed a motor using benzene as fuel. In the same year a German by the name of Paul Haenlein was using a four-cylinder internal combustion motor. Attempts were even made to develop a motor that could be operated on the same kind of gas that was used to inflate the envelope of the airship.

In 1898, two years after Major Andrée had attempted to reach the Pole by balloon, a diminutive Brazilian named Santos-Dumont, then resident in Paris, demonstrated that a cigar-shaped balloon could be steered and driven through the air by a gasoline motor. His early airship could be steered but it could not resist a stiff wind and it was far from being a rigid structure. Five years later his ship and his motor had both progressed to a point where he was able to fly his ship on a closed course. From a suburb of Paris he flew to the Eiffel Tower, made a sharp turn around it and returned to his starting point, six and three-quarter miles away. He remained in the air for a period of about an hour and a half. This flight won for him a substantial prize and world-wide recognition. By 1905 he was using a more rigid structure equipped with two motors for propulsion. This ship was able to travel at a speed of twelve miles per hour.

Santos-Dumont was not the only man working on airships during the last years of the last century. During these same years, across the border in Germany, Count Ferdinand von Zeppelin was also at work on an airship. There was a strange though characteristic contrast between these men. Santos-Dumont was small, slight of build, quick of movement, alert, inventive, experimental in all his approaches, working as an individualist with private funds. Zeppelin was an older man who had first observed balloons in America during the Civil War. He was large, grave, not to say pompous, methodical. He was working in the military interests of the German nation and, when he could get them, using official subsidies in the development of his projects.

It was somehow in keeping with his character that he should be the pioneer of the large and rigid airship. His work progressed slowly and involved large expenditures. His first ship to take the air was launched in 1900 and was soon wrecked. It was only after a number of ships had developed and after the German government began to support Zeppelin with heavy subsidies, which it did in 1908, that the rigid dirigible was able to demonstrate its value.

In the meantime an entirely different principle of controlled flight had been demonstrated in the early airplanes. The airplane, or heavier-than-air flying machine, was not strictly speaking a new invention. As early as 1842 an Englishman by the name of William S. Henson had made designs and plans for a monoplane type structure that was to be driven through the air by aerial propellers deriving their power from a steam engine. A few years later John Stringfellow demonstrated in London a steam-driven model plane which was capable of limited flight.

From then on experimental planes were occasionally built and often projected. Failures were so frequent that the wisest students of flight, like Otto Lilienthal in Germany and Octave Chanute and the Wright brothers in America, toward the end of the last century turned to the building and flying of gliders or motorless planes. In this way they sought to find out how the air behaved when it came in contact with the plane surface.

They sought also the answers to other questions: how much weight various sizes and shapes of plane surface could support at constant speed; how this support varied with an increase in speed; how a machine, made up of plane surfaces, could be controlled in the air. These men all hoped finally to succeed in power-driven flight but they were aware that they needed to know more and to have better machines before they could risk putting power into them.

Two of the most important problems were the problem of sufficient power in relation to weight of the engine and the problem of stability and control. The first man to feel confident that he had solved both these problems was Professor Samuel P. Langley who was then the head of the Smithsonian Institution in Washington.

Langley devised a type of machine that was in effect a tandem bi-plane with the supporting surfaces virtually in the same horizontal plane. At the extreme end of the framework there was placed a sort of tail of intersecting plane surfaces that were to provide control by acting as horizontal and vertical rudders. For this machine Langley coined the name "aerodrome." As early as 1896 Langley created a model of a machine of this type and designed for it a miniature steam engine. When launched from the roof of a houseboat on the Potomac this model flew for 3,000 feet.

As a result of this demonstration Langley secured from President McKinley a grant of funds to permit the construction of a man-carrying aerodrome. By this time the gasoline motor was proving its general efficiency and its ability to develop relatively large horsepower at low weight. Therefore Langley and his associates decided to try the aerodrome with a gasoline engine rather than with steam.

The engine was built by Charles M. Manley, Langley's assistant. Manley devised a novel and highly interesting engine. He arranged five cylinders in a radial design, thus cutting down the weight of the crankshaft and crankcase. Thus, he achieved an engine delivering fifty-two horsepower at a weight of only 120 pounds.

His radial engine was the first example of what was to be for many years one of the basic successful types of aircraft motors. Manley, who had solved the motor problem, also served as pilot. On two successive attempts to achieve flight the machine fell into the river when launched from a houseboat on the Potomac. It appears that the machine was inherently unstable and also lacked adequate control surfaces.

It was just nine days after Langley's machine flopped into the Potomac for the second time that the Wright brothers made the world's first flight in a power driven heavier-than-air machine. Langley was a well-known scientist. His experiments and his aerodrome were financed out of public funds. He was known to the President and his experimental flights attracted great public interests in the nation's capital.

The Wright brothers were a contrast to Langley in almost every respect. They were young and obscure. They earned, begged and borrowed the funds of less than $1,000 required to build their first machine. They had no scientific reputation and no special scientific training, being for the most part self-taught. They worked in obscurity from choice and carried on their open air experiments at Kill Devil Hill on the seacoast of North Carolina. This location suited them not only because the weather bureau had said that it was here that they could find the strongest and steadiest winds but also because it was so remote that sightseers and attendant publicity would not encumber their efforts.

For a number of years the Wright brothers in Dayton and at Kitty Hawk worked on the problem of flight. They had evolved the idea of warping the wings of a plane as a method of providing stability and control. Their glider experiments began at Kitty Hawk in 1900 and continued through the succeeding years. During this time they also built the first wind tunnel for their experiments. In 1902, in their third glider, they completed more than 1,000 successful glides. By 1903 they had built their own four-cylinder gasoline engine and mounted it in a biplane.

In December of that year they achieved several flights, the longest of which kept them in the air for almost a minute and covered 852 feet against a twenty-mile wind. Their flights were witnessed by some of the personnel of the coast guard station and one or two people from a nearby town.

These early flights attracted little public attention; in fact, the country was so skeptical that only three newspapers carried any accounts of the event and these were extremely inaccurate. It was some months before the first adequate description of the machine and of the flights were put in circulation.

Throughout 1904 and 1905 they continued to build and rebuild and fly machines in a field near Dayton. The first official recognition their accomplishment received was from the British government which sent a representative to visit them at Dayton at the end of 1904, confirmed by a letter from the War Office of February 11, 1905, asking the Wright brothers to submit terms for the purchase of their machine. At the same time the United States government disclaimed any interest in the Wright brothers' machine.

In 1906 the French secured an option to purchase a Wright machine and in this year also Santos-Dumont and other European aviators began making first flights in machines of their own design. Bleriot completed his first monoplane in 1907.

The Wright brothers were continuing to extend the power of their machine and the range of their flights. Interest in Europe had mounted to such a point that Wilbur Wright sailed for Europe in May of 1907 to demonstrate an airplane and to complete contracts with Great Britain, France, Italy and Germany.

By 1908 the United States government had relented. Orville Wright, in September, staged a demonstration at Fort Meyer, Virginia, making a flight of forty-five miles. A few months later Wilbur Wright at LeMans in France extended the record to seventy-seven miles. This was spectacular for a heavier-than-air machine, but at the same time Count Zeppelin took one of his dirigibles on a flight across the Alps to Italy for a distance of 235 miles and then returned safely to his base. Thus, already there was a competition for public attention and confidence between the two alternative methods of air travel that were finally to compete for the honor of making the first transatlantic crossing.

The next few years were critical and were of great importance in the history of aviation. Encouraged by the success of the Wright brothers, many inventors and aviation enthusiasts who had been secretly nursing the notion to fly began translating their dream into new forms of planes and motors. Many new forms of planes were developed. There was a hot contest between those who believed in the biplane and those who believed in the monoplane and there were experiments with triplanes and other strange devices.

Many new fliers developed and a number of these began developing their own style of ship. In France there was Henri Farman, Breguet, Bleriot and Voisin. Even Santos-Dumont, who had started out in the dirigibles, became a plane enthusiast and designed a little parasol of a monoplane which was so small and handy that he could fly it around the streets of Paris.

In America Glenn Curtiss, at Hammondsport, New York, was experimenting in the fields with a new form of plane he called the "June bug" and on the lake he was developing another form that would rise from water. W. Starling Burgess turned his attention from designing yachts long enough to design some new planes. Many were taking to the air; there was Loughhead, Glenn Martin, the Stinsons and many others. Some of these learned from the Wright brothers and other early fliers and many taught themselves by trial and error on machines of their own design.

By 1909 the Wright brothers began a systematic training of army pilots under a contract with the government. The Wrights, Curtiss, Glenn Martin and others organized companies to produce and sell airplanes and the famous suit between the Wright brothers and Glenn Curtiss was instituted. In this year the first large-scale airplane show was held in Rheims, France and its counterpart, an International Air Meet, was held at Belmont Park on Long Island in the succeeding year.

This was also the year in which Bleriot flew his monoplane across the English Channel from the French coast to a landing in a field above Dover. It took him thirty-seven and a half minutes and in this time he not only won a prize of $25,000 but also made the first overwater flight across any part of the Atlantic Ocean in a heavier-than-air machine.

1910 was the year for money prizes and cross-country flights. Paulhan, competing against Claude Graham-White, made a flight from London to Manchester, a distance of 183 miles, and won a *London Daily Mail* prize of $50,000. In America Glenn Curtiss won $10,000 by flying from Albany to New York City and Charles K. Hamilton won a similar amount by flying from New York to Philadelphia and returning within a twenty-four-hour period.

1910 was also the year in which an American named Walter Wellman made a serious attempt to fly the Atlantic Ocean. For this purpose he had built a dirigible which he christened *America*. This machine was driven by gasoline motor. Wellman knew that his airship could not lift into the air a sufficient load of gasoline to carry him from the American continent to Europe but he thought he had a plan for overcoming this difficulty. In addition to having the usual gas tank carried in the car of the machine, he expected to take along a supply in a sort of tail or drag rope which he intended to tow behind the dirigible. Ropes, trailing from the after part of the dirigible car, had gasoline containers attached to them at intervals.

At the start of the flight, most of these containers would be floating on the sea, trailing behind the ship. As gasoline was used up, the rope would be drawn up into the car, the gasoline transferred from the drums into the tank and the drums abandoned at sea. It was a logical plan on paper; in practice, it nearly wrecked the ship and cost Wellman his life. The trailing drums were a terrific drag on the machine and in addition, when the sea was at all rough, the tail jumped from one wave to another and nearly shook the aircraft to pieces. Nonetheless, Wellman made a long flight in the machine and was finally, by good fortune, rescued at sea.

About this time the ladies also began to take to the air. Miss Harriet Quimby was the first woman in America licensed to fly. In 1911 she was the first woman to fly an airplane over the English Channel. Ruth Law and Katherine Stinson also joined the slim ranks of lady aviators.

By 1911 it was possible for a young American enthusiast, by the expenditure of a little money and a great deal of patient effort, to make flights in some of the early French machines. One of the aviation centers consisted of some large fields surrounded by sheds at Buc, a suburb of Paris. This field was at its busiest at night and just after sunrise. The early French machines of 1911 were all underpowered and imperfectly controlled and were, therefore, not able to cope with adverse winds. The theory was that the air was quietest at about the time of sunrise and most flights were made at this ungodly hour. Taking a flight or flying lesson meant either getting up long before dawn or else staying up all night.

Early in the summer of 1913 one of the sheds at Buc provided an unusual spectacle. Lashed to the rafters was a simple skeleton framework to which a little bucket aviation seat was attached in an upside down position and a man was sitting in this seat, also upside down, kept there by a simple harness of webbing and leather. The man hung there for minutes at a time working controls which, as nearly as possible, were the exact models of the controls of his airplane. This was the French aviator, Pegou, seeking experience and orientation for a type of flying that no man had yet attempted.

A few days later Pegou astonished Europe by completing a vertical loop and also flying his plane in an upside-down position. Pegou was, I believe, the first aviator to have accomplished these feats though the honor is also claimed for an American aviator, Lincoln Beachey, flying a Curtiss plane, who completed a loop in November of 1913. Pegou was killed while attempting a high altitude flight over the Alps.

Back in 1911 it was also possible to make a really extensive flight with Count Zeppelin in a rigid dirigible. By this time he was operating out of the fashionable resort Baden-Baden. Here large fields had been cleared for the use of the count's machines and an enormous shed built to house them. He was then operating and demonstrating a huge dirigible called the *Schwaben,* either the third or fourth machine of that name, making triangular flights from Baden-Baden to Koblenz, Strasburg or other points along the Rhine Valley.

Even the casual observer knew that the various forms of flying had military value and that the nations were subsidizing aviation in one way or another because of this potential value, but few people were able to foresee that the machines were, in effect, already being groomed for an impending war. In 1913 Lord Northcliffe hopefully offered a prize of $50,000 for the first successful nonstop transatlantic flight and Rodman Wanamaker entered into a contract with Glenn H. Curtiss for the design and construction of a flying boat capable of crossing the ocean. The resulting ship, christened the *America,* was tested in July, 1914, but before any attempt could be made on the crossing, war broke out.

The history of aviation for the next five years was largely the history of machines developed for military purposes. Nonetheless, during this time aviation made great strides that were ready for civilian application at the end of the war.

At the beginning of the war our planes were used to reconnoiter positions for spotting the results of gunfire, for directing gunfire and for rapid communication. In the process of carrying out such errands machines from the opposing sides occasionally encountered each other. On such occasions the aviators began to take pot shots at each other with rifles, revolvers or whatever arms they could get into their machines. Presently machine guns were being mounted in the planes and air duels and dogfights began to take place in no man's land and over the lines.

Presently a Dutch aviator and engineer named Anthony Fokker devised a method of synchronizing the fire of a machine gun with the rotation of the airplane propeller in such a way that the bullets from the gun always passed harmlessly between the rotating blades of the propeller. This gave an enormous stimulus to the development of combat planes. What was required for such work was a small ship that had great power and speed, which could be translated into ability to outclimb any opposing machine with the premium also set on rapid maneuverability.

Aside from beginning to fight each other, the pilots of the early and simple planes, by flying on their missions for information, discovered also that they had a natural advantage over the enemy's troops on the ground. They began dropping hand grenades and simple hand bombs on the enemy's trenches. At the same time they discovered that the enemy could occasionally hit them with rifle or machine-gun fire. This gave an impetus to the use of larger and larger bombs and better methods of carrying and dropping them.

The carrying and management of larger bombs soon showed the need for an airplane especially designed for this service. What was needed in such a plane was not so much speed and maneuverability as large size, driven by an engine that had great power and reliability. Weight-carrying capacity and endurance were the bomber's virtues.

Thus, the war brought about rapidly great divergencies in the size, speed and equipment of two radically different forms of airplane and intermediate forms also developed for special purposes. While the war speeded up the development of different types of machines, it also speeded up the development of aviators. In all the combatant countries, thousands of young men suddenly became aviators and learned to fly many different kinds of machines propelled by many different kinds of motors. Their life literally depended upon their ability to acquire experience and skill rapidly and they crowded into months or even weeks of military flying knowledge and experience that it would have taken them years to acquire in times of peace.

At the close of the war many of the military planes were retired and scrapped and many of the World War I aviators returned to civilian pursuits, but a number of the planes, motors and men found a place in the early development of commercial civilian flying. Immediately after the war nearly all the European countries made efforts to establish national commercial air lines and these utilized the experience and sometimes the very ships that had come out of the war. In England this was the experience of companies like Handley-Page and Armstrong-Whitworth. In Holland there was Anthony (Tony) Fokker and the various machines he had developed for sale during the war. In Germany there were various ships based on Dr. Junker's war experiences including the use of low-wing all-metal machines and also the Dornier ships.

The United States had been slow in the development and delivery of fighting planes but it had trained and supplied many aviators. In 1918 air-mail service commenced with the establishment of flights between Washington and Philadelphia. The air-mail system enjoyed a fairly rapid growth but the transport of passengers by air was slow to develop in the United States in contrast with the number of routes that were rapidly established in Europe.

By 1919 aviation was ready to make an assault on the transatlantic flight. The United States Navy was the first to make the attempt. The navy had adopted a design of a seaplane produced for it by

Glenn Curtiss. This class of ship was designated as the NC, standing presumably for "Navy-Curtiss" boats. Four of them were built and given number designations. In May of 1919 three of them took off from Trepassy in Newfoundland on a course that was to carry them to Europe by way of the Azores. Navy vessels patrolled the coarse and a world relaxing from the war took a sportsman's interest in the outcome. Only the NC-4 succeeded in completing the crossing.

Also starting from Newfoundland, H. G. Hawker made a valiant effort to complete the flight from Newfoundland to the British Isles. The first successful flight was also made in this season by Captain J. Alcock and Lieutenant A. Whitten-Brown. They ran into foggy and difficult weather and finally succeeded in reaching the west coast of Ireland and in landing their machine in a bog. The flight lasted sixteen hours and was the first nonstop flight across the Atlantic. Thus, they qualified for the $50,000 prize.

A few weeks after the completion of the Alcock-Brown flight a large British dirigible known as the *R-34* flew from Edinburgh to New York and back to England. Naturally a flight such as this of a dirigible carried across the ocean many more people than were represented in all the early flights of heavier-than-air machines. A number of dirigibles had been developed not only in England but also in Germany and the United States. Atlantic crossings to North and South America of dirigibles were fairly common up to the time of the disastrous burning of the great German airship *Hindenburg* which took place in 1937.

One notable flight of this class was that made by the airship *Los Angeles* in 1924. This ship, in command of Dr. Hugo Eckener, made a flight of 5,066 miles from Friedrichshafen, Germany, to Lakehurst in New Jersey. This was also the year in which United States Army planes completed a flight around the world. They met with many delays and difficulties but their flying time was 371 hours.

By this time it had been fairly well established that flights could be made across the Atlantic from Europe to North America or Europe to South America. In 1926 aviators began to turn their attention to polar exploration. In May of that year there was a race on to see what man, in what kind of machine, could first get to the North Pole. On May 29 the honor went to Lieutenant Commander (later Admiral) Richard E. Byrd and Floyd Bennett when they flew an airplane from Spitsbergen to the North Pole and returned by the same route. It was only a few days later that the semi-rigid airship the *Norge* carried Ronald Amundsen, Lincoln Ellsworth and General

Nobile from Spitsbergen across the North Pole to a landing in Alaska.

In 1927 a New York merchant of French descent named Raymond Orteig had offered a prize of $25,000 for a nonstop flight from New York to Paris. In the spring of that year many well-known aviators were grooming machines for long-distance flights apparently with this prize in mind. These included Richard Byrd and Clarence Chamberlain, each of whom had fairly large ships at their disposal and crews of several persons.

In September, 1926, René Fonck, a French aviator, in an attempt to make the nonstop flight to Paris, crashed on the take-off from Roosevelt Field, Long Island. Fonck and another crew member survived the crash but two members of the crew were killed.

In April 1927 Lieutenant Commander Richard Byrd cracked up the *America* in a test flight preparatory to attempting the New York to Paris nonstop flight and, about the same time, Commander Noel Davis and his partner were killed in another contending ship called the *American Legion.*

Almost unknown at the time was a young aviator named Charles Lindbergh who had asked a young manufacturer named Ryan at San Diego, California, to build and equip a ship for just this flight. Lindbergh's ship was small and fast and he was flying it alone. He claimed the ship in San Diego, flew it to St. Louis where he paused briefly to see some of the gentlemen of that city who had backed his venture. His next hop carried him to Roosevelt Field outside of New York. This was already a remarkable performance and his unheralded arrival attracted a good deal of publicity.

The small ship, the young flier, the lone venture made a combination to arouse the greatest popular interest. Taking advantage of an apparent break in the weather, Lindbergh got under way from Roosevelt Field on May 20 and to the general surprise of the world completed the flight successfully. By this time many people had flown across the Atlantic, but Lindbergh's flight served to dramatize and in a way to popularize the crossing.

Following the flight Lindbergh was, for a number of years, successfully advised in matters of public relations and by extending his travels and aerial explorations was able to create, particularly in the United States, a lively interest in air travel. This was finally utilized by a number of the air lines that were then beginning to succeed with commercial air operations.

Lindbergh's popularity stole the limelight from another very important flight made in the same year. This was the remarkable achievement of USA Lieutenants Maitland and Hegenberger in making a nonstop flight from Oakland, California to Honolulu.

It is interesting to observe that the North Atlantic weather system that was such a problem to the sailing ship captains was now also proving to be a great problem to aviation pilots. Our chapter on the packets serves to illustrate how the prevailing system of westerly winds that troubles the North Atlantic in most seasons of the year was a great advantage to eastbound ships and a great handicap to those making the passage to the west. They played the same part in airplane travel and this accounts for the fact that while the first flight from North America to Europe took place in 1919 it was nine years later, that is, one year after Lindbergh's flight, before an airplane succeeded in flying from Europe to the American continent. This was accomplished by a German Junker ship called the *Breman* commanded by a Captain Koehl.

The carrying of passengers by airplane across the Atlantic which had long been anticipated and projected began in a tentative and experimental way at the end of the 1930's. In March of 1939 a Pan American Airways ship, christened the *Yankee Clipper,* made a survey flight under the command of Captain Harold E. Gray from Baltimore to Europe carrying twenty-one passengers. In May of that year Pan American Airways began the first North Atlantic air-mail service on a route that ran between Port Washington, Long Island, the Azores, Portugal and Marseille, France. About this time also, Imperial Airways of Great Britain and other foreign companies began pioneer flights from Europe to America by a variety of routes.

So far as civilian services were concerned, transatlantic flying was curtailed by the outbreak of war in Europe. However, this Second World War speeded up developments in the aviation industry and in this respect was similar in its effects to the First World War.

Throughout the war period there was a steady demand for increased speed and climbing ability for the pursuit ships and the fighters and great increases in power, range and capacity of the bombers and transports. Again, types of aircraft and of motors developed during the war were subsequently made available for the improvement of civilian flying services.

When the war began flight across the Atlantic still wore the air of a special or unusual event but it was not long before the crossing became a matter of scheduled and routine operation. In June of 1940 fifty-five attack bombers were flown from Mitchel Field, Long Is-

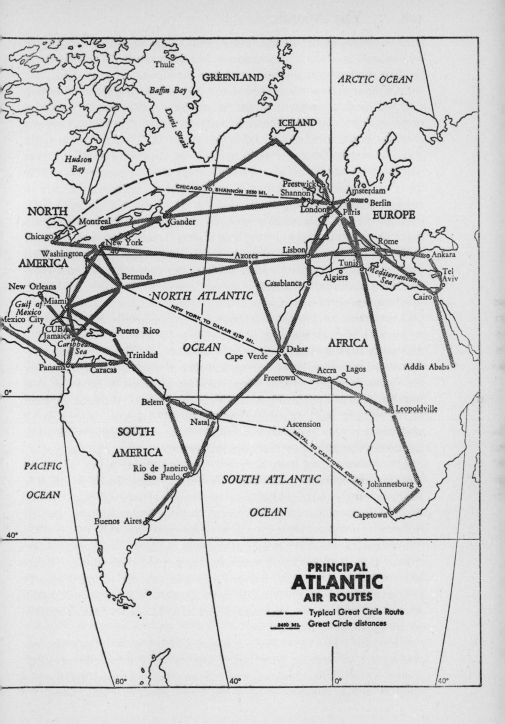

PRINCIPAL
ATLANTIC
AIR ROUTES

——— Typical Great Circle Route
⎯3460 MI.⎯ Great Circle distances

land, to Nova Scotia in the first air delivery of fighting planes. By September American and Canadian pilots were meeting in Montreal to form the first transatlantic ferry group. By June of 1941 the Army Air Corps was organizing the ferry command to fly airplanes, manufactured in this country, across the ocean for delivery in England. Later in the same year Pan American Airways completed an agreement for delivery of planes to Africa and the Middle East.

A Naval Air Transport service was established in January of 1942 to carry personnel and cargo in connection with navy operations and the Air Transport Command, under Major General Harold L. George, commenced operations to all parts of the world on the first of June. In the fall, it took over the African line operations previously carried out by Pan American Airways. The size and scope of military air operations is well illustrated by the fact that the United States 8th Air Force, in order to carry out a raid over northwest Germany at the end of 1944, assembled a fleet of over 1,300 heavy and medium bombers.

Commercial air transport services over the Atlantic were resumed in January of 1945 and have been steadily growing in reliability and popularity and frequency of offered services. By the year 1950 over half a million transatlantic air passengers departed from or arrived at American airports. The exact figure is given as 515,154. Of this number approximately 75 per cent were being carried on United States air lines and approximately 25 per cent on foreign air lines. Overseas air mail amounted to approximately nine million pounds and overseas cargo to nineteen million pounds.

The number of air passengers carried is a significant fraction of all first-class transatlantic passenger services including those of the steamship lines. The carrying of half a million passengers, however, in both directions is less impressive when compared with the ten millions of people that entered this country in a single year during the period of large volume transatlantic services before the world wars began. The carrying of air mail, of course, is significant and important but the volume of goods carried by the transatlantic air lines is insignificant when contrasted either with the needs of transatlantic services or the services actually performed by the transatlantic cargo carrying ships on the sea. Taken all in all, even at its present high level of performance aircraft are now performing something like 1 per cent of the total volume of transatlantic services required in normal times.

It was once thought that aircraft would open up new routes and channels of communication which would form on the earth, or on a map representing the earth, a pattern of commerce radically different from that of the conventional methods of land travel and conventional lanes of steamer travel on the ocean. This was a reasonable expectation and in the future aircraft may well open up transpolar routes between North America and Europe and North America and Asia. Under present political conditions such routes have not developed to any significant degree, although Scandinavian Airlines now flies from Los Angeles to Europe via the polar routes, and similar flights to Asia seem imminent.

On the contrary, it is interesting to notice that for the most part the lines of air travel both over sea and over land tend to follow the pattern and precedents of the carriers that operate on the earth's surface both in direction of route and in relative volume of services offered. The reasons for this are perfectly simple. Like other forms of communication, the air lines depend for their economic existence on providing connections between the major centers of population. Most of the major centers of population have been established for some time and the routes between them carefully worked out by land services such as railways, highways, truck routes, rivers, channels, etc. Along these lines of travel important secondary and even primary centers of population have appeared.

Consequently, even though the air lines might theoretically and even technically follow different lines of travel their natural desire for a large volume of traffic constrains them to operate between the major centers of population. Safety of operation also constrains them to follow prescribed routes.

In the case of transatlantic travel it appeared for a time as though the passage from Europe to America might be made from Spain or Lisbon to the Azores, to Bermuda and then to some American port such as Norfolk or Baltimore. During a developmental stage such routes were, in fact, pursued by airplanes and they thus revived an early route of the sailing ships. The reasons why the planes followed this route were exactly the same reasons that appealed to the captains of the old sailing vessels, namely, that on this route there were convenient island stops for the replenishment of supplies and for the comfort of passengers. Also, this route, in a measure, avoided the prevailing westerlies of the northern latitudes which were such a handicap both to ships on the sea and ships in the air making the passage from Europe to America.

Since that time the fuel capacity and the range of aircraft has greatly increased and the ability of the aircraft to seek routes in higher altitudes has also increased their ability to deal with adverse weather conditions. The air lines from America to Europe are now almost entirely operating from New York to the British Isles or some other nearby north European port and population center. They are, thus, closely following the lanes across the Atlantic that were laid out first by the captains of the Yankee whalers, then by the New York packets, then by the Yankee clippers and that were finally stabilized as accepted international lines of travel following the original suggestion of Matthew Fontaine Maury.

The reasons are exactly the same. New York, London and Paris are still the great centers of population of the modern Western World and the operators of transport services by sea and by air are both anxious to make their arrivals and departures as close to these cities as is practicably possible. The surface vessels have long since traced out and followed great circle courses from a point off the Grand Banks to the Channel ports.

Theoretically the airplanes are free to fly a little longer and a little closer to ideal great-circle courses. In practice weather conditions frequently make a deviation from such courses either necessary or desirable and in any event, the pattern of intercontinental travel by air now looks startlingly like the pattern of intercontinental travel by way of the sea. Admittedly the future may bring changes but at the present time there is a rather amusing parallel as anyone can observe for themselves by looking at a reliable series of maps showing world transport systems.

Transatlantic air travel is an established aspect of modern living. These international services are steadily improving with respect to safety, reliability and volume of service. Short of a catastrophic war it is difficult to see what condition might arise that would prevent their continued growth. The other conspicuous features of air travel are luxury services, speed, a certain amount of flexibility and along with these factors a natural ability to meet emergency situations.

The ferrying of supplies to China over the "Hump" during the last war, the air lift to Berlin, the supply of materials to Korea and the return of the wounded from Korea to the United States are all examples of the extraordinary services that can be performed by aircraft in emergencies. Naturally, such services are possible only through extraordinary efforts of organization, extraordinary devotion of individuals to the enterprise and extraordinarily high costs. In warfare the huge costs of delivering troops, equipment and supplies by air may be justified; they may even represent national economy if they avoid defeat or win victory.

Military marvels, however, are hardly precedent for what reasonably may be expected under the condition of normal healthy growth. Air travel and air transport are still luxuries and special services operating in what must be regarded as a rather specialized field in the general economy. The cost to the individual of air passage to or from Europe is, to be sure, now comparable to rather superior first-class ocean passage but these are not true costs in either class of travel for the true costs are concealed in a multiplicity of economic and political factors including both direct and indirect subsidies.

In a sense air travel across the Atlantic is now competing with steamship travel, but the steamship lines appear, year after year, to be doing a good normal business and there is as yet no evidence that the gain in air travel is won at the expense of steamer operation even in first-class services. Given an adequate defense of the Atlantic and a period of even reasonable peace and prosperity, there appears to be no inherent reason why air travel should not turn out to be a supplement to rather than a substitute for ocean passenger services. The healthy international economy about the Atlantic may, in the future, demand the best in all types of services.

When it comes to the matter of the transportation of goods, it will be a long time before air services fill any appreciable part of the general international demand for transport. Here cost is the greatest single consideration. Ocean freights formerly carried in sailing ships are now carried in steam and motor vessels and have each in their various times been the greatest in volume and the lowest in cost of all transport services.

It is axiomatic that, per ton mile, transportation of goods on the sea has always been and is today a small fraction of the cost of transporting goods on land. The ocean freighters and the humble freight train share the honor of being mankind's most indispensable servants. Upon them, in peace and in war, depends the whole structure of the modern world.

Chapter 25

ATLANTIC WARFARE TODAY

IN New York, London, Paris and other capitals of the
world, on January 1, 1900, a new century was ushered in by celebra-
tors who looked forward with bright curiosity, with enthusiasm,
with confidence. There had been a long period of relative peace and
prosperity and of growing trade all about the Atlantic. Popular education was making great strides; social conditions were often bad but
it was only a matter of time until they would improve under the attack of a new generation of social workers. Industrial relations could
be improved by intelligent trade unionism, enlightened management
and scientific control. Surgery, medicine, public health were beginning to make progress against ill health and disease—in this campaign tuberculosis, "the great white plague," was public enemy number one. In the new century man was to achieve many goals through
energetic and intelligent action: social progress through better legislation; industrial prosperity through improved management, ease
and happiness through mechanical and scientific progress. Peace was
to be achieved through the ever expanding and strengthening web of
international trade and international good manners. Someday this
would lead perhaps to international courts and laws.

In this program there were admittedly occasional hitches, interruptions, even wars. There was the little affair between the United
States and Spain, and the British had counterparts in the Boer War,
the Afghan War, etc. These were regarded as temporary and remote

affairs taking place somewhere on the fringes of civilization. When the Japanese launched an unprovoked and unannounced war against Russia the explanation was that though they had been very quick in absorbing Western mechanical progress they had been a little slow in catching on to Western social and ethical ideas. The development of a major war among Christian countries was regarded as a remote improbability.

Today it is hard to recover the feeling of confidence and hope that marked the beginning of the century. Yet though we may smile at some of its vain and naïve expressions, the spirit of the early part of the century has a strong survival value and is not beaten yet. From 1890 to 1914 there was a great period of expansion and construction. We are, in fact, still engaged in a struggle testing the institutions and relationships then established.

At the time the critics and doubters were few. The main thing was to get on with the job—extend the railroads, run faster trains, build bigger and faster ships, open up new mines, explore new territories.

To express its pride in progress and its confidence in the future, the Western World held a number of international expositions or world's fairs at the beginning of the century. There was the Paris Exposition in 1901 with a moving sidewalk that carried people all around the exposition grounds. Horseless carriages were seen on the avenues of Paris and people who rode in the captive balloon could look down on the people who were riding to the top of the Eiffel Tower.

In England Queen Victoria, who had celebrated her diamond jubilee in 1897, lived on into the new century and was succeeded by her aging son, Edward VII, who, despite his long years of waiting, took up the responsibilities of the throne with energy as well as social grace.

In Germany the new emperor, the energetic and aggressive William II, had forced Bismarck into retirement and had progressively revised or displaced the Bismarck policies. At the beginning William showed considerable aptitude and tact in social and political organization. Under his rule German industry and trade expanded enormously. Germans everywhere were recognized for the ingenuity and inventiveness of their science, the scope and thoroughness of their scholarship. On the Atlantic the liners of the North German Lloyd and the Hamburg-American began to rival the best that the English builders and operators could do. All of these things seemed to disguise or excuse the fact that Germany was at the same time endlessly, untiringly and rigidly building up a large navy and the most ruthless war machine the world had yet seen.

In America President McKinley was attending an exposition in Buffalo when he was assassinated on September 14, 1901 and Theodore Roosevelt, lately the colonel of Rough Riders, succeeded to the presidency. Energetic, tireless, patriotic, he once gave utterance to the motto, "Speak softly but carry a big stick." There were times when he forgot the first part of this injunction but he kept the stick by him all the years he was in the White House. In the program and purposes of his administration Roosevelt incorporated three projects designed to give the United States a more secure position in the Atlantic. These were: the building up of an adequate merchant marine, the building of the Panama Canal and the rehabilitation and increase of the United States Navy.

If in the first of these projects he met with no success at all you may be sure this was due neither to lack of desire nor energy on his part. It was just the old American preoccupation with work and wealth ashore; neither labor nor capital found it inviting to go to sea in competition with other seafaring people. Back in the 1890's people became alarmed because only 12.5 per cent of United States foreign commerce was carried in American bottoms and Congress passed two acts proposed by Senator Frye of Maine designed to strengthen the merchant marine. In the 1900's, after Frye and Roosevelt had done their best, the figure had dropped to less than 10 per cent.

The canal was largely a Theodore Roosevelt triumph even though it was not completed until years after he had left office. He showed how urgently it was needed in the Spanish war; how it would increase naval strength; benefit commerce; be of value to all nations. He judged the times and the opportunities; bought out the French failure; took advantage of local interests and the local revolt; selected and supported the right men and methods. In the matter of the navy he met both failure and success. He never got the advanced and efficient ships he knew the navy needed and he never got the department reorganized but he improved gunnery and morale and technical competence and in numbers he parleyed some dozens of obsolescent ships into a navy that stood next to Great Britain's in size.

There was much to be built into the new navy that had not previously found a place in the battleships; inventions and new ideas in naval warfare had been accumulating for over a century. Some of these remained undeveloped and many had not yet been tested in battle. There is a paradox about military defense that works to the disadvantage of democratic and free peoples and often gives an advantage to the determined aggressor. In times of peace Congress will not vote funds for adequate defense. In wartime, when the ships are essential to the lives of the people and the nation, the funds are suddenly voted but it is then too late to build the best and most effective ships. A warship cannot be hastily assembled; it is the most intricate and complex of all human structures.

Warship design had been changing. One of the reasons for the changes was an accumulating progress in the art of building and using guns, and the warship and the gun are interdependent instruments—the effectiveness of the one depending upon the effectiveness of the other. As early as 1824 a French gunnery expert named Henri J. Paixhans had introduced a revolution in gunnery when he designed shells and guns for firing shells. Up to this time guns had fired shot, which were simply solid masses of metal of various shapes and sizes. Shot were sometimes preheated so that they might set fire to a ship or any other target which they struck. The shell was a hollow projectile which carried an explosive charge and greatly increased the effectiveness of gunfire. Paixhans shells exploded on impact. The fuse which determined when and where a shell was to explode was a later development.

Though the shell gun was an important discovery in itself its value was enhanced in 1836 when Johann Dreyse in Prussia developed the so-called needle guns, an important feature of which was a safe and effective breech-loading device. The discovery that rifling in the barrel of a gun would improve the range and accuracy of fire was being applied by Sir Joseph Whitworth and W. G. Armstrong in 1855. In 1860 the Winchester repeating rifle appeared and two years later Richard J. Gatling patented and developed the rapid-firing gun. This was a clumsy forerunner of the machine gun and its first immediate use was in land warfare, but subsequently the ideas which it launched had an effect on naval gunnery and consequently on the character of naval vessels.

None of the ideas and inventions that we have mentioned here, and many others that were actually involved in the development of gunnery, found an instant and ready application. All of them went through many stages of adaptation and development. Thus the first

Paixhans gun to be mounted on a United States naval vessel was placed on *Fulton II* in 1837 but the old naval cannon throwing shot continued to be used for many decades after that time.

The arts and skills of gunnery were modified again toward the end of the century with the development of high explosives and of smokeless powder. As early as 1886 the French chemists were leading in these developments but again it took a lapse of some time for their inventions to become absorbed in effective naval use.

Different from the guns but related to them as a substitute or adjunct was the development by Robert Whitehead in 1866 of the first effective self-propelled torpedo. This gave rise to a whole succession of changes in naval architecture. First there was the fact that the torpedo required a launching device or tube. The original idea was that a special vessel was needed to store and handle the torpedoes and to carry or incorporate the launching tubes. This gave rise to the torpedo boat. The appearance of torpedoes naturally called for defensive measures such as nettings which could be hung outside the hull of the vessel to catch or arrest the torpedo before it could do damage to the hull. Another defensive measure was the idea of attacking torpedoes at their source through the construction and use of very rapid and nimble vessels called torpedo-boat destroyers. Presently torpedo tubes were mounted or incorporated in many varieties and sizes of vessels and the torpedo boat itself disappeared. Its enemy, that is the vessel to which it gave rise, dropped the "torpedo" part of its name but has continued to the present time a busy life as a "destroyer."

The submarine also had made its appearance. The idea was at least as old as Leonardo Da Vinci, who had sketched one along with his other fancies, and a one-man submarine had been built in America and tried unsuccessfully against the flagship of Lord Howe during the Revolution. The first submarines of sufficient size and power and ability to stay under water to be of practical value were constructed by a number of different inventors in the last decade of the nineteenth century.

The developments mentioned above relate to firearms and other methods of attack so they were bound to have an influence on the design of ships of war. The development of new fuels and new ways of utilizing power was also bringing about changes in naval warfare and the design of ships. The burning of oil instead of coal came by stages to be incorporated in naval vessels. The Parsons steam turbine and the oil engine of Rudolf Diesel both came into use before

1900 and found a place not only on liners and cargo vessels but in the fighting ships as well.

Scores of other inventions and discoveries came into the warships, some after delay and some by devious routes: Edison's incandescent light; Bell's telephone; Maxwell's and Hertz's radio waves (1885) which Marconi utilized for local signals (1895) and made into transatlantic wireless (1901); hydraulic and then electric elevators; machinery for moving and handling heavy weights. The list in full would be almost endless for nearly every development that is important in civilian life is either directly useful in naval structures or has some naval counterpart. Even the child's spinning top made a contribution to naval development: it suggested to Ludwig Obry the gyroscope (1896) and the gyroscope was used first to control the direction of torpedoes; later it was used to stabilize ships in rough waters; in the Sperry gyro-compass and "metal mike" or automatic steerer for ships and planes and in many other ways.

While it was true that such new devices were absorbed at a tardy and uneven pace it was also true that the unevenness sometimes included a big jump. The British took such a jump in 1906 when they floated upon the Atlantic the latest product of their shipyards, H.M.S. *Dreadnaught*. She was not only new—she was a surprise package. She was the largest (18,000 tons), fastest (twenty-one knots), most heavily armed (ten twelve-inch rifles) battleship afloat. Of course her importance was measured neither by speed nor size nor firepower but by the fact that the three qualities supported each other. The size would have made her an easy target without the speed; the heavy armament would have burdened a smaller vessel and been wasted in a slower one. Taken together the three superlatives reinforced each other. No other navy had afloat or building a vessel like her or anything else to rival her power. She gave her name to a new class of vessels—the Dreadnaughts—the all-big-gun ships.

This move brought forth a number of different responses, some of them characteristic. The immediate response was that many nations began building ships more or less along the *Dreadnaught* pattern. In addition to stepping up her big ship program, Germany began looking for alternative sources of strength. This led her to an even more intense program of army training and to the expenditure of special efforts on submarines and submarine warfare.

In the United States there could be no immediate response in terms of a building program, for this was peacetime and Congress kept all naval appropriations to a minimum. Theodore Roosevelt took what steps he could. He encouraged the navy in the study and development of a new program; he demanded better training of officers and many active exercises to improve gunnery; he ordered navy ships on a round-the-world cruise. He believed in activity and in publicity. If he could not have new ships he could at least put the ships he had on parade.

It was not a bad move. It was a way of saying in many ports of many nations that the U.S.A. had become a world power. The fleet was well received and in many quarters the tacit statement was accepted at its face value. It was also a way of waking America up to the fact that it had a navy and needed a navy. While news of the cruise was still ringing in the daily press another alarm also began dinging in American ears. *McClure's Magazine* opened the year 1908 with an article by Henry Reuterdahl exposing the defects of the navy ships of which the nation was beginning to be so proud. Reuterdahl had much general and also some special or inside information on naval programs and designs and many of his points were well taken and important: the ships were armored but the low placement of the armor plate rendered the ships vulnerable to enemy fire; the ships had too little freeboard resulting in the big guns being located at insufficient elevation so that passing waves and rolling of the ship would cut down the time during which they could be fired; turrets and handling equipment were poorly designed and so on through a list of technical errors. He attacked also the seniority system and bureau organization within the Navy Department. This and related articles aroused almost universal interest and gave rise to resounding debates. It provided Roosevelt with a fresh incentive for another attempt at Navy Department reorganization. The immediate program failed and Taft became President in 1909, but the nation had become aware that it had a problem of naval defense and commitments in many parts of the world to be protected. What Reuterdahl had said and Roosevelt had done affected naval policy and naval growth in the critical years leading to World War I.

There were, of course, a score of general or background reasons why the U.S.A. was almost certain to become involved in this war and why its interests lay with the Allies. Among these were many loosely defined but strong sympathies such as those due to racial descent and even family connection in England, Scotland, Ireland, France, Belgium; cultural, linguistic and intellectual ties with England; political sympathies and a sense of comradeship-in-arms shared with France; resentment at the disruption of the general peace joined with a general feeling that Germany was the aggressor; violation of law and morality in the unprovoked invasion of Belgium; disregard for other treaties; dislike of Prussian arrogance and Prussian philosophy, etc. None of these sympathies or feelings, however, were effective in bringing the United States into the struggle until an amazing series of immediate and concrete provocations had accumulated. Indeed Germany had to mismanage her campaign on a lavish and reckless scale in order to arouse a sluggish America to a consciousness of responsibility and danger.

For some time America's relation to the war was intellectual and emotional rather than active. Wilson believed it was his destiny to be the great peacemaker and he was correspondingly reluctant to appear as the head of a nation at war.

What America suffered first from the war was a restriction on her international commerce, interference with her ships on the high seas, sinking of ships and loss of American lives.

In 1914, at the beginning of the war, the British fleet in the North Sea numbered about twenty dreadnaughts based on Scapa Flow in the Orkneys and two ports in Scotland. The German fleet in North Sea ports counted only thirteen dreadnaughts. The Germans were not therefore disposed to risk a major engagement at sea. In August British cruisers raided Heligoland and the German cruisers came out to drive them off. Then Sir David Beatty, coming up with battle cruisers, sank three German ships. Later the German battle cruisers did well in an engagement at Dogger Bank (1915) and occasionally threw some shells at British ports like Yarmouth, Scarborough, etc. Meanwhile German ships in remote foreign ports put to sea and became wreckers and raiders. Admiral Graf von Spee, coming from Japan with the cruisers *Scharnhorst, Gneisenau* and *Nürnberg,* bombarded Papeete and ruined Fanning Island cable station. In company with other German vessels he won his way into the South Atlantic where he met three old British cruisers and sank two of them. Then he decided the Falkland Islands would make an easy target as he sailed by on his way home. He was wrong. A hastily assembled Allied fleet caught him there; four German ships were sunk and von Spee and his two sons lost their lives.

From the beginning Germany placed considerable confidence in the use of mines and of submarines, and when her efforts with surface craft proved fatal or turned out inconclusive she intensified her efforts in mines and submarines.

These activities soon reached Americans even though America had few merchant ships at sea. From the beginning Britain and France were severe in the matter of contraband and neutral shipping. Wilson protested and their interpretations, if altered at all, grew more rigid. On February 4, 1915, Germany declared a submarine blockade around the British Isles. Wilson protested. On March 28 a German submarine sunk *Falaba,* a passenger ship; May 1, an American ship, *Gulflight,* was sunk without warning and two Americans died; May 7, *Lusitania* was torpedoed by a German submarine and 1,198 were lost; 124 of them were Americans. Wilson sent diplomatic notes of protest to Germany but in a public speech at home said, "There is such a thing as a man being too proud to fight." Among Americans there was much debate as to the President's meaning. The Germans seem to have had no doubts for the sinking continued and Wilson's notes continued. Shooting war started in Europe in August 1914 and it was July 1915 before it occurred to Wilson to inquire how the army and navy might be strengthened. It was February 3, 1916, before he asked the country to build and support a strong navy. Congress spent eight months in talk before passing the Navy Bill in August 1916.

In May 1916 Germany, in response to more of Wilson's protests, agreed to respect neutral shipping and to warn merchant vessels before sinking them. On January 31, however, Germany changed her policy again. She had decided that her submarines could sink 600,000 tons of shipping per month and that this would starve England into defeat. She also decided that America might intervene but that even in that case she would be too late and too slow to produce any serious opposition. Germany announced unrestricted submarine warfare. In March 1917 five American merchant vessels were sunk by German submarines. By April 6, 1917, the President and Congress agreed a state of war existed between the United States and Germany.

At the time the United States entered the war the prospects for an ultimate Allied victory were not bright. On paper the Allies had many advantages. Overnight, on the declaration of war, the United States Navy became a part of the belligerent forces and though its building program had been neglected and though many of its ships were out of date, judged by the best European standards, the total number of vessels of the American and British fleets far exceeded the German Navy or any navy the Germans could possibly build. Likewise in merchant shipping the combined Allied resources seemed to be adequate for the movement across the Atlantic of men, foods and the materials of war, but that represented the crux of the entire war problem. The French, to hold the western front, depended in great measure on British support, not only on British troops to hold an important part of the front but also to supply its corresponding part of foods, arms, ammunition, etc. The ability of the British to maintain their section of the western war depended on shipping and the protection of shipping not only from the British Isles to the continent but from all the dominions and colonies also to the British Isles. On top of this the American contribution in turn depended on securing or building up adequate transatlantic transport with naval protection adequate to give the transport a reasonable prospect of safe arrival at the ports of Great Britain or of France.

On May 31 and June 1, 1916, the English Grand Fleet under Jellicoe and the German High Seas Fleet under Scheer met in the North Sea in the Battle of Jutland. The big ships in the major fleets might have come to blows but actually did not. Most of the actual fighting took place between the German battle cruisers under Hipper and the British battle cruisers under Admiral Beatty. In this engagement, though the Germans had fewer ships, they proved themselves superior in battle tactics and in gunnery so that with a loss of six small ships they destroyed six sizable British vessels. Had the large ships composing the major fleets actually met it was anticipated that the British would have inflicted serious losses on the Germans for they were superior in numbers and in firepower, but Scheer was able to effect an escape for his fleet.

In April 1917 the prospect of safe arrival of Allied shipping to the continent was not reasonable. In the submarine attack on merchant vessels, armed and unarmed, belligerent and neutral, the Germans had invented a new, ruthless and therefore effective type of warfare. The captains and crews of the vessels that were then crossing the Atlantic from various scattered points to converge on the British Isles were experiencing a new form of war about which they were poorly informed, for which they were ill-equipped and almost unarmed and in the conduct of which they were at this time without leadership.

The individual ships were left pretty much to their own devices and they pursued varied individual courses under the belief that in this way they presented less of a target to enemy attack. Special devices for detecting and combating submarines had not yet come into effective use. Through countless watches they scanned the horizon for the death-dealing enemy they had never seen and might never see, knowing that a growing toll of vessels like themselves had been hit without warning and sunk without trace.

In April 1917 the Germans had at least 120 submarines and this number was increasing month by month. In April 1917 875,000 tons of Allied shipping were sunk. This exceeded by almost one-half the rate which the Germans had set as a measure of assured victory.

People in the Allied lands were generally aware of a high rate of submarine sinkings but only the British Admiralty knew the exact record or the extent to which this threatened the health and strength of the British war effort. Once the American declaration of war was made the Admiralty lost no time in presenting the picture to Rear Admiral Wm. S. Sims in London so that he might fully inform Washington.

There was a desperate need for destroyers and for small fast anti-submarine craft that could be quickly built, for nobody had fore-seen the character and extent of unlimited submarine warfare. On April 14 Sims requested the maximum available number of destroy-ers. By May 24 six destroyers sailed from Boston under Commander J. K. Taussig and reported to Vice-Admiral Sir Lewis Bayly in Queenstown, Ireland, on May 4. This was a welcome addition to the thirteen coal-burning sloops which together with hastily assembled trawlers and drifters was all the force that Bayly had for the protec-tion of merchantmen sailing to Liverpool or entering the English Channel.

In an attempt to relieve the desperate situation five aged coal-burning destroyers were ordered to proceed from Manila to Gibraltar by way of the Suez Canal and made the trip successfully. The first fleet of destroyers from America was followed by seven submarines and a tender and by the fall of 1917 the American destroyer fleet, assisting the British, had increased to thirty. Because it was promptly delivered at the time it was most needed, this was one of the most effective contributions that America made to World War I.

Synchronizing with the arrival of the American destroyers, in May 1917 there came into use another effective antisubmarine device. This was the development of the convoy system for merchant ves-sels. Of course the convoy system had been known and effectively employed for centuries, but it took time to realize that it might be effectively employed against the submarine. There were, in fact, vio-lent objections raised against the idea: collected merchant ships could be an easy target for the submarines, the merchant ships would be too slow and they would fail to follow prescribed courses, etc. A trial convoy of eight-knot merchantmen was finally assembled at Gibraltar and, under destroyer protection, made the passage to England with perfect operation and without loss of a vessel.

Other defenses against the submarine developed rapidly. The "depth charge" demonstrated its value and came into wider and more effective use. In essence, the depth charge was simply a large steel drum filled with high explosives. This was detonated by a device set to go off at a predetermined pressure and therefore, of course, at a predetermined depth. A considerable number of depth charges were mounted at the stern of destroyers and other vessels and simply plopped overboard by a light explosive charge. The depth charge was not a missile and it was not necessary for it to hit a submarine in order to be effective. It was only necessary for the depth charge to explode in the water in the vicinity of the submarine in order to set up a shock wave sufficient to damage the plates of the underwater craft.

A number of other developments came along to make the use of the depth charge more effective and to build up a submarine defense complex. These elements included an increased use of destroyers for escort purposes, the use of large numbers of small high-speed antisubmarine vessels, the development and use of improved listening devices for detecting the noise of a submarine and therefore its location, the use of seaplanes and other aircraft for spotting submarines by air—radio being employed for contact between the aircraft and the antisubmarine surface vessel. Thus, for example, a seaplane and a number of antisubmarine vessels would jointly be assigned for the protection of a particular area of the ocean or coastline. When the airplane on patrol sighted a submarine it would use the radio to inform one or more of the antisubmarine boats as to the exact location and estimated depth of the submarine. The high-speed surface craft would then converge on this point and drop their depth charges or otherwise attack the vessel.

The Germans expected and the Allies feared that during the days of long sunshine which mark the spring in northern waters the submarines would sight their targets for many more hours and that consequently in May and June and the later summer months the toll of submarine sinkings would rise. Actually nothing of this kind happened even though the number of German submarines increased to

134. On the contrary, the American destroyers, the use of the convoy system and the other measures of submarine defense began to prove effective.

By October the number of submarine sinkings had dropped to 458,723 tons. This was encouraging even though by this time the total of sinkings had accounted for the loss of 8,000,000 tons of shipping. The Germans, however, were suffering losses. It was later ascertained that they had lost fifty submarines. This was a loss and a drain on resources that Germany could ill afford. By April of 1918, one year after American entry into the war and after the subs had established their record sinking, Allied shipping losses had dropped to 277,934 tons. The joint web of British and American defenses extended from the North Sea into the Mediterranean. The German unrestricted submarine warfare was proving itself a costly failure and America was in the war to stay to the bitter end.

As a part of its contribution to submarine defense the United States undertook the principal responsibility for laying a North Sea mine barrage. This involved the development of a new type subsurface mine and the conversion of steamers from the eastern seaboard of America into mine layers. These ships succeeded in placing a little less than 600,000 of these mines; the British in the meantime placing over 13,000. The mine barrage extended from Scotland to Norway—a distance of 250 miles. Hemmed in by the mines and chased by the aircraft and surface vessels, a trip on a German submarine could hardly be rated as a health cruise. It became increasingly difficult to man the remaining German submarines.

The American shipbuilding program was formulated as part of the answer to the submarine war but was slow and bungling in its approaches to the task of creating adequate ships and services. The Emergency Fleet Corporation got off to a bad start in projecting a program of wooden ship construction. The shipping board was therefore compelled to assemble ships by every conceivable means and from every conceivable source. Vessels were bought (233) from foreign nations, chartered (331) and seized (97) from the enemy, including the *Vaterland*, which became the *Leviathan*, a transport capable of accommodating 12,000 troops. One of the uses of this hastily assembled emergency fleet was to transport to Europe about half of the 2,000,000 men that America contributed to the war effort —the other half being transported in vessels of British registry.

During 1918 the Emergency Fleet Corporation began getting ships into the water under a revised building program. As though to atone for many mistakes and delays, this program was undertaken on a vast scale. In these plans standardization of design and prefabrication of parts of the vessels played a part. Thus, plants far from the sea could be utilized in the shipbuilding program. Shipyards were also increased. By 1919 there were 223 shipyards in the United States with a combined capacity of over 1,000 ways. At peak operation the yards employed 625,000.

It was not until after the conclusion of the war that the great shipyard at Hog Island succeeded in regularizing the flow of materials and hit its stride but it was then able to deliver two 7,500-ton ships a week. By 1921, when there was no longer need for such a vast armada, the shipping board had accumulated 1,792 vessels amounting to over 10,000,000 tons. The so-called "bridge of ships" to win the war had cost the shipping board and the nation over $3,000,000,000. Lack of foresight and delay accounted in great measure for the large size of the bill and the ineffectiveness of the expenditure.

Even though the cost of an adequate merchant marine to carry a substantial part of the country's trade in times of peace and to serve the armed forces in times of war might have involved considerable expenditures, it would have in the long run proved a great economy in either of the world war periods. Ships that must be acquired rapidly in order to save the nation's life are always expensive whether they are acquired by lease or by purchase or by a building program. At the close of the war there was no further use of "the bridge of ships" to win the war and many of them were put in moth balls; that is to say, anchored in large fleets in unused coastal waters where they could rust away in idleness.

By the fall of 1918 the pressure on Germany had built up to such a point that political changes within the country were inevitable. The unlimited submarine campaign had failed and after refusing an armistice Wilson, on October 21st, had secured from Germany a declaration that U-boats would no longer attack passenger ships. Germany was losing ground on the western front. The civil population was hungry and war weary and increasingly impressed by Wilson's fourteen-point surrender program. The emperor and a new chancellor, Prince Max von Baden, began making sweeping concessions with the object of winning an armistice before the western front collapsed.

Then on November 3 the fleet at Kiel, which had waited and fumed in idleness for so long, was shaken by mutiny and many ships scuttled and sunk. Ashore, workers went on strike, and the *Land-*

wehr troops revolted behind the lines. The emperor fled to Holland and after Germany had agreed to withdraw across the Rhine and other concessions, an armistice was signed on November 11, 1918.

At the time of the Paris Peace Conference it was clear that the United States had emerged from the war as a great naval and commercial power with a merchant marine second only to that of England. Britain was surprised and shocked and Wilson found that her views on naval affairs were as strong and tough as those of Clemenceau and Orlando on boundaries and armies ashore.

Naval disarmament and limitation were discussed at Paris without profitable result. However, by 1921 Harding was able to call a naval conference in Washington. By this time all the nations, with the possible exception of Japan, were clamorous in their pursuit of "normalcy" or peacetime pursuits and were anxious to cut down war expenditures and commitments. Prices were high and cumulative war debts enormous. Secretary of State Charles Evans Hughes opened the meeting by declaring that the United States would abandon its building program and scrap fifteen battleships, representing 845,700 tons; England was to lop off 583,370 tons and Japan 448,928 tons. The United States was thus generously offering to cut its lead in capital ships. A final agreement provided a ratio among the leading nations, i.e., Britain, U.S.A., Japan, France and Italy of 5-5-3-1.7-1.7. Joined to a Four Power Treaty to preserve the peace in the Pacific and a Nine Power Treaty covering an "open door" policy in China, the prospect of reduced armaments seemed quite real. The trouble was that the United States had sacrificed her outstanding position in capital ships but gained little, for there was no agreement made on cruisers, destroyers, submarines, etc. Later, in 1927, a further conference on naval matters called at Geneva to cover the lesser ship categories bogged down in disagreements. In 1929 a London conference resulted in a nominal 15-15-9 ratio on capital ships for England, U.S.A., Japan, and some control program for lesser ships, but France and Italy came to no agreement and did not sign. No doubt these treaties were in part effective but their limited and partial character doomed them to ultimate failure. It was also an ironical fact that the great depression which began with the stock market crash in 1929 exercised a more austere control over naval programs than any international agreements and in the United States a "treaty navy" did not come into existence until the world was again at war.

At the time of the complete defeat and surrender of Germany it appeared as though the last resistance to the Allied cause and triumphant democracy had been overcome. The war-weary world was disposed to ignore, neglect and forget the tyranny and terror that the Bolsheviks were busily instituting in Russia.

However, the weakened and disunited states of Central Europe offered attractive fields for the progressive exploitation and conquest of determined fascist and communist tyrants. Czechoslovakia was from the first beset by racial and minority problems of her own and it was the three million or so Sudeten Germans she had absorbed who provided an excuse for the Hitler invasion. No League of Nations saved her, but her fate and that of Poland finally showed England and France the importance of resistance to Hitler.

Within a few hours of the declaration of war by England a German submarine torpedoed and sank the *Athenia*. The *Athenia* was a passenger vessel, westbound from Scotland, heavily laden with American tourists returning from Europe. This was open evidence of Germany's continued belief in the effectiveness of unrestricted submarine warfare.

As once before in history, the first reaction of Uncle Sam was to put his hands in his pockets and try to preserve his balance on an island of neutrality that was rapidly being washed away from under his feet.

In October a Pan-American Conference proclaimed a safety zone of 300 miles around the shores of the western continents and declared a general neutrality. The United States had already imposed an embargo on the shipment of all arms to belligerents which greatly embarrassed France and England who, in good faith, had ordered arms and equipment from the United States before the declaration of war when they were both neutral countries. It was November before Congress passed and the President signed an amendment permitting the delivery of arms on a "cash-and-carry" basis. This meant not only that the free European countries had to pay for their war goods on delivery but also that delivery had to be made in their own vessels.

At the same time American merchant vessels were forbidden to arm themselves or to enter a belligerent port. American citizens were barred from combat zones. Submarine captains, however, could not read and cared not whether the vessel they attacked was armed or unarmed, neutral or belligerent. This time the submarine war was conducted on an enormous scale. The German submarine ranged everywhere, at various times staging raids off the American coast and entering the Caribbean, and in June, 1942, a German submarine even landed eight enemy agents on Long Island.

The effectiveness of the submarine campaign so far as the British were concerned is reflected in the following figures: when the war started the British merchant fleet accounted for a trifle less than 18,000,000 gross tons; an additional 8,000,000 had been captured from the Axis. Over 26,000,000 tons might be considered an impressive and satisfactory fleet were it not for the fact that 4,000,000 tons were continually in demand by the British army and navy for their own purposes. The remaining vessels were everywhere in demand. As the war progressed and Poland fell, Denmark and Norway were invaded, Holland, Belgium and France successively occupied by the German army, England was cut off from many sources of supply of foods and raw materials that were customarily open to her. The Mediterranean was unsafe and routes to the east led again around South Africa. In fact, no waters were then safe from submarine attack.

Before 1941 the British had lost over 5,000,000 tons of shipping. At this time British ships were being sunk faster than the replacement rate of all British shipyards combined. Great Britain then ordered sixty ships built in American yards according to an old and familiar British pattern on which the American publicity methods fastened the name of "Liberty" ships. Fortunately under the Maritime Commission the pace of American shipbuilding was experiencing an acceleration of its own. In January 1941 Roosevelt asked for an additional 200 Liberty ships.

That Britain could benefit from the increased rate of American shipbuilding was assured in March by the so-called Lend-Lease Bill under which any country could receive by sale, transfer, exchange or lease, any articles required for its defense provided that the President deemed that the defense of that country was vital to the defense of the United States.

In the meantime, while the ships were being built, steps were also gradually being taken which improved the defense against submarine attack. On September 3, 1940, Roosevelt announced the completion of an executive agreement under which fifty American destroyers of a type used in World War I had been given to Britain in exchange for the right to build and operate naval and air bases in British possessions in the Western Hemisphere. Protective sea and air patrols were already in operation along the seaboard of the United States.

The acquisition of the new bases at once permitted the extension of this defensive patrol for the bases extended from Newfoundland to Bermuda, into the Bahamas, to St. Lucia, Antigua, Trinidad and British New Guinea. This at once had the effect of moving the protective defenses of the shores of the United States hundreds of miles out to sea. American ships and planes operating from these bases could develop a patrol over the whole western half of the Atlantic basin. When, on their patrols, the planes and warships detected a German submarine, they would naturally notify their respective bases by wireless and there was nothing to prevent the British ships or shore stations from overhearing such reports.

In April of '41 the United States reached an agreement with Denmark under which the former became responsible for the defense of Greenland in exchange for the right to construct air and naval bases, and in July Iceland asked the United States to supply them with adequate defense, relieving the British who, up to this time, had been providing these services. Under these arrangements, air and naval base facilities were constructed in Iceland. These two agreements again extended the continental defenses. A glance at the map will show that ships operating from these bases could maintain patrol over the western Atlantic far from the American shores in a most effective manner. Patrols of aircraft operating from these bases benefited even more in the extension of the area which they had under effective observation. All the effective sea routes were comprehended in these patrols.

Many developments had come into the field to make submarine defenses more effective. The speed of destroyers and other vessels protecting convoys had been stepped up, their armament intensified; the small but extremely light and fast PT boats had come into the picture; listening devices for the detection of submarines had been greatly improved; a special outgrowth of wireless telegraphy or radio had gradually been nursed into a new device called "radar."

Way back in the 1920's two young experimentalists, Dr. Albert Taylor and Leo C. Young, working in Washington with high-frequency radio signals, had observed that when their instruments were placed on opposite sides of the river the passage of a ship deflected or disturbed their signals. After a little reflection they concluded that such deflection of their signals might be used for the detection of enemy ships passing between two vessels equipped with the proper instruments. No attention was paid to their report but fortunately the building of a new naval research laboratory permitted them to continue their experiments. Later they were involved in the building of an aircraft landing system which also required the use of high-frequency emissions. Again they observed that their emissions were disturbed by an airplane flying within the field.

It was already known that the Kennelly-Heaviside layer of the atmosphere had the effect of bouncing back or returning certain types of radio signals, high-frequency emission being especially susceptible. It was not necessary to transmit signals from one ship or station to another. Signals could be sent out from one ship in all directions and, when picked up on their return, could be made to show on a luminous screen a pattern of the objects by which they had been deflected in their flight.

Experimental radar was installed on the USS *Leary* in April 1937 and a finished set was installed on the USS *New York* in December 1938. Radar had the advantage of operating day and night through any kind of weather and eventually of bringing in signals and patterns over long distances. It gave rise to many various devices for detecting enemy ships and planes of all types and even for training and firing guns at an unseen enemy.

Surface vessels and aircraft co-operated in the detection and destruction of enemy submarines, and the battle finally swung in favor of the submarine defenses. However, before this happened the toll of shipping had been tremendous. In 1939 the world tonnage for merchant ships was 68,500,000. Of this amount a half was destroyed in the course of the next five years. Though aircraft and other means gave able assistance in this destruction, the major part of it was attributable to the submarines. Finally the defense became an offense. The enemies of the submarines were now not only the destroyers but the destroyer escorts, the frigates and the corvettes. Seaplanes were less in use but they had been replaced by long-range aircraft. Aircraft were no longer confined to flights from land stations but were based on mobile carriers.

In 1944 this warfare on the submarine had reached such a state of development that two German submarines were sunk for every merchantman that they were able to torpedo. This was a ratio that not even the Germans could stand. It is estimated that Germany lost a total of 713 submarines, 100 of which were attributed to mines laid by the British Bomber Command and to other types of destruction where the record was imperfectly known. Of the remaining 613 there was a rough balance between those sunk by ships and those sunk by aircraft. It is interesting to note that in twenty-six cases one submarine sank another submarine.

At the end of the war the Germans were developing the *schnör-kel* or breather-tube submarine which could draw air for crew and motors through an extensible pipe while still running submerged. This late development was incorporated in a submarine that had a higher than usual rate of speed when on the surface of the water and also when submerged. It had no effect on the late war but the pattern or patterns to which it gave rise will undoubtedly prove important in any war of the future.

While the submarine war was developing and being brought to its fortunate conclusion many other forms of warfare were simultaneously being conducted on the Atlantic and on the Continent. The submarine war and these other forms of war were definitely related in the sense that the other wars could not be won, in fact they could not even be vigorously pursued until the menace of the German submarine had been reduced and controlled. Thus the air patrols operating from Norway, working jointly with submarines lurking beneath the surface of the sea, took a heavy toll of the convoys carrying goods and supplies to the Russian ports from Iceland.

Other important sea lanes were similarly harassed. Prolongation of the submarine war could have delayed American assistance to the war in Europe in a serious and possibly even in a critical way. As it worked out, however, it took some time to accumulate effective American participation and during this time the submarine threat was abated, but until the submarine war was won it would have been impossible to stage the American landing in North Africa or the delivery of the American Army in England.

During the war there were many spectacular occurrences in which naval vessels were involved and the navy and marine corps were indispensable to the successful conduct of the most important operations but there were few naval engagements of the old pattern.

British naval forces made a gallant effort to assist Norway during the German invasion of 1940. This began in February with the rescue of over 300 prisoners of war from the German ship *Altmark*. On April 8 the French and British announced that they had mined the waters of southern Norway to prevent the passage of German vessels. Nonetheless the German attack one day later was successfully carried out by sea-borne troops as well as those carried by air. Important coastal cities such as Oslo, Bergen, Trondheim, etc., were occupied. Despite the surprise of the attack, Norway put up a good resistance and the operation cost Germany four cruisers and four troopships. The Norwegians drove the Germans out of Trondheim and Bergen.

In mid-April British naval units staged a raid on Narvik, sinking all the enemy ships in that harbor and occupying the town until the second week in June.

In the meantime an Anglo-French expedition in southern Norway was less successful, having to withdraw in the early part of May. These were gallant efforts but doomed to failure because they were hastily improvised and therefore poorly supported whereas the combined German attacks by land and sea were based on plans developed months, probably even years, before they were executed.

About the time the naval units were being withdrawn from Narvik, naval and all other resources of the British were being taxed to the utmost to evacuate the British, French, Belgian and Polish forces marooned on the beaches at Dunkerque. Between May 28 and June 4 215,000 British and 120,000 French were returned to England. Naval vessels protected this operation and assisted in it. However, the navy did not have available either the numbers of ships or the types of ships required for such a transport operation. The size of the ships that could be used were strictly limited because of the lack of port facilities; a great number of small ships and boats were required. Transportation was improvised and every kind of craft that could keep afloat and be propelled across the Channel by any means whatsoever was pressed into service.

The collapse and capitulation of France created some serious questions about the integrity of the Atlantic defenses not only in London but also in Washington. For whatever it might be worth, the United States obtained from Marshal Petain, the nominal ruler of all that was left of France, a promise that the French Navy would never be surrendered to the Germans. Nor was the loss of the French Navy the only problem that worried America. At this time it was generally known that the German High Command was developing plans for the invasion of the British Isles. Twenty-five divisions were involved in these plans. The success of the *Blitzkrieg* in Poland, Belgium, France raised the possibility that Britain would be invaded if not conquered. In this case what would happen to the British Navy? In what proportions might it be captured, sunk, surrendered or saved by flight?

Faced with such possibilities the country suddenly awoke to the need and advantage that resided in an adequate navy and on July 20, 1940, Congress passed a bill calling for a two-ocean navy.

So far as the French fleet was concerned, a partial answer was given in July when the British Navy staged an attack on the port of

Oran in North Africa. It was anticipated that the French officers were sympathetic with the British and with the resistance forces headed by General Charles de Gaulle, then in London. When surrender was refused the British sank three ships and captured the remainder of the French fleet.

The fate of the British Navy at this juncture was determined not by its own activity but by that of the Royal Air Force. Here was another example of a situation where one type of warfare had to be solved before another type could swing into action. While the English and German fighter planes and bombers were flashing back and forth across the Channel in almost continuous raids, no self-respecting naval vessel of either side wanted to be caught in these waters.

The Battle of Britain which was fought day and night in the air lasted until the end of October. Estimates vary but in general it appears that somewhere around 2,400 German planes were destroyed, which this time contrasted with the loss of 800 British planes. The loss of life and of property in Britain had been very severe but the victory in the air was decisive. It was clearly demonstrated that Germany was not going to establish aerial control over the Channel and that without that control she could not hope to succeed in an invasion.

Occasionally small naval engagements turned up in various widely scattered parts of the world to illustrate the widespread character of modern warfare. A familiar name turned up in the news in December 1939. Many who were alive during World War I remembered the gallant fight to the death of Admiral Spee when he was cornered in the Falkland Islands. In his memory a large German warship had been christened the *Graf Spee* and assigned to operations in the South Atlantic. After receiving some severe damage in an engagement with British cruisers she made for the port of Montevideo. Finding no refuge here her commander preferred to blow her up rather than to surrender her.

An individual German battleship surprised the world again in the spring of 1941. The British believed that they had the major elements of the German fleet surrounded, cut off from the open Atlantic and under almost continuous observation. However, on May 24, one of the largest and newest of German battleships, the *Bismarck,* eluded the blockade and made her presence felt by sinking the British dreadnaught *Hood.* The *Bismarck* escaped from the action and for a time it appeared that the British forces had completely lost contact with her. However, she was relocated and sunk by a combined naval and air attack on May 27.

The new phase of Atlantic naval warfare—in fact, of naval warfare anywhere—made its first appearance in 1942. Briefly put this was the use of concentrated navy units to support a massive landing and invasion of enemy-held territory. This has been called an amphibious operation but usually involves a concerted attack by sea, land and air forces. In such undertakings the purpose of the naval action is not primarily to attack or sink the vessels of another navy, though this may be incidentally involved, but to destroy the enemy's shore installations and to lay down a screen of fire under the protection of which the landings may be effected. An operation of this kind involves the use of ships of all sizes and purposes from the largest battleship to inflatable rubber boats, including new and specially devised craft such as those designed to carry and land tanks, combat personnel, ammunition, supplies, etc.

The first operation of this kind took place on November 8, 1942, and involved a concerted landing and invasion of a large strip of coast in French North Africa. This extended from Oran and Algiers at the Mediterranean end to Safi, which is 125 miles south of Casablanca, at the Atlantic end. It is said that before spreading out to take their positions for this attack the combined task forces covered over twenty-five square miles of sea area. The movement of the American forces and the British forces had to be carefully timed, co-ordinated and integrated. The difference in scale between this and the historic types of naval operation may be judged from the fact that, counting the warships, transports and cargo vessels, over 850 ships were involved in the operation. Obviously the planning of such an operation required both speed and patience and the decision to invade North Africa had been made by the joint chiefs of staff four months before it was carried out.

There was some resistance on the part of the French at Fedala and Casablanca but this was overcome within a few days. Resistance petered out after Admiral Jean François Darlan, who was the commander in North Africa for Petain's government, was designated by the Americans as the continuing commander of the French forces in North Africa. In exchange for this recognition Darlan ordered the termination of resistance. The task of the operation, however, was by no means over.

The Germans, in retaliation for their losses, sent troops into "Unoccupied France." The part of the French fleet that had not been disposed of at Oran had been guarded in the harbor of Toulon. Here the officers sank their vessels in preference to having them fall into the hands of the advancing Germans.

Besides their total occupation of France the Germans made a last desperate effort in their submarine war against the supplies that now were continuously needed in Russia, Britain and North Africa. To maintain the forces in North Africa and to permit their successful advance, each soldier required one and one-half tons of supplies each month. In the first three months after the North African invasion 800 ships were engaged in transporting 6,500,000 tons of supplies and equipment.

The number of vessels involved in the North African operations seem modest when compared with those that were required to stage the next landing and invasion operation. This took place in stages— the first stage being the landing and occupation in Sicily on July 10, 1942, which involved the use of over 2,500 vessels. There were no ports in Sicily and no landing facilities for handling even a sizable fraction of this enormous flow of men and materials. The whole movement depended on new and revised techniques of a landing operation. More and more landing craft had been built and put into use. Floating piers had been prefabricated and were assembled on the spot. The rest of the month of July and all of August was devoted to the thorough occupation of Sicily and to preparation for the next phase which came on September 3 with the brief step from Sicily to the Italian mainland.

The conquest in Italy proceeded but progress on the whole was slower than anticipated. The advance up the peninsula in bad weather and over rugged territory stalled at Cassino. A second landing of troops was successfully carried out at Anzio but the invading forces were hemmed in largely by reason of the dogged resistance of the Germans. Even after the Italian forces surrendered and the Italian fleet fled to the Allied side, the German forces in Italy maintained a strong resistance.

These difficulties in Italy increased the need for a plan that had already been under discussion, namely a more direct drive on Germany to be made by invasion of the French coast. This was not an easy move to contemplate for the Germans had been busy creating along the Atlantic coast structures for both offensive and defensive operations. The offensive structures included gun emplacements, launching platforms for "buzz bombs" and rockets, landing fields for aircraft, etc. Among the defensive structures were fortifications, pillboxes, barbed wire entanglements, barricades and ditches against tanks, a man-trap to catch parachute troops, etc.

The growing strength of these German preparations demanded speed from the Allies if their invasion was not to face insurmountable obstacles. At the same time the invasion could not be undertaken without enormous increases in amphibious trucks and specialized landing craft. Also, before the invasion could be undertaken the American participating forces together with all their supplies and equipment had to be ferried across the Atlantic.

This operation commenced toward the end of the year 1943 and proceeded at the rate of 150,000 men a month together with food, weapons and supplies; not only those that were immediately needed but those that would be required in the final invasion itself. By June 1944 1,500,000 American soldiers together with all their arms and supplies had been landed on the British Isles. The only elements of the invasion force that did not have to be shipped across the Atlantic were the planes which were ferried over by way of Newfoundland, Iceland and Scotland. However, this ability of the planes to get themselves to Europe was far from relieving the pressure on ocean transport, for large fleets of tankers had to transport the gasoline that those planes were to use and cargo ships had to carry the bombs that they expected to drop on the enemy.

On top of this the convoys of tankers and of cargo ships required naval protection. General Dwight Eisenhower was the supreme commander of the Allied Expeditionary Force while Admiral Sir Bertram Ramsey of the Royal Navy was in charge of the naval operations including the American naval contribution which numbered over 100,000 officers and almost 2,500 warships and landing craft.

The prelude to the operation was some days of intensive aerial bombing of the German installations in France. The operation itself began at 2 A.M., June 6, 1944, when three air-borne divisions were landed in Normandy with orders to disrupt all types of communications serving the Germans in that area. An hour later heavy bombers began flying over the beaches dropping high explosives and clearing the way for the landing. Mine sweepers moved in to clear the Channel and the approaches to the beaches so that the naval vessels could move in and commence bombarding the coast. At dawn the actual landing operations commenced. The warships supplied shellfire and rocketfire to protect the landing, to which was added a continuous cover of fighter planes.

Despite the huge scale of the plan, preparation and execution the first forces to land were hampered by German machine gun and mortar fire. This was gradually suppressed by fire from the ships and wave after wave of troops were landed on the beaches—the landing ships and cargo carriers maintaining a steady ferry service between the Normandy beaches and the English ports.

Artificial ports of two types were constructed to assist in the landing operations. The larger type, called "Mulberries," were made by floating concrete caissons into position and sinking them. The Mulberries were equipped with floating pierheads, and floating causeways connected them with the shore. They were built on such a scale that they could accommodate ocean-going vessels. Multiple smaller harbors to accommodate smaller vessels were built out of damaged or obsolete warships and merchantmen and were known as "Gooseberries."

Day after day these improvised ports were in use and the landing and supply operation proceeded as was anticipated until June 18, when a three-day gale hit the Channel, interrupted operations and destroyed some of the harbors. This speeded the determination to attack Cherbourg, which was carried out on June 25 by a combined sea and land attack. Despite the fact that the port of Cherbourg had been wrecked and mined by the Germans it began to be of some service in the early part of July and supplemented the enormous traffic that was still flowing over the beaches.

The invasion beaches extended for sixty miles—the naval bombardment to establish control of this area involved eighty warships firing 800 large guns. Air control was supplied by the United States Eighth and Ninth Air Forces and the British Royal Air Force and involved the use of 10,000 planes.

Despite the success of the landing in North Africa and in Sicily, the German General Staff continued to believe that a beachhead type of invasion of such volume and so well sustained was impossible. Their defensive preparation had chiefly been made at the ports. Their lack of imagination cost them the war. By the end of July the invasion forces began a concerted advance inland. Shortly thereafter other ports such as Dieppe in August and Le Havre in September fell into Allied hands. The beaches of Normandy had served their purpose.

This brief account indicates some of the features of war as it has been fought in the Atlantic of our time. Were a new war to develop in the Atlantic today it would have features that are not reflected in this account. Some of these were first developed and used against Japan in America's continuation of World War II in the Pacific.

Among these was the use of a carrier task force as an element in an amphibious landing; the use of the Construction Battalions, or "Sea Bees," as a part of such operation. Their task was to create or improve harbor facilities, construct emergency landing strips and larger airports, etc., and finally, of course, the handling, transport and delivery of the atomic bomb.

The schnorkel submarine is a development that originated with the the Germans but has since passed both to Russia and to the United States. However effective the development of the schnorkel submarine may be it will undoubtedly be replaced by the atomic submarine. It seems sure that an atomic submarine would participate in any future Atlantic wars.

The use of atomic power for carriers and for aircraft is already under discussion and may shortly be under development and construction. Beyond this, what effects new inventions might have on some future Atlantic war we can only conjecture. Much is shrouded in necessary national secrecy and much will depend on the timing of the event.

Instruments of war are often developed and put into use for a number of years and then neglected in favor of some newer development only to find a place in some later war. Apparently there are fashions in arms as well as in clothes. Rocket propulsion seems to have figured in some of these fashions. The principle of rocket propulsion was first discovered in China, then passed to India where in the eighteenth century it was used against the British. A British army officer improved the design and brought it to Europe and then to America where it appeared in the War of 1812. After lying idle for the better part of a century it came into use again in World War II.

Small rockets fired in salvos were extensively and effectively used by the United States Navy in support of amphibious landing operations. The very large-size long-range military rocket was, however, first developed and used by the Germans. Rockets of a type called the "V2" were used in the bombardment of the British Isles.

Since then some of the German rocketeers have passed under Russian control. Dr. Wernher von Braun and some of the others have come to America and become a part of the American Rocket Research Program. Guided missiles and long-ranged rockets have developed to such a degree that they would almost certainly form a part of any present war in the Atlantic and would have an effect on the character of its development and operation.

For obvious and good reasons we do not know the exact present status or the present products of the research and development programs in rockets, guided missiles and other related instruments that might be used in war. The most ambitious plans concern the establishment of a permanent station in space which could be occupied by human beings. Obviously such a station in space would be of incalculable value as a center for scientific research in time of peace and offer a decisive advantage in time of war. It requires some imagination to picture and write about a man-made station in space. Much more difficult to understand and to describe are the elusive but pervasive elements that have entered into the science of our time and have also found a place in military and naval arms.

One of these elusive developments is the extensive and increasing use of automatic, usually electronic, devices which can be used as substitutes for human direction and control of machines or processes. In their simplest forms these are called "servo mechanisms." A servo mechanism might be used to determine when and how far a valve should be opened or closed. A familiar form of servo mechanism would be a thermostat that controls the operation of your furnace.

Servo mechanisms have been extensively used in aircraft; in fact, without servo mechanisms it would be almost impossible for a crew to operate a modern bomber. In recent years they have grown up and been transformed into very complicated devices. In one direction they have led into the field of machines that perform mechanical operations—the calculating machines and the so-called "mechanical brains."

The problems of the army and the navy and the air corps have absorbed a large proportion of the time of these machines as fast as they could be constructed. Recently machines have become available but are especially devoted to business research, to control of industrial processes and for many special uses. In the military and naval fields also special devices have been developed not only to calculate and plot but also to completely control the flight of aircraft, guided missiles, etc. Joined with the use of radar, such machines are able, in the black of night, to detect a target and direct against it the fire of a gun or the maneuvering of a whole airplane or a vessel.

Undoubtedly the "push-button" war that was under discussion some years ago still lies somewhere in the indefinite future, but machines already built are daily assisting man in naval research in arriving at quick and reliable decisions in the conduct of maneuvers, in the direction and control of vessels, the fire of vessels, the handling and operation of carrier-based aircraft, etc. All these things would inevitably be a part of any Atlantic warfare waged today.

Chapter 26

ATLANTIC HEALTH, WEALTH AND SANITY

WHAT is the value of an ocean?

This is a big question and one that it is possible to answer in various ways. One way is to rephrase the question. What is there in the ocean that man finds valuable?

A hasty answer might be, "I can find nothing in sea water—it's free —it has no value because there is so much of it."

This is too hasty an answer. Actually, though it cannot be seen, sea water contains, dissolved within itself, practically every mineral or chemical that man finds valuable including silver, gold, uranium, etc., and there is so much sea water that the sum total of what is dissolved in the sea becomes a fabulous storehouse of value. If all the solids that are dissolved in the ocean waters were suddenly dropped out of them, or as the chemists say precipitated, the amount in metric tons of these solids could be expressed by the figure five with sixteen zeros following it. This would form a layer on the crust of the earth of forty-five meters or about 150 feet; or, if the solid matter were squeezed out of the ocean and deposited only on the land, the layer would be 153 meters thick or roughly 500 feet.

Now man judges the value of his things in gold and silver which he uses in his currency. Therefore the amount of gold and silver in the sea might give us one way of judging its value. First, it would appear that the precious metals were very poorly represented in sea water. A rough calculation would seem to establish, however, in there being over 8,500,000 tons of gold floating around in the oceans. With gold at $35 per ounce, this would give a value of $9,520,000,000,000. The silver in the ocean is represented by 426,000,000 tons and with silver at $.92 per ounce, this would represent a value of $12,541,440,-000,000.

This is a sizable value but nobody has made any money out of the gold and the silver in the sea except the confidence men who some years ago were able to interest gullible people in investing in secret methods for getting the gold out of sea water. In the laboratory gold can be extracted from sea water, but at present its recovery takes more equipment, time and energy than the gold is worth. Methods of recovering gold improve from time to time but long before it becomes profitable to extract precious metals from the ocean we will be taking out of sea water other less spectacular but more useful products.

For hundreds of years, people living along tidal lowlands in warm climates have found it profitable to extract salt from the sea by a process of evaporation. There are some modern industries that utilize sea water and extract products from it that have a commercial value. There is an older way of extracting chemicals from sea water which does not require as much of an initial investment and this is to let the plants and animals of the sea do the work for us. Thus there is a bony, oily, little fish, menhaden, that breeds rapidly and travels in great schools. Profitable enterprises have been established on catching these fish and converting them into fertilizer. There was formerly a profitable business in the extraction of iodine from marine growths. Large fields of kelp were harvested and processed and this was our chief source of iodine. More recently iodine has been discovered in salts and brines in the earth. These are undoubtedly the fossil remains of the seas of former geological ages.

Bromine is still extracted from the sea because that is where most of it is stored. In the sea it is found dissolved in the sea water and also in the bodies of plants and animals to which it imparts special colors. As found in the body of a shellfish called *murex* it formed the basis of one of the oldest and most widely used dyes, known to the ancient world as Tyrian Purple.

An extremely modern and growing industry is that based on the extraction from sea water of the light metal magnesium. Under certain conditions magnesium burns and gives off an intense light. It is, therefore, used in flares, flash powder and for tracer bullets, but it can also be produced in a more stable state as a lightweight metal and is then extensively used in the aircraft industry and in other places where extreme lightness is desirable.

The extraction of bromine dye from the shellfish *murex* and of iodine from the seaweeds are early and crude examples of the use of plants and animals in extracting chemicals from the sea. Already there has been talk of the possibility of raising and gathering the plankton of the sea so that they might serve as a source of food energy. Hardy, hungry and heroic souls like those on the raft *Kon-Tiki* have reported the use of plankton soup but I suppose it would be generally agreed that plankton were not a delicate and possibly dangerous diet for man. Presumably, therefore, plankton, algae and other lowly forms of life would be used as nourishment by some other plant or animal which in turn would be eaten by man.

Possibly this is neither so fantastic nor so far in the future as we would at first suppose. The micro biologists have already discovered a number of ways in which microscopic forms of life can be put to work in the service of man. They are willing servants not yet covered by Social Security and labor laws and on special processes more skillful chemists than men themselves. They have been put to work making chemical syntheses that have been proved to be difficult, expensive or impossible of attainment by other means.

At the present writing the latest census shows that the population of the world continues to grow at a surprising and probably dangerous rate. The danger, of course, resides not so much in the absolute number of people as in the relationship between the known and definite rate of population increase and the probable practical rate of increase in the production of food, shelter, power and other facilities needed to provide a minimum of health and comfort for human beings.

Related to this is another problem that is often concealed or ignored by those who are prone to argue that science is infinitely resourceful and can always be counted upon to find new foods or increase the production of old foods. The problem that remains is the problem of distribution. Even when a new product or process comes into existence it takes time and a great range of social readjustments to make it available where it is most needed. Time is the very core of the problem, for while time passes the population has again increased and often we are no better off than we were before. Furthermore, neither socialism nor communism provides an answer to this problem. Even sympathetic accounts that reach us from behind the iron curtain show that faulty distribution grows alongside of inadequate production as one of the twin roots of communist poverty.

Trends may reverse themselves and no one knows enough about all the elements and ingredients to be quite positive of the future. The probability, however, is that population will continue to increase, that our soil over large areas will be overused and depleted of elements that make it fertile and that make its products healthful and nourishing to man. The ocean is the ultimate recipient and storehouse of the great majority of all these elements. It seems likely, therefore, that men will increasingly turn to the oceans as a source of needed foodstuffs, of chemicals, of minerals and maybe someday also of heat and power.

Another kind of valuation might be put upon an ocean because it contains the important fisheries of the world and thus supplies a constituent of human diet. The products of the different fisheries are recorded in weight of the annual catch and a million pounds of fish per annum forms a convenient unit. On this basis, annual production for the world is 55,000 million pounds. Of this amount European fisheries (exclusive of the USSR) account for 13,200 million pounds—these would be entirely Atlantic Ocean fisheries. North and Central America account for 8,300 million pounds. This would be split between Atlantic and Pacific fisheries. South America, despite its long coastline on both the Atlantic and the Pacific Oceans, produces only 1,100 million pounds. Oceania, despite the fact that it is everywhere embedded in the ocean, produces only 300 million pounds. Asia (exclusive of the USSR) produces 26,400 million pounds. This includes the Indian Ocean as well as Pacific Ocean fisheries.

The above comments sound as though the ocean fisheries were the only ones contributing to the human diet. This is almost but not quite the case. Included in the above figures are also the fresh water fisheries, but of all the fish caught 40,000 million pounds come from the ocean fisheries.

Now another interesting fact emerges, namely, that the deep waters and open oceans contribute few fish that are eaten by man. The primary reason is that edible fish in large numbers breed and live in the shallow slopes of the ocean and in the shallow seas. Supplementary reasons may be that fishermen, for the most part, lack the methods, the equipment and the ships to make deep-water fishing possible. Also, if it were possible, it might not prove economically valuable.

One authority puts the matter this way. The shallow ocean waters and the shallow seas account for only 7 per cent of the total ocean area of the world yet it is from these waters that man obtains practically all of the fish that find a way to his table. Again, the annual take of the fisheries may be rated at twenty million metric tons. Ninety-five per cent of this amount is taken from the shallow ocean waters of the northern hemisphere with only 5 per cent coming from all other sources combined.

Owing to fluctuations in currency value and to the different monetary units employed in the markets where fish is sold, it is extremely difficult to put a dollars and cents valuation on the ocean fisheries but the above facts are enough to suggest the value and the critical importance of the Atlantic Ocean fisheries.

This importance will probably increase in the future rather than diminish particularly if populations continue to build up at the present rate. Some people seem to think that all that is necessary in order to secure more fish for the hungry world is to send more fishing boats to sea apparently in the general belief that the sea is an unending source of foodstuffs. They leave out of account the limited area referred to above in which food fishes breed in adequate numbers to make fishing an economic possibility.

Oysters, clams, mussels, crabs, lobsters and fish are in themselves palatable and add an interesting element to the human diet. The contribution, however, that they make to the total volume of human food consumed is small as compared with the production and consumption of grains, vegetables and the meat of fowls and land animals. Again, it takes an extraordinary amount of time and labor to catch fish even on the more productive and profitable fishing grounds. An equal amount of time and energy expended on the production of food on dry land still seems a more certain way of adding to the total of the world's food supply. Thus, the best Iowa corn land can produce 2,000 pounds of corn per acre per year while the English Channel, which is one of the world's best fishing areas, produces an estimated yield of about five pounds per acre per year.

Again, it is not safe to assume that more fishing produces more fish. In the past an increase in the number of boats fishing has sometimes increased the total catch of fish. But as years go on the limitation for a number of commercial fisheries is the rate at which the fish can breed and the amount of feed available. Thus it has been pointed out that in times of war and of food shortages, intensive fishing in the North Sea has resulted in a smaller daily catch and in a reduction in the size of fish taken. Even to preserve the present rates of production of many of the fisheries it is necessary to organize international boards for the control of the fishing areas.

There is an idea as yet undeveloped and tried only in a limited way which may change the present, not very bright, prospect for good fishing. This is the idea that practically all of our efforts to secure food from the sea are like hunting expeditions and not like agricultural enterprises. On land, in most areas, men long ago gave up the effort of trying to feed himself by gathering wild fruits and vegetables or by shooting the natural game of the region. Instead he turned to the cultivation of the soil and the raising of domesticated livestock.

At sea we are still at the hunting stage; there are a few exceptions. The European oyster is not entirely a natural production and in a way has been domesticated. To some extent in England, but more particularly in France, different varieties of oysters are bred and raised under controlled conditions and profitably marketed. There seems no inherent reason why the idea of sea-farming cannot be gradually extended. This demands the development of methods of protection and control over certain shore areas.

So far in America control of shellfish beds and of marine fisheries seems to have been mostly negative in character and in results. There has been, at least on the eastern seaboard, a steady pollution of waters and a steady retreat of fishing areas farther and farther offshore. It is always possible, however, that once matters become sufficiently desperate a concerted effort may be made to improve them. There are examples of fisheries that have been successfulyl protected and controlled and even built up after it would seem they were about to become depleted. Someday we may find it profitable to make a real effort to restore and render sanitary shallow waters for the cultivation of the American oyster; we may have a few rivers that are sweet enough to attract an annual run of healthy shad; we may have lobster farms and fish ranches.

It is plain that there are many ways in which the Atlantic Ocean is of value to man and that some of these ways could be assigned a dollars-and-cents value and that in the future these values are likely to become higher rather than lower.

None of the values we have been discussing above, however, represent the true value of the ocean or the contribution which it makes to human welfare. This value and contribution is something that cannot be assigned a monetary value because it is too broad and deep and comprehensive. The value and the strength of the ocean lies in its relationship to man—in the ways it has affected his history and development, the uses he has made of it in the past and the uses he may make of it in the future.

This, of course, has been the main subject of our book. The time has come now to look back over the course we have been sailing and to abstract from our log some of the entries that illustrate the ways the Atlantic has served us in the past and what opportunities it holds open today. As to the future, it should become clear to us that the health, wealth and sanity of the Western World depends upon the judicious use and development of the Atlantic Ocean. Atlantic power resides partly in the position of this ocean. It is the central valley of the land hemisphere; its margins are the great land masses of the world; it is the only ocean that reaches five major continents.

Atlantic power resides partly in its service as a drainage basin. It not only touches the continents, it penetrates them. It happens that the continents that lie to the east of the Atlantic have continental divides that lie to the east far removed from the Atlantic shores and, correspondingly, continents that lie to the west of the Atlantic have their rocky spines on their western borders. So the Atlantic serves as the drainage basin for the continents and receives most of the great navigable rivers of the world.

Practically all of the great temperate zone agricultural areas of the world lie along rivers that drain into the Atlantic. Another group of rivers such as the Amazon, the Congo, the Orinoco drain the great tropical rain forests; a third group penetrates the cold forests of the Northern Hemisphere.

Atlantic power lies partly in the structure of the ocean itself. The fact that the Atlantic is not as large as the Pacific contributes to its beauty and its utility. It is a compact, well-organized ocean with clearly defined systems of winds and of currents. The Atlantic Ocean holds a large proportion of the world's northern shallow seas. These are of value because they constitute the world's major fishing areas such as the English Channel, North Sea, Icelandic fisheries, the Grand Banks of Newfoundland, etc. For the most part, however, the Atlantic is marked by clean-cut and well-defined shores with a wealth of subsidiary seas, sounds and estuaries. Therefore, it is rich both in navigable waters and in suitable harbors.

The value of the Atlantic rests not only in itself as an ocean but in its relationship to the land where man resides. How the land juts into the sea and how the sea reaches into the land determines the value of the ocean to man. This close relationship between the Atlantic and the continents is expressed by the fact that the Atlantic has a longer coastline than the Pacific and the Indian Oceans combined.

This structure of the Atlantic increases the value of two other services that the ocean performs. The first of these is the ocean's effect on climate; the second is its service as a means of communication and transport. The well-organized system of winds and currents of the Atlantic are of the utmost importance in tempering our climate and regularizing our lives. All of the world's heat and power ultimately derives from the sun and most of the sunlight that falls upon the world falls upon ocean water. Air heats up quickly and cools quickly but fortunately ocean water has a capacity to absorb heat, to store it and convey it and to give it up slowly.

This difference between air and water is of the greatest practical importance. If you want to warm up by one degree, ten cubic feet of air, you will expend in the process a certain amount of heat. To warm ten cubic feet of water will require 3,000 times as much heat. This relationship helps us to understand how the Atlantic performs a useful service in slowly absorbing great volumes of excess heat poured on it in the tropics, later giving up the heat in our northern climates where it is so badly needed. For, of course, this system works both ways, for when our ten cubic feet of water cools off by one degree in a northern climate, it will heat by one degree a volume of air 3,000 times as great as itself.

The human air conditioning of buildings depends on the extraordinary capacity of water (or some other fluid) to absorb heat so that a small volume of water can influence a very large volume of air. In somewhat the same way the perpetually moving waters of the ocean influence the weather and the climate of the continents. In particular, Europe may be said to have an air-conditioned or rather a water-conditioned climate benefiting from the very extraordinary movements of the Gulf Stream system.

Considering the size of the continent, Europe is fortunate in possessing a relatively large proportion of productive agricultural soil. It benefits from the warm climate imparted by the Gulf Stream. At the same time it is a territory well up in northern latitudes so that it has the advantage of long and uninterrupted hours of spring and summer sunshine. This is an almost unique and unbeatable combination of geographic blessings.

The greatest of Atlantic powers, and the greatest benefit it confers on man, is its service as a method of transport and communication. In this service all other features of the Atlantic are combined: the length of the rivers, the fertility of soil, the fortunes of climate, the wealth of interlocking waterways and of harbors, the organization of winds and ocean currents, the accessibility of large land masses—the one to the other.

The prelude to transport was discovery and we have seen how the organization of the Atlantic helped to shape the rate and direction of human progress. The Norsemen sailed their courses in latitudes above the prevailing westerlies where winds, though strong, were variable. This was a condition that served them well on their relatively short passages from Norway to the Faeroes, to Iceland, Greenland, Labrador and other portions of the American coast.

The first Atlantic explorations of the Portuguese were not made to the west but to the south, thus they utilized the southward flowing current that flowed so steadily off their shores and also the prevailing northeast wind which was the beginning of the northeast trades that carried them to Madeira and the shores of Africa. The long period that intervened between the early voyages initiated by Henry the Navigator and the rounding of the Cape of Good Hope were not due to the hostility of the African tribes so much as to the resistance of the southeast trades and the Benguella Current. When the Portuguese boldly struck out to sea it was the winds and currents of the South Atlantic that sped them smartly around the cape. They seem to have overdone matters somewhat in the case of one Portuguese navigator for it was a combination of the South Atlantic Current and a southeasterly storm that caused Cabral to discover the eastern tip of Brazil when he thought he was on his way around the Cape of Good Hope to India.

Columbus, with his round-bodied, clumsy and simply rigged vessels, would hardly have survived to reach the West Indies had he not been favored with the northeast trades and the north equatorial currents that swung him southward to the Canaries and then westward to the Bahamas. So, of course, Columbus' successors benefited by the same ocean blessings, soon adding to them a favorable return from the Caribbean and the Gulf of Mexico by way of the Florida Straits and the Gulf Stream.

Nor were the benefits of the Atlantic monopolized by the Portuguese and the Spaniards for it was variance of these routes that permitted the Dutch to develop their island colonies in the West Indies and that accounted for the early prosperity of Barbados and of the British West Indies at a time when the northern colonies were still fighting for a foothold on the continent.

Man's desires are not always favored by nature even by the fortunes of the Atlantic, and human determination too has been essential to the utilization of the ocean. The establishment of the northern sea routes in the latitudes of the prevailing westerlies represents a hard-won but successful compromise between human inventiveness and natural environment. Once established, the difference between the northern and the southern sea routes across the Atlantic had an important bearing on the whole pattern of human migration to the Western World and had a bearing even on the routes that the migrants followed on their western penetration of the continent. The North and the South were separated not only by the Mason and Dixon Line but also by the Gulf Stream, and the Gulf Stream came first.

The Atlantic routes that were followed by the explorers and colonists became at once the routes of transport and communication between the colonists and those who had remained behind in Europe. The colonists needed trade as well as the homeland and despite disagreements on matters of politics, religion and ways of life, trade grew and persisted. With few exceptions the early routes became the strong threads in a web of trade and communication that knits the Atlantic nations into a community of reciprocal interests.

Among the powers and capacities with which the Atlantic Ocean has endowed mankind, one of the most fundamental is the power of transport. The map of Basic World Transport presented on page 409 should now have a fuller meaning for us. The map illustrates how central to human undertaking and how important in volume is the network of transatlantic transport. Air transport is not included in this map because we are talking about major transport activities which can be represented on a tonnage basis. On a tonnage basis, air transport at the present time would be represented by something considerably less than 1 per cent. Our picture, therefore, of combined service transport represents rather more than 99 per cent of all world transport.

Land transportation, of course, is important to and within each country but for the most part it is the water transport that is international and intercontinental. The ordinary cargo vessel is the cheapest and most effective means of transport that man has ever devised in cost per ton of pay load. This could be illustrated with many lengthy and complicated schedules but here a characteristic example must serve. A bale of crude rubber weighs 250 pounds. It can be moved by freighter from Singapore to New York City for a cost of approximately $2.00. The distance is 9,000 miles. Its destination is Akron, Ohio—by rail, about 500 miles from New York. It will cost just as much to get the bale from New York to Akron as it cost to get it from Singapore to New York, that is to say, $2.00.

This means that the transportation per ton mile by rail is about eighteen times as expensive as oceanic transportation.

Now let us suppose that the bale of rubber were shipped the whole way by air. At current rates the charge would be about $600.00 or three hundred times as expensive as the transport by sea.

In practice, of course, rates will fluctuate one way or another as between the different methods of transport depending in part on the distances covered and the types of goods conveyed, but these fluctuations are trivial when we compare them with the great jumps in cost from one method of transport to another.

Another illustration of the economy of ocean transport contrasted with other charges involved in the handling of produce was supplied by a merchant doing business in Oriental commodities. The case involved a large shipment of rice from an Oriental port by way of New York to a port in South America. The ship from the Orient was to dock in Staten Island, a part of New York harbor. The ship for South America was to depart from a Manhattan pier. Fortunately, in time, the merchant discovered that it was going to cost him more to convey the shipment from Staten Island to the outward bound vessel in Manhattan than it cost him to transport it from the Orient to New York. The problem was solved and solved economically by shipping the rice to Hamburg and trans-shipping from there to the South American port.

These examples illustrate the effectiveness and low cost of ocean transport contrasted with the high costs of land transport and ruinous harbor charges. However, reliable low-cost ocean freights were not an automatic gift of God and nature; they were not won at a single stroke; they do not stand alone; they can be lost.

Many inventions went into the development of low-cost ocean freights. First the improvement of ships from the Phoenician vessel to the superliner through all the special types we have seen crossing the Atlantic—the galleon, packet, clipper, etc. Then the wiser use of the ocean and its lanes that began with Maury and quicker and more accurate methods of navigation. To this we must add an array of special services: charts and pilot books; lights and markers for coasts and harbors; equipment for handling cargo aship and ashore; fire protection and safety equipment; radio, radar, sonar, etc.

A part of the success and economy of ocean transport arises from the ships and the other concrete inventions that we have mentioned above but a part arises also from ideas that have grown up both on the sea and ashore. Among these are the services of insurance to cover losses either of the ship or its cargo; the idea of economy to be won by regularity and speed of service; the idea of massed transport which is naturally connected with the development ashore of mass production.

Clearly these are all related in a way to our fundamental beliefs in the virtues and advantages of a free economy. Effective low-cost ocean transport is thus partly a product of our industrial and economic system but at the same time it is a peaceful contributor to the success of these systems. In peace and in war it is a major element in supplying raw materials at reasonable cost and distributing products to profitable markets.

Finally, these ocean services are also an expression of prevailing ideas and philosophies. Into these services have entered the movements for the protection of the rights of seamen beginning with their freedom from impressment on the high seas and the idea of the free use of the open oceans as highways for international commerce. Freedom of the seamen and freedom of the seas are ideas that could only have grown up in a community of nations that valued their national and individual liberty on the seas as well as ashore.

About the Atlantic economic freedom and political freedom have grown hand-in-hand. About the Atlantic representative government and democratic institutions have had their origin and their longest periods of development and trial. It may be significant that Iceland, situated on an island in the very middle of the Atlantic, has been governed by the Althing, the oldest representative deliberative body, with a record of unbroken service that now runs well over 1,000 years.

An examination of the Atlantic story shows that there has grown up about this ocean a group of nations that have many characteristics in common: They have participated in successive waves of migration and colonization; they have sought the same types of political and personal liberty; they have developed farm lands and utilized natural resources; established productive industries; built up across the Atlantic lines of communication, of travel and of trade. Likewise in philosophy and science, in literature and the arts, they have exchanged ideas back and forth across the Atlantic and up and down its length.

Naturally over so large an area and with so many different national, racial and religious groups participating in a common adventure, extended over so great a period of time, there are wide variations in the accepted and standard patterns. But even variations are a sort of admission that there are standards or central tendencies of a basic Atlantic culture.

Warfare is often a test of basic relationships and ultimate allegiances. It is often assumed that the Atlantic Ocean has been a kind of buffer separating Europe from America in times of peace and serving as a line of protection or defense in times of war. This seems to be based on a general misunderstanding of how mankind reacts to an ocean. An examination of cultural history shows that, once the ocean was crossed, Europe and America combined to use it continually as a highway for commerce.

An examination of Atlantic warfare shows that even in the earliest colonial times, when ships were small and Atlantic crossings relatively difficult, there was hardly a colony that enjoyed any immunity from recurring European wars. Thus the English colonists fought the Spanish colonists when England and Spain were at war, and when England and the Netherlands were at war New Amsterdam became New York. Even so domestic a struggle as our Civil War deeply affected the economy of Europe. At one stage England's sympathy for and possible assistance to the South vitally influenced the war plans of the Union. At the close of the war England paid a large indemnity for acts hostile to the United States committed by her citizens.

Again, it is usually taken for granted that war is always a totally hostile opposition of irreconcilable interests or philosophies. There were certainly wars of this kind in the past and there may be again in the future. There are also wars that are admissions of common interests. There is even agreement that certain things are worth fighting about. Thus in the Revolution the Americans were seeking for themselves economic and political freedoms that England in large measure already granted to her citizens and denied only to the colonists. Insofar as the freedom of ships and seamen were involved this was true also of the War of 1812.

In modern times the Atlantic did not protect the United States or the other western nations from involvement in two World Wars. In each case, with the passage of time, it became apparent that it was the Atlantic itself which had to be protected. Once it was so protected it became the path of ultimate victory. Even more important is the fact that on these two occasions the great majority of all the Atlantic nations were no longer fighting among themselves but against philosophies and policies which they regarded as of remote and alien origin and hostile to their somehow common interests in a free world.

People sometimes jump to the conclusion that international agreements formed in time of war such as the North Atlantic Treaty Organization or various Pan American agreements are pure inventions or the expedient devices of harassed but agile national leaders. On the contrary, an examination of Atlantic history will show that they are based on old but persistent associations and interests which have already found a partial expression in the past. To the extent that they represent real cultural interests and not political inspiration, they have proved effective and to that extent they may prove effective in the future.

The conviction grows that in the Atlantic community we have what is worth defending in the world today and that in the Atlantic Ocean we have a strategic asset for such defense. We should be quite clear about what this means. It does not mean that the Atlantic Ocean is an automatic defense or a natural protection to any nation or any set of ideas no matter how admirable or desirable. The Atlantic Ocean is only of value to those who will cultivate it persistently and use it courageously. To such it must prove a realm of economic prosperity in time of peace and a bulwark of defense in time of war. This belief in the ultimate utility of the Atlantic is at the heart of the seaman's often unexpressed belief about the world.

If we believe that the Atlantic Ocean is worth utilizing and worth protecting, it follows that we must take a permanent and effective interest in the establishment of a strong merchant marine and a strong navy not only in our own country but also in the other countries that are our partners. To this extent the Atlantic story is an argument for a large and effective navy but it would be the greatest mistake to assume that this could be left as a partisan matter or that this was all that was involved.

In the real world and under the existing circumstances a strong navy or navies seem indispensable not only for the protection of Canada and the United States and the Western World in general but also for the defense of the Atlantic communities on both sides of the water. It is equally an argument for the development of an adequate merchant marine, serviceable in peace as well as in war; an argument for a strong air force or strong air forces and for the progressive development of a great variety of air services in time of peace. It could equally be interpreted as an argument for improved port services on both sides of the Atlantic.

The essential idea is that the Atlantic and its associated nations form a natural strategic area. It is so essential to the preservation of a desirable world that in its defense every arm of national service and every effective weapon now existing must be available for use and research must continually be developing new defensive and offensive weapons. Apart from the possibility of a sudden sneak air atomic attack from behind the Iron Curtain, there are certain dangers that threaten the integrity of the Atlantic circle of nations even though they remain nominally at peace. One of them would be the further encroachment or aggression by which Soviet Russia or its satellites would acquire the use and control of further Atlantic ports. For example, by combined use of pressures and threats and force such as she has already employed in other cases, Russia might push her way through Finland and Norway to reach the northern part of the Norwegian coast and then edge southward, or extend her control from East Germany westward. Such acts would at least involve the threat of open and general warfare.

Two other types of danger lie within the area of aggression or penetration in time of "peace." One type is represented by the attempt to take over a territory like British Guiana or the seizure of Guatemala by a band of political adventurers who claim they are establishing a form of communism and who are at least potential allies of Soviet communism.

The other kind of threat is the disruption of Atlantic services and Atlantic ports by communist controlled unions or by unionists that are unwittingly serving communist purposes.

Discussion of the threats to our ports and to our sea services is not hostile to the liberties or economic interests of the honest working man. This is just the reverse of the truth. There is always the claim that a strike, slow-down or a disruption of service is made in the interest of the working man and is made to secure better hours or working conditions. There is always the hope that this old-fashioned claim will be believed by the press and the public. Many strikes and stoppages are actually only phases of a war for power waged between rival unions or rival labor leaders. In them the workers have little to gain and much to lose no matter who wins the battle. In fact all citizens are losers. When such conflicts persist for long periods of time in our defense plants and in our ports, a breach has been made in the ramparts of our national security.

There was a time when the improvement of port services could be provided for largely by the creation of deeper harbors, longer piers, better unloading and handling facilities. This is still true in a limited measure but what we need chiefly today is an elimination of the crime, graft and corruption that infects our harbors.

It is, of course, erroneous to believe that the problems of our ports and longshore services are local problems. This might be the case if our ports and dockside services operated continually, efficiently and economically. The ports serve all parts of the nation—the interior as well as the seaboard. They have become a national problem and a threat to national security and it seems doubtful if improvements can be made other than in a thoroughgoing fashion and on a national scale.

There are some who believe that an ocean—the Atlantic Ocean in particular—is of limited interest or importance because they say we have advanced into something called the "Air Age." This of course is a very limited view and represents either a willful misinterpretation or an incomplete knowledge of the capabilities and limitations of aircraft. It is exactly because we find an increasing use for aircraft that we should examine our relationship to the ocean.

The political, naval, military, commercial, cultural relationships that have grown up about the Atlantic have been established as a result of oceanic communication. As far as we can foresee they will be served by oceanic communication in time of peace and varying forms of defensive and offensive operation in time of war. Air transport and armed air forces have appeared as a useful and sometimes crucial adjunct to the oceanic services. There a few, but a very few, points at which they compete. For the most part they complement and supplement each other. Much, of course, depends upon the point of view.

Modern war is so complex that partisans of any service or particular forms of activity can point to their particular contribution and claim that it was a main or crucial contribution to victory. The case may sound impressive as long as they ignore the claims of other services. The strategic bombers might point to the destruction of means of production in industrial cities of Germany or to the destruction of railroads, bridges or other means of communication before and during the invasion of Normandy. But back of these efforts, as we already know, lay tremendous services of ocean transport and of naval protection for that transport and back of that again the uphill battle in submarine warfare.

Should the argument arise that the whole matter may be changed because airplanes now have greater fuel capacity or a greater radius of operation, it requires only a little reflection to see that this only partially affects the situation. In fact, many of the newer and faster planes, including the jets, have a higher rate of fuel consumption than ever before and are more dependent on supplementary services. It is still economically inexpedient and logistically wasteful to anticipate that aircraft will service themselves at advanced bases though this may occasionally be resorted to for particular purposes. In general planes are too costly and too much needed for other services. Ocean transport will still supply the planes with the fuel they burn and the bombs they drop.

The most recent pride and joy of the United States services is the new advanced air base in the Arctic at Thule, Greenland. From one point of view this may become a signal contribution of the air arm, but from another point of view it is also a triumphant naval service. The base did not fly to Greenland. It took the vast skill and experience of many technical services to make it possible at all and its initial establishment involved the services of an armada of some fourscore ships operating over thousands of miles of ice-encrusted waters. All will agree that the base is an invaluable asset in peace as well as in war and might be designated as one of the latest completed products of "air-age" thinking—yet it also represents a combined sea-air accomplishment.

The Atlantic as a strategic area in peace and in war remains. It is a complex structure; in part an unalterable feature of the physical world and in part a product of human history. Nothing that we have written here is to be interpreted as derogatory of nations in the non-Atlantic parts of the world. World-wide associations may prove valuable and may become necessary but the ability of the Atlantic nations to preserve their freedom and to be of any service in other parts of the world depends upon their integrity in their own area. It is a cardinal mistake for one of the free Atlantic nations to seek power or curry favor in the Orient if at the same time they are losing territory or losing control on their own doorstep.

The importance of the Atlantic as a strategic area is not altered by the creation of new weapons or round-the-world bombers. The arms and the planes exist simply to attack or to defend the area. We are not going to live in the air. The Atlantic basin is our home. The nation or nations that control the Atlantic basin control the heart of the world. Even if we hang a satellite station in space or if we reach the moon, the Atlantic Ocean will still be the center of the human world.

ACKNOWLEDGMENTS
AND SUGGESTIONS
FOR FURTHER READING

It is always a pleasure to acknowledge, whenever possible, the hints, clues, suggestions, ideas, facts, information, services and aids of all kinds that assist one in the making of a book. In the case of the present volume this pleasure must be restrained for a variety of reasons.

In the first place, the Atlantic has always been of interest to me, and the book has been a matter of slow growth. Much of it is a matter of personal observation and experience, such for example as my cruise in *Kinkajou* and passages in many other vessels. I have tried always to check, supplement and support my observations by reference to written authority, but even with the best intention it has not always been possible to show exactly where authority left off and observation began. At certain points where authority seemed lacking or silent, I have ventured to express my own observations.

In the second place, other parts of the book are based on observations made in museums and exhibits and on reading and research extending over many years. To document the account and to supply it with a full set of notes and references would have made it more difficult to read and more expensive to produce. The author and publisher early agreed that they wished to interest the general reader and to make his trip through the book as easy, pleasant and profitable as possible.

Finally, while it is only fair to acknowledge facts and statements derived from another author, it is unfair to involve him in matters of opinion or judgment. The present author wishes, therefore, not only to thank such authorities as may be named here or in the body of the book for their assistance, but also to free them from involvement in or responsibility for interpretations of facts or judgments of value expressed in this book.

My first indebtedness is to those who taught me to sail and imparted in other ways some understanding of ships and the sea. The list would be too long to mention in full. It would begin with quiet, simple people like the ex-whaler captain who taught me how to "hand, reef, and steer" in the waters of Nantucket; Captain Schwartz of *Hickory* on Biscayne Bay; Jimmie Thompson with whom I sailed the Gulf Stream and explored the keys, cuts and banks of lower Florida. It would include old shipmates like Henry Anderson, Michael Cumberlege, Oliver Hazard Perry and crews, amateur and professional, of my little ships, and inventive and technical fellows, interested in the aerodynamics of sail, like Jasper Morgan, Manfred Curry and C. Townsend Ludington, and "Skipper" Herbert Stone of *Yachting,* who in his quiet way knew so much of so many subjects. I could not omit memorable but all-too-brief talks with some of the great men of the sea of our time, William McFee, H. M. Tomlinson, Captain Sir David Bone, Joseph Conrad and John Masefield.

I acknowledge also a debt of gratitude to institutions that maintain museums and libraries dealing in whole or in part with ships and the sea, and to some of their officials who have aided my study, as follows:

> The Naval War College at Newport, Rhode Island, and Captain R. N. S. Clark who secured for me permission to use its library and map collections, with particular thanks to Miss Heffernan, Librarian;
>
> The Mariner's Museum of Newport News, Virginia, for opportunities to study its extensive exhibits of ships and engines, and to utilize its well-organized library;
>
> Marine Historical Society and Mystic Seaport, Mystic, Connecticut, for study of its exhibits and use of volumes in its library;
>
> The Model Collections and Library of the New York Yacht Club, with special thanks to Critchell Rimington;
>
> The Whaling Museum, New Bedford, Massachusetts;
>
> the library of the American Museum of Natural History, with special thanks to Dr. Robert Cushman Murphy;
>
> the library of the Union Club, with special thanks to its Librarian, Miss Irwin;

Of American institutions, last, but by no means least,

> the library and map collection of The American Geographical Society of New York City, with special thanks for encouragement and assistance to its director, Dr. Charles Hitchcock.

Of institutions abroad, special reference should be made to:

the ship-model collections and marine exhibits of the Science Museum, South Kensington, London;

The National Maritime Museum, Greenwich, London, which also houses the Macpherson Collection of Naval and Marine Art;

the excellently presented and very extensive pictures, models, and exhibits of the Marine Museum, Rotterdam, Netherlands;

the collections and exhibits of the Oceanographic Museum established at Monte Carlo by Prince Albert of Monaco.

There is no intention here to supply documentary references or bibliography. My main bibliography runs to several thousand items, and it is supplemented by a compilation in card-catalog form to which I attached the title "Annals of the Sea." This records in chronological order the names of ships, the main features of their structure and their performances, and also notes special events, innovations, inventions, laws, decrees, etc., taking place at sea or affecting life at sea. These are too much to reproduce.

I wish, however, to acknowledge my indebtedness to a few special authors and books either because they are unique and meet some special need, or because they are general and supply excellent summaries of information. Some I mention also because they may assist the interested reader in further study.

On oceanography, marine biology and related matters, the best and most comprehensive general text is *The Oceans:* Their Physics, Chemistry and General Biology, by Harold V. Sverdrup, Martin W. Johnson and Richard H. Fleming, published by Prentice-Hall, New York, 1942.

I believe that at the time this volume was written, all the authors were associated in the work of the Scripps Institute of Oceanography, La Jolla, California. This volume contains all the basic facts and theories and has many passages that would be of interest to the general reader. It is also, however, highly technical and of necessity employs involved mathematical formulations and presentations which discourage casual reading.

An easier but still authoritative general introduction to most of these subjects is supplied in *The Sea* by Captain H. A. Marmer, published by Appleton & Co., New York, in 1930. The same author also supplied a very useful volume, *The Tide,* published by Appleton in 1926. Though no longer quite up to date, these volumes form good introductions, and can be supplemented by current reading.

Miss Rachel Carson's delightful volume *The Sea Around Us* is so well known as to require no special commendation here. It is, however, useful to note that it is fortunate for the reader that Captain Marmer is at his best in oceanography and the physics of the sea, whereas Miss Carson is at her best in marine biology. Her recommendations regarding further reading are sound and useful.

A man with a full, clear and active mind and a gracious manner of speaking is a treasure to his time. When he speaks on any subject he is qualified to extend its meaning and is worth listening to. Thus Dr. Robert Cushman Murphy of the American Museum of Natural History, while he is primarily an orinthologist, is also a serious student in Oceanography. His *Oceanic Birds of South America,* published in 1948 by the Museum and The Macmillan Company, contains many clear and interesting descriptions of the ocean's structure and behavior. This reminds me that I should also thank Dr. Murphy for permission to study his personal notebooks on oceanographic subjects.

Submarine Geology by Francis P. Shepard, New York, Harper's, 1948, still seems to be the first and only book on this special subject.

The *Geographical Journal* of the American Geographical Society frequently contains articles and reviews of oceanographic and geophysical interest.

Readers interested in the ocean should secure for themselves copies of the United States Pilot Charts. In addition to offering the monthly chart, this publication usually prints on the reverse of the chart some interesting and timely article or study covering such subjects as: Seasonal Variations in the Limits of Arctic Ice; The Drift and Behavior of Icebergs; The Courses of Cyclonic Storms; Studies of the Gulf Stream, etc.

On the history of ships and shipping, and on special types of vessels, there are literally hundreds of volumes. I shall mention only some special cases, and some useful general works. Starting with these, the reader can work his way into any eras or subjects that particularly interest him.

Ancient Ships, by C. Torr, London, Oxford University Press, 1894, was an early study of early navigation, and is still a sound point of departure.

Sailing Ships by W. L. Clowes, published by the Science Museum at South Kensington, London, is based on materials in their collections. These are, however, so extensive that the volume becomes more than a catalog, it is also a good general reference work.

Conquest of the Seas, by Frank C. Bowen, London, Heffner (no date), is a general account. Mr. Bowen has also written many volumes on special ships.

The Story of the Ship by Charles E. Gibson, New York, Schuman, 1948, is a very comprehensive and constructive general account.

The History of the American Sailing Ships by Howard I. Chapelle, New York, W. W. Norton, 1935, is a little too episodic to quite justify its title, but that is not of great importance. The book is composed of interesting, valuable, and technically excellent studies of important types of American vessels, with full plans and drawings.

Maritime History of Massachusetts by Samuel Eliot Morison, Houghton, Mifflin, Boston, 1921, is a book that could easily be overlooked, but should not be. It has a more general interest and a greater importance than the title suggests.

Of volumes on special subjects, *Square-riggers on Schedule* by Robert Greenhalph Albion, Princeton University Press, 1938, is of unusual value. It is our only thorough and reliable account of American packetship operations, and I am indebted to it for much of the material included in my chapter on this subject.

On the subject of the clippers of America there are a number of volumes, some of them good. *The Clipper Ship Era* by Capt. Arthur H. Clark, G. P. Putnam's Sons, New York, 1910, is good. Scholars have asserted that some of his facts, figures and memories are not exactly accurate, but that does not destroy the value of the general account, nor dull its vividness and enthusiasm.

Greyhounds of the Sea by Dr. Carl C. Cutler, G. P. Putnam's Sons, New York, 1930, has produced a most valuable and accurate record of year-by-year clipper-ship operation.

In the matter of illustrated works, few painters or draughtsmen can rival, and none can excel, the work of Gordon Grant. He grew up in the old square-riggers, he is a careful historian and natural artist, and his works therefore have a rare combination of knowledge, accuracy and beauty. Books illustrated by him, *Book of Old Ships, Greasy Luck* (a pictorial record of a whaling cruise), *Unrolling the Map,* etc., will always have an extra value because of his work.

There are many works on the activities of the United States Navy and the American Merchant Marine at various stages in our history. A fine general account is *The Sea and The States* by Samuel W. Bryant. I found this entertaining as well as informative. It is in the Growth of America Series, published by Thomas Y. Crowell, New York, copyright 1947.

There are a number of books on slave ships and slaving. The Marine Research Society of Salem, Massachusetts, published a volume of collected pieces on this subject. There is also *The American Slave Trade* by John R. Spears, 1901, and *The Atlantic and Slavery* by H. A. Wyndham, London, Oxford University Press, 1935. Chappelle in the work referred to above deals with the form of the slave ship.

The Ocean Tramp by Frank C. Hendry, London, Collins, 1939, is a special volume.

On the liners there are a number of volumes of variable value, such as *Passenger Liners of the Western Ocean* (1838 to 1952), by C. R. Vernon Gibbs, London, Staples Press, 1952: this work is the latest and best; *The Story of the Liner,* S. Jackson, London, Harrap (no date); *Lives of the Liners,* Frank O. Braynard, New York Cornell Maritime Press, 1947.

There is no writer whose works give us so complete and revealing a picture of the changes that have taken place in the life of the ocean in our time as those of Sir David Bone. He has experienced it all in peace and in war, from the time he was an apprentice in square-riggers to the time when he commanded great modern liners. He knows what stores of knowledge and reserves of strength are needed to insure the safety and comfort of travelers at sea. He can describe not only the outward changes of forms of ships and fashions of travel, but also suggest how accompanying changes in tempo and spirit have affected travelers and crews and captains, and so altered life at sea. The record begins with *The Brassbounder,* continues in *Merchantman at Arms* and others, and culminates in his recent work, *Landfall at Sunset.*

I am grateful to Cass Canfield, Jr., for his patient and discerning work as editor of this volume.

In the end, my greatest debt is to the late Thomas R. Coward, publisher, who believed in this book; my greatest regret is that he could not see it completed; my greatest hope is that it will justify his judgment.

LEONARD OUTHWAITE

Long Beach, California
May, 1957.

Index

Academy of Sciences, French, 394
Adam of Bremen, 112, 119
Adams, John, 370
Adelaide, packet ship, 305
Aeolian Islands, 74, 77
Agamemnon, cable ship, 318
Agassiz, Alexander, 258
Airplanes, 398 ff.
Airships, 397-98, 401, 402, 403-04, 406
Alabama, C.S.S., 385
Alameida, steamship, 341
Albert I, of Monaco, 259
Albion, packet ship, 247, 349
Albion, R. E., 233, 242
Albuquerque, Alfonso de, 143
Alcock, Captain J., 68, 406
Alexander VI, Pope, 120
Alexander the Great, 100
Alfonso V, King, 139
Alfred, King, 201
Alfred the Great, 104, 118
Ali Pasha, 360
Allaire, John P., 302
Allen, John, 296
Allen, William H., 241
Allen Line, 308, 349
Alliance, U.S.S., 368
Almeida, Francisco de, 143
Altmark, 433
America, dirigible, 402
America, dory, 333
America, flying boat, 404, 407
America, yacht, 288-89
American Legion, airplane, 407
American Mediterranean, 25, 27
American Rocket Research Program, 440
Amherst, General Geoffrey, 366
Amity, packet ship, 235
Amundsen, Ronald, 406

Anchor Line, 341
Anderson, Henry, 286
Andrea Doria, steamship, 352-53
Andrée, Major S. A., 396, 397
Andrews, W. A., 331-32
Anne, yacht, 285
Antarctica, 59
Antarctic basin, 30
Antarctic Current, 53
Anthony, Marc, 359
Antilles Current, see Bahama Current
Antillia, 95
Antipodes Island, 58
Arctic, steamship, 304
Arctic Mediterranean Ocean, 24, 27
Arctic Mediterranean Sea, 21, 40, 48
Ariel, clipper ship, 306
Ariel, steamship, 385
Aristides, 359
Aristotle, 101
Armada, the, 363-64
Arminger Current, 39
Armstrong, W. G., 417
Army Air Corps, 410
Around the World Alone, 327
Ascension, 28
Asiento, 224
Aswan, 99
Athenia, steamship, 350-51, 429
Atlantic, schooner, 290-91
Atlantic, steamship, 304
Atlantic Circle, 326
Atlantic Ridge, see Mid-Atlantic Ridge
Atlantis, 29, 93-95, 97
Aubert, 124
Avienus, 82, 83
Azores, 28, 29, 48, 96, 123, 138, 320

Bacon, Roger, 161
Baden, Prince Max von, 427

Baffin Land, 126
Bahama Current, 49, 51
Bahama Islands, 47, 49, 144, 147, 171
Bailey, David G., 303
Bailey, J. W., 256
Baines, James, 275
Baines, James, clipper ship, 273
Balboa, Vasco Nuñez, 149, 156
Balenny, Captain, 213
Balloons, 393-97
Baltic Sea, 25
Baltimore Clippers, 228-29, 264-65
Bancroft, George, 375
Barbarigo, 360
Barents, William, 201-02
Barents Sea, 21
Barker, Captain, 307
Barnum, P. T., 245, 331
Bates, Joshua, clipper ship, 275
Bayly, Sir Lewis, 424
Beachey, Lincoln, 403
Beagle, 137
Beatty, Sir David, 421, 423
Bell, Alexander Graham, 419
Bell & Brown, 268, 270
Bellinghausen, Admiral F. G., 266
Benguela Current, 53, 54
Bennett, Floyd, 406
Berengaria, steamship, 345
Bering Sea, 24
Bering Strait, 20, 207, 212
Bermuda, 29, 52
Berryman, O. H., 256, 316
Biddle, Nicholas, 368
Bingham Foundation for Oceanography, 259
Biscay, Bay of, 23, 48
Biscoe, Captain, 213
Bismarck, battleship, 435
Bismarck, Otto von, 415
Bismarck, steamship, 344-45
Bjarne, 113
Black Ball Line, 236, 237, 240, 241, 245, 247, 267, 295, 303
Blackburn, Howard, 332-33
Black Death, 158-59, 168
Blake, survey vessel, 258
Blanchard, Jean Pierre François, 394
Bleriot, Louis, 401, 402

Blessing of the Bay, 191
Block, Captain Adrian, 178, 285
Blommaert, Samuel, 179
Blue Water, 326
Boit, John, Jr., 328
Bojador, Cape, 138
Bone, Captain David, 342
Bon Homme Richard, 370
Boole, Albenia, 270
Boone, Daniel, 181
Borchgrevink, Carsten, 213
Bosphorus, 24
Boston, 247, 271
Botelho, Diogo, 81, 327, 335
Bowne, William, 235, 236
Brassey, Lord, 317
Brazil Current, 53
Brequet, 401
Breman, airplane, 408
Breman, motor vessel, 345, 346
Brendan, St., 107
Brindle Cow, 130
Britannia, steamship, 301
Brøgger, A. W., 84, 107
Brooke, John Mercer, 256, 316, 377, 378
Broughton, Captain, 368
Brudel, Captain, 328-29
Brunel, Isambard Kingdom, 300, 303, 304, 306, 318-19
Bryer, Captain, 242
Buchanan, 377, 379
Buck, Dr. Peter, 86
Buckley, J. C., 329
Bulloch, Captain James D., 385
Burgess, W. Starling, 401
Butler, General B. F., 382
Byrd, Admiral Richard E., 406, 407

Cabeza De Vaca, Alvarez Nuñez, 171
Cables, 312-23
Cable ships, 322-23
Cabin class liners, 342
Cabot, John, 122-23, 124, 143, 148
Cabot, Sebastian, 123
Cabral, 54, 142, 149
Cabrillo, Juan Rodriguez de, 173
Cadamosto, 138
Cadillac, Antoine de la Mothe, 175
Cadiz, 82

Caesar, Julius, 76, 96, 100-01, 106, 282
Calhoun, John C., 181
Cambria, steamship, 301
Campbell, John, 325-26
Canada, steamship, 305
Canadian Arctic Islands, 27
Canaries basin, 29
Canary Current, 49
Canary Islands, 29, 49, 95, 97, 136, 138, 142, 144
Canaveral, Cape, 47
Cancer, Luis da, 155, 172
Cano, Sebastian del, 150
Cape Verde Islands, 29, 138
Cárdenas, Garcia Lopez de, 173
Caribbean Sea, 25
Carpini, 133
Carson, Rachel, 114
Cartier, Jacques, 125
Cavendish, Henry, 363, 394
Cayman Trench, 30
Cellini, Benvenuto, 160
Celtic, steamship, 344
Centennial, dory, 330
Cervera, Admiral, 389
Challenger, H.M.S., 258
Chamberlain, Clarence, 407
Champlain, Samuel de, 126-27, 174, 175
Chanute, Octave, 398
Chappelle, Howard I., 229, 288
Chariot of Fame, packet ship, 271
Charles, J. A. C., 394
Charles II, King, 284
Chesapeake, U.S.S., 370
Chesapeake Bay, 51
Christian I, King, 120
Christianson, Captain, 178
Christian Typography, 101
City of Flint, tanker, 350
City of New York, steamship, 343-44
City of Paris, steamship, 343-44, 345
City of Ragusa, lifeboat, 329
Civil War, American, 226, 258, 366, 376, 377-87
Clemenceau, Georges E. B., 428
Cleopatra, 73, 359
Cleopatra Selene, 96
Clermont, steamship, 297, 298
Cleveland, Captain J., 327

Clinton, De Witt, 233
Clipper ships, 262-78, 306
Cobb, Nathan, 237, 241
Cobra, H.M.S., 308
Cochran, Alexander Smith, 291
Codorus, steamship, 305
Collins, Edward Knight, 244, 266, 304
Columbia, 194
Columbus, Christopher, 100, 118, 122, 124, 143, 144-48, 151, 171, 220
Columbus, Fernando, 144
Condry, Dennis, 271
Congo River, 143
Congress, U.S.S., 370, 378, 379
Conrad, Joseph, 342
Conrad, yacht, 307
Constellation, U.S.S., 370
Constitution, U.S.S., 369, 370
Cook, Captain James, 163, 212
Cordoba, Francisco Hernández de, 150
Coronado, Francisco Vásquez de, 173
Corsair, yacht, 307
Corte-Real, Gaspar, 123
Corte-Real, João (John) Vaz, 122, 124
Corte-Real, Miguel, 123-24
Cosmas, 101-02
Courier, packet ship, 235, 236, 245, 271, 295
Cove, 207
Covilhã, Pedro de, 140, 141
Crapo, Thomas, 330
Crete, 94
Crisis, packet ship, 247
Crockett, David, 181
Cruise of the Dream Ship, The, 326
Cruise ships, 343
Cumberland, U.S.S., 378, 379
Cunard, Samuel, 301, 304
Cunard Line, 245, 341, 344, 345
Curaçao, steamship, 300
Currier & McKay, 271
Curtiss, Glenn H., 401, 402, 404, 406
Cutler's Year by Year Analysis of the Activity of the Clippers, 276
Cutty Sark, clipper ship, 306
Cyprus, 77

D'Abbans, Marquis, 296
Da Gama, Vasco, 142, 162

Dahlgreen, 384
Dale, Governor, 189
Darius Hystaspis, 81
Dark Secret, 331
Darlan, Admiral Jean François, 436
D'Arlandes, Marquis, 394
Darwin, Charles, 137
Dauntless, schooner, 290
Davila, Pedrarias, 155, 156
Da Vinci, Leonardo, 160, 418
Davis, F. T. B., 291
Davis, John, 125-26, 127
Davis, Noel, 407
Davison, Anne, 334
Davis Straits, 51, 202
Day, Thomas Fleming, 326
Daydream, yawl, 325-26
DeBlois, John S., 211
De Gaulle, General Charles, 435
Delano, Joseph C., 240
Delano, Warren, 240
De la Vaulx, Count Henri, 396
Delaware Bay, 42
Delaware River, 180
De Lôme, Dupuy, 397
Depths of the Sea, The, 258
De Rozier, Jean Pilâtre, 393-94
De Soto, Hernando, 172, 173
Desnouettes, Count Lefevbre, 247-48
Deutschland, steamship, 344
Dewey, Commodore George, 390
Diaz, Bartholomeu, 140-42
Diaz, Diniz, 138, 140
Diaz, João, 140
Dickens, Charles, 245
Diesel, Dr. Rudolf, 307, 418
Dirigibles, 397-98, 401, 402, 403-04, 406
Discovery, 127
Discuil, 107-08
Disko Island, 111, 113, 115
Doenitz, Admiral Karl, 351
Dohrn, Anton, 259
Dolphin, U.S.S., 316
Doldrums, 46-47, 230-31
Dominia, cable ship, 322
Donaldson Line, 350
Dorade, schooner, 291
Doria, Andrea, 360
Drake, Sir Francis, 166, 363, 364

Dramatic Line, 240, 244, 266, 267, 304
Dreadnaught, H.M.S., 419
Dreadnaught, packet ship, 238
Dreyse, Johann, 417
Drottningholm, steamship, 308
Dundas, Charlotte, steamship, 298
Dutch East India Company, 126
Dutch Princess of Saba, schooner, 287
Dutch West India Company, 178, 188

Eagle, balloon, 396
East Greenland Current, 51, 115
Eckener, Dr. Hugo, 406
Edison, Thomas A., 341, 419
Edward VII, King, 415
Egede, Hans, 115
Egypt, 78
Eisenhower, General Dwight D., 438
Elder, John, 302
Elena, schooner, 291
Elgar, John, 305
Elizabeth, steamship, 298
Elizabeth I, Queen, 363
Ellesmere Island, 21
Ellis, John, 125
Ellsler, Fanny, 303
Ellsworth, Lincoln, 406
Emancipation Proclamation, 226
Emergency Fleet Corporation, 426
Enderby, Captain, 213
England, packet ship, 247
English Channel, 25
Enterprise, steamship, 299
Eratosthenes, 98, 99
Eric of Pomerania, 121
Ericsson, John, 298, 378, 379, 380
Ericsson, Lief, 112, 117, 119, 128
Eric the Red, 110-11, 114, 119, 128
Erie Canal, 233
Eriksson, Gudrid, 112-13
Eriksson, Thorstein, 112-13
Eudoxus, 81
Eugene, bark, 334

Faeroe Islands, 24, 27, 28, 108, 126
Falmouth, U.S.S., 251
Fanning, Captain Edmund, 213
Fanning Island, 213
Farewell, Cape, 51, 111, 115, 123

Farman, Henri, 401
Farragut, Admiral David G., 378, 382
Felicity Ann, sloop, 334
Ferrel, James, 307
Field, Cyrus, 255, 313, 315, 316, 317
Fighting ships, 357-91
Fillmore, President, 253
Firbo, George, 333-34
Fish & Grinnel, 237
Fitch, Captain, 328
Fitch, John, 296
Florida, 171, 172
Florida, C.S.S., 385
Florida Current, 39, 49, 50-51
Flying Cloud, clipper ship, 253, 271, 272, 273
Fokker, Anthony, 404, 405
Fonck, René, 407
Fore-and-afters, 279-92
Fortunate Islands, 95, 96
Fortune, 190
Four Power Treaty, 428
Fox, Richard K., 333
Fox, skiff, 333-34
Foyen, Sven, 213
Fraenkel, Knut, 396
Fram, 40
François I, packet ship, 244
Franklin, Benjamin, 232-33, 392, 394
Franklin, steamship, 304
Fremont, Major, 375
French and Indian War, 366
French Atlantic Telegraph Company, 319
French Line, 342, 345, 349
Frobisher, Martin, 125, 363
Frye, Roger P., schooner, 292
Frye, Senator, 416
Fugitive Slave Law, 226
Fulton, Robert, 298
Fulton II, U.S.S., 418
Furuseth, Andy, 214

Gambia River, 138
Garay, Blasco de, 295
Gardar, 108
Gardener, Captain, 276
Gatling, Richard J., 417
Gatty, Harold, 87, 88

Gazelle, S.M.S., 258
George, Harold L., 410
Gibraltar, Straits of, 20, 52, 75, 80, 91, 92, 93, 94, 95
Gibson, Charles E., 282
Giffard, Henri, 397
Gneisenau, 421
Gold Coast, 139
Golden Eagle, privateer, 368-70
Gomez, Esteban, 150
Good Hope, Cape of, 20, 80, 81, 141, 150
Gourgues, Chevalier de, 173
Grace Line, 341
Graf Spee, warship, 435
Graham-White, Claude, 402
Grant, Gordon, 215
Grasse, Admiral Comte de, 371
Gray, Harold E., 408
Great Britain, steamship, 303, 304
Great Eastern, steamship, 303-04, 306, 318-19, 322, 344
Great Explorations and Discoveries, The, 121
Great Harry, 362
Great Nassau Balloon, 396
Great Republic, clipper ship, 271, 272, 273-74, 306
Great Republic, sloop, 333
Great Western, sloop, 333
Great Western, steamship, 300, 301, 303
Greek fire, 358-59
Green, Charles, 395-96
Greene, Henry, 127
Greenland, 21, 24, 27, 39, 40, 110-12, 115, 119, 120, 201, 202
Greenland Ice Cap, 40
Greenland Sea, 21
Greyhound, yacht, 385
Griffiths, John Willis, 248, 265, 267, 268-69, 272, 275
Grijalva, 150
Grinnel, Minturn & Co., 237
Guanches, 97
Guided missiles, 440-41
Guinea, 138, 139
Guinea, Gulf of, 22, 23
Guinea Current, 43
Guiscard, Bohemund, 105

Guiscard, Robert, 105
Gulf Stream, 16, 28, 39, 43, 49, 50, 53, 54, 62, 63, 177, 178, 181, 233, 255, 299; map, 38
Gunpowder, 161
Gustavus Adolphus, King, 179

Hackstaff, William G., 242-43
Haenlein, Paul, 397
Hague, U.S.S., 368
Hakluyt, Richard, 201
Half Moon, 126, 127
Hamburg-American Line, 344, 415
Hamilcar, 82
Hamilton, Charles K., 402
Hannah, schooner, 368
Hanno, 67, 82
Hannu, 77-78, 79, 81-82
Hanseatic League, 129, 130
Happy Return, 203
Haraden, Captain Jonathan, 368
Harding, Warren G., 428
Hardrada, Harald, 105, 112
Harmony, 210
Harold, King, 105
Hartford, U.S.S., 383
Hatshepsut, Queen, 73, 78
Hatteras, Cape, 48
Hatteras, gunboat, 385
Haushofer, 69
Hawker, H. G., 406
Hawker, Harry, 68
Hawkins, Sir John, 363
"Heartland," 69
Hegenberger, Lieutenant, 408
Helland-Hansen, 28
Helluland, 113
Hencken, H. O'Neil, 84
Henlopen, Cape, 42
Henry VI, King, 121
Henry VIII, King, 362
Henry the Navigator, 54, 135-39, 160, 163, 227
Henson, William S., 398
Herald of the Morning, 210
Herjolf, 108
Hermann, steamship, 304
Hermannsson, Professor, 108
Herne Island, 82

Herodotus, 80-81, 97-98
Hero of Alexandria, 295
Herreshoff, 291
Hesiod, 97
Heyerdahl, Thor, 334
Hibernia, steamship, 301
Hickory, schooner, 286
Higham, Captain, 277
Hildebrand, Arthur, 326
Himilco, 67, 82, 83, 84
Hindenburg, dirigible, 406
Hipparchus, 98
Hipper, Admiral, 423
History of American Sailing Ships, 229
Hitler, Adolf, 69, 351
Holand, Hjalmar, 120-21
Holland, Robert, 395
Home, steamship, 305
Homer, 73-76, 90, 91, 94, 358
Hood, H.M.S., 435
Horn, Cape, 21
Hottinguer, packet ship, 246
Houqua, clipper ship, 240, 266, 268
Houston, Samuel, 181, 250
Howard, Lord, 363
Howe, Lord, 418
Howland & Aspinwall, 265, 267, 268
Hrolf, the Ganger, 104-05
Hudson, Captain H. B., 328
Hudson, Henry, 124, 126-27, 178, 202
Hudson Bay, 20, 25, 27, 127
Hughes, Charles Evans, 428
Huguenots, 172
Hull, H. J., 213
Hulls, Jonathan, 296
Humboldt, steamship, 304
Humphreys, Joshua, 370
Huntsville, packet ship, 266, 267
Hussey, Christopher, 203
Hutchinson, Anne, 183
Hy-Brasil, 95

Iberia basin, 29
Iberian Peninsula, 132
Iberville, 175
Iceland, 24, 28, 29, 86, 98, 106, 108-10, 111, 119, 120, 122, 133, 144
Ile de France, steamship, 342, 345, 352
Immigration Act (1924), 348

Imperator, steamship, 344
Indian Ocean, 19, 25, 59, 98, 100
Industrial Revolution, 159-60, 168
Inman Line, 343
Institute of Marine Biology, 259
International Hydrographic Bureau, 259
Intrepid, clipper ship, 276, 277
Ireland, 95, 119
Irish Sea, 25
Isabella, Queen, 153, 220
Islander, yacht, 326

Jackson, Andréw, 181
Jackson, Charles T., 314
James, Arthur Curtis, 127, 307
James, King, 189
Jamestown, 177, 179, 188-89, 221
Japan, steamship, 306
Jason, 213
Jeanette, 40
Jefferson, Thomas, 370
Jeffreys, John, 394
Jellicoe, Admiral, 423
Jenny, yacht, 285
João II, of Portugal, 139-40, 143
Johnson, Alfred, 330-31
Joliet, Father, 175
Jones, Catesby, 377, 379
Jones, John Paul, 368, 370
Juan Fernandez Island, 211
Junker, Dr., 405

Kaiser Wilhelm der Grosse, steamship, 341, 344
Kansas-Nebraska Act, 226
Karlsefni, Thorfinn, 113, 117, 119, 164-65, 170
Kearsarge, U.S.S., 385, 386
Kelvin, Lord, 317
Kemp, Captain, 213
Kensington, Minn., 121
King George's War, 365
King Oscar Land, 213
King William's War, 365
Kinkajou, schooner, 137, 229, 325, 336
Kipling, Rudyard, 76, 325
Knor, 120
Knupsson, Bishop Eric, 119

Knutson, Powell (Paul), 120
Kuehl, Captain, 408
Kristiansen, Captain Leonard, 213
Kronprincessin Cecilie, steamship, 344
Kronprinz Wilhelm, steamship, 344

Labrador, 24, 122
Labrador basin, 30
Labrador Current, 51, 111, 115
Lady Adams, 210
Lagrange, 250
Laird, John, 306
Lamont Observatory of Geology, 259
Lanchester, F. W., 374
Land, Captain, 269
Landfall, schooner, 291
Land Hemisphere, 59
Langley, Samuel P., 399-400
Larsen, C. A., 213
Las Casas, Bartolome de, 153, 154-55, 172, 220
La Salle, Ferdinand, 175
Laudonnière, René de, 172
Law, Ruth, 403
Lawlor, Josiah W., 332
Lawson, Thomas W., schooner, 290, 292, 307
Leary, U.S.S., 432
Lee, William, Jr., 247
Lempe, First Lieutenant, 351
Lepe, Diego de, 149
"Letter Concerning Lanes for Steamers," 254
Leviathan, steamship, 345, 426
Lightning, clipper ship, 272, 273, 275
Lightning, H.M.S., 258
Lilienthal, Otto, 398
Lincoln, Abraham, 181, 381
Lindbergh, Charles A., 68, 407
Lion, 210
Lipari Islands, 74
Liverpool, packet ship, 244, 247
Livingston, Robert R., 298
Log Book for Grace, 216
Los Angeles, dirigible, 406
Loughhead, 401
Louis XVI, King, 393
Low, A. A., 266
Low, Charles Porter, 266

Low & Brother, A. A., 266
Lucania, steamship, 345
Lucas, Eliza, 222
Lusitania, steamship, 344, 346, 349-50, 351, 422
Luxury liners, 339-56

Macauley Island, 82
MacKinder, Sir Halford J., 68-69
Madeira Islands, 96, 136, 138
Magellan, Fernão de, 143, 150-51, 156, 163
Magnusson, King, 120
Mahan, Admiral, 12
Maine, Gulf of, 42,
Maine, U.S.S., 389
Maitland, Lieutenant, 408
Majestic, steamship, 345
Mallory, Stephen Russell, 377
Mamby, Aaron, 305
Manhattan Island, 178-79
Manley, Charles M., 399
Manly, Captain John, 368
Maps, 56-57; air routes, Atlantic, 409; Atlantic shipping, 193; drainage into the Atlantic Ocean, 15; Gulf Stream, 38; Taylor drift voyage, 41
Marconi, Guglielmo, 419
Marie Antoinette, Queen, 393
Markland, 113, 114, 120, 123
Marquette, Father, 175
Marshal, Benjamin, 235
Marshal, C. H., 240
Marshal & Co., C. H., 240
Martin, Glenn, 401, 402
Mary, yacht, 284-85
Masefield, John, 88
Mason, Monck, 395
Mataura, sailing ship, 306
Matthew, 123
Mauretania, steamship, 344, 346, 349
Maury, Matthew Fontaine, 233, 250-57, 304, 309, 313, 315-17, 377, 412
Mayflower, 177
McKay, Donald, 247, 248, 253, 265, 270-75, 306
McKay, Donald, clipper ship, 273
McKay, Lauchlan, 270, 273, 274
McKim, Ann, clipper ship, 265

McKim, Isaac, 265
McKinley, William, 389, 399, 416
Means, 114
Medici, Lorenzo de, 149
Mediterranean Sea, 21, 24, 25, 75-76, 91-92
Mediterranean water, 52
Melville, Herman, 210, 212
Menéndez de Avilés, 173
Mensura Orbis Terrae, 107
Mercator projection, 56
Mermaid, dory, 332
Merrimac, C.S.S., 376, 377-81
Merton, Phillip, 325-26
Messina, Straits of, 74, 91, 92
Meteor, packet ship, 237
Mexico, Gulf of, 20, 25, 38, 50, 150
Mid-Atlantic Ridge, 28-29
Minuit, Peter, 178, 179
Mississippi, U.S.S., 375
Mississippi River, 25, 60, 171, 172, 173, 175, 176
Missouri, U.S.S., 375
Missouri Compromise, 226
Moby Dick, 212
Monitor, U.S.S., 376, 377-81
Monroe, James, packet ship, 295
Montgolfier brothers, 393
Montojo, Admiral, 390
Moonshine, 125
Morgan, Henry, 166
Morgan, Thomas W., 215
Morrison, 212
Morrison, Admiral, 12
Morse, S. F. B., 245, 314-15
Moscoso, Luis, 172
Mossel Bay, 141
Müller, 81
Murphy, Robert Cushman, 216
Murray, Sir John, 14, 258, 261
Muscovy Company, 202
Mystic, 202, 214-15

Naddodd, 108
Nansen, Fridtjof, 40, 260
Nares, Sir George, 258
Narvaez, Pánfilo de, 171
Natchez, packet ship, 267, 269
National Observatory, 251, 256

Naval Air Transport, 410
Necham, Alexander, 135
Necho, King, 80, 90, 97, 141
Nelson, Admiral Lord, 374-75
Neptune's Car, clipper ship, 276
New Bedford, 202, 214
Newfoundland, 51, 52, 112, 122, 124, 126, 170, 201, 316
New Orleans, 176
Newport, Captain, 179, 188
New Sweden Company, 179
New World, packet ship, 271
New York, U.S.S., 432
New York City, 232, 246
Niagara, cable ship, 318
Niehof, Ilah, 342
Nicolet, Father, 175
Nicolas, Pope, 120
Nicolls, Colonel Richard, 365
Nine Power Treaty, 428
Nobile, General, 406-07
Norge, airship, 406
Normandie, steamship, 342, 345, 349
North American basin, 29
North Atlantic Ocean, 19-20
North Atlantic Drift, 39, 49, 62, 109, 177, 178, 299
North Cape, 20
Northcliffe, Lord, 404
North Equatorial Current, 43, 49, 50, 53, 229
North German Lloyd, 345, 346, 415
North Polar Seas, *see* Arctic Mediterranean Ocean
North Sea, 25, 107
Norway, 120
Norwegian Sea, 21, 24, 28
Nürnberg, 421

Obry, Ludwig, 419
Ocean, The, 99
Oceanic, steamship, 344
Oceanic Steam Navigation Company, 304
Octavius, 96, 359
Odo, Count, 105
Olympic, steamship, 344
Oñate, Juan de, 173
Oriental, clipper ship, 266, 267

Orkney Islands, 118
Orteig, Raymond, 407
Ortiz, Juan, 172
Osborne, Henry Fairfield, 97
Othere (Ottar), 118, 201
Oviedo, 155

P. & O. Steamship Co., 299
Pacific, packet ship, 235, 236
Pacific, steamship, 305
Pacific Ocean, 19, 25, 58, 86-88, 149
Packet ships, 232-48, 295
Paddock, Peter, 210
Paixhans, Henri, 417
Palmer, N. B., 213, 240, 248, 265-67, 272, 274
Palmer, N. B., clipper ship, 275, 277
Panama, 149, 165
Panama Canal, 416
Pan American Airways, 408, 410
Pan-American Conference, 429
Papin, Denis, 295-96
Paris Peace Conference, 428
Parsons, Sir Charles A., 307-08
Patapar, steamship, 345
Patten, Joshua, 276-77
Paulhan, 402
Pegou, 403
Pell, William W., 245, 314
Penn, William, 180
Pennsylvania Dutch, 180
Pepperell, Colonel William, 365
Pereira, Duarte Pacheco, 148
Perry, Commodore Matthew Calbraith, 376
Perry, Commodore N. C., 212
Pet, Christopher, 285
Pet, Peter, 285
Petain, Marshal, 434
Philadelphia, 180
Philippine Deep, 33
Phillip II, King, 360, 363
Philosophical Society of Philadelphia, 394
Physical Geography of the Sea, 254, 255
Pickering, privateer, 368
Pidgeon, 326-27
Piggott. C. S., 261

Pillars of Hercules, *see* Gibraltar, Straits of,
Pineda, Alvarez de, 150, 171
Pining, 120
Pinzon, Vicente, 149
Pius V, Pope, 360
Plato, 93-95
Plimsoll, Samuel, 353-54
Pliny, 82
Po, Fernando, 139
Polar Sea, *see* Arctic Mediterranean Sea
Polk, James K., 181
Pollard, George, Jr., 210-11
Polo, Marco, 67, 133, 144
Ponce de Leon, Juan, 149, 171
Pook, S. H., 269, 273
Porcupine, H.M.S., 258
Porter, 378
Porto Bello, 165-66
Portugal, 132-43
Portuguese trade winds, 48
Posidonius, 99, 100
Pothorst, 120
Power, Tyrone, 245
President, U.S.S., 370
Princeton, U.S.S., 375
Privateers, 367-70
Propontis, steamship, 302
Ptolemy, 100, 101
Puerto Rico, 30, 149, 171
Pythias, 83, 84, 90, 95, 98-99, 106

Queen Anne's War, 365
Queen Elizabeth, steamship, 345
Queen Mary, steamship, 345
Quimby, Harriet, 403

R-34, dirigible, 406
Radar, 432
Raeder, Grand Admiral, 351
Raft Book, 87
Rainbow, clipper ship, 268-69, 272
Raleigh, Sir Walter, 177
Rameses II, 80
Ramsey, Sir Bertram, 438
Rapid, clipper ship, 276, 277
Raven-Floki, 108

Red, White and Blue, lifeboat, 328
Redjacket, clipper ship, 273
Red Star Line, 237, 241, 242, 247
Renaissance, 159-60
Rennels, 81
Reuterdahl, Henry, 420
Ribaut, Jean, 172
Richelieu, Cardinal de, 174
Rio Grande River, 60
Robert brothers, 395
Roberts, Captain, 301
Roberval, 125
Robinson, Andrew, 287
Robinson Line, 246
Rochambeau, General, 371
Rockets, 440-41
Rodney, Admiral, 374
Rogers, Stanley, 215
Rolph, John, 189
Romer, Captain Franz, 333, 335
Roosevelt, Franklin D., 240, 430
Roosevelt, Theodore, 389-90, 416, **420**
Roscius, packet ship, 244
Ross, James Clarke, 207
Royal African Company, 224
Royal Air Force, 435
Royal William, steamship, 300
Rubruck, 133
Rumsey, 296
Russell, Samuel, clipper ship, 266, 275

Sahuri, King, 77
Sailing Ship—A Study in Beauty, 215
St. Brandan's Isle, 95
St. Helena, 28
St. Lawrence, Gulf of, 25
St. Lawrence River, 125, 127
St. Michael's, 83
St. Paul's Rocks, 28, 29, 42-43
Salva, 313
Samuels, Captain, 242
Samuelson, Frank, 333-34
San Roque, Cape of, 21
Santa Clara, bark, 307
Santa Cruz, 360
Santa Maria, 145
Santos-Dumont, Alberto, 397-98, 401
São Roque, Cape, 22, 53

Sapolio, 332
Sardinian Sea, 99
Sargasso Sea, 25, 51, 178
Sataspes, 81
Savannah, steamship, 54, 299, 309
Scandinavian Airlines, 411
Scandinavian Peninsula, 23
Scharnhorst, 421
Scheer, Admiral, 423
Schooners, 286-92
Schurz, Carl, 245
Schwaben, dirigible, 403
Schweiger, Lt. Capt., 349
Scorsby, William, 213
Scorsby, William, Jr., 213
Scotland, 95, 119
Scripps, Edward W., 260
"Sea Bees," 440
Sea Bird, yacht, 326
Sea Witch, clipper ship, 267, 269
Semmes, Captain Ralph, 377, 385
Senegal River, 138
Sertorius, 96
Seti, I, 80
Seven Seas, yacht, 307
Seville, Diogo de, 138
Sheffield, packet ship, 242
Shenandoah, C.S.S., 385, 387
Sherbro Sound, 82
Sherman, General, 384
Shetland Islands, 21, 27, 28, 118-19
Sicily, 77
Sierra Leone basin, 29
Sims, Rear Admiral Wm. S., 424
Sirius, steamship, 300-01
Sita, bark, 334
Slave trade, 217-31, 288
Sloat, Commodore John Drake, 375
Slocum, Joshua, 327
Sloops, 285-86
Small-boat voyages, 324-36
Smith, Captain John, 126, 191
Snorri, 114
Solis, Juan Diaz de, 150
South Antilles basin, 30
South Atlantic Ocean, 19-20
South Equatorial Current, 53, 54
Southern Cross, 213

Sovereign of the Sea, clipper ship, 271,
    272, 273
Sovereign of the Seas, steamship, 305,
    308
Spain, 132, 138, 143
Spanish-American War, 389-91
Spee, Admiral Graf von, 421, 435
Spitsbergen, 28
Spray, yawl, 327
Staffordshire, packet ship, 271
Stag Hound, clipper ship, 271, 272, 273
Stanton, John, 235
Star of the Empire, packet ship, 271
Steamships, 293-311
Steers, George, 288
Stefansson, Vilhjalmur, 79, 83, 117, 121
Stevens, John, 296-98
Stevens, Robert L., 378
Stevens, Robert L., steamship, 298
Stinson, Katherine, 403
Stock, Ralph, 326
Stockholm, motorship, 352-53
Stockton, Captain Robert F., 375
Story of the Ship, The, 282
Strindberg, Nils, 396
Stringfellow, John, 398
Stuyvesant, Peter, 179
Submarine plow, 321-22
Submarine telegraph, 312-23
Suez Canal, 80, 289, 310
Sully, packet ship, 244, 245, 313-14
Surprise, clipper ship, 269
Swallowtail Line, 237, 240, 244, 245
Swedish American Line, 308
Swinburne, Algernon Charles, 60
Syene, 99

Taeping, clipper ship, 306
Taft, William Howard, 420
Taussig, Commander J. K., 424
Taylor, Dr. Albert, 431
Taylor, Fred B., 40-42
Teneriffe, 96
Thames, steamship, 298
Themistocles, 359
Thetis, steamship, 302
Thirteenth Amendment, 226
Thompson, Francis, 235

Thompson, Jeremiah, 235, 236
Thomson, Sir C. Wyville, 258
Thomson, William, 317
Thorhall, 113
Thorolf, 108
Thule, 95, 106; see also Iceland
Thule air base, 48
Thumb, Tom, 245
Tidal Institute, The, 260
Tinker, Captain, 305
Titanic, steamship, 336, 344, 345, 351-52
Toronto, steamship, 305
Torricelli, 146
Trade winds, 47-48, 53
Trafalgar, Cape, 47
Train, Enoch, 247, 271
Transylvania, steamship, 341-42
Trave, S.S., 40
Trimountain, sailing ship, 305
Trinble & Co., Byrnes, 236
Tristan da Cunha, 28
Trondhjem, 119
Tryggvason, Olaf, 112
Turbinia, Diesel ship, 307-08
Tusitala, yacht, 307
Tyng, Captain, 365

Ulfsson, Gunnbjorn, 110
Union, 210
United States, packet ship, 247
United States, steamship, 346
United States, U.S.S., 370
United States Coast and Geodetic Survey, 260
United States Line, 345
Unrolling the Map, 121
Urquhart, Captain, 305
Usselinex, William, 179
Ussher, Bishop, 95
Utrecht, Treaty of, 224

Van den Bergh, 34
Vanderuen, Captain Timotheus, 203
Vaterland, steamship, 344, 426
Velazquez, Diego, 149
Veniero, 360
Vera Cruz, 165, 166
Verde, Cape, 22, 47, 138
Verrazano, Giovanni da, 124-25, 143

Vespucci, Amerigo, 148-49
Vesta, steamship, 304
Vestmannaeyjar, 109
Victoria, Queen, 308, 415
Victorian, turbine ship, 308
Victory, H.M.S., 373
Viking ships, 106
Ville de Havre, steamship, 305
Villeneuve, Admiral, 374
Villiers, Allen, 307
Vincennes, U.S.S., 251
Vineland, 112-13, 119
Viper, H.M.S., 308
Virgil, 92
Virginian, packet ship, 244
Virginian, turbine ship, 308
Voisin, 401
Vraad, lifeboat, 329

Waldseemüller, Martin, 149
Walker, Delia, clipper ship, 271
Wanamaker, Rodman, 404
Warfare, naval, 357-91, 414-39
Washington, George, 367-68, 370, 392, 394, 395
Washington, steamship, 304
Water Hemisphere, 58-59
Waterman, Robert H., 248, 267, 269
Watkinson, James, 235
Watt, John, 302
Weather Bureau, 254
Webb, Isaac, 268, 270
Webb, William, 268
Weddell, James, 213
Weddell Sea, 26
Wegener, Alfred, 22-24, 29
Wellman, Walter, 402-03
Westerlies, 48
West European basin, 30
West Greenland Current, 51, 115
West Indies, 47, 147, 151, 165-66, 217, 222
Westward, schooner, 291
Weyler, General, 389
Whaling industry, 199-216
White Diamond Line, 271
Whitehead, Robert, 418
White Sea, 24
White Star Line, 341, 344

Whitman, C. O., 259
Whitney, Eli, 224
Whitten-Brown, A., 406
Whitworth, Sir Joseph, 417
Wild Pigeon, 275
Wilkes, Captain John, 328, 329
Wilkins, Sir Hubert, 27
Wilkins, John, 305
William II, Emperor, 415
Williams, John, 235, 248
Williams, Roger, 183
William the Conqueror, 105
Wilson, Hubert, 341
Wilson, Woodrow, 349-50, 421, 422, 428
Wind and Current Charts of the North Atlantic Ocean, 252
Windward Islands, 47, 49
Winslow, Captain John A., 385
Winsor, Phineas, 276, 277
Winthrop, Governor John, 191
Wise, John, 396

Wolfe, General James, 366
Woods Hole, 259
Worden, John L., 380
World War I, 421-29
World War II, 429 ff.
Wright, Orville and Wilbur, 398, 399-401
Wright, W. H. D. C., barque, 253
Wright & Son, Isaac, 235
Wyville Thompson Ridge, 28

Yankee Clipper, airplane, 408
Yorkshire, packet ship, 303
Young, Leo C., 431
Yucatan, 150
Yucatan Channel, 50
Yu Yun-wen, 162

Zambesi River, 61, 140, 143
Zeppelin, Count Ferdinand von, 398, 401, 403-04

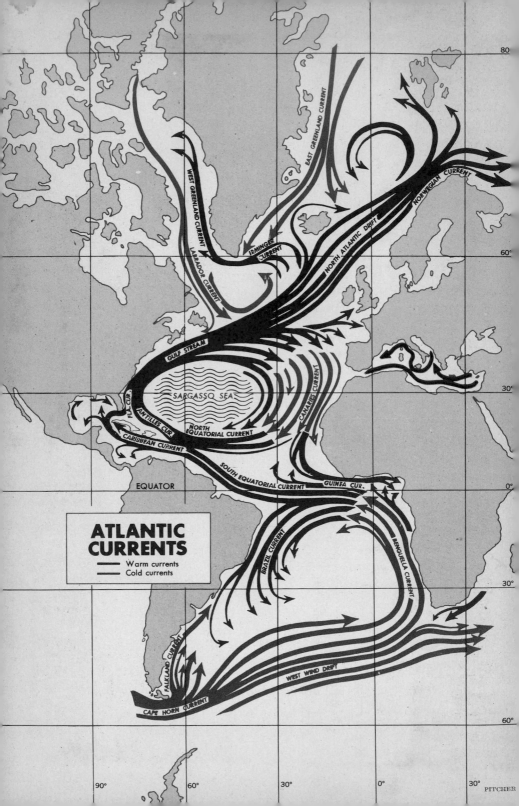

ATLANTIC CURRENTS

— Warm currents
━ Cold currents

WEST GREENLAND CURRENT
EAST GREENLAND CURRENT
LABRADOR CURRENT
IRMINGER CURRENT
NORTH ATLANTIC DRIFT
NORWEGIAN CURRENT
GULF STREAM
SARGASSO SEA
CANARIES CURRENT
FLA. CUR.
ANTILLES CUR.
NORTH EQUATORIAL CURRENT
CARIBBEAN CURRENT
SOUTH EQUATORIAL CURRENT
GUINEA CUR.
EQUATOR
BRAZIL CURRENT
BENGUELA CURRENT
FALKLAND CURRENT
WEST WIND DRIFT
CAPE HORN CURRENT

80
60°
30°
0°
30°
60°

90°
60°
30°
0°
30°

PITCHER